perspectives

Women's Studies

perspectives

Women's Studies

Academic Editor
Renae Moore Bredin
California State University at Fullerton

coursewise
publishing
inc.

St. Paul • Bellevue • Boulder • Dubuque • Madison

Our mission at **coursewise** is to help students make connections—linking theory to practice and the classroom to the outside world. Learners are motivated to synthesize ideas when course materials are placed in a context they recognize. By providing gateways to contemporary and enduring issues, **coursewise** publications will expand students' awareness of and context for the course subject.

For more information on **coursewise** visit us at our web site: http://www.coursewise.com

To order an examination copy, contact Houghton Mifflin Sixth Floor Media: 800-565-6247 (voice); 800-565-6236 (fax).

coursewise publishing editorial staff

Thomas Doran, ceo/publisher: Journalism/Marketing/Speech
Edgar Laube, publisher: Geography/Political Science/Psychology/Sociology
Linda Meehan Avenarius, publisher: **courselinks**
Sue Pulvermacher-Alt, publisher: Education/Health/Gender Studies
Victoria Putman, publisher: Anthropology/Philosophy/Religion
Tom Romaniak, publisher: Business/Criminal Justice/Economics
Kathleen Schmitt, publishing assistant

coursewise publishing production staff

Lori A. Blosch, permissions coordinator
Mary Monner, production coordinator
Victoria Putman, production manager

Copyright © 1998 by **coursewise publishing**, Inc. All Rights Reserved.

Library of Congress Catalog Card Number: 98-072189

ISBN 0-395-90252-5

Printed in the United States of America by **coursewise publishing**, Inc.
1559 Randolph Ave., St. Paul, MN 55103

10 9 8 7 6 5 4 3 2

from the
Publisher

Sue Pulvermacher-Alt
coursewise publishing

Passion *(noun): extreme, compelling emotion*

As a publisher, I've worked in several different discipline areas, and I've seen many passionate professionals who believe profoundly in what they are doing. Many believe that they are doing important work—work not to be taken lightly. Never, however, have I seen the passion I've witnessed in women's studies. Let me offer two examples:

One day in the fall of 1997, the front page of *The New York Times* featured four women—Princess Diana, Mother Teresa, Janet Reno, and Queen Elizabeth—in four different cover stories. Participants on a women's studies listserv had an extended discussion about that particular *New York Times* issue. They discussed and debated the value to women of this front-page prominence. One participant made this passionate (and unfortunately, sad) concluding remark: "Too bad half those women had to die first...."

I witnessed another example of passion early in the development of this volume. Renae Bredin, the Academic Editor (see below for more on her talents), had suggested a large number of articles for possible inclusion in the reader. Before taking the article list to the Editorial Board for feedback, she and I were talking about how to winnow the long list. Coming purely from the standpoint of a publisher of public print, I made the editorial suggestion that we not use articles containing the word *fuck* if a different article of comparable quality was available. After careful thought, Renae made it very clear to me that she couldn't continue in the role of Academic Editor if I put such editorial constraints on the selection of articles. Her passion for the field of women's studies struck me. Let me just say that Renae continued in the role of Academic Editor, and you'll find only the best !#@^* articles here!

Good for you for taking a women's studies course. Whether or not you start this course feeling passionate about the important issues in women's studies, I'll bet you won't get through the course without feeling some passion—some intense emotions. For your sake, I hope I'm right. Whatever your position on a number of issues—women's place in family and community, gender and sexuality, feminist activism, gender bias, sexual harassment, body image—you will be challenged to explore other perspectives. Along the way, you'll read articles and explore web sites that will invoke emotions. Our goal is to help you better understand these complex issues so you can support your passion with rational reasoning.

I worked with a talented group to develop these materials—both this reader, *Perspectives: Women's Studies,* and its accompanying **courselinks**™ site. I had the good fortune to work with Renae Bredin as the Academic Editor for the reader. I'm glad Renae chose women's studies because her drive and commitment serve this discipline well. She knows her stuff and is a self-proclaimed technology addict. She's an English graduate who has gravitated to women's studies. Renae is currently teaching at California State University at Fullerton.

Renae and I were helped by a top-notch Editorial Board. At **course-wise**, we're working hard to publish "connected learning" tools—connecting theory to practice and the classroom to the outside world. Articles and web sites are selected with this goal in mind. Members of the Editorial Board offered some critical feedback and posed some interesting challenges. They know their content and are a web-savvy bunch. Take a look at the Editorial Board page and read the bios. Can you sense the passion that each Editorial Board member brings to the field? My thanks to Renae and the entire Editorial Board.

Before I close, I want to invite you to share your passion with me. I feel strongly that we made some good choices in the articles and web sites we've included in both this volume and at the **courselinks**™ site. What do *you* think?

Sue Pulvermacher-Alt, Publisher
suepa@coursewise.com

from the
Academic Editor

Renae Moore Bredin
The College of New Jersey

Renae Moore Bredin is assistant professor of Women's and Gender Studies at The College of New Jersey. She previously served as acting director of Women's Studies at Rutgers University–Newark, where her addiction to technology began. She has published essays about the relations between indigenous and white women in the United States in places like *Studies in American Indian Literature*. Her most recent essay appears in the new anthology, *Other Sisterhoods: Literary Theory and U.S. Women of Color.*

Teaching interdisciplinary materials in Women's Studies has always posed special challenges—especially that of finding and putting together materials that are current, multidisciplinary, and gender relevant. *Perspectives: Women's Studies* fills a void for instructors and students looking for cogent, contemporary discussions of critical issues in Women's Studies from sources both inside and outside of academic publishing.

This volume includes a wide range of voices and media, from *The Village Voice* to *The Women's Rights Law Reporter* to *Social Text*, to supplement traditional, critical readings in Women's Studies. In addition, **coursewise publishings** groundbreaking connections to the Internet for this volume offer access to a multitude of conversations about women's issues around the globe. Linking Sallie Tisdale's work on body image to the "Distorted Barbie" web site brings alive the questions raised in Naomi Wolf's often anthologized essays in *The Beauty Myth.*

Sections 1 and 2 cover sexual harassment, body image, and representation—issues that are still central in the political and social climate of the 1990s. Sections 3 and 4 deal with the complex debates surrounding the social and biological reproduction of gender and sexuality. Section 5 explores women's places within different kinds of communities, while Section 6 exposes and examines women's place in the global economy of techno-eco-nomics. Finally, Section 7 highlights the larger questions of feminist thinking and activism, with the final reading from Gerda Lerner delineating a brief history of patriarchy, male dominance, and female subordination. I have placed this essay last, as a way of thinking through issues, and then determining the underlying causes. It seemed right that Lerner have the last word, at least in print, because her contributions to our understanding of the history of women's lives has laid the groundwork for so much of what has been done in Women's Studies.

The Internet offers exciting, wide-ranging links between the study of women's lives and activist efforts on behalf of women. These links promise a kind of synthesis or synergy between these two endeavors that has often failed to materialize in the past. I have appreciated the opportunity to be part of this effort to bring together disciplines, discourses, and media as a means of enhancing Women's Studies in a wholly new form.

My appreciation goes to the students in the Gendered Techno-culture classes at TCNJ in the fall of 1997, for their wide-ranging web searches, as well as to Sue Alt, AnaLouise Keating, and Fran Bartkowski, for their crucial contributions on behalf of this book.

Editorial Board

We wish to thank the following instructors for their assistance. Their many suggestions not only contributed to the construction of this volume, but also to the ongoing development of our Women's Studies website.

WiseGuide Introduction

Critical Thinking and Bumper Stickers

The bumper sticker said: Question Authority. This is a simple directive that goes straight to the heart of critical thinking. The issue is not whether the authority is right or wrong; it's the questioning process that's important. Questioning helps you develop awareness and a clearer sense of what you think. That's critical thinking.

Critical thinking is a new label for an old approach to learning—that of challenging all ideas, hypotheses, and assumptions. In the physical and life sciences, systematic questioning and testing methods (known as the scientific method) help verify information, and objectivity is the benchmark on which all knowledge is pursued. In the social sciences, however, where the goal is to study people and their behavior, things get fuzzy. It's one thing for the chemistry experiment to work out as predicted, or for the petri dish to yield a certain result. It's quite another matter, however, in the social sciences, where the subject is ourselves. Objectivity is harder to achieve.

Although you'll hear critical thinking defined in many different ways, it really boils down to analyzing the ideas and messages that you receive. What are you being asked to think or believe? Does it make sense, objectively? Using the same facts and considerations, could you reasonably come up with a different conclusion? And, why does this matter in the first place? As the bumper sticker urged, question authority. Authority can be a textbook, a politician, a boss, a big sister, or an ad on television. Whatever the message, learning to question it appropriately is a habit that will serve you well for a lifetime. And in the meantime, thinking critically will certainly help you be course wise.

Question Authority

Getting Connected

This reader is a tool for connected learning. This means that the readings and other learning aids explained here will help you to link classroom theory to real-world issues. They will help you to think critically and to make long-lasting learning connections. Feedback from both instructors and students has helped us to develop some suggestions on how you can wisely use this connected learning tool.

WiseGuide Pedagogy

A wise reader is better able to be a critical reader. Therefore, we want to help you get wise about the articles in this reader. Each section of *Perspectives* has three tools to help you: the WiseGuide Intro, the WiseGuide Wrap-Up, and the Putting It in *Perspectives* review form.

WiseGuide Intro

In the WiseGuide Intro, the Academic Editor introduces the section, gives you an overview of the topics covered, and explains why particular articles were selected and what's important about them.

WiseGuide Intro

Also in the WiseGuide Intro, you'll find several key points or learning objectives that highlight the most important things to remember from this section. These will help you to focus your study of section topics.

At the end of the Wiseguide Intro, you'll find questions designed to stimulate critical thinking. Wise students will keep these questions in mind as they read an article (we repeat the questions at the start of the articles as a reminder). When you finish each article, check your understanding. Can you answer the questions? If not, go back and reread the article. The Academic Editor has written sample responses for many of the questions, and you'll find these online at the **courselinks**™ site for this course. More about **courselinks**™ in a minute. . . .

WiseGuide Wrap-Up

Be course wise and develop a thorough understanding of the topics covered in this course. The WiseGuide Wrap-Up at the end of each section will help you do just that with concluding comments or summary points that repeat what's most important to understand from the section you just read.

In addition, we try to get you wired up by providing a list of select Internet resources—what we call R.E.A.L. web sites because they're Relevant, Exciting, Approved, and Linked. The information at these web sites will enhance your understanding of a topic. (Remember to use your Passport and start at http://www.courselinks.com so that if any of these sites have changed, you'll have the latest link.)

Putting It in *Perspectives* Review Form

At the end of the book is the Putting It in *Perspectives* review form. Your instructor may ask you to complete this form as an assignment or for extra credit. If nothing else, consider doing it on your own to help you critically think about the reading.

Prompts at the end of each article encourage you to complete this review form. Feel free to copy the form and use it as needed.

The courselinks™ Site

The **courselinks**™ Passport is your ticket to a wonderful world of integrated web resources designed to help you with your course work. These resources are found at the **courselinks**™ site for your course area. This is where the readings in this book and the key topics of your course are linked to an exciting array of online learning tools. Here you will find carefully selected readings, web links, quizzes, worksheets, and more, tailored to your course and approved as connected learning tools. The ever-changing, always interesting **courselinks**™ site features a number of carefully integrated resources designed to help you be course wise. These include:

- **R.E.A.L. Sites** At the core of a **courselinks**™ site is the list of R.E.A.L. sites. This is a select group of web sites for studying, not surfing. Like the readings in this book, these sites have been selected, reviewed, and approved by the Academic Editor and the Editorial Board. The R.E.A.L. sites are arranged by topic and are annotated with short descriptions and key words to make them easier for you to use for reference or research. With R.E.A.L. sites, you're studying approved resources within seconds—and not wasting precious time surfing unproven sites.

- **Editor's Choice** Here you'll find updates on news related to your course, with links to the actual online sources. This is also where we'll tell you about changes to the site and about online events.

- **Course Overview** This is a general description of the typical course in this area of study. While your instructor will provide specific course objectives, this overview helps you place the course in a generic context and offers you an additional reference point.

- **www.orksheet** Focus your trip to a R.E.A.L. site with the www.orksheet. Each of the 10 to 15 questions will prompt you to take in the best that site has to offer. Use this tool for self-study, or if required, email it to your instructor.

- **Course Quiz** The questions on this self-scoring quiz are related to articles in the reader, information at R.E.A.L. sites, and other course topics, and will help you pinpoint areas you need to study. Only you will know your score—it's an easy, risk-free way to keep pace!

- **Topic Key** The Topic Key is a listing of the main topics in your course, and it correlates with the Topic Key that appears in this reader. This handy reference tool also links directly to those R.E.A.L. sites that are especially appropriate to each topic, bringing you integrated online resources within seconds!

- **Web Savvy Student Site** If you're new to the Internet or want to brush up, stop by the Web Savvy Student site. This unique supplement is a complete courselinks™ site unto itself. Here, you'll find basic information on using the Internet, creating a web page, communicating on the web, and more. Quizzes and Web Savvy Worksheets test your web knowledge, and the R.E.A.L. sites listed here will further enhance your understanding of the web.

- **Student Lounge** Drop by the Student Lounge to chat with other students taking the same course or to learn more about careers in your major. You'll find links to resources for scholarships, financial aid, internships, professional associations, and jobs. Take a look around the Student Lounge and give us your feedback. We're open to remodeling the Lounge per your suggestions.

Building Better Perspectives!

Please tell us what you think of this *Perspectives* volume so we can improve the next one. Here's how you can help:

1. Visit our **coursewise** site at: http://www.coursewise.com

2. Click on *Perspectives*. Then select the Building Better *Perspectives* Form for your book.

3. Forms and instructions for submission are available online.

Tell us what you think—did the readings and online materials help you make some learning connections? Were some materials more helpful than others? Thanks in advance for helping us build better *Perspectives*.

Student Internships

If you enjoy evaluating these articles or would like to help us evaluate the **courselinks**™ site for this course, check out the **coursewise** Student Internship Program. For more information, visit:

http://www.coursewise.com/intern.html

Brief Contents

Contents

section 1

Working Girls: Women, Wages, and Work

section 2

Gazing Back: Representation and Stereotypes

section 3

Having (a) Sex: Gender, Sexuality, Reproduction

section 4

Playing Around: Gender Equity in School, at Play and Growing Up

section 5

Togetherness: Family and Community

section 6

Techno-eco-nomics: Technology, Eco-Feminism, Global Economies, Women's Health

section 7

Good Girls/Bad GRRRLS: Feminism and Patriarchy

Topic Key

This Topic Key is an important tool for learning. It will help you integrate this reader into your course studies. Listed below, in alphabetical order, are important topics covered in this volume. Below each topic, you'll find the reading numbers and titles, and also the R.E.A.L. web site addresses, relating to that topic. Note that the Topic Key might not include every topic your instructor chooses to emphasize. If you don't find the topic you're looking for in the Topic Key, check the index or the online topic key at the **courselinks**™ site.

section 1

- Despite recent gains in wages and rising numbers of women in managerial and professional jobs, women's earnings are still only 75 percent of men's earnings.

- As women continue to dominate low-paying, low-status job categories, these feminized occupations, such as clerical, service, and teaching jobs, help maintain traditional power relations of male dominance and female subordination.

- Representational practices which associate women with sex is a basis for gender discrimination in the workplace.

- Class structures facilitate divisions between working women, setting upper- and middle-class women's interests at odds with the interests of working-class and pink collar women workers.

Working Girls: Women, Wages, and Work

 Women have always worked, but most women have done so under conditions of inequality. The problem of the gender wage gap has been well documented, if not resolved, and the issues of discriminatory hiring practices and sexual harassment have also received a great deal of attention in the media and from activist groups.

Less obvious means of discriminating against women in the workforce have been overlooked. Subtle forms of exclusion and stereotyping often function effectively to keep women from moving out of lower-paying, nonmanagerial positions. The feminization of some job categories, associated with lower wages and little power, as well as lower prestige, is sustained by social and cultural definitions of appropriate feminine traits and behaviors.

In Section 1, readings focus on some of these hidden practices. "Facts on Working Women" and "The Memoirs of a Token" highlight the strategies of separating, ghettoizing, and patronizing women as discriminatory practices. "What I Learned at College" argues that, while some women in certain groups move into previously masculine arenas, women in other groups, particularly those in such pink collar jobs as have been traditionally feminized, are left behind. The tensions between these groups functions to keep women from forming coalitions to improve wages and conditions for women from different classes. Perhaps even less obvious is the means by which sex work is both empowering and oppressive, as Barbara's story in "It's a Pleasure Doing Business with You" demonstrates.

Questions

Reading 1. What are the occupational categories with greatest participation by women? Compare the salaries of men and women in similar jobs, particularly predominantly female jobs. What avenues are open to women to increase their salaries and autonomy?

Reading 2. What are the divisions within women's movements? What responsibilities do the academic feminists at Barnard College have to the women on strike?

Reading 3. How is sex work an entrepreneurial enterprise for women? Compare and contrast the tasks, both implicit and explicit, of secretaries, wives, and sex workers.

Reading 4. What are some of the reasons Borsook offers for the masculine sensibility of magazines like *Wired*? How was Borsook discriminated against at the magazine? What actions could she have taken to facilitate changes?

What are the occupational categories with greatest participation by women? Compare the salaries of men and women in similar jobs, particularly predominantly female jobs? What avenues are open to women to increase their salaries and autonomy?

Facts on Working Women

20 Facts On Women Workers

1. There were **103 million** women age 16 and over in the United States in 1995. Of that total, a record **61 million** were in the civilian labor force (persons working or looking for work).

2. Women's share of the total labor force continues to rise. Women accounted for **46 percent** of total United States labor force participants in 1995 and are projected to comprise **48 percent** in the year 2005.

3. Nearly six out of every ten women—**58.9 percent**—age 16 and over were labor force participants (working or looking for work) in 1995.

4. Women between the ages of 20 and 54 had labor force participation rates of at least 70 percent. Even half the Nation's teenage women ages 16–19 were labor force participants— 52 percent (see Table 1).

5. Labor force participation by marital status varies for women. Divorced women have higher participation rates mainly because they are the primary or the only wage

Table 1	Labor Force Participation Rates For Women by Age Groups, 1995
Age Groups	**Participation Rate**
All Women	58.9
16 to 19	52.2
20 to 24	70.3
25 to 34	74.9
35 to 44	77.2
45 to 54	74.4
55 to 65	49.2
65 and over	8.8

Source: U.S. Department of Labor, Bureau of Labor Statistics, *Employment and Earnings*, January 1996.

Table 2	Female Labor Force Participation, by Marital Status, March 1995
Marital Status	**Participation Rate**
All women	58.9
Never married	65.5
Married, spouse present	61.1
Married, spouse absent	62.0
Divorced	73.7
Widowed	17.5

Source: U.S. Department of Labor, Bureau of Labor Statistics, Unpublished Data, March 1995.

earners in their families (see Table 2).

6. Unemployment for all women in 1995 was only **5.6 percent.** For white women it was 4.8 percent; 10.2 percent for black women; and 10.0 percent for Hispanic women.

7. Nearly **58 million** women were employed in 1995 with the largest proportion still working in technical, sales, and clerical occupations.

Source: U.S. Department of Labor, Bureau of Labor Statistics, Unpublished Data, March 1995.

Table 3 Employed Women by Occupational Group, 1995 (in millions)

Occupation	No. Employed
Total	57.5
Management and profession specialty	16.9
Technical, sales and administrative support	24.1
Service occupations	10.2
Precision production, craft, and repair	1.2
Operators, fabricators, and laborers	4.4
Farming, forestry, and fishing	0.7

Source: U.S. Department of Labor, Bureau of Labor Statistics, *Employment and Earnings*, January 1996.

Table 4 Women as Multiple Jobholders, 1995 (numbers in thousands)

Age	Total Employed	Multiple Job Holders	Percent
16–19 years	3,127	196	6.3
20–24 years	5,779	424	7.3
25–34 years	14,647	896	6.1
35–44 years	15,828	1,007	6.4
45–54 years	11,421	753	6.6
55–64 years	5,163	238	4.6
65+ years	1,558	38	2.5

Source: U.S. Department of Labor, Bureau of Labor Statistics, Unpublished Data, Annual Averages 1995.

Table 5 Median Weekly Earnings, Selected Traditionally Female Occupations, 1995

Occupation	Earnings	
	Women	Men
Registered nurses	$693	$715
Elementary school teachers	627	713
Cashiers	233	256
General office clerks	360	389
Health aides, except nursing	285	345

Source: U.S. Department of Labor, Bureau of Labor Statistics, *Employment and Earnings*, January 1996.

8. Women have made substantial progress in obtaining jobs in the managerial and professional specialties. In 1985 they held one-third (35.6 percent) of managerial and executive jobs and nearly half (49.1 percent) of the professional jobs. By 1995 they held 48.0 percent of all managerial/executive positions and over half (52.9 percent) of professional occupations.

9. Women are not only more likely to work outside the home today than in the past, but they also spend more time at work than did women in earlier years. Women have increasingly opted to work both full time and year round, partly due to economic necessity, but also due to movement into occupations that require full-time, year-round work.

10. Of the **57.5 million** employed women in the United States in 1995, 42 million worked full time (35 or more hours per week); 16 million worked part time (less than 35 hours per week). Two-thirds of all part-time workers were women (68 percent).

11. Many women who work part time are multiple job holders. In 1995, **3.6 million** women held more than one job. The highest rates of multiple jobholding was among women 20 to 24 years old and single women—7.3 percent and 7.2 percent, respectively.

12. Of all women who were multiple job holders in 1995, those in the 35 to 44 age group were most likely to hold 3 or more jobs.

13. The ratio of women's 1995 median weekly earnings to men's was **75.5 percent.** Even in traditionally female occupations where women outnumber, women still earn less than men (see Table 5).

14. With women still concentrated in lower paying occupations and having overall earnings about three-fourths that of men, it is predictable that more adult women than men are below the poverty level (see Table 6).

15. Of the 14 million families maintained by women, **4.2 million** were below the poverty level in 1994. This

Table 6 — Persons Below Poverty Level, by Age and Sex, 1994 (numbers in thousands)

Age	Below Poverty Level	
	Women	Men
Total, 18 years and over	14,140	8,632
18 to 24 years	2,833	1,705
25 to 34 years	3,359	2,104
35 to 44 years	2,539	1,929
45 to 54 years	1,348	1,033
55 to 64 years	1,337	921
65 years and over	2,724	939

Source: U.S. Department of Commerce, Bureau of the Census, *Income, Poverty, and Valuation of Noncash Benefits: 1994.*

Table 7 — Percent Distribution of the Labor Force by Educational Attainment, Sex, and Age, 1995

Category	Women	Men
25 years and over	100.0	100.0
Less than a high school diploma	9.2	12.2
High school graduate, no college	34.2	32.3
Some college or associate degree	30.0	26.1
College graduates	26.6	29.4

Source: U.S. Department of Labor, Bureau of Labor Statistics, Unpublished Data, Annual Averages, 1995.

Table 8 — Median Income of Persons, by Educational Attainment and Sex, Year-Round, Full-Time Workers, 1994

Level of Education	Women	Men
9th to 12th grade (no diploma)	$15,133	$22,048
High school graduate	20,373	28,037
Some college, no degree	23,514	32,279
Associate degree	25,940	35,794
Bachelor's degree or more	35,378	49,228

Source: U.S. Department of Commerce, Bureau of the Census, *Income, Poverty, and Valuation of Noncash Benefits: 1994.*

represents 34.6 percent of all families with female householders.

16. Women have, however, made great strides in becoming entrepreneurs. According to the latest Census Bureau data, women owned over 6.4 million of all U.S. businesses in 1992, employing over 13 million persons and generating $1.6 trillion in business revenues.

17. Nearly three-quarters of these women owned firms operated as a service or retail trade in such businesses as apparel and accessory stores; automobile dealerships; gasoline service stations; miscellaneous retail stores; business services; health services; and personal services.

18. In 1995, 3.4 million women were self-employed workers in nonagricultural industries. A large number of these self-employed women worked in the following industries: wholesale and retail trade; professional services; personal services; and social services.

19. Of all labor force participants age 25 years and over in 1995, women were more likely than men to have completed high school. **Ninety-one percent** of female labor force participants held the minimum of a high school diploma, compared with 88 percent for men. A slightly lower percentage of female labor force participants than men were college graduates—27 percent compared with 29 percent.

20. Employment and earnings rates rise with educational attainment for both females and males, but earnings are lower for females than for males with the same education.

U.S. Department of Labor Women's Bureau Regional Addresses

Region I: Boston
Ms. Jacqueline Cooke, RA
John F. Kennedy Federal Building
Room E-270
Boston, MA 02230
Phone: (617) 565-1988

Fax: (617) 565-1986
(Connecticut, Maine, Massachusetts, New Hampshire, Rhode Island, Vermont)

Region II: New York City
Ms. Mary C. Murphree, RA
201 Varick Street, 601
New York, NY 10014-4811
Phone: (212) 337-2389
Fax: (212) 337-2394
(New Jersey, New York, Puerto Rico, Virgin Islands)

Region III: Philadelphia
Ms. Cornelia Moore, RA
Gateway Building, Room 2450
3535 Market Street
Philadelphia, PA 19104
Phone: (215) 596-1183
1-800-379-9042
Fax: (215) 596-0753
(Delaware, District of Columbia, Maryland, Pennsylvania, Virginia, West Virginia)

Region IV: Atlanta
Ms. Delores L. Crockett, RA/Field Coordinator
1371 Peachtree Street, Room 323
Atlanta, GA 30367
Phone: (404) 347-4461
Fax: (404) 347-1755
(Alabama, Florida, Georgia, Kentucky, Mississippi, Carolina, South Carolina, Tennessee)

Region V: Chicago
Ms. Sandra K. Frank, RA
230 S. Dearborn Street, Room 1022
Chicago, IL 60604
Phone: (312) 353-6985
1-800-648-8183
Fax: (312) 353-6986
(Illinois, Indiana, Michigan, Minnesota, Ohio, Wisconsin)

Region VI: Dallas
Ms. Evelyn Smith, RA
Federal Bldg., Suite 735
525 Griffin Street
Dallas, TX 75202
Phone: (214) 767-6985
Fax: (214) 767-5418
(Arkansas, Louisiana, New Mexico, Oklahoma, Texas)

Region VII: Kansas City
Ms. Rose Kemp, RA
Center City Sq. Building
1100 Main St., Suite 1230
Kansas City, MO 64105
Phone: (816) 426-6108
1-800-252-4706
Fax: (816) 426-6107
(Iowa, Kansas, Missouri, Nebraska)

Region VIII: Denver
Ms. Oleta Crain, RA
1801 California Street, 905
Denver, CO 80202-2614

Phone: (303) 391-6756
1-800-299-0886
Fax: (303) 391-6752
(Colorado, Montana, North Dakota, South Dakota, Utah, Wyoming)

Region IX: San Francisco
Ms. Barbara Sanford, Acting RA
71 Stevenson Street, Suite 927
San Francisco, CA 94105
Phone: (415) 975-4750
Fax: (415) 975-4753
(Arizona, California, Guam, Hawaii, Nevada) North

Region X: Seattle
Ms. Karen Furia, RA
1111 Third Avenue, Room 885
Seattle, WA 98101-3211
Phone: (206) 553-1534
Fax: (206) 553-5085
(Alaska, Idaho, Oregon, Washington)

Note: These names, addresses, and phone numbers may have changed. For the most current information, please check the Web site at: http://www.dol.gov/dol/wb/public/info_about_wb/regions/regions.htm

 Article Review Form at end of book.

What are the divisions within women's movements? What responsibilities do the academic feminists at Barnard College have to the women on strike?

What I Learned at College

On feminism, class, and my delayed diploma

Sasha Cagen

This is a story about how I changed at college. It's a story about naïveté, growing up and shedding the blinders of privilege that have kept me, a white, middle-class quasi-riot grrrl, from dealing with the blemishes and elitism of the mainstream women's movement. Until my last semester, I never saw the problems with such clarity.

Over the last four years, I have taken in many critiques of feminism, from writers like Audre Lorde, bell hooks, Dorothy Allison, and Gloria Anzaldua. But it often takes a real-life experience to fully digest an abstract critique. In this case it was the nine-week-and-still-going strike by workers at my (now) alma mater, Barnard College, the women's college affiliated with Columbia University.

Like any strike, the standoff has exposed otherwise submerged class rifts. But this strike has an ideological twist—the union, 165 predominantly female clerical and dormitory workers, is striking against a feminist institution. And with banners reading "Barnard Cuts Women and Children First" strung up at the entrance to the college and picketers chanting, "2-4-6-8, Barnard discriminates," the enduring fault lines of liberal feminism—race and class—have become visible and audible to everyone who walks by Barnard's tiny campus in Morningside Heights.

Here's part of what I learned my senior year: Barnard is vehement about promoting its women students—future lawyers, scientists, and CEO's. But as for other women, like the striking clerical workers, Barnard doesn't like to talk about them.

And the media doesn't shine its spotlight on them very often either. On the other hand, when seven Barnard seniors (me included) were threatened with delayed diplomas after a four-hour sit-in to support the union, Local 2110, we had no trouble landing on the front page of the *Time* Metro section. Withholding our diplomas was Barnard's way of telling us to behave at commencement. But the delay was not exactly the kind of issue that the entire country needed to read about. The media pounced on the Ivy League "diploma debacle," barely mentioned the strikers, and turned the story into a debate over whether the sit-in had been an exercise in free speech or civil disobedience.

As it turns out, the Student Strike Committee had voted on a silent protest for commencement, so for two hours, I sat in my cap and gown, polite and ladylike, listening to our commencement speaker, State Supreme Court Justice Judith Kaye, Barnard class of '58, tell the class of '96 that for today's women "the opportunities are limitless."

From Sasha Cagen, "What I Learned at College" in *Village Voice*, June 4, 1996. Reprinted by permission of the author.

Please consider this article the commencement address I so sorely wished someone had made.

One brilliantly sunny February afternoon, when the strike had just begun, I was planted by the picket line, trying to gather signatures. A constant stream of hurried students brushed by. That morning I had overheard two students whining about the two extra blocks they had to walk because their classes had been moved off campus, and I remember thinking with some disbelief: Barnard might really get away with mouthing feminist rhetoric while it goes after the lowest-paid women who work here.

Many of the women on the picket line are black and Latino, many sole breadwinners for their families. Their salaries are modest, averaging $24,000 a year, so employer-paid health-care benefits are crucial to them.

The college wants them to start contributing to their premiums, and it wants the union to switch to the health plan used by faculty and administrators. Local 2110 (which also represents *Voice* workers) opposes both demands. The dispute involves a tiny amount of money, but according to union president Maida Rosenstein, "It's really an issue of power, and setting the tone for the future."

The college's latest proposal asked that only new employees make a small co-pay for health care. But that proposal would introduce a two-tiered system that would divide new and old workers and open the door to contributions from all, which, says the union, was Barnard's original objective anyway. There have

been no negotiations for over six weeks.

This is the longest strike in the last 50 years at Columbia University. The directive comes from the hip of President Judith R. Shapiro, an anthropologist who did her work on transsexualism. When she was inaugurated last school year, President Shapiro delighted many of us with her refreshingly feminist point of view. Disappointingly, this strike has shown us the limitations of her feminism.

Even more disappointing, few students enrolled in women's studies seemed to notice the discrepancy between what Barnard practices and what it teaches. Barnard continues to sponsor conferences on Women and Politics, Women and Poverty, Women and This, That or the Other, while outside on the sidewalk, actual women enter another paycheck-less week.

I had hoped that more students at a women's college would understand that feminism is about more than networking and dressing for success. But why should most of my classmates, coming of age in a reactionary time, be unlike the rest of white, middle-class America—who have the peculiar quirk of believing that they live in a classless, caste-less society? Barnard is also a school that charges tuition and fees of $27,000 a year, more than the average salary of the clerical workers.

My bottom floor of naïveté dropped out that February afternoon, just like the day I figured out the United States isn't really trying to make the world safe for democracy. I was left on the sidewalk, rethinking my values, alliances and priorities.

In the seventh week of the strike, I was sitting with my friend Tamar in the library, mired in the last stretch of final exams. Distracted, I wandered over to the magazine rack and picked up Barnard's alumnae rag. When I showed Tamar the cover story, we gave each other knowing looks and cackled like the hags we have become. The cover story is headlined "Our Money, Our Selves: Why Women are Bullish on Investment Clubs." When we stopped laughing, Tamar told me, with a barely concealed smile, "We're Barnard Feminists. We're going to take over the world."

The Barnard library is full of promise in other places, like the stacks housing books by more-visionary feminists. I hold on to this definition: "Feminism is the political theory and practice to free *all* women: women of color, working class women, poor women," said Barbara Smith at the 1979 National Women's Studies Association convention. "Anything less than this is not feminism, but merely female self-aggrandizement."

Ironically, the women who stood to gain the most from the women's movement, women who worked before they had the option, have arguably seen the least-meaningful changes in their lives. Since the '70s, the second-wave women's movement has brought, among many other wonderful things, a momentous influx of women into the professions of law, medicine, and business.

But by 1990, 80 percent of working women were still clustered in undervalued sex-segregated jobs, like clerical work, in which wages are artificially low, at 70 cents on the male dollar. And in the last two decades, we have also seen the "feminization of poverty." Increasingly, single mothers in the pink-collar ghetto are the sole support of their families. If current trends continue, some scholars estimate that by the year 2000, the poverty population will be composed entirely of women and children.

Women activists need to undertake some critical reconsideration before they take over the world. Simply dismantling barriers to female advancement only succeeds if all women are able to take advantage of those opportunities, and without structural change, sisters will remain unequal.

For these lessons in feminist political education, I leave Barnard grateful to the bigwigs who gave me a semester-long independent study in "Liberal Feminist Myopia." I just opened my mailbox, to find my first invitation to contribute to Barnard's alumnae fund. I will have to respectfully decline.

 Article Review Form at end of book.

How is sex work an entrepreneurial enterprise for women? Compare and contrast the tasks, both implicit and explicit, of secretaries, wives, and sex workers.

It's a Pleasure Doing Business with You

"Barbara"

A next-door neighbor of mine worked as an escort. She always drove terribly smart cars and always looked absolutely fabulous. I wondered what she did. Then we became very good friends, and one night, over a couple of bottles of wine, she told me how she made her money. I was absolutely fascinated. She kept telling me I ought to try it, but making that first phone call was terrifying. Eventually I phoned the agency, had a chat with them, and sent them a photograph. I was quite insecure and described myself as average, but when they got the photograph they said: "Oh, you are really, really nice!" Women have internalized so much insecurity! So I went to work with them. They were very, very good—highly professional. I worked there for three months, and in those three months I paid off all my debts and gained an enormous amount of confidence.

The first job was terrifying. I kept thinking that someone was going to scream "Fraud!" or find something wrong with me. I nearly had a heart attack every time in the beginning; it took me a while to gain self-confidence. When you begin, you really plunge in at the deep end. There's no training, as it's very difficult to describe to someone else exactly what to do. It's up to you to decide, for example, when the right moment is to go to the bedroom. That's where the art of it comes in, especially if the client is nervous. You have a little chat, make them feel that you are interested in them, then you pick the moment when they've relaxed. An experienced client, though, usually can't wait to get on with it. Before seeing a client for the first time, you are running on adrenaline, and you can become quite addicted to that feeling in the beginning. Then, as you go on, you become more and more confident.

Escort work is not what people think at all. It doesn't involve men just paying for your time, and telling you what to do. It's not that way at all. Nine times out of ten, all the men want you to do is seduce them. Men are sick, fed up, and tired with taking the sexual initiative. I always say to them: "Well, I suppose now you want me to rape you, don't you?" And they look at me, and say: "Yes!"—with their tongues lolling out of their mouths. Most of all, the clients want a woman to take the initiative for once. Most women who are in the escort business are adventurous types to begin with, and that's what the clients want.

I've got some regulars who are brilliant. Others are very businesslike, and just go through the motions. Then you get the regulars who get emotionally involved with you, and want to start a deep relationship. That's much harder. It's very difficult when they become emotionally involved, because you have to be so careful about what you say. You have to be so careful not to hurt their feelings, and also not to get emotionally involved yourself.

I've taught some men an awful lot about women. Some married men have only had sex in one position: under the covers with the lights out. I hope that they learn something from me. There are an awful lot of repressed people out there who want to know more, but who are just too frightened. I've had a few virgins and I feel an enormous responsibility with them. You want to make it as wonderful for them as possible. I've got one client who I see quite regularly now, and I saw him first as a virgin. I know he's never seen anybody else. Each time I see him, I try to introduce something different. And I try to be sensitive to the fact that when he does get a girlfriend, when he finds the confidence to do it, that he looks after *her* as well. That's a different kind of responsibility. If you see someone who is virgin territory, you want to teach them that in sex they're *two* people involved, and they're *both* supposed to enjoy it. I suppose I end up educating a lot of people.

There are some very confused men out there, who can ask me things they can't ask any other woman. It's very important that you ask them open questions, especially if they are nervous. You get them talking about themselves. The next thing you know, they can't stop. They get all these things off their chests and they feel so much better, especially if they are young single guys who aren't used to dating or who aren't confident. They can ask me things about women that they can never ask anyone else. They can't ask their mothers or their sisters. They can't talk about them to anyone except me.

I felt so, so sorry for one man. He'd been married for twenty years and his wife was going to leave him. And after twenty years she told him that she'd never, ever enjoyed sex with him. He had no idea of what he was doing. He had no idea what a clitoris was, or what it looked like! I remember being at school, and we found a pile of old magazines. There was an old women's magazine, dating back to just after the war. The headlines were: "Lie Back and Think of England." This was what was instilled into women. I was sexually active at

an early age and I always knew that I enjoyed sex, but I never orgasmed from just sexual penetration except with one man, and that was marvelous.

You also get the types who are all mouth and no trousers, the bull-shitters who want to impress you: aren't they wonderful, and shouldn't you feel privileged to be in their company? They make me laugh. They don't really believe themselves. They just want someone else to believe them. You just think: arsehole.

The worst are the ones who want to rescue you. They are totally, totally dangerous. They are the ones who are liable to flip. They see you as someone who needs saving—as someone who needs rescuing. And when you say you don't want to be rescued, that seems to trigger something in their brains: "Right, I'll go for you then." Their fantasy is that they're going to rescue you from your life of drudgery, and thereafter you'll be eternally grateful to them and will kiss their feet when they walk through the door. And when they find out that you don't want to be rescued at all, that in fact you live a wonderful life, and that you enjoy your work, it shatters their world. You have to be so terribly, terribly careful with those ones, and avoid them like the plague.

The only really bad client I ever had was this nice guy in his mid-thirties who lived in a fabulous house. It was worth over a million and a half. But after one minute he started talking about my new job! Two minutes later he got on to the "And when we get married" business. I'd only known him a matter of four minutes! I was more naive then, and I just burst out laughing. He absolutely flipped. At one point he was running around with a

knife, saying: "Well, one of us will end up dying." You always think you'll panic if something like that happens. But I didn't. I suddenly became more calm and more clear thinking than I've ever been in my life. Everything became completely focused. I was so calm, I thought: "This isn't me. This is someone else talking." And I actually managed to convince him that we'd go for a picnic the next day to discuss everything. I gave him the number of the local taxi form, and pretended it was my home phone number. I talked a whole load of rubbish and he believed it all. Then I left, went to the nearest pub, had six large brandies, and then phoned A—. And she got him blacklisted by everybody.

I absolutely hate it when they say: "And what's a nice girl like you doing a job like this for?" I always feel like saying: "Earning four times as much as you do!" Because it's true. Though it's fatal to generalize, that's what a lot of men resent. Here you are, taking charge of your own life: doing it because you want to. They resent the fact that you are not in a "normal" relationship; that there isn't a man looking after you; that you want to do what you are doing. Especially if you are good-looking. They really don't understand that at all.

If I could change one thing, I'd change the publicity around escort work. It makes me furious when women are portrayed as walking, down-trodden victims. If you portray women as victims, you are *encouraging* attacks on them. Men will attack women who they think are victims. Why are girls always portrayed the way they are in the media? We are portrayed as women who stand on street corners, who wear microscopic miniskirts, who are foul-mouthed junkies, who are violent, with severe psychiatric disorders, and who were abused as kids. Why are we not portrayed as completely normal people? I remember one day I was in Tesco's. My pager went off, so I called up A—, and she gave me a number to ring a client. There I was—in Tesco's, talking to the client, and you could hear the check-out noises in the background. So I said: "I'm sorry about this, but you caught me in Tesco's, doing my shopping." And he said to me: "My God, you're normal!"

People don't realize that we are completely normal people. When you first meet people, after five minutes, they say: "But you're intelligent! Why are you doing this when you are intelligent?" In this business, you've *got* to be intelligent; you've got to stay one step ahead of the game. You've got to have more brains than the clients have! And it takes great guts. But it's also a great deal of fun.

If you're getting paid for it, you feel justified for all the times when men presume sex is just for them. When I started working, my marriage had just broken up and I wasn't in a particularly I-love-men mood. And it made me feel much better because I was in control. It wasn't so much the money, but that I was taking the *sexual* lead in everything. I could turn the situation into what I wanted. That sense of power made me feel very good.

It's important to intimidate the client slightly in the beginning. You have to set the ground rules and show that you are in control of that situation. The first thing you do is take your coat off and give it to them. "Hang that up!" Not in a rude way, but in the

way that you say: "I'm taking control of this situation." It is also very important to be honest with them. There's one client who is particularly small. I couldn't help it: one day I was in a wicked mood, and I shouted, "Hold on a minute. I'll go and see if I can find a six-man search party." Most men would have been totally destroyed. But he knows he's microscopic and he laughed with me about it. Mind you, I haven't seen him recently.

When you think, "What is the ideal girl that the client wants?" you might think: someone who is pretty, sweet, and submissive. And yet in actual fact, if you play that role with clients, nine times out of ten you won't see them again. Clients genuinely don't like submissive women. They want women who have spunk and who have a sense of humor. They don't just want you to roll over and put your legs up in the air. They want that spark, to get the repartee going. They really like it when you criticize them. They like it when you criticize their dress sense. They like it when you criticize their house and say things like, "Oh my God, you really live here?" I've played some awful tricks on my clients, and they just love it.

There was one man who used to come through regularly. In the beginning, he was so rude to three of the girls at A—'s, that he quite upset them. So A— phoned me up. She said: "Look, he comes over really brusque. You can deal with him." So I spoke to him on the phone, and went to see him, and he started saying: "Sit down there. Take your coat off." I said: "Hold on one minute. You set down there. You take my coat." And I said: "Right, so where do I put the taxi rank for the other girls to queue up so you

can make up your mind?" After that, he came to see me three times a week. They really don't want you just to be polite, sweet, and submissive.

The ruder you are to them, I've found, the more they love it. I had real trouble coming to terms with this in the beginning, because I thought it was wrong. One very good client phoned up A— at some ridiculous time for me in the morning once, completely drunk. And she called him a prat, and next time he said: "That was wonderful. Nobody ever calls me a prat!"

In this job, you're supposed to be really hard, cynical, and never have feelings. But I find it's the opposite. It's made me far more receptive to people's feelings. There are some really lonely people out there. Men are so scared of being rejected. They are tired of wining and dining women and spending a fortune on them, and getting nowhere. At least this way, they know that they are going to get somewhere. You get a lot of men these days, especially the single ones, who think that they've been used. They're too frightened to start a relationship. But the problem is that once they get to know you, they decide you're wonderful, and then they do want to start a relationship with you.

Some men phone an escort agency rather than a dating agency. A lot of men really don't want just to pay you for your time and have sex. What they really want is a relationship, a deep, meaningful relationship. And that's when it gets hard. You know you are going to lose them as a client, because they start to make demands of you that you can't fulfill. They are not just after sex: sometimes the whole romance is the fantasy. They want to feel that you really do care for them. And you don't want to hurt their feelings, but you don't want to boost their feelings either. It's a very thin line you have to walk. Sometimes the involvement is not intended.

There's one client who I've seen over a period of about eight months. And just before Christmas we realized that it was becoming more than it was supposed to be, and he said: "I can't see you any more." So I was highly professional about it and said: "Okay, then, fine. No problem." Then he called up a week ago, and I was just so pleased to hear from him! And we ended up spending the whole night together—still safe-sex and everything. But then I really, totally, and utterly screwed up—and I don't think I'll ever see him again— because in the morning I asked him for my money. And I saw the look on his face! But I thought: "Damn it, we agreed on a contract. You ought to stick to it." But I left there thinking: "Damn it, I really screwed up. I'll never see him again." That's when it gets really hard.

If I'd got the money up front, it would have been okay. But there's nothing worse than asking for it afterwards. The majority of clients pay up front. But there's about 5 percent of clients, where I know if I ask for the money afterwards, I get twice as much. If you are talking about respectable, honorable people, after you've seen them a couple of time, they like to feel there's a trust between you. So if you ask them for the money up front all the time, I suppose they feel insulted. And you always end up running overtime, so they always give you more. It's something you have to judge.

You have days when it's easy to say the right thing, and be well behaved. It's like any other job. Then they are days when you are feeling pissed off, and you say completely the wrong thing. Everyone has their bad days, and there are occasional ones that you don't enjoy at all. But some of them are terribly enjoyable experiences. It's like any other job. It's as exciting and as interesting as you want to make it.

A lot of the job is being a psychologist, a counselor. It always amazes me how much people respect my opinion. I have got quite a good group of regular clients and they'll ask me things like: "Should I buy a Jaguar or a BMW?" I say: "The BMW." The next week they say: "I took your advice and bought the BMW." One client is a solicitor. I saw him the other week coming out of court as I was doing my shopping, but he didn't see me. When he phoned up, I said: "Oh, I thought I saw you the other day, but it couldn't have been you." And he said: "Why not?" And I said: "It looked like you were wearing somebody else's suit. It was a couple of sizes too small for you." And he phoned up the other day and said: "I've taken your advice and I've bought six new suits." They love someone to tell them these things. They even ask my business advice. They tell me things about their business that they wouldn't dream of even telling their wives. If I wanted to go into insider trading now, I'd probably do terribly well.

It's fatal to generalize about men, but you can divide clients into four or five different groups. There's your married businessman who just wants a quickie: very pleasant, very nice, no problem. Then there's your married guy, who also wants more of a relationship. Then there's your single guy, who wants more of a

relationship. Then there's the kinky ones. I can in fact tell on the telephone what type of client it is. I play little games with myself. I guess on the phone whether they're wearing boxers or briefs, which is of course a class thing. I don't know how I do it, but I'm never wrong now. I've even got to where I can guess whether they are cotton or silk. You get to suss them out pretty easily.

I used to play games to liven things up, though I've stopped some of them now. You always get the ones who want to hear your life story. So I'd tell everybody something different. Then they'd say: "Oh, well, of course, you were a brain surgeon once, weren't you?" It got very difficult remembering who I'd told what. Regulars, of course, stick in your memory, but most clients I have no recollection of at all. I've also been to see clients who haven't realized that they've seen me before. I saw one man who, halfway through the evening, said: "You've been here before!" And I said: "Yes, I know." And he said: "We've had this conversation before!" And I said: "Yes, I know."

There are some men who don't want sex at all, who I really do just go out to dinner with. It's an all-round service. During the day, it tends to be businessmen, and just straight sex, not too many frills. Whereas during the evening, you spend a lot more time with people. You tend to get more involved. I have a few kinky clients, but not that much, though that's a growing market. The AIDS thing is making everyone more kinky. A lot of men don't like condoms, so they try to get their kicks in different ways.

The fetish scene is easier. But you have to be able to keep a straight face until you can run to the bathroom. You have to be a bit of a mind reader—to look in their eyes and know what they are thinking. I don't want to specialize in the fetish scene, though. I used to be convinced that this job would never change me. But it does. It changes you dramatically. There's one man who's really kinky, and I feel quite disturbed afterwards. I feel disturbed that I have that much power over somebody. He likes being dominated completely. He wants to be slapped around the face and to kiss my shoes. He never, ever touches me physically. I don't even take my clothes off. I haven't got that much of a kinky wardrobe, but he likes slicked-back hair, six-inch stilettos, and black clothes. But I always feel disturbed that I have that much power. He's ridiculously wealthy. He wants me to go off to the Caribbean with him; he'll book a five-star suite, and he wants me to chain him to the radiator and make him sleep on the floor, and embarrass him in public. Poor bloke, he wants to be utterly mistreated. His ideal fantasy is for me to go out with him, tie him to a tree, smack him around the face a little, and then leave him there for the night. When I leave, I feel frightened, not about the physical side of it, but the mental. He says things like: "If you ordered me to marry you, I'd obey." He's worth millions and millions and millions! But I couldn't cope with that. I'd end up in the funny farm. You have to decide what level you're happy with. The kinky ones tend to be people who have trouble expressing themselves emotionally—which happens to be the vast majority of the population!

In general I'd say it's nine to one men that want to *be* dominated. They want to be abused by a woman. But I like people, and I respect people, and I find it really difficult to do it. And it's so difficult not to laugh as well. I've had to run out of the room, once, in hysterics. I ran out of the hotel room, had hysterics in the corridor, and then ran back in again. But at the end of the day, especially if you like someone, it upsets me. They say: "Smack me around the face." I say: "I can't." I smacked one man so hard I nearly sent him flying across the room, and he loved it. I find that very difficult.

You get to where you can almost look at someone and tell if they are kinky or not, simply by how reserved and businesslike they are. The more powerful they are, the more submissive they want to be. One of my theories is that they spend all day bawling people out and they like to be submissive for a while. It is completely stress-free being told what to do, rather than having to make all the decisions. I can understand that. Women do the same in relationships. You get women who are very businesslike and very dominant and successful at work, but always seem to find some man they can play the little woman role with.

I've only ever met one client who wanted to be dominant. I didn't like him on the phone, so I asked for £450 for two hours. He's absolutely paranoid, this chap. You meet the odd client who checks the cupboards for reporters. He'd park his car at least a mile away and walk the last bit. I know from a bit of investigation that he is an MP. He was really into submissive women. He was this other woman's client, and she was there, and I didn't like what he was doing. After twenty minutes he turned to me and said: "You don't like me, do you?" And I said: "No, personally, I think you're an arsehole and I hate your guts." And he gave me my £450, and he said: "You can go."

I don't like seeing a man who's had a few to drink. It's very difficult if you know the client, and he sounds sober on the phone. The worst men are the ones who don't turn you on and think that all women have to have about six orgasms before they will penetrate them. Some men think this is normal. There are men who get their sexual experience from watching porno movies. Now women who work in porn have twenty minutes in between takes to relax, before faking again. But if you have to fake six on the trot, that's hard work! If I were to act out how I have a real orgasm, they wouldn't believe I'd had one! They'd say: "That wasn't a real orgasm. You've faked that!" So you have to do this dramatic, over-the-top fake. And they manage to really believe it. They really do. Sometimes they'll say things like: "Oh, that was a fake." And I say: "Oh, no it wasn't." And they smile. They want that bit of reassurance. They want to believe it. They really do. But I don't fake all the time. Sometimes I do get turned on. Sometimes I get turned on very much. But if you were to have a real orgasm, they wouldn't believe you. They are so, so funny. And they all like to think that they're different.

It's really important for people to understand it's okay not to have an orgasm. Even for men. The first time a guy faked on me—this wasn't a client—I knew, I knew. You can tell the difference. I told him: "Why the hell didn't you tell me? There was no need to fake it."

If I don't like the sound of a client on the phone, I'll make some excuse. If I do like the sound of them, before I see them, I check them out through directory inquiries to make sure that the telephone number and address match. I can also find out if they have a track record, which quite a few of them do. Escort agencies can advertise. Some newspapers will take advertising, some won't. We wondered if advertising was soliciting, and we borrowed a police manual, and it says there that you can only solicit on a face-to-face basis. So soliciting by telephone or newspapers has to be legal. Ask any friendly policeman.

I've had policemen come to see me. One policeman, I knew at once what he did, because he hadn't changed his boots. The second time he came to see me, he said: "You have no idea what I do for a living, do you?" As he was about to come out with the big confession, I thought, oh to hell with it, I'm not going to give him the pleasure. And I said: "Yes, I do know what you do. You're a policeman, aren't you?" He was so shocked. He said: "How on earth did you know?" I said: "Your boots. If nobody's ever told you, they're a dead giveaway."

The one that really shattered all my illusions was the Catholic priest. He was Canadian and was staying with the mission in X—. He had "Jesus Loves You" and a cross on the bottom of his glasses. I wondered if he was going to try to convert me. Not at all! It was just straight off up to the bedroom. I go to the church up the road once a month, and I thought, "God, if he's kinky, I'm going to die." But it was just straight sex. Later, I said to A—: "This is going to end them all—a Catholic priest!

It's quite usual to see lords or earls, but now I'm going to have to set my cap on the pope. Nothing less will do!"

A girl I know is paid £150 an hour by a priest. He's seen her about six times now. He sits her down, and talks to her about the error of her ways. He tells her Jesus loves her, and that she shouldn't be doing it. She doesn't mind at all. He doesn't ask for anything. He's just a born-again Christian, doing God's work. She takes the money and laughs her head off. He thinks he's saving souls, and she's just having hysterics.

There really are big cultural differences between countries. English people have real problems with sex. English men are so repressed. They don't like talking about things; they *can't* talk about things. On the other hand, I think American men tend to dissect things and go into them too much. With American men you can spend ten minutes having sex and ten hours talking about it afterwards. Give me a Continental man any day.

Women paying for sex is a Continental thing. My ex-husband used to be an escort. He worked in an agency where the women used to call out the men, more than the men called out the women. It's a cultural thing. English women are repressed. American women *think* they are more open. But Continental women are far more aggressive about their pleasure. In Scandinavian countries it's quite usual for a woman to call out an escort. But, of course, they don't expect the man always to perform; men can't always get it up. I was fascinated about this and asked my husband all sorts of questions. It was just a question of the woman being satisfied: as long as she gets her

orgasm. It was also usually a whole experience. Dinner first. Then sex for the woman afterwards—either orally or with a vibrator, massaging them. In Scandinavian counties it's not that unusual at all. It's coming to Britain, but in a very odd way. It's rich, bored housewives clubbing together for a laugh. It's not being taken seriously. And I think that's a real shame. On my birthday I'm going to treat myself to a male escort.

A lot of the women working as escorts are married. Their husbands know and don't mind. They know it's just business. Some of the husbands drive them around, and sit outside, and wait for them. Not as a form of pimping, but just if the girls can't drive. They know it helps pay the bills and they just see it as being a job. I've spoken to other girls who have got boyfriends, and the men all go through the same syndrome. We've identified the patterns. The first week they are nervous to ask, but they are worried about whether or not you enjoyed it. And they are worried about your safety. The second week, it's like being on Mastermind. They want to know every single detail—in *great* detail. They want to know everything that happened and everything that was said. The third week, they're more relaxed, but they moan when you get out of bed at one in the morning, and get dressed, and go out. And finally they end up accepting it and stop putting you through the Spanish Inquisition. But they all suffer from insecurity; they're all afraid you're going to fall in love with a client and run off with him. So you do try to draw the line. Business is business. But it doesn't always work.

You set your own prices, but all the girls charge basically the same. Recently around here, though, some girls have started undercutting drastically. But then the men soon realize that they're not getting the service they want. Here, the agency fee is £30. My fee is £100 for an hour. If someone wants something extra special, you might charge more. If you're going to be with someone longer than an hour, you negotiate, because you can't bonk all the time. Sometimes it's only twenty minutes. You're flexible.When sixty minutes is up, you don't set off an alarm and dash out with your clothes. You don't leave things dangling in midair. Some girls do work like that; but I don't.

Our biggest grudge is with the media. If you want to put a call girl in a film, you cast someone who looks like a total disaster area, who has got every vice going. Girls just aren't like that. If there was one thing I could do, it would be to get rid of the stigma. It's very important to change the laws, but that will not get rid of the stigma. Only public awareness can. I'm a mother, for example, and you couldn't find a better-looked-after child. I know I do spoil her, but when she's not with me I know she is getting quality care. She goes to a terribly good school. She doesn't lack anything. She has an extremely happy home. She's not exposed to any dangers. She has no idea what goes on. How can anyone say I'm not a good mother? If I didn't do what I do, and we were living on the breadline, surely that would make me a worse mother.

I admire the girls who work the streets. I think they are enormously brave. I feel genuinely sorry for them, because of the laws. The laws have to be abolished, but people also need to be protected. We can't be that relaxed that anything goes. I would like girls to have health checks, for their own sakes. But girls shouldn't be harassed. Nobody's going to have sex without a condom or do anything stupid like that. But there should be drop-in centers where people can get confidential care. I couldn't tell my doctor what I do. I can afford to go privately, but what about all the people who can't?

Most of the time the clients are highly sensible and very well behaved about condoms. Generally, I have no problems with men about using condoms, especially with Continental men. The funny thing is, the one group of men who should be more aware than anyone else, but aren't, are American men. You have to try to build it up and say things like: "Rubber turns me on." For some reason it seems to hurt their egos to wear one.

Clubs where women can't use condoms should be closed down. I think there should be more women running the industry and making the decisions. For example: what exactly does "living off immoral earnings" mean? We've tried to get a definitive ruling on that. I pay my nanny out of my earnings. Does that mean that he is living off immoral earnings and breaking the law? I spend money in the local shops. Does that mean they are living off immoral earnings? But pimps ought to be eradicated. There *are* girls who get beaten up and sent out there, and that's got to be stopped. Personally, I don't like working for men and I won't work for men.

It's not a job that most women can do. And it's not a question of looks. It doesn't really matter how you look, but it takes a certain type of person. Some of the busiest girls are the ones who are not the prettiest, who are far older, but who just have the personality. You need the right personality. You also have to like sex and be very sexually aware of yourself. If people know that you absolutely despise sex . . . you shouldn't lie there as if you want to be somewhere else. You have to like sex or be a terrifically good actress—or a bit of both! The worst thing is kissing: if you don't want to kiss them and they want to kiss you. Instinctively, you pull back.

Some girls go in like a steamroller, and say: "I'll do this, this, and this, and I won't do that, that, and that." That's a turnoff. You can set boundaries more subtly by saying: "I want this and this and this, and that turns me on." At the end of the day they want to please you. If I didn't fake, some of them would be devastated! It's their egos. It's not just the sex; they need the whole experience. If it was just sexual desire, they'd lock themselves in a closet with a dirty magazine. But I've met some men who were so sexually frustrated that they were bordering on violence. It was an urgent need, a deep frustration that they weren't getting their share. If you can let them pay for it, and soothe their egos at the same time, you are providing a really worthwhile service.

Nothing I do is illegal. One of the first clients I saw was a solicitor. I thought, I know he's paying for this, but damn it, I'm going to pump him for information, and I did. What I do isn't illegal, but I have about £2,000 of clients' bounced checks that I haven't bothered chasing up. If you take them to the small claims court, they want to know all about it. I know some girls who've done it, but I'm still sitting on the fence. One girl even sent in the bailiffs. I take checks very, very carefully, but bounced checks are quite a problem—it's "taking services by deception." The last thing we want to do is involve the police, but I would have no qualms about calling them. And I always let clients know that I'm not breaking the law in any way. If they think that

what I'm doing is illegal, they might think that they can abuse the situation and get away with it.

Men-for-men prostitution has been in this country for an awful long time. It's a huge business, almost bigger than our business. And they are so much better at it! My friend M— can't understand why I'm not dripping in Cartier jewelry. But I'm just not that mercenary. At the end of the day, men are far more mercenary.

Money plays an important role in it all, though again you can't generalize. Some men get a kick out of paying for it. Others

resent having to pay. Some guys like to think you are going to fall so madly in love with them that you won't ask for money. Others say on the phone: "Well, I'm really young and I'm really good-looking. . . . " As if that is going to bring the price down! You just laugh at them and say: "Look, I don't particularly care if you look like Quasimodo! It's the same price." They don't seem to be able to understand that at all.

 Article Review Form at end of book.

What are some of the reasons Borsook offers for the masculine sensibility of magazines like *Wired*? How was Borsook discriminated against at the magazine? What actions could she have taken to facilitate changes?

The Memoirs of a Token

An aging Berkeley feminist examines *Wired*

Paulina Borsook

I suppose it all came to a head one night past midnight in the spring of 1995. I lay awake on the couch in the living room thinking dark thoughts until past three in the morning. *Wired* magazine had brought me to that too-often described "aha" state of women and ethnic minorities and gays and anyone else who feels marginalized and badly done by, when they reach the epiphany that requires leaving policies of appeasement behind—wounded pride, self-disgust, the infant impulse to lash out.

Wired is the hottest, coolest, trendiest new magazine of the 1990s. Within its first three years, it has received a National Magazine award, started sister publications in England and Japan and become the coffee table ornament/lifestyle indicator/ print-based fashion accessory *du jour*. This consumer magazine that makes computers and communica-

tions and video and technology sexy and glamorous even shows up in IBM's television commercials. *Wired* marks its readers as being with-it one-planet high-tech high-touch global citizens of the 1990s.

And *Wired* has certainly been the most successful magazine launch San Francisco has seen since *Rolling Stone* in the mid-1960s. Like *Rolling Stone,* it seeks to both shape and reflect an emerging, media-driven world-wide culture, one that's creative and anarchic and playful and loose in the hips. And like *Rolling Stone*'s founder, Jann Wenner, *Wired* co-founder Louis Rossetto is well on his way to creating a media empire of his own, everything from the online *HotWired* to HardWired Books to rumors of Wired TV.

Memories of Underdevelopment

But here's where things get tricky and uncomfortably gendered:

When *Rolling Stone*, the chronicle of sixties sex'n'drugs'n'rock'n'roll culture came into being, sixties feminism hadn't really yet hit the streets. Hippie chicks were all into free love and making bread, and Janis and Grace sure could wail; but somehow girls weren't much relevant (o, sixties concept!) to making it all happen. The second wave of feminism hadn't yet spawned its kazillions of cultural commentators (How many feminists does it take to screw in a light bulb? One to do it, and four to write about it).

The counterculture was supposed to affect us all—however, you wouldn't know that women were up to much, really, after reading *Rolling Stone*. Women getting uppity (as they did as the sixties turned into the seventies and into the eighties) were intrinsically *not* considered entertaining—nor of much interest to the fifteen-year-old boys (*Rolling Stone*'s true subscriber base) who read the magazine in the rec room of their parents' basement, and to whom the magazine represented the fantasy lives they wished to live: hip, smart, irreverent. *Rolling Stone*, like *Wired*, like all consumer magazines, acts out its readers' fantasy lives (consider that half of the subscribers to *Vogue* are size 12 or larger, and that many of those who subscribe to poetry magazines are would-be poets who hope to get published themselves someday).

Thirty years have passed since Jann Wenner started *Rolling Stone*, yet *Wired*, its spiritual child, both interpreter and vanguard of the Next New Generational Thing, is also turning out to be largely by guys and for guys. It's as if women hadn't infiltrated, at least to some degree, every kind of traditionally male bastion since the 1960s—and as if it wouldn't be perilous and foolish and shortsighted to conceive of and record any kind of global transfiguration of culture that didn't include them.

We're not quite as invisible or handmaidenly this time around, but *Wired* doesn't seem to have paid much mind. We have in us, if only as ancestral genetic memory, the experience of women civil-rights workers who began to wonder why they weren't allowed to participate in the revolution they came to foment—and who came to demand a commensurate place in it, and in their own lives overall.

Nonetheless, *Wired* has consistently and accurately been compared in the national media to *Playboy*. It contains the same glossy pictures of certified nerd-suave things to buy—which, since it's the nineties, includes cool hand-held scanners as well as audio equipment and cars—and idolatrous profiles of (generally) male moguls and muckymucks whose hagiography is not that different from what might have appeared in *Fortune*. It is the wishbook of material desire for young men.

And as with *Playboy*, whose articles can be both *great* and about things that count society-wide, women tend to be put off by *Wired*, as they seem not to be by *Wired*'s more wacked-out sister-spirit competitor publications, *boing boing* and *Mondo 2000*. When thirty women at a San Francisco talk about women and the Internet (a pretty self-selected bunch relatively comfortable with technology) were asked if they read *Wired*, they all raised their hands. And when they were asked if they hated *Wired*, they all raised their hands. It appears women, even the techno-initiated, generally do *not* like *Wired*.

Looks Count

Which poses an uncomfortable question: If something looks sleek and whiz-bang, does that mean it *can't* appeal to most women? That is, if a publication exudes the smell of new machines, celebrates the whizzy and the zippy—are there subtle gendered cues that say "Boys club! Fun for us! None of that cuddly touchy-feely serious crap that reminds us of moms/girlfriends/schoolmarms!" And does that also telegraph to women the message "trancelike boy-absorption in silly fetishizing junk on the order of model airplanes—who needs it?"

Would art directors and style-setters worldwide ape the *Wired* style if it telegraphed *girls* just having fun? Put the *Wired* visual gestalt in the same box as other mostly-male-reader mags such as *Popular Science* or *PC Magazine*. If they looked like *Ladies Home Journal* or *Martha Stewart Living*, would male readers refuse to pick them up? Why aren't the similarly tacit appeals to out-there lifestyle choices of *Interview* as gendered as those of *Wired*? Is it because *Interview*, with just as tendentious an à la mode look and feel as *Wired*, is nominally about *people* and *Wired* is about *machines*?

The Second Sex

The very success of *Wired* raises another unpleasant revenant: It's a sociocultural commonplace that when a profession, hitherto a male dominion, becomes more accessible to women, it loses status. Clerks, bank tellers, secretaries, pharmacists, schoolteachers, English professors, psychiatrists, were at one time prac-tically all men—these are occupations that lost money, status and power as they became more female-dominated. Does this mean that a trade and a subculture can't possibly be of the moment and desirable and highcaste and way-cool and possessed of societal *juju* if it is seen as being female? Or even, female-friendly? It's a truism that women wear male clothing (either the real thing, or reinterpreted for them), but few men wear women's clothing—unless they are into gender-fuck or transgressive behaviors in general. A certain sexually charged salability aside (Swedish bikini team or dyke chic), girl-associated culture isn't perceived as cutting edge.

Wired says that 20 percent of its readership is women. Would *Wired* ever run an article of more appeal to women than men, just to favor for once one of those 20-percenters? Would its core readers feel betrayed?

Material Culture

The wild success of *Wired* also touches on other equally creepy gender-oriented uneasiness. A peculiarly awful, misogynistic boss I once had at a now-defunct computer magazine in the early 1980s once made the dismissive remark that no general-interest magazine whose audience was mostly women could survive commercially (witness the problems with *Ms* and *Psychology Today*)—unless it was a female service-magazine such as *Redbook*. But magazines whose readership was largely male (such as *PC World*) could flourish. That ignores all the niche hobbyist magazines largely for women, and the nominally-unisex-but-really-for-women titles such as *Vanity Fair* and *Gourmet* and elides the important distinction that computer magazines, in some sense, are very much business and trade publications.

But his point still nags: Since women generally don't fetishize and aren't tool and object junkies to the extent that men are (though of course there are exceptions), maybe there can't be a magazine that guarantees to a set of advertisers (and it is advertisers, and not subscribers, who subsidize a magazine) a captive audience of readers interested in particular kinds of goods and services they have to sell. The idea is, women aren't interested in objects, unless it's the bland health/grooming/fitness/beauty/Kitchen Bouquet chachkas that show up mostly in the pages of rags such as *Good Housekeeping.*

You Do the Math

When all else fails, you can, as they say in Internet slang, RTFM (read the fucking manual). That is, IRL (in real life), examine the text at hand. I sat down with all *Wired* issues published as of late spring 1995 and performed the lame, plodding, numerical analysis so annoyingly a part of feminist studies and employment-discrimination class-action lawsuits. I counted how many men and how many women were authors of *Wired* stories and subjects of *Wired* features, and how many were listed on the *Wired* mastheads.

It would be intellectually dishonest to expect *Wired* to practice what a male *Wired* editor calls "affirmative-action journalism," that is, to expect more women to appear in the magazine than actually scrabble around in the world of digital convergence. The best figures available seem to indicate that about one third of Internet accounts are now owned by women, but historically that has not been the case. And it's clear to anyone who spends time online that even now women aren't taking up one-third of the bandwidth. And only about 10 to 15 percent of computer-science majors (both graduate and undergraduate) are women.

And thus it appears: Women were the subject of about 15 percent of *Wired* articles and only one cover out of twenty-five as of June 1995. There are vague in-house grumbling intimations by women on staff of likely accomplished females being shot down as article-subjects in *Wired* editorial meetings and of no-account off-point numb-nut guys being celebrated instead—but that's par for the course in any mostly-male arena.

Where *Wired* numbers become dismaying lies in who is doing the article writing. The community of writers capable of writing for *Wired* is not made up of the same kinds of people who might be considered net geeks or multimedia content developers—or who in their fantasy-life might want to imagine themselves to be such.

Schools of journalism overall attract and graduate women in equal or greater numbers than men; even the staffs of male-oriented magazines such as *Playboy* are made up of sizable numbers of women. What's more, within the specialty of technical journalism, women make up 30 to 50 percent of its work force, much as women dominate technical writing and documentation—because that's where the jobs are.

But only 15 percent of *Wired* authors are women.

Because computer journalism as a specialty has been around for at least ten to fifteen years, plenty of women have been able to acquire the chops to make it to the journeyman, and even expert, ranks of this specialized writing guild. But these women seldom show up in the pages of *Wired.*

These dreary *Wired* statistics fit with what many, many women have told me: that they had pitched *Wired* and gotten nowhere, not even the courtesy of a formal rejection.

Is it that women who habitually *do* write about technology simply can't phrase their queries in ways that *Wired* guys like? Is it their choice of subjects? Is it that they look at the magazine, think "boys and their toys; no way they'd want *me*" and don't even try? And as for the women who are simply damned fine writers and could write about anything if asked (you know, like Janet Malcolm or Katha Pollit or Cynthia Heimel)—are they not asked? Would they laugh if they were? Would the whole magazine strike them as being inaccessible and adolescent-male-wet-dream and, therefore, not worthy of their efforts? Highly paid, highly visible male writers want to be in *Wired* regardless of the pay because it's the current guy magazine of record, whereas women writers of similar status appear to not know it exists, not care, or maybe figure it's too much of a boy's club to even bother.

Historically the editorial positions of creativity, power and prestige at *Wired* have been held by men, while editorial pooper-scooper jobs, the copy editors and fact-checkers and everyone else who has to clean up and rewrite copy into acceptable shape for publication, have been held largely by women. They have contended with substandard prose written by male writers all the time (where'd they get these guys?). Are the women who can't even get in the door worse than the guys who are already in? Do the women's shoes have to be shined twice as bright? four times as bright? eight times? to compete with the boys whose output makes *Wired* staffers' eyes roll?

As for the women authors who do make it into *Wired*, they seem to write an inordinate number of articles on sex'n'dating, or profiles of other women; can they not think of anything else to write about? Or is this the equivalent of what happens in big corporations, where no one knows if it's due to women unconsciously seeking their comfort zones or men unconsciously ghettoizing their female hires? Women in management inevitably show up in human resources ("so good with people"). In the legal community they end up in family law, in urban planning they cluster in housing.

As for the masthead, it reflects who a magazine considers its stable of contributors to be, even if they haven't written a thing in months: It's a way to list membership in its club of the cool, the equivalent to "of counsel" on a law firm's letterhead.

Sad to say, in my survey of *Wired*, women made up only 8 percent of the writers listed on the masthead. There was one month when I was the only woman on the masthead. Month to month, I have been in the company of only one or two others.

Does this issue of the gender of authorship matter? To me gender and agency are inextricably bound up with each other, though necessarily not in a one-to-one causal relationship: For example, it's still the case that women legislators, regardless of party affiliation, care more about childcare and education and family-leave than male legislators do. And just as in fiction, where men trying to write from a woman's point of view can create fascinating work that to me almost always rings false, I think it does matter that so few of the voices printed in *Wired* are female. It probably doesn't occur to the men writing for *Wired* to think about issues that might be of more importance to women than to men.

The Personal Is the Political

Then there's my own history with *Wired*, which explains how I ended up such a wreck that night on the couch. Of course, all kinds of folks feel marginalized and dismissed by the *Wired* sensibility and the *Wired* powers-that-be. Indeed, my sense of the magazine's rejecting me with a foreign-body reaction was probably just

as much a function of my own intolerance of their wacky, techno-naive libertarian worldview (technology = good, government = bad; free market = good, regulation = bad; digital = good, analog = bad) as it was the magazine's trivialization of the token girl. Although *Wired* maintains a posture of celebrating all the cacophony and lack of prior restraint net global culture has to offer, in fact, it is not open to points of view other than its own, as bounded a set as *National Review* or *The Advocate*.

Ultimately, gender and gender politics are simply part of the political mix of all humans operating in groups, and not everything can be squished through the narrow cognitive-filter of feminist critique.

That being said, commence my lament:

Back in the winter of 1993, before I'd returned to live in San Francisco, I had dinner with John Markoff, computer correspondent for the *New York Times*. Markoff is someone I've known more socially than professionally, if tangentially, for years, and he asked me if I knew about these nice, interesting people at this new startup, *Wired*, which had billboards on buses all over town. No, I hadn't heard of them, but Markoff had written for the magazine's first issue, so I figured the founders might be engaged in something decent.

A few weeks later, I received a free copy of the first issue of *Wired* through a one-time mass mailing. The magazine had obtained my name and address from the membership roster of the Electronic Frontier Foundation (EFF), a non-profit cofounded by Lotus 1-2-3 entrepreneur Mitch Kapor and Grateful Dead lyricist John Perry Barlow and dedicated to the preservation of First and Fourth Amendment rights in cyberspace; I'd been a charter card-carrying member.

I describe this periphrastic backstory so that it's clear *why* I thought *Wired* was an association of kindred spirits, communicators whose larger view on technology was not so different from my own. At its start, and at the commencement of my connection with it, *Wired* and I seemed to be cohabiting the same small sector of the galaxy, and there seemed a certain synchronistic rightness to the connection. But I digress. . .

When I looked over that first issue of *Wired*, with its glossy literate tone (plus a Q+A with Camille Paglia, the counterfeminist of the moment), I thought, "Hmm, maybe they'd get my fiction." My MFA thesis written for Columbia University's School of the Arts was a series of interconnected short stories depicting how the new information technologies deform relationships, focusing on but not limited to email. I'd been receiving Miss Congeniality award rejections on it for months, often written on manual typewriters ("you're a very good writer, and this is very interesting, but no one cares about this email nonsense and this is all unrealistic anyway").

After asking editor in chief Rossetto by email if he'd be interested (in those days, he was easily reachable), I asked my agent to FedEx the manuscript. They received it on a Friday and agreed to publish its concluding novella, "Love Over the Wires," the following Monday. I was told they were thrilled to have a Pushcart Prize-nominated writer publishing fiction with them, and they started throwing nonfiction projects my way.

Working on my first *Wired* profile, a portrait of the Hannah Arendt/Jeane Kirkpatrick of the computer industry, Esther Dyson, I included a section on gender-politics, because I had been struck in my reporting by how often I was asked "Who is Esther dating?"—a question that had *never* come up when I had done profiles of other computer folks, that is, guys. I was also struck by the personal quality of what her detractors had to say; that is, people made snotty remarks about her clothes or manners that I had once again never heard applied to equally socially aberrant guys. And finally, Esther was interesting as a woman who had succeeded in a male-dominated field.

Making Esther neither a feminist exemplar nor a martyr, I simply described in a limited portion of my article the comments and questions about her that I had found curious, indicated that such an anomalous set of reactions had to be related to her gender, and asked Esther how she felt about the ways her life-path had been affected by her being a woman.

Executive editor Kevin Kelly called me up to complain. Wasn't it sexist of me to call attention to Esther's gender at all? "I don't even think of whether or not Esther is a woman." Of course he didn't; Esther-the-uncoupled-off-tomboy is one of the best women I've ever met at being one of the guys. Wasn't it irrelevant of me to bring up all these feminist issues. I responded that it would be of interest to other women to see how a woman negotiated all the compromises and contradictions of making it in a male-majority polis. "Gee, I never thought about how it might be interesting to women to hear about another woman's experience." And on it went, back and forth. That section

remained; it is the part of the article I have gotten the most compliments and comments on; but, of course, as Deborah Tannen has pointed out in her books, anytime a woman raises an issue of gender-politics, or a relationship issue, she is branded as troublesome, regardless of how polite or righteous her cause.

I'd never had a conversation quite like this with an editor before; puzzled, I trotted off to. . .

The Salon

I was asked to participate in a roundtable discussion with various people considered Interesting and Worthy by *Wired*, perhaps modeled on the monthly Reality Club meetings of New York literary agent John Brockman (who handles clients such as *Whole Earth Catalog*'s Stewart Brand and John Markoff). I was amused and flattered and thought it would be fun.

Alas, what resulted was one of those click-inducing, radicalizing smashups I'd heard about and read about since 1969 but never before experienced for myself.

The Friday-night salon turned out to be just like those conclaves that women who attend graduate school in male-dominated fields in science report on and that women in the business world complain about. In other words, no one paid me, one of the few women invited, the smallest amount of attention.

Some of my problems that night were no doubt structural: My female tendency towards rhetorical politeness (not wanting to barge in or raise my voice to overmaster someone else's speech) and my softer voice, were, I'm sure, part of the problem. And a male friend I ran into later commented on the bombastic, bad energy in the place that night, so gender probably wasn't the only determinant of bottom-dog status.

Nonetheless, at this confab at *Wired*'s South of Market offices, I was rendered mute. When I would start to talk, the other salon attendees would simply act as if I weren't present. If I made a point, it was simply ignored, evidently not worth responding to. One participant was a guy I had coincidentally interviewed on the phone a few hours before for a non-*Wired* project—he acted as if I were not even there.

The climax of the evening came when virtual-reality spokesmodel Jaron Lanier started babbling on about how "we" (who we? *Wired?* the technology community? self-absorbed guys with large and fragile egos? monomaniacs?) needed to seek out artists and humanities people, people whose comments and critiques were not normally heard. Meanwhile I had been sitting right next to him all evening, and he hadn't even acknowledged the volume of air I was displacing. I felt like grabbing him by the dreds and saying, "Asshole, I studied with Kenneth Rexroth and published poetry in little magazines whose names even I have forgotten! I've been hanging out with arty types like Leo Castelli hangers-on at places like Max's Kansas City since 1973!"

But I couldn't see what such defensiveness and such protestations and such borching would accomplish. I was appalled at having been put in a position where it was assumed I was a null set, useless until I proved otherwise. Not being inclined towards scenes, I said nothing at the time. I did throw a hissy fit afterwards, (for I had never been ignored just like that), and naturally, was not invited back.

The events at the *Wired* salon were a sign that something very odd was going on with this community/culture/cult. I hadn't expected bleeding-edge guys from their twenties to their fifties to act like the board members of General Motors sometime in mid-1957, and it's certainly not been borne out by my encounters with the Real World Out There that technophiles are, to a man, male chauvinist pigs. The manners of the *Wired* salon participants were quite different, say, from what I had run into with the friendly geeks of the Internet technical community. Those Internet technocrats were attentive, verging on courtly, once they saw I meant no harm and was at least educable.

Tending toward the dense, I couldn't reconcile the cognitive dissonance between *Wired*'s representation of itself (egalitarian, democratic) and *Wired*'s operational nature.

Cut a year later to. . .

Femxpri

In the summer of 1994, a woman started the topic "WIRED . . . gendered? (oh no!)" in the *Wired* conference on the WELL, the online conferencing system/BBS I've lurked on for years. The predictably accurate but hopeless comments were posted: the aggressive, swaggering look and feel of the mag (most likely appealing to guys, probably off-putting to gals), the emphasis on expensive toys likely to induce male vasocongestion and capable of being used as display and territorial markers (women, to the extent they care about such things at all, generally are interested in the utilitarian value, not fetish-worthiness, of tools), the generally unconscious but annoyingly present small sexisms, and so on.

Publicly I posted a few remarks, mostly to the effect that guys have this amazing "off" switch that makes them simply not want to hear women complaining about men, or talking about topics exclusively of interest to women—unless it's about sex in a way guys find exciting and not threatening. But what signified more is that while I was posting that publicly, I wrote what I *really* felt in a private women's conference on the WELL, femxpri (a conference at least nominally for Generation X women). This public-private duality in part sprang from my not wanting to violate the confidences told to me by female *Wired* staffers. I also didn't want to jeopardize my position at the magazine. Not totally. Not at that time. *Wired,* like many entrepreneurial organizations, is very much of the either-you-are-with-us-or-you-are-against-us mentality. It pronounces anathema on those who defect for any reason and cannot abide criticism or deviation from its tiny cel of the world-kaleidoscope. I knew to write all I thought and felt would end my career as The Woman Writer They Respect and Can Point to When People Accuse Them of Being Sexist. I was well aware, like many tokens in high-profile scenes before me, that I had a position of some status that I enjoyed and wasn't ready to relinquish.

This dodge is somewhat allied to the phenomena I'd observed in social or professional situations where it came out that I'd written for *Wired.* Suddenly I would be perceived to be more interesting/intelligent/attractive than I had been in the seconds before this revelation was made. But sickeningly enough, I came to feel this highly favorable response may have had *less* to do with the reflected sheen of *Wired* and more to do with the oddity of such an unprepossessing creature (a frowzy, lumpy, bookish, middle-aged woman) creating content capable of appearing in *that* mag. Didn't Dr. Johnson make a misogynistic remark to that effect: that women preaching is on a par with a dog's walking on its hind legs; the marvel is not that they do it well, but that they do it at all. . . .

Which feeds, sheepishly enough, into a confession regarding . . .

Writer Vanity and Thin-Skinnedness

Anyone who works for applause (actors and film editors and writers) cares if his or her work is displayed to maximum advantage, is leveraged for optimum narcissistic gratification. Which in the negative, means it's really easy to start throwing all manner of slights into one's own private cauldron of discontent: Never a cover story. Screwups on layout and design and type. Not being invited to A-list parties. Unreflective slap-dash press-release journalism rewarded lavishly in others. Never being paid on acceptance, as my contract stipulates.

As a consequence, it's hard to disentangle the inevitable gripes stemming from the general *Wired* cavalier attitude toward its writers (I know of no one, regardless of gender, currently writing for them that is happy with the magazine); the personal-to-me lack of fit between my worldview and that of *Wired;* and the instinctive antipathy I've always had toward star fucking and status seeking, which *Wired* is tending toward more and more. But considering I've been with the

damned thing from the beginning, that I've been told repeatedly that I am valued as one of their best writers (when I was applying for a job at *The Economist* in the spring of 1994, the managing editor of *Wired* told the Brits that they could have me only if I was still allowed to write for him), why did I feel shunted aside? I'm not that paranoid. . . .

Which leads to the blowout/couch-huddling/coup de grâce incident triggered by women technopagans.

Around the same time as the femxpri discussions on the WELL, I finished writing a controversial profile for *Wired,* this one of Paul Allen, the other billionaire founder of Microsoft. This was a project beset by false starts, blind alleys, confidential sources, massive use of the computer industry's bush telegraph, and reliance on the sources—and the reputation for accuracy and fairness—I'd built up over years. It was investigative reporting of the classic kind: as such, it got lots of people upset and required the services of the *Wired* libel lawyer—and exposed me to serious censorship. Rossetto deleted material that didn't fit his ideological praxis. The article took six months, eight drafts, and was exhausting for all parties concerned.

So for my next project, I wanted to do something fun, where no one would be disposed to get mad and no moneyed interests were at stake. It was a story idea I'd had in mind for a long time: technopagans, high-tech folks practicing neopaganism, nerds making like wizards on their nights off or actually using technology in their rituals. I thought they were a hoot, and I relished writing as an

inquiring anthropologist from Mars about a subculture I found entertaining. And it seemed like a pure-form emergent-culture *Wired* feature.

Wired hemmed and hawed; wouldn't say yes, wouldn't say no. I kept presenting my case to John Battelle, the managing editor, who had always served as my first-line editor. He was lukewarm at best.

But at the same time, in a fit of pique + divine madness, my then-roommate Andy Reinhardt (fellow humanities-geek/executive editor for *PC World*) and I wrote a spoof treatment of a TV show, "beverly_hills.com." It was silly and satirical and in the tradition of a *New Yorker* literary parody, sketching out the madcap doings of a gang of cool Gen X kids as they searched the Information Superhighway for love and adventure.

Still undecided about technopagans, Battelle dithered about actually reading "beverly_hills.com" for weeks. When he finally did read it, he quickly snagged it for the magazine. But he had also decided to give the technopagans assignment to a *Village Voice* writer, Erik Davis, whose query came in after mine. Doing a little damage control, Battelle suggested we go out for dinner and a chat.

At dinner, he told me that *Wired* had been blown away by "beverly_hills.com"; hadn't realized I was capable of playfulness (in other words I had been typed as the conscientious but humorless shrew; remember what Deborah Tannen said about the bad rep that attaches itself to women who kick up a fuss?), which presented the magazine with a quandary: I *was* on the masthead and *did* have seniority and *had* pitched the technopagan idea first; nevertheless, they had wanted to give the very-cool Mr. Davis a chance in the magazine.

Implicit, of course, is that my pitching the proposal didn't make it a worthwhile subject. As an aside, it turns out that another writer, another woman, had tried to pitch the same story to *Wired* months earlier than I had and had gotten even more nowhere than I had. But when Davis pitched the story, it suddenly became more legit. But "beverly_hills.com" for *Wired* revealed another side of my writing, and now *Wired* was chagrined. I found it puzzling (and to be honest, I was miffed) that they hadn't thought me capable of lightness or deftness or insouciance: I had been communicating with them, by phone, email and in person for two years; they'd been reading and editing my writing for two years; they'd read my fiction—sheesh!

Battelle suggested I do a sidebar to Davis's story. Davis okayed this and came up with the idea of a sidebar on women technopagans. Davis has impeccable feminist-male credentials and is as tuned into gender politics as a guy could be; and he and I were equally cognizant of, and uncomfortable with, the notion of ghettoizing the female aspects of the subject into their own pink-beribboned little add-on. We agreed that, best case, women would have been woven into the story naturally (unusual in tech culture, women are key players in technopaganism), but that assigning me the femme concerns was a natural and easy way to create a companion piece to round out the narrative.

Anyway, as awkward as it was for me to sequester the women

pagans off by themselves (the stealth affirmative-action journalism I practice means making sure I include as many women sources as I can in a story, so that women are heard, but weaving female issues and ideas and experiences in where it fits—the best way to combat sexism is to render women visible, but not to make a big deal about them as Other), I was happy to have *part* of my story back and glad to sneak some women-centric writing into the mag.

Battelle promised that Davis's piece would run around three thousand to four thousand words, and mine around fifteen hundred words.

So I wrote my piece on girl technopagans, careful as I always am not to engage in childish "woman = good, man = bad" false dichotomies (if anything, as a straight but not narrow het who from one year to the next is likely to have more male chums than female ones, I am a male apologist and insist on seeing and describing the world in all its non-binary shades-of-gray nuance); Davis wrote his main bar; he and I talked and swapped proto-drafts. His piece had to undergo a massive rewrite, so I heard nothing about my "The Goddess in Every Woman's Machine" until months after I turned it in.

At the last minute, arriving by email after 11 p.m. one night, only a few days before the package of articles was to head off to its final staging areas of layout and art and fact-checking and the printer—and I was off to New York for a business trip, and consequently had little time to do much squawking—I received "The Goddess in Every Woman's Machine" from managing editor Battelle. It has been cut to five hundred words and was anno-

tated with the comment that he wasn't sure he could salvage it at all with executive editor Kelly and editor in chief Rossetto, especially since it was so different from what Davis had written.

I went berserk. I *knew* that if the article had been on cryptography and technopagans, hot sex chat and technopagans, any *Wired* hot-button topic and technopagans—hell, pretty much anything other than women technopagans—there wouldn't have been a question of trying to get it past the executive editor and editor in chief. I also knew there was no standard magazine practice dictating that an article accompanying a main article had to be like it in any obvious way: in fact, the more variety, the better.

And the threat of killing it was particularly galling, for women really matter in technopaganism; it wouldn't be honoring the reality of that special parallel universe to leave them out. That was the message I left on Battelle's voicemail: that *Wired* would look foolish, as if it had done a shoddy job, it if didn't talk about The Girls of Technopaganism. The story did run, but cut to 750 words.

So all of this, run-ins past and thwartings present, was eating at me the night of the Pagan Girl Massacre. I was gagging on the loss of face, full of self-loathing for having thought I was exempt from the second-class treatment other women had experienced at *Wired*, seething with impotent rage at knowing that if I no longer wrote for *Wired*, I'd lose access to *the* high-gloss, high-visibility, high-cachet venue for my writing, and most of all, wearily confronting one of Joan Didion's home truths. In her essay "On Self-Respect," Didion was talking about writers and Hollywood but her thesis rang true: it's a loser's game when you're trying to win the approval of people for whom you have contempt.

Where had I ever gotten the idea that being the house eccentric at *Wired*—its resident feminist/humanist/skeptic/Luddite, the one they could point to as their woman writer, the writer who takes nothing at face value and refuses to cheerlead—could succeed? Silly, vain, foolish girl. . .

My *Wired* Problem, and Maybe Yours

Where things stand now, after getting much grief and much flack, is that the editorial boykings of *Wired* are finally promoting some women out of the pink-collar ghetto of back-office functions and support roles. A very credentialed woman was recently hired as a features editor. The research editor was recently made a features editor (meaning she can seek out and edit writers and story ideas on her own). Another woman was promoted to the position of assistant managing editor. Perhaps things really will change in the years to come.

But as I write now, I feel not very different from the very distinct minority of women I've met in high-tech who have made it there—and who quit in disgust after coming to what feels to them like their right minds and their senses. They come to feel that it's just not worth it, that it's a game not worth playing. They don't want to deal with the racket of male elephant-seal-like trumpeting and jostling for status.

If one is not interested in participating in circle-jerk exercises and paying homage to the alpha male of the moment, what is there left to do at *Wired?* All magazines engage in the happy talk of crowing about their subjects—unless their characters, like that of *The Atlantic Monthly,* are to be contrarian. In all fairness, I know it's my predisposition to ironic distance, my Petronius-Arbiter-of-Rome act, as much as my feminist malcontentions, that cause me trouble with *Wired*.

If I were more bluff and bully, if I had the heart and stomach and bile and spleen—not to mention the spirit and will—to keep slogging it out, in spite of knowing I do not belong, I would keep on writing for *Wired*. I would owe it to the principle of speaking truth to power and Not Wimping Out to assert that voice of agonized humanism and female snarkyness. But as with most folks of artistical temperament, I mostly want to be left alone to do my work, to get at that still silent voice within, and not be fighting ideological battles my editors at *Wired* might not even consciously realize they are engaging in. Progress means exchanging one set of problems for a more interesting set of problems—but my struggles with *Wired* have been generating problems of ever-decreasing interest. I strive to have other, better, more rewarding and less stupid battles to fight.

Being a token calls for tremendous carbohydrate-reserves, reserves ready to rush to the spirit-body's defense. And by 1995, in the field of publishing, where women have been present in large numbers for decades, it just seems as if this shouldn't be necessary; these are kilocalories best expended elsewhere: On the subject at hand. On saying things as best you can. On doing some small part to decrease the weight of human misery in the world or create good art. You shouldn't have to have the tirelessness of a revolutionary, or the sauciness of a turncoat, to be a woman and regularly write for *Wired*.

 Article Review Form at end of book.

WiseGuide Wrap-Up

- Women face continued discrimination in the workplace, in wages, jobs, and opportunities for power and recognition.

- Both overt and subtle means are employed to maintain current workforce patterns, as well as to reproduce continuing assumptions about femininity.

- Race, class, and sexuality are sites of both coalition and confrontation between women and between men and women.

R.E.A.L. Sites

This list provides a print preview of typical **coursewise** R.E.A.L. sites. (There are over 100 such sites at the **courselinks**™ site.) The danger in printing URLs is that Web sites can change overnight. As we went to press, these sites were functional using the URLs provided. If you come across one that isn't, please let us know via email to: webmaster@coursewise.com. Use your Passport to access the most current list of R.E.A.L. sites at the **courselinks**™ site.

Site name: Dataline—The Glass Ceiling
URL: http://cyberwerks.com:70/1s/dataline
Key topics: Work
Why is it R.E.A.L.? Tracks recent developments in management hiring and promotional practices in Fortune 500 companies. Includes reports from women in management about their own experiences.
Activity: Review the entire site, and develop a news report that details for the public the current state of women and management. Include information from Article one to support your claims.

Site name: PENet—Prostitutes Education Network
URL: http://bayswan.org/penet.htm/
Key topics: Work
Why is it R.E.A.L.? Contains current information, videos, and links developed and maintained by sex workers and advocates. Special page in site specifically for students studying the issue.
Activity: Take a tour of the web site; then send a question to the student resource page.

Site name: Department of Labor/Women's Bureau Home Page
URL: http://dol.gov/dol/wb/welcome.html
Key topics: Work, Discrimination
Why is it R.E.A.L.? The Women's Bureau tracks current trends for women in the workforce. This information is generally the most-up-to-date available on a continuing basis.
Activity: Go to the publications page, review the articles, and develop a set of recommendations for the women on strike at Barnard College.

section 2

Key Points

- Media and popular culture influence the construction of appropriate feminine appearance and behavior.

- Appropriate femininity is also class- and race-based. Representations of suitable behaviors for different groups of women are shown on TV, and in movies and magazines.

- The cult of beauty engages women in constructing a passive self. Cultural practices reward women who take up very little space and starve themselves of food and fulfillment.

Gazing Back: Representation and Stereotypes

 **WiseGuide Intro**

Appropriate feminine traits and behaviors are produced and reproduced in popular culture through television icons, toys designed for boys or girls, and other mass-produced items that are gender inflected. Girls and women are likely to understand themselves, and to construct their identities, based on these images. While some women may resist the stereotypes offered them in the media, others may buy into them and, in doing so, modify their bodies and behaviors in ways that sustain male dominance and female subordination.

These messages about women's bodies and behaviors are focused on female bodies as objects to be looked at by men, and on female behaviors that are passive and willing to be the objects of men's looks or gaze. Dieting, hair alterations such as straightening, perming, and dyeing, and plastic surgery are not in and of themselves actions which subordinate women to men, but, when they become, along with other rituals of passivity and beautification, the primary pastimes of women, they reduce the potential for women to participate in public life in more important ways.

The essays and poem in Section 2 cover the ways in which these behaviors affect girls and women. In "In Magazines (I Found Specimens of the Beautiful)," Omosupe links the images of white, blonde women that surround her to her own sense of herself. Lisa Jervis outlines the history of MTV's images of women, which have changed from strong and powerful to ornamental since MTV's inception. Finally, Sallie Tisdale narrates the effects of a culture of thinness on the bodies and self-identities of real girls and women.

Questions

Reading 5. How does the narrative voice in the poem transform the "negative print" into something more positive?

Reading 6. What archetypes of women prevailed in the early days of MTV? What has replaced these archetypes?

Reading 7. What are some of the effects of the "compulsion to diet" on self-esteem and identity? What connections are there between Tisdale's and Omosupe's realizations about their own bodies?

How does the narrative voice in this poem transform the "negative print" into something more positive?

In Magazines (I Found Specimens of the Beautiful)

Ekua Omosupe

Once
I looked for myself
between the covers of
Seventeen
Vogue
Cosmopolitan
among blue eyes, blonde hair, white skin, thin bodies,
this is beauty.
I hated this shroud of
Blackness
that makes me invisible
a negative print
some other one's
nightmare.

In a store front window
against a white back drop
I saw a queenly head of nappy hair

and met this chiseled face
wide wondering eyes,
honey colored, bronzed skin
a mouth with thick lips
bowed painted red
smiled purple gums and shining pearls
I turned to leave
but this body of
curvaceous hips
strong thighs
broad ass
long legs
called me back to look again at likenesses of
African Queens, Dahomey Warriors, statuesque Goddesses,
I stand outside those covers meet
Face to Face
Myself
I am the Beautiful

Article Review Form at end of book.

From *Making Face, Making Soul: Haciendo Caras* © 1990 by Gloria Anzaldua.

What archetypes of women prevailed in the early days of MTV?
What has replaced these archetypes?

Amazon Women on the Moon

Images of femininity in the video age

Andi Zeisler

Like some grizzled old-timer sitting on the porch of the homestead talking about the good old days, I think back to the first time I saw MTV and pity the prepubescents of today who didn't have the luck to see, as I did, the wonder of MTV when it first aired. I was eight years old, alone in my living room, and somehow I knew that I was witnessing a tremendous event: a connection with something that just wasn't accessible through after-school cartoons of *Gilligan's Island* reruns. When I recall what I saw back then, I may remember some of the details wrong, but that doesn't matter. It's my perception of those early videos that creates the memory, that resonates in my tv-addled mind as the truth. And what I remember best are the images of women that I saw on MTV. I'm aware of those representations in a different way than I was in those first golden days when I sat glued to the small screen, clutching a handful of Fritos. What I say about these im-

ages now comes from filtering them through a screen of theory and history and related bullshit, but it still comes from what I saw back then. The women of MTV were not merely women; rather, they were on-screen archetypes of what a video-age woman could be, and they were indelibly printed on my young brain.

The Androgyne

By the time the first little MTV spaceman planted his flag on the screens of cable-blessed homes, androgyny in rock music was old news. This was, after all, the post glam-rock early 1980s. The New York Dolls, Patti Smith, David Bowie and many others had been praised up and down not only for their musical achievements but for their knack of appropriating/mocking the styles of the opposite sex. But the legions of suburban tykes lounging in our beanbag chairs in front of the tube didn't know about that. All we knew was that there were a huge number of girly-looking guys staring out at us from the other side of the tv screen, and we were

mesmerized. Through Adam Ant and Duran Duran, I absorbed the concept of androgyny unconsciously as I giggled dreamy-eyed over these grown men with made-up faces, these boys who looked too much like girls to be the "opposite" sex.

But then there were the actual girls: Joan Jett, who wore head-to-toe black leather and reveled in crunchy cock-rock riffs in her video for "I Love Rock n' Roll;" skinny, imperious Chrissie Hynde of the Pretenders. These women's physical images incorporated a litany of bad-boy references, from pre-zirconium Elvis to Marlon Brando to Keith Richards. They were appropriating the style of men whose blatant sexuality made them "dangerous." Not so much rejecting femininity as cloaking it in the historical acceptibility of male rebellion, these women were insinuating themselves into the badass canon. I didn't consciously think that they looked like boys, but when I saw the video for the Pretenders' "Brass in Pocket" I thought that Chrissie Hynde in a waitresses' uniform was all wrong. And the

"Amazon Women on the Moon" originally appeared in *Bitch Magazine*, Vol. 1, #1. Copies of *Bitch* are available by writing to: 3128 16th St. #201, San Francisco, CA 94103.

end of the video, when she runs out of the diner and hops on the tough guy's motorcycle—well, that was all wrong too. Anyone who had seen "Tattooed Love Boys" knew that Chrissie would never let her ass be grabbed by a customer and then go for a ride on his hog. She'd get on her own motorcycle and peel out of the diner parking lot, spraying that loser with a mouthful of gravel.

Perhaps the most memorable androgyne of early MTV was Annie Lennox of the Eurythmics. In their first video, "Sweet Dreams (Are Made of This)," Annie wore a man's black suit and held a riding crop (or maybe it was a pointer); her bright-orange flattop rose out of the ensemble like a placid mask of Ziggy Stardust-style unrealness. The dangerous sexuality of Joan and Chrissie's leather pants was here replaced by the more danger-ous sexuality of total gender un-recognizability. No real precedent for female-to-male cross-dressing had been set on television at this point, although the madcap hilar-ity of men impersonating women had been proven many times over, from Milton Berle to *M.A.S.H.* The employment of cross-dressing for non-comedic purposes, and by a woman, was jarring. The whispering among my elementary-school friends about this video yielded only one possible conclu-sion—that Annie Lennox must be a lesbian.

The Future Freak

The second image that appeared consistently on early MTV can best be described as the space-age, futuristic freak. The SAFF, like the Androgyne, took more than one form. There was the faraway-eyed, operatic Kate Bush, the future-Barbie frontwomen of Missing Persons and Berlin, and the space-age amazon Grace Jones, among others. But unlike the Androgyne, the SAFF had no basis in history other than the col-lective projection of "the future" that held 1980s media in its thrall. Computers, NASA, and ever-expanding medical and industrial technologies were spurring us on to the future, but what about hu-manity? The fears of future dehu-manization, particularly of women, were given paranoid form in movies like *Blade Runner* and *Liquid Sky,* where futuristic fe-males invariably took on the form of alien succubi, preying on the hapless male hero. The sexual fe-male, given power, mutated into something evil that had to be stopped by the likes of Harrison Ford. The message of these films? Future women are going to be scary, castrating sexual deviants. The video counterparts of these cinematic women presented an al-ternative to traditional notions of what constitutes femaleness. The SAFF was not soft, not yielding, and seemed entirely her own in-vention. Her voice was clearly that of a woman, yet it was not a "feminine" voice—it was robotic, as Grace Jones's was, or it was the ethereal, oth-erworldly siren song of Kate Bush.

But the SAFF's physical image was hyperfeminized, caricatured. In the video for Missing Persons's "Destination Unknown," lead singer Dale Bozzio sported a floor-length white mane, a mylar-and-bubble wrap dress, and spike heels, and

MTV realized that their audience was adolescent boys and their hard-ons. The marketing dynamic took over and these women all but vanished.

she sang in a high-frequency baby-doll voice while staring at her own bizarre face in a smoky mirror. This image plays into clas-sic notions of woman as the infant-like, narcissistic other. But despite the contradictions inher-ent in the SAFF persona, she de-fined the future—unknowable, cloudy, and scary.

The Bad Girl

This MTV archetype was perhaps the most familiar one. As tough as the Androgyne but less mascu-line, earthier than the Future Freak, the Bad Girl was like a canny, fun older sister—smart and sexy and cut-the-shit direct. All her songs spoke directly to some-one—presumably a guy—who was trying to mess with her, and she wasn't having it. Pat Benatar, Toni Basil, the Flirts, the Waitresses, and Patti Smythe of Scandal all embodied a kind of fishnet-stockinged consciousness that allowed them to seem like slutty girls while harboring a clearheaded intelligence and the occasional subversive agenda. Toni Basil's "Mickey" video ex-ploited the whole good girl/bad girl cheerleader motif, with Toni cart-wheeling around, pompoms in hand, while delivering the gen-derfuck line "Come on and give it to me, any way you can/ Any way you wanna do it, I'll take it like a man." Pat Benatar took the Bad Girl role one step further, using the video format to star in mini-movies in which she took on the persona of *other* bad girls. In "Shadows of the Night," she por-trays a 1940s Rosie-the-Riveter type who dreams of being a ruth-less, glamorous double agent. And in "Love is a Battlefield," probably the *tour de force* of her video career, Pat plays a teenage runaway whose foray into the big city leads to her working in a seedy dance parlor with other unlucky women. But Pat mobilizes the women into a line-dance uprising against their evil pimp, and liberation ensues. Go on with your bad self, Pat!

Sadly, these would turn out to be the salad days of the Bad Girl, because once MTV realized that their main audience was comprised of adolescent boys and their hard-ons, the marketing dynamic took over and these women all but vanished. Pat Benatar and Toni Basil were replaced by nameless inflato-breasted bimbos who writhed in videos by poufy-haired "metal" bands like Warrant and Poison, portraying groupies, porn actresses, and girlfriends. MTV wanted you to believe that *this* was what a Bad Girl was, but even those of us just graduating from our training bras knew the vast difference between a player and a plaything.

Even those of us just graduating from our training bras knew the vast difference between a player and a plaything.

Little by little, the archetypes of early MTV disappeared from the screen, displaced by the ever-increasing popularity of the channel and its ability to create and crush images and fads with heartless precision. The use of women primarily as cheese-metal video ornaments made it necessary for those women who were actual musicians to protect themselves from winding up as yet another babe spread-eagle on top of a Camaro. So women like Tracy Chapman, Suzanne Vega, and the Indigo Girls ushered in a new era of no-frills videos—no leather pants, no bubble wrap dresses, no Benatar-esque role playing. They played solid, admirable music that also happened to make boring-as-hell video viewing. Having experienced the myriad over-the-top moments of MTV's first inception, there was no substitute. Well, there was Madonna, who aimed

to amass all the aspects of the Bad Girl and the SAFF and the Androgyne into one package, but that's a whole other essay, and Camille Paglia has got it covered.

Those early images and videos were powerful. They were novelty and stereotype and affirmation. They provided young girls with ideas of rebellion, sex, and self-sufficiency that couldn't be found in the pages of *Young Miss*. They allowed us to think critically and find fault with other images of women that we saw not only on MTV, but in other media. They inspired us to rock out. If you turn on MTV today, in between segments of "Beauty and the Beach" and "The Real World," you might—if you're lucky—see something that reminds you of what MTV once was: that brave new world where the women talked tough and the men looked pretty.

 Article Review Form at end of book.

What are some of the effects of the "compulsion to diet" on self-esteem and identity? What connections are there between Tisdale's and Omosupe's realizations about their own bodies?

A Weight That Women Carry

The compulsion to diet in a starved culture

Sallie Tisdale

Sallie Tisdale is a contributing editor of Harper's Magazine. *Her most recent book is* Stepping Westward: The Long Search for a Home in the Pacific Northwest. *Tisdale's essay "Talk Dirty to Me" appeared in the February 1992 issue of* Harper's.

I don't know how much I weigh these days, though I can make a good guess. For years I'd known that number, sometimes within a quarter pound, known how it changed from day to day and hour to hour. I want to weigh myself now; I lean toward the scale in the next room, imagine standing there, lining up the balance. But I don't do it. Going this long, starting to break the scale's spell—it's like waking up suddenly sober.

By the time I was sixteen years old I had reached my adult height of five feet six inches and weighed 164 pounds. I weighed 164 pounds before and after a healthy pregnancy. I assume I weigh about the same now; nothing significant seems to have happened to my body, this same old body I've had all these years. I

usually wear a size 14, a common clothing size for American women. On bad days I think my body looks lumpy and mis-shapen. On my good days, which are more frequent lately, I think I look plush and strong; I think I look like a lot of women whose bodies and lives I admire.

I'm not sure when the word "fat" first sounded pejorative to me, or when I first applied it to myself. My grandmother was a petite woman, the only one in my family. She stole food from other people's plates, and hid the debris of her own meals so that no one would know how much she ate. My mother was a size 14, like me, all her adult life; we shared clothes. She fretted endlessly over food scales, calorie counters, and diet books. She didn't want to quit smoking because she was afraid she would gain weight, and she worried about her weight until she died of cancer five years ago. Dieting was always in my mother's way, always there in the conversations

> The number on the scale became my totem, more important than my experience. I thought if I could change that number I could change my life.

above my head, the dialogue of stocky women. But I was strong and healthy and didn't pay too much attention to my weight until I was grown.

It probably wouldn't have been possible for me to escape forever. It doesn't matter that whole human epochs have celebrated big men and women, because the brief period in which I live does not; since I was born, even the voluptuous calendar girl has gone. Today's models, the women whose pictures I see constantly, unavoidably, grow more minimal by the day. When I berate myself for not looking like—whomever I think I should look like that day, I don't really care that no one looks like that. I don't care that Michelle Pfeiffer doesn't look like the photographs I see of Michelle Pfeiffer. I want to look—think I should look—like the photographs. I want her little miracles: the makeup artists, photographers, and computer imagers who can add a mole, remove a scar, lift the breasts, widen the eyes, narrow the hips, flatten the curves. The final product is what I see, have seen my whole adult life. And I've seen this: even when big people become celebrities, their weight is constantly re-marked upon and scrutinized; their successes seem always to be *in spite of* their weight. I thought my successes must be, too.

I feel myself expand and di-minish from day to day, some-times from hour to hour. If I tell someone my weight, I change in their eyes: I become bigger or smaller, better or worse, depend-ing on what that number, my weight, means to them. I know many men and women, young and old, gay and straight, who look fine, whom I love to see and whose faces and forms I cherish, who despise themselves for their weight. For their ordinary, human bodies.They and I are simply big-ger than we think we should be. We always talk about weight in terms of gains and losses, and don't wonder at the strangeness of the words. In trying always to lose weight, we've lost hope of simply being seen for ourselves.

My weight has never actu-ally affected anything—it's never seemed to mean anything one way or the other to how I lived. Yet for the last ten years I've felt quite bad about it. After a time, the number on the scale became my totem, more important than my experience—it was layered, metaphorical, *metaphysical,* and it had bewitching power. I thought if I could change that number I could change my life.

In my mid-twenties I started secretly taking diet pills. They made me feel strange, half-crazed, vaguely nauseated. I lost about twenty-five pounds, dropped two sizes, and bought new clothes. I developed rituals and taboos

around food, ate very little, and continued to lose weight. For a long time afterward I thought it only coincidental that with every passing week I also grew more depressed and irritable.

I could recite the details, but they're remarkable only for being so common. I lost more weight until I was rather thin, and then I gained it all back. It came back slowly, pound by pound, in spite of erratic and melancholy and sometimes frantic dieting, dieting I clung to even though being thin had changed nothing, had meant nothing to my life except that I was thin. Looking back, I remem-ber blinding moments of shame and lightning-bright moments of clearheadedness, which inevitably gave way to rage at the time I'd wasted—rage that eventually would become, once again, self-disgust and the urge to lose weight. So it went, until I weighed exactly what I'd weighed when I began.

I used to be attracted to the sharp angles of the chronic dieter—the caffeine-wild, chain-smoking, skinny women I see sometimes. I considered them a pinnacle not of beauty but of will. Even after I gained back my weight, I wanted to be like that, controlled and per-severing, live that underfed life so unlike my own rather sensual and disorderly existence. I felt I should always be dieting, for the dieting of it; dieting had become a rule, a given, a constant. Every or-dinary value is distorted in this lens. I felt guilty for not being completely absorbed in my diet, for getting distracted, for not car-ing enough all the time. The fat person's character flaw is a lack of narcissism. She's let herself go.

So I would begin again—and at first it would all seem so . . . easy. Simple arithmetic. After all, 3,500 calories equal one

pound of fat—so the books and articles by the thousands say. I would calculate how long it would take to achieve the magic number on the scale, to succeed, to win. All past failures were sup-pressed. If 3,500 calories equal one pound, all I needed to do was cut 3,500 calories out of my intake every week. The first few days of a new diet would be colored with a sense of control—organization and planning, power over the self. Then the basic futile misery took over.

I would weigh myself with foreboding, and my weight would determine how went the rest of my day, my week, my life.When 3,500 calories didn't equal one pound lost after all, I figured it was my body that was flawed, not the theory. One friend, who had tried for years to lose weight fol-lowing prescribed diets, made what she called "an amazing dis-covery." The real secret to a diet, she said, was that you had to be willing to be hungry *all the time.* You had to eat even less than the diet allowed.

I believed that being thin would make me happy. Such a pernicious, enduring belief. I lost weight and wasn't happy and saw that elusive happiness disappear in a vanishing point, requiring more—more self-disgust, more of the misery of dieting. Knowing all that I know now about the biology and anthropology of weight, knowing that people naturally come in many shapes and sizes, knowing that diets are bad for me and won't make me thin—some-times none of this matters. I look in the mirror and think: Who am I kidding? *I've got to do something about myself.* Only then will this vague discontent disappear. Then I'll be loved.

For ages humans believed that the body helped create the

personality, from the humors of Galen to W. H. Sheldon's somatotypes. Sheldon distinguished between three templates—endomorph, mesomorph, and ectomorph—and combined them into hundreds of variations with physical, emotional, and psychological characteristics. When I read about weight now, I see the potent shift in the last few decades: the modern culture of dieting is based on the idea that the personality creates the body. Our size must be in some way voluntary, or else it wouldn't be subject to change. A lot of my misery over my weight wasn't about how I looked at all. I was miserable because I believed *I* was bad, not my body. I felt truly reduced then, reduced to being just a body and nothing more.

Fat is perceived as an *act* rather than a thing. It is antisocial, and curable through the application of social controls. Even the feminist revisions of dieting, so powerful in themselves, pick up the theme: the hungry, empty heart; the woman seeking release from sexual assault, or the man from the loss of the mother, through food and fat. Fat is now a symbol not of the personality but of the soul—the cluttered, neurotic, immature soul.

Fat people eat for "mere gratification," I read, as though no one else does. Their weight is *intentioned*, they simply eat "too much," their flesh is lazy flesh. Whenever I went on a diet, eating became cheating. One pretzel was cheating. Two apples instead of one was cheating—a large potato instead of a small, carrots instead of broccoli. It didn't matter which diet I was on; diets have failure built in, failure is in the definition.

Fat is seen as antisocial and curable. It is a symbol of the soul—the cluttered, neurotic, immature soul.

Every substitution—even carrots for broccoli—was a triumph of desire over will. When I dieted, I didn't feel pious just for sticking to the rules. I felt condemned for the act of eating itself, as though my hunger were never normal. My penance was to not eat at all.

My attitude toward food became quite corrupt. I came, in fact, to subconsciously believe food itself was corrupt. Diet books often distinguish between "real" and "unreal" hunger, so that *correct* eating is hollowed out, unemotional. A friend of mine who thinks of herself as a compulsive eater says she feels bad only when she eats for pleasure. "Why?" I ask, and she says, "Because I'm eating food I don't need." A few years ago I might have admired that. Now I try to imagine a world where we eat only food we need, and it seems inhuman. I imagine a world devoid of holidays and wedding feasts, wakes and reunions, a unique shared joy. "What's wrong with eating a cookie because you like cookies?" I ask her, and she hasn't got an answer. These aren't rational beliefs, any more than the unnecessary pleasure of ice cream is rational. Dieting presumes pleasure to be an insignificant, or at least malleable, human motive.

I felt no joy in being thin—it was just work, something I had to do. But when I began to gain back the weight, I felt despair. I started reading about the "recidivism" of dieting. I wondered if I had myself to blame not only for needing to diet in the first place but for dieting it-

Concern with my weight evokes the meanest parts of me. I look at another woman passing on the street and think, "at least I'm not *that* fat."

self, the weight inevitably regained. I joined organized weight-loss programs, spent a lot of money, listened to lectures I didn't believe on quack nutrition, ate awful, processed diet foods. I sat in groups and applauded people who'd lost a half pound, feeling smug because I'd lost a pound and a half. I felt ill much of the time, found exercise increasingly difficult, cried often. And I thought that if I could only lose a little weight, everything would be all right.

When I say to someone, "I'm fat," I hear, "Oh, no! You're not *fat!* You're just—" What? Plump? Big-boned? Rubenesque? I'm just *not thin*. That's crime enough. I began this story by stating my weight. I said it all at once, trying to forget it and take away its power; I said it to be done being scared. Doing so, saying it out loud like that, felt like confessing a mortal sin. I have to bite my tongue not to seek reassurance, not to defend myself, not to plead. I see an old friend for the first time in years, and she comments on how much my fourteen-year-old son looks like me—"except, of course, he's not chubby." "Look who's talking," I reply, through clenched teeth. This pettiness is never far away; concern with my weight evokes the smallest, meanest parts of me. I look at another woman passing on the street and think, "At least I'm not *that* fat."

Recently I was talking with a friend who is naturally slender about a mutual acquaintance who is quite large. To my surprise my friend reproached this woman because she had seen her eating a cookie at lunchtime. "How is she going to lose weight that way?"

my friend wondered. When you are as fat as our acquaintance is, you are primarily, fundamentally, seen as fat. It is your essential characteristic. There are so many presumptions in my friend's casual, cruel remark. She assumes that this woman should diet all the time— and that she *can*. She pronounces whole categories of food to be denied her. She sees her unwillingness to behave in this externally prescribed way, even for a moment, as an act of rebellion. In his story "A Hunger Artist," Kafka writes that the guards of the fasting man were "usually butchers, strangely enough." Not so strange, I think.

Reduction is the opposite of feminism. Smallness is what feminism strives against, the smallness that women confront everywhere.

I know that the world, even if it views me as overweight (and I'm not sure it really does), clearly makes a distinction between me and this very big woman. I would rather stand with her and not against her, see her for all she is besides fat. But I know our experiences aren't the same. My thin friend assumes my fat friend is unhappy because she is fat: therefore, if she loses weight she will be happy. My fat friend has a happy marriage and family and a good career, but insofar as her weight is a source of misery, I think she would be much happier if she could eat her cookie in peace, if people would shut up and leave her weight alone. But the world never lets up when you are her size; she cannot walk to the bank without risking insult. Her fat is seen as perverse bad manners. I have no doubt she would be rid of the fat if she could be. If my left-handedness invited the criticism her weight does, I would want to cut that hand off.

In these last several years I seem to have had an infinite number of conversations about dieting. They are really all the same conversation—weight is lost, then weight is gained back. This repetition finally began to sink in. Why did everyone sooner or later have the same experience? (My friend who had learned to be hungry all the time gained back all the weight she had lost and more, just like the rest of us.) Was it really our bodies that were flawed? I began reading the biology of weight more carefully, reading the fine print in the endless studies. There is, in fact, a preponderance of evidence disputing our commonly held assumptions about weight.

The predominant biological myth of weight is that thin people live longer than fat people. The truth is far more complicated. (Some deaths of fat people attributed to heart disease seem actually to have been the result of radical dieting.) If health were our real concern, it would be dieting we questioned, not weight. The current ideal of thinness has never been held before, except as a religious ideal; the underfed body is the martyr's body. Even if people can lose weight, maintaining an artificially low weight for any period of time requires a kind of starvation. Lots of people are naturally thin, but for those who are not, dieting is an unnatural act; biology rebels. The metabolism of the hungry body can change inalterably, making it ever harder and harder to stay thin. I think chronic dieting made me gain weight— not only pounds, but fat. This equation seemed so strange at first that I couldn't believe it. But the weight I put back on after losing was much more stubborn than the original weight. I had lost it by taking diet pills and not eating much of anything at all for quite a long time. I haven't touched the pills again, but not eating much of anything no longer works.

When Oprah Winfrey first revealed her lost weight, I didn't envy her. I thought, She's in trouble now. I knew, I was certain, she would gain it back; I believed she was biologically destined to do so. The tabloid headlines blamed it on a cheeseburger or mashed potatoes; they screamed OPRAH PASSES 200 POUNDS, and I cringed at her misery and how the world wouldn't let up, wouldn't leave her alone, wouldn't let her be anything else. How dare the world do this to anyone? I thought, and then realized I did it to myself.

The "Ideal Weight" charts my mother used were at their lowest acceptable-weight ranges in the 1950s, when I was a child. They were based on sketchy and often inaccurate actuarial evidence, using, for the most part, data on northern Europeans and allowing for the most minimal differences in size for a population of less than half a billion people. I never fit those weight charts, I was always just outside the pale. As an adult, when I would join an organized diet program, I accepted their version of my Weight Goal as gospel, knowing it would be virtually impossible to reach. But reach I tried; that's what one does with gospel. Only in the last few years have the weight tables begun to climb back into the world of the average human. The newest ones distinguish by gender, frame, and age. And suddenly I'm not off the charts anymore. I have a place.

A man who is attracted to fat women says, "I actually have less specific physical criteria than most men. I'm attracted to women who weigh 170 or 270 or 370. Most men are only attracted to women who weigh between 100 and 135. So who's got more of a fetish?" We look at fat as a problem of the fat person. Rarely do the tables get turned, rarely do we imagine that it might be the viewer, not the viewed, who is limited. What the hell is wrong with *them,* anyway? Do they believe everything they see on television?

My friend Phil, who is chronically and almost painfully thin, admitted that in his search for a partner he finds himself prejudiced against fat women. He seemed genuinely bewildered by this. I didn't jump to reassure him that such prejudice is hard to resist. What I did was bite my tongue at my urge to be reassured by him, to be told that I, at least, wasn't fat. That over the centuries humans have been inclined to prefer extra flesh rather than the other way around seems unimportant. All we see now tells us otherwise. Why does my kindhearted friend criticize another woman for eating a cookie when she would never dream of commenting in such a way on another person's race or sexual orientation or disability? Deprivation is the dystopian ideal.

My mother called her endless diets "reducing plans." Reduction, the diminution of women, is the opposite of feminism, as Kim Chernin points out in *The Obsession.* Smallness is what feminism strives against, the smallness that women confront everywhere. All of women's spaces are smaller than those of men, often inadequate, without

privacy. Furniture designers distinguish between a man's and a woman's chair, because women don't spread out like men. (A sprawling woman means only one thing.) Even our voices are kept down. By embracing dieting I was rejecting a lot I held dear, and the emotional dissonance that created just seemed like one more necessary evil.

A fashion magazine recently celebrated the return of the "well-fed" body; a particular model was said to be "the archetype of the new womanly woman . . . stately, powerful." She is a size 8. The images of women presented to us, images claiming so maliciously to be the images of women's whole lives, are not merely social fictions. They are *absolute* fictions; they can't exist. How would it feel, I began to wonder, to cultivate my own real womanliness rather than despise it? Because it was my fleshy curves I wanted to be rid of, after all. I dreamed of having a boy's body, smooth, hopeless, lean. A body rapt with possibility, a receptive body suspended before the storms of maturity. A dear friend of mine, nursing her second child, weeps at her newly voluptuous body. She loves her children and hates her own motherliness, wanting to be unripened again, to be a bud and not a flower.

Recently I've started shopping occasionally at stores for "large women," where the smallest size is a 14. In department stores the size 12 and 14 and 16 clothes are kept in a ghetto called the Women's Department. (And who would want that, to be the size of a woman? We all dream of being "juniors" instead.) In the

> I suddenly remembered the Lane Bryant shopping bag in my hand, the sheer heaviness of that brand name shouting to the world that I've let myself go.

specialty stores the clerks are usually big women and the customers are big, too, big like a lot of women in my life—friends, my sister, my mother and aunts. Not long ago I bought a pair of jeans at Lane Bryant and then walked through the mall to the Gap, with its shelves of generic clothing. I flicked through the clearance rack and suddenly remembered the Lane Bryant shopping bag in my hand and its enormous weight, the sheer heaviness of that brand name shouting to the world. The shout is that I've let myself go. I still feel like crying out sometimes: Can't I feel *satisfied?* But I am not supposed to be satisfied, not allowed to be satisfied. My discontent fuels the market; I need to be afraid in order to fully participate.

American culture, which has produced our dieting mania, does more than reward privation and acquisition at the same time: it actually associates them with each other. Read the ads: the virtuous runner's reward is a new pair of $180 running shoes. The fat person is thought to be impulsive, indulgent, but insufficiently or incorrectly greedy, greedy for the wrong thing. The fat person lacks ambition. The young executive is complimented for being "hungry"; he is "starved for success." We are teased with what we will *have* if we are willing to *have not* for a time. A dieting friend, avoiding the food on my table, says, "I'm just dying for a bite of that."

Dieters are the perfect consumers: they never get enough. The dieter wistfully imagines food without substance, food that is not food, that begs the definition of food, because food is the problem. Even the ways we *don't eat* are based in class. The middle class don't eat in support groups. The poor can't afford not to eat at all. The rich hire someone to not eat with them in private. Dieting is an emblem of capitalism. It has a venal heart.

The possibility of living another way, living without dieting, began to take root in my mind a few years ago, and finally my second trip through Weight Watchers ended dieting for me. This last time I just couldn't stand the details, the same kind of details I'd seen and despised in other programs, on other diets: the scent of resignation, the weighing-in by the quarter pound, the before and after photographs of group leaders prominently displayed. Jean Nidetch, the founder of Weight Watchers, says, "Most fat people need to be hurt badly before they do something about themselves." She mocks every aspect of our need for food, of a person's sense of entitlement to food, of daring to *eat what we want.* Weight Watchers refuses to release its own weight charts except to say they make no distinction for frame size; neither has the organization ever released statistics on how many people who lose weight on the program eventually gain it back. I hated the endlessness of it, the turning of food into portions and exchanges, everything measured out, permitted, denied. I hated the very idea of "maintenance." Finally I realized I didn't just hate the diet. I was sick of the way I acted on a diet, the way I whined, my niggardly, penny-pinching behavior. What I liked in myself seemed to shrivel and disappear when I dieted. Slowly, slowly I saw these things. I saw that my pain was cut

from whole cloth, imaginary, my own invention. I saw how much time I'd spent on something ephemeral, something that simply wasn't important, didn't matter. I saw that the real point of dieting is dieting—to not be done with it, ever.

I looked in the mirror and saw a woman, with flesh, curves, muscles, a few stretch marks, the beginnings of wrinkles, with strength and softness in equal measure. My body is the one part of me that is always, undeniably, here. To like myself means to be, literally, shameless, to be wanton in the pleasures of being inside a body. I feel *loose* this way, a little abandoned, a little dangerous. That first feeling of liking my body— not being resigned to it or despairing of change, but actually *liking* it—was tentative and guilty and frightening. It was alarming, because it was the way I'd felt as a child, before the world had interfered. Because surely I was wrong; I knew, I'd known for so long, that my body wasn't all right this way. I was afraid even to act as though I were all right: I was afraid that by doing so I'd be acting a fool.

For a time I was thin. I remember—and what I remember is nothing special—strain, a kind of hollowness, the same troubles and fears, and no magic. So I imagine losing weight again. If the world applauded, would this comfort me? Or would it only compromise whatever approval the world gives me now? What else will be required of me besides thinness? What will happen to me if I get sick, or lose the use of a limb, or, God forbid, grow old?

By fussing endlessly over my body, I've ceased to inhabit it. I'm trying to reverse this equation now, to trust my body and enter it again with a whole heart. I know more now than I used to about what constitutes "happy" and "unhappy," what the depths and textures of contentment are like. By letting go of dieting, I free up mental and emotional room. I have more space, I can move. The pursuit of another, elusive body, the body someone else says I should have, is a terrible distraction, a sidetracking that might have lasted my whole life long. By letting myself go, I go places.

Each of us in this culture, this twisted, inchoate culture, has to choose between battles: one battle is against the cultural ideal, and the other is against ourselves. I've chosen to stop fighting myself. Maybe I'm tilting at windmills; the cultural ideal is ever-changing, out of my control. It's not a cerebral journey, except insofar as I have to remind myself to stop counting, to stop thinking in terms of numbers. I know, even now that I've quit dieting and eat what I want, how many calories I take in every day. If I eat as I please, I eat a lot one day and very little the next; I skip meals and snack at odd times. My nourishment is good—as far as nutrition is concerned, I'm in much better shape than when I was dieting. I know that the small losses and gains in my weight over a period of time aren't simply related to the number of calories I eat. Someone asked me not long ago how I could possibly know my calorie intake if I'm not dieting (the implication being, perhaps,

> By giving up dieting, I free up mental and emotional room. I have more space, I can move.

that I'm dieting secretly). I know because calorie counts and grams of fat and fiber are embedded in me. I have to work to *not* think of them, and I have to learn to not think of them in order to really live without fear.

When I look, *really* look, at the people I see every day on the street, I see a jungle of bodies, a community of women and men growing every which way like lush plants, growing tall and short and slender and round, hairy and hairless, dark and pale and soft and hard and glorious. Do I look around at the multitudes and think all these people—all these people who are like me and not like me, who are various and different—are not loved or lovable? Lately, everyone's body interests me, every body is desirable in some way. I see how muscles and skin shift with movement; I sense a cornucopia of flesh in the world. In the midst of it I am a little capacious and unruly.

I repeat with Walt Whitman, "I dote on myself . . . there is that lot of me, and all so luscious." I'm eating better, exercising more, feeling fine—and then I catch myself thinking, *Maybe I'll lose some weight*. But my mood changes or my attention is caught by something else, something deeper, more lingering. Then I can catch a glimpse of myself by accident and think only: That's me. My face, my hips, my hands. Myself.

 Article Review Form at end of book.

WiseGuide Wrap-Up

- Media and popular culture influence the construction of femininity.

- There are multiple versions of femininity, based on race and class affiliations.

- Dieting functions not only as a means of controlling the appearance of women, but also of containing their efforts to increase their access to power.

R.E.A.L. Sites

This list provides a print preview of typical **coursewise** R.E.A.L. sites. (There are over 100 such sites at the **courselinks**™ site.) The danger in printing URLs is that Web sites can change overnight. As we went to press, these sites were functional using the URLs provided. If you come across one that isn't, please let us know via email to: webmaster@coursewise.com. Use your Passport to access the most current list of R.E.A.L. sites at the **courselinks**™ site.

Site name: Excerpt: *Forever Barbie*
URL: http://desires.com/1.2/words/docs/lord2.html
Key topics: Beauty Myth, Stereotypes
Why is it R.E.A.L.? The recent unauthorized biography of the most known doll in history uncovers many of the cultural stereotypes of femininity that girls learn as they group up.
Activity: After reading this excerpt from Barbie's biography, write an autobiography for Barbie as a response to what you either agree with or disagree with in the excerpt.

Site name: The Distort Barbie
URL: http://www.users.interport.net/~napier/barbie/barbie/html
Key topics: Stereotypes, Identity Politics
Why is it R.E.A.L.? These startling and controversial images of alternative representations of Barbie resist most current ideologies about beauty, Barbie, and identity. Mattel successfully forced the site's creator to make changes to some of the images.
Activity: Read the e-mail submitted to the site about its contents; then check all of the artwork on the site. Send an e-mail to the creator with your response, indicating how you see the site—do these images really resist current power relations? Include material from one of the e-mails already posted.

Site name: BLO
URL: http://www.reed.edu/~cosmo/art/BLO/BLO.html
Key topics: Technology, Beauty Myth
Why is it R.E.A.L.? The Barbie Liberation Organization is a group of guerrilla fighters in the gender wars. They recently brought attention to gender stereotyping in Barbie and Ken with their "surgical reconstruction" of Barbie.
Activity: Listen to the audio clips. Do a web search for more information about the Barbie Liberation Organization. Choose another cultural icon that stereotypes gender roles for women, and, using the information you have gathered about BLO as well as the audio clips, develop your own set of "guerrilla" tactics for exposing these stereotypes.

section 3

Key Points

- Binary biological sex categories divide the world by male and female, categories which may not be the only possibilities, because DNA and sex organs aren't always clearly within the limits of these categories.

- Sex and sexuality are implicated in the system of gender relations that assigns masculinity and male biological sex a dominant position, and femininity and female biological sex a subordinate position, making heterosexual relations normative and marking out other possibilities as deviant.

- Gender roles are also grounded in culture, race, and ethnicity.

- Attempts to maintain the subordinated status of female sexuality are linked to the control and containment of women's reproductive choices, often at great risk to their health and safety.

Having (a) Sex: Gender, Sexuality, Reproduction

 WiseGuide Intro

Three concepts are often referred to when using the same word—*sex*. The concepts of biological sex, sex as an activity, and sex as a set of behaviors associated with a particular group with similar characteristics are all linked by both biology and social norms. Biological sex is the primary meaning associated with the word *sex*. DNA, body composition, and sex organs are the primary means of determining a person's sex as female or male. *Gender* is the term most appropriate for referring to masculine or feminine roles and behaviors, which are assigned to those with male or female sex characteristics. Finally, sex as an activity would appear to be self-explanatory.

Each of these concepts is marked by power. Cultural systems reproduce dualistic sets of relations through the continued replication of assumptions that biology is destiny. In other words, if you are born with certain sex characteristics, then appropriate gender roles and sexual behaviors are assigned to you. Deviance from these two categories of male/masculine–female/feminine leads to multiple sanctions from the larger group. These systems of power are most manifest in the ongoing struggle of who controls reproduction in the female body, seen most pointedly through the hotly contested arena of abortion. This debate, like the split between male and female, has been divided between the pro-choice and pro-life camps, leaving no in-between space for compromise or negotiation.

Anne Fausto-Sterling offers an alternative to this rigid dualism in "The Five Sexes." She argues that, biologically, there are more than two possible genders at birth but that babies are assigned one of the two categories. The power of sexuality and its representation are the subject of Chapkis' essay "The Meaning of Sex." Finally, in the *Women's Rights Law Reporter*, Román explores a single piece of the puzzle surrounding reproductive rights, through her brief summary of the attempt to ban the D & E procedure.

? Questions ?

Reading 8. What factors determine whether a newborn is male or female? What are the consequences if Fausto-Sterling's argument about the existence of more than two sexes is correct?

Reading 9. What is the primary difference in the positions of what Chapkis calls "anti-sex"

feminists, "positive sex" feminists, and "sexual libertarians"? How does Ariane Amsberg's exploration of prostitution relate to Barbara's assessment of the situation in Section 1?

Reading 10. Who benefits from the continued efforts to ban some abortion procedures?

What factors determine whether a newborn is male or female?
What are the consequences if Fausto-Sterling's argument about the
existence of more than two sexes is correct?

The Five Sexes

Why male and female are not enough

Anne Fausto-Sterling

*Anne Fausto-Sterling is a developmental
geneticist and professor of medical science
at Brown University in Providence. The
second edition of her book* Myths of
Gender: Biological Theories about
Women and Men, *published by Basic
Books, appeared last fall. She is working on
a book titled* The Sex Which Prevails:
Biology and the Social/Scientific
Construction of Sexuality.

In 1843 Levi Suydam, a
twenty-three-year-old resident of
Salisbury, Connecticut, asked the
town board of selectmen to vali-
date his right to vote as a Whig in
a hotly contested local election.
The request raised a flurry of objections from the opposition party,
for reasons that must be rare in
the annals of American democracy: it was said that Suydam was
more female than male and thus
(some eighty years before suffrage
was extended to women) could
not be allowed to cast a ballot. To
settle the dispute a physician, one
William James Barry, was brought
in to examine Suydam. And, presumably upon encountering a
phallus, the good doctor declared
the prospective voter male. With
Suydam safely in their column the
Whigs won the election by a majority of one.

Barry's diagnosis, however,
turned out to be somewhat pre-
mature. Within a few days he
discovered that, phallus notwithstanding, Suydam menstruated
regularly and had a vaginal opening. Both his/her physique and
his/her mental predispositions
were more complex than was first
suspected. S/he had narrow
shoulders and broad hips and felt
occasional sexual yearnings for
women. Suydam's "feminine
propensities, such as a fondness
for gay colors, for pieces of calico,
comparing and placing them together, and an aversion for bodily
labor, and an inability to perform
the same, were remarked by
many," Barry later wrote. It is not
clear whether Suydam lost or re-
tained the vote, or whether the
election results were reversed.

Western culture is deeply
committed to the idea that there
are only two sexes. Even language
refuses other possibilities; thus to
write about Levi Suydam I have
had to invent conventions—*s/he*
and *his/her*—to denote someone
who is clearly neither male nor female or who is perhaps both sexes
at once. Legally, too, every adult is
either man or woman, and the difference, of course, is not trivial.
For Suydam it meant the fran-

chise; today it means being available for, or exempt from, draft
registration, as well as being subject, in various ways, to a number
of laws governing marriage, the
family and human intimacy. In
many parts of the United States,
for instance, two people legally
registered as men cannot have
sexual relations without violating
anti-sodomy statutes.

But if the state and the legal
system have an interest in maintaining a two-party sexual system,
they are in defiance of nature. For
biologically speaking, there are
many gradations running from female to male; and depending on
how one calls the shots, one can
argue that along that spectrum lie
at least five sexes—and perhaps
even more.

For some time medical in-
vestigators have recognized the
concept of the intersexual body.
But the standard medical literature uses the term *intersex* as a
catch-all for three major sub-
groups with some mixture of male
and female characteristics: the so-
called true hermaphrodites,
whom I call herms, who possess
one testis and one ovary (the
sperm- and egg-producing vessels, or gonads); the male pseudo-
hermaphrodites (the "merms"),

This article is reprinted by permission of *The Sciences* and is from the March/April 1993 issue. Individual subscriptions are $28 per year. Write to:
The Sciences, 2 East 63rd St., New York, NY 10021.

who have testes and some aspects of the female genitalia but no ovaries; and the female pseudo-hermaphrodites (the "ferms"), who have ovaries and some aspects of the male genitalia but lack testes. Each of those categories is in itself complex; the percentage of male and female characteristics, for instance, can vary enormously among members of the same subgroup. Moreover, the inner lives of the people in each subgroup—their special needs and their problems, attractions and repulsions—have gone unexplored by science. But on the basis of what is known about them I suggest that the three intersexes, herm, merm and ferm, deserve to be considered additional sexes each in its own right. Indeed, I would argue further that sex is a vast, infinitely malleable continuum that defies the constraints of even five categories.

Not surprisingly, it is extremely difficult to estimate the frequency of intersexuality, much less the frequency of each of the three additional sexes: it is not the sort of information one volunteers on a job application. The psychologist John Money of Johns Hopkins University, a specialist in the study of congenital sexual-organ defects, suggests intersexuals may constitute as many as 4 percent of births. As I point out to my students at Brown University, in a student body of about 6,000 that fraction, if correct, implies there may be as many as 240 intersexuals on campus—surely enough to form a minority caucus of some kind.

In reality though, few such students would make it as far as Brown in sexually diverse form. Recent advances in physiology and surgical technology now enable physicians to catch most intersexuals at the moment of birth.

Almost at once such infants are entered into a program of hormonal and surgical management so that they can slip quietly into society as "normal" heterosexual males or females. I emphasize that the motive is in no way conspiratorial. The aims of the policy are genuinely humanitarian, reflecting the wish that people be able to "fit in" both physically and psychologically. In the medical community, however, the assumptions behind that wish—that there be only two sexes, that heterosexuality alone is normal, that there is one true model of psychological health—have gone virtually unexamined.

The word *hermaphrodite* comes from the Greek name Hermes, variously known as the messenger of the gods, the patron of music, the controller of dreams or the protector of livestock, and Aphrodite, the goddess of sexual love and beauty. According to Greek mythology, those two gods parented Hermaphroditus, who at age fifteen became half male and half female when his body fused with the body of a nymph he fell in love with. In some true hermaphrodites the testis and the ovary grow separately but bilaterally; in others they grow together within the same organ, forming an ovo-testis. Not infrequently, at least one of the gonads functions quite well, producing either sperm cells or eggs, as well as functional levels of the sex hormones—androgens or estrogens. Although in theory it might be possible for a true hermaphrodite to become both father and mother to a child, in practice the appropriate ducts and tubes are not configured so that egg and sperm can meet.

In contrast with the true hermaphrodites, the pseudohermaphrodites possess two gonads of the same kind along with the

usual male (XY) or female (XX) chromosomal makeup. But their external genitalia and secondary sex characteristics do not match their chromosomes. Thus merms have testes and XY chromosomes, yet they also have a vagina and a clitoris, and at puberty they often develop breasts. They do not menstruate, however. Ferms have ovaries, two X chromosomes and sometimes a uterus, but they also have at least partly masculine external genitalia. Without medical intervention they can develop beards, deep voices and adult-size penises.

No classification scheme could more than suggest the variety of sexual anatomy encountered in clinical practice. In 1969, for example, two French investigators, Paul Guinet of the Endocrine Clinic in Lyons and Jacques Decourt of the Endocrine Clinic in Paris, described ninety-eight cases of true hermaphroditism—again, signifying people with both ovarian and testicular tissue—solely according to the appearance of the external genitalia and the accompanying ducts. In some cases the people exhibited strongly feminine development. They had separate openings for the vagina and the urethra, a cleft vulva defined by both the large and the small labia, or vaginal lips, and at puberty they developed breasts and usually began to menstruate. It was the oversize and sexually alert clitoris, which threatened sometimes at puberty to grow into a penis, that usually impelled them to seek medical attention. Members of another group also had breasts and a feminine body type, and they menstruated. But their labia were at least partly fused, forming an incomplete scrotum. The phallus (here an embryological term for a structure that during usual development goes on to form either a clitoris or a penis) was between 1.5 and 2.8 inches long; nevertheless, they urinated through a urethra that opened into or near the vagina.

By far the most frequent form of true hermaphrodite encountered by Guinet and Decourt—55 percent—appeared to have a more masculine physique. In such people the urethra runs either through or near the phallus, which looks more like a penis than a clitoris. Any menstrual blood exits periodically during urination. But in spite of the relatively male appearance of the genitalia, breasts appear at puberty. It is possible that a sample larger than ninety-eight so-called true hermaphrodites would yield even more contrasts and subtleties. Suffice it to say that the varieties are so diverse that it is possible to know which parts are present and what is attached to what only after exploratory surgery.

The embryological origins of human hermaphrodites clearly fit what is known about male and female sexual development. The embryonic gonad generally chooses early in development to follow either a male or a female sexual pathway; for the ovo-testis, however, that choice is fudged. Similarly, the embryonic phallus most often ends up as a clitoris or a penis, but the existence of intermediate states comes as no surprise to the embryologist. There are also uro-genital swellings in the embryo that usually either stay open and become the vaginal labia or fuse and become a scrotum. In some hermaphrodites, though, the choice of opening or closing is ambivalent. Finally, all mammalian embryos have structures that can become the female uterus and the fallopian tubes, as well as structures that can become part of the male sperm-transport

system. Typically either the male or the female set of those primordial genital organs degenerates, and the remaining structures achieve their sex-appropriate future. In hermaphrodites both sets of organs develop to varying degrees.

Intersexuality itself is old news. Hermaphrodites, for instance, are often featured in stories about human origins. Early biblical scholars believed Adam began life as a hermaphrodite and later divided into two people—a male and a female—after falling from grace. According to Plato there once were three sexes—male, female and hermaphrodite— but the third sex was lost with time.

Both the Talmud and the Tosefta, the Jewish books of law, list extensive regulations for people of mixed sex. The Tosefta expressly forbids hermaphrodites to inherit their fathers' estates (like daughters), to seclude themselves with women (like sons) or to shave (like men). When hermaphrodites menstruate they must be isolated from men (like women); they are disqualified from serving as witnesses or as priests (like women), but the laws of pederasty apply to them.

In Europe a pattern emerged by the end of the Middle Ages that, in a sense, has lasted to the present day: hermaphrodites were compelled to choose an established gender role and stick with it. The penalty for transgression was often death. Thus in the 1600s a Scottish hermaphrodite living as a woman was buried alive after impregnating his/her master's daughter.

For questions of inheritance, legitimacy, paternity, succession to title and eligibility for certain professions to be determined, modern Anglo-Saxon legal systems require that newborns be regis-

tered as either male or female. In the U.S. today sex determination is governed by state laws. Illinois permits adults to change the sex recorded on their birth certificates should a physician attest to having performed the appropriate surgery. The New York Academy of Medicine, on the other hand, has taken an opposite view. In spite of surgical alterations of the external genitalia, the academy argued in 1966, the chromosomal sex remains the same. By that measure, a person's wish to conceal his or her original sex cannot outweigh the public interest in protection against fraud.

During this century the medical community has completed what the legal world began—the complete erasure of any form of embodied sex that does not conform to a male–female, heterosexual pattern. Ironically, a more sophisticated knowledge of the complexity of sexual systems has led to the repression of such intricacy.

In 1937 the urologist Hugh H. Young of Johns Hopkins University published a volume titled *Genital Abnormalities, Hermaphroditism and Related Adrenal Diseases*. The book is remarkable for its erudition, scientific insight and open-mindedness. In it Young drew together a wealth of carefully documented case histories to demonstrate and study the medical treatment of such "accidents of birth." Young did not pass judgment on the people he studied, nor did he attempt to coerce into treatment those intersexuals who rejected that option. And he showed unusual evenhandedness in referring to those people who had sexual experiences as both men and women as "practicing hermaphrodites."

One of Young's more interesting cases was a hermaphrodite

named Emma who had grown up as a female. Emma had both a penis-size clitoris and a vagina, which made it possible for him/her to have "normal" heterosexual sex with both men and women. As a teenager Emma had had sex with a number of girls to whom s/he was deeply attracted; but at the age of nineteen s/he had married a man. Unfortunately, he had given Emma little sexual pleasure (though *he* had had no complaints), and so throughout that marriage and subsequent ones Emma had kept girlfriends on the side. With some frequency s/he had pleasurable sex with them. Young describes his subject as appearing "to be quite content and even happy." In conversation Emma occasionally told him of his/her wish to be a man, a circumstance Young said would be relatively easy to bring about. But Emma's reply strikes a heroic blow for self-interest:

> Would you have to remove that vagina? I don't know about that because that's my meal ticket. If you did that, I would have to quit my husband and go to work, so I think I'll keep it and stay as I am. My husband supports me well, and even though I don't have any sexual pleasure with him, I do have lots with my girlfriends.

Yet even as Young was illuminating intersexuality with the light of scientific reason, he was beginning its suppression. For his book is also an extended treatise on the most modern surgical and hormonal methods of changing intersexuals into either males or females. Young may have differed from his successors in being less judgmental and controlling of the patients and their families, but he nonetheless supplied the foundation on which current intervention practices were built.

By 1969, when the English physicians Christopher J. Dewhurst and Ronald R. Gordon wrote *The Intersexual Disorders*, medical and surgical approaches to intersexuality had neared a state of rigid uniformity. It is hardly surprising that such a hardening of opinion took place in the era of the feminine mystique—of the post–Second World War flight to the suburbs and the strict division of family roles according to sex. That the medical consensus was not quite universal (or perhaps that it seemed poised to break apart again) can be gleaned from the near-hysterical tone of Dewhurst and Gordon's book, which contrasts markedly with the calm reason of Young's founding work. Consider their opening description of an intersexual newborn:

> One can only attempt to imagine the anguish of the parents. That a newborn should have a deformity . . . [affecting] so fundamental an issue as the very sex of the child . . . is a tragic event which immediately conjures up visions of a hopeless psychological misfit doomed to live always as a sexual freak in loneliness and frustration.

Dewhurst and Gordon warned that such a miserable fate would, indeed, be a baby's lot should the case be improperly managed; "but fortunately," they wrote, "with correct management the outlook is infinitely better than the poor parents—emotionally stunned by the event—or indeed anyone without special knowledge could ever imagine."

Scientific dogma has held fast to the assumption that without medical care hermaphrodites are doomed to a life of misery. Yet there are few empirical studies to back up that assumption, and

some of the same research gathered to build a case for medical treatment contradicts it. Francies Benton, another of Young's practicing hermaphrodites, "had not worried over his condition, did not wish to be changed, and was enjoying life." The same could be said of Emma, the opportunistic hausfrau. Even Dewhurst and Gordon, adamant about the psychological importance of treating intersexuals at the infant stage, acknowledged great success in "changing the sex" of older patients. They reported on twenty cases of children reclassified into a different sex after the supposedly critical age of eighteen months. They asserted that all the reclassifications were "successful," and they wondered then whether reregistration could be "recommended more readily than [had] been suggested so far."

The treatment of intersexuality in this century provides a clear example of what the French historian Michel Foucault has called biopower. The knowledge developed in biochemistry, embryology, endocrinology, psychology and surgery has enabled physicians to control the very sex of the human body. The multiple contradictions in that kind of power call for some scrutiny. On the one hand, the medical "management" of intersexuality certainly developed as part of an attempt to free people from perceived psychological pain (though whether the pain was the patient's, the parents' or the physician's is unclear). And if one accepts the assumption that in a sex-divided culture people can realize their greatest potential for happiness and productivity only if they are sure they belong to one of only two acknowledged sexes, modern medicine has been extremely successful.

On the other hand, the same medical accomplishments can be read not as progress but as a mode of discipline. Hermaphrodites have unruly bodies. They do not fall naturally into a binary classification; only a surgical shoehorn can put them there. But why should we care if a "woman," defined as one who has breasts, a vagina, a uterus and ovaries and who menstruates, also has a clitoris large enough to penetrate the vagina of another woman? Why should we care if there are people whose biological equipment enables them to have sex "naturally" with both men and women? The answers seem to lie in a cultural need to maintain clear distinctions between the sexes. Society mandates the control of intersexual bodies because they blur and bridge the great divide. Inasmuch as hermaphrodites literally embody both sexes, they challenge traditional beliefs about sexual difference: they possess the irritating ability to live sometimes as one sex and sometimes the other, and they raise the specter of homosexuality.

But what if things were altogether different? Imagine a world in which the same knowledge that has enabled medicine to intervene in the management of intersexual patients has been placed at the service of multiple sexualities. Imagine that the sexes have multiplied beyond currently imaginable limits. It would have to be a world of shared powers. Patient and physician, parent and child, male and female, heterosexual and homosexual—all those oppositions and others would have to be dissolved as sources of division. A new ethic of medical treatment would arise, one that would permit ambiguity in a culture that had overcome sexual division. The central mission of medical treatment would be to preserve life. Thus hermaphrodites would be concerned primarily not about whether they can conform to society but about whether they might develop potentially life-threatening conditions—hernias, gonadal tumors, salt imbalance caused by adrenal malfunction—that sometimes accompany hermaphroditic development. In my ideal world medical intervention for intersexuals would take place only rarely before the age of reason; subsequent treatment would be a cooperative venture between physician, patient and other advisers trained in issues of gender multiplicity.

I do not pretend that the transition to my utopia would be smooth. Sex, even the supposedly "normal," heterosexual kind, continues to cause untold anxieties in Western society. And certainly a culture that has yet to come to grips—religiously and, in some states, legally—with the ancient and relatively uncomplicated reality of homosexual love will not readily embrace intersexuality. No doubt the most troublesome arena by far would be the rearing of children. Parents, at least since the Victorian era, have fretted, sometimes to the point of outright denial, over the fact that their children are sexual beings.

All that and more amply explains why intersexual children are generally squeezed into one of the two prevailing sexual categories. But what would be the psychological consequences of taking the alternative road—raising children as unabashed intersexuals? On the surface that tack seems fraught with peril. What, for example, would happen to the intersexual child amid the unrelenting cruelty of the school yard? When the time came to shower in gym class, what horrors and humiliations would await the intersexual as his/her anatomy was displayed in all its nontraditional glory? In whose gym class would s/he register to begin with? What bathroom would s/he use? And how on earth would Mom and Dad help shepherd him/her through the mine field of puberty?

In the past thirty years those questions have been ignored, as the scientific community has, with remarkable unanimity, avoided contemplating the alternative route of unimpeded intersexuality. But modern investigators tend to overlook a substantial body of case histories, most of them compiled between 1930 and 1960, before surgical intervention became rampant. Almost without exception, those reports describe children who grew up knowing they were intersexual (though they did not advertise it) and adjusted to their unusual status. Some of the studies are richly detailed—described at the level of gym-class showering (which most intersexuals avoided without incident); in any event, there is not a psychotic or a suicide in the lot.

Still, the nuances of socialization among intersexuals cry out for more sophisticated analysis. Clearly, before my vision of sexual multiplicity can be realized, the first openly intersexual children and their parents will have to be brave pioneers who will bear the brunt of society's growing pains. But in the long view—though it could take generations to achieve—the prize might be a society in which sexuality is something to be celebrated for its subtleties and not something to be feared or ridiculed.

 Article Review Form at end of book.

What is the primary difference in the positions of what Chapkis calls "anti-sex" feminists, "positive sex" feminists and "sexual libertarians"? How does Ariane Amsberg's exploration of prostitution relate to Barbara's assessment of the situation in Section 1?

The Meaning of Sex

Wendy Chapkis

The sexualization of the female body historically has been a concern for women's rights activists. According to feminist historian Sheila Jeffreys, many prominent suffragists at the turn of the century believed that the "sexualization of women led to her being considered fit for no other career than that of sexual object and affected the opportunities of all women for education, work, and general self-development."[1] As a result, they often endorsed purity campaigns which aimed "to free women from the 'degradation of her temple to solely animal uses,' so that she might take a full part in all the areas of life previously arrogated to man."[2] Women's identification with sex was understood, then, to be an important obstacle in the recognition of women as civil subjects rather than simply sexual objects.

Other early women's rights activists challenged this understanding of sex as primarily an expression of women's oppression, arguing instead that sex could and should be an arena of expanded freedom for women. *Freewoman* magazine, for example,

founded in 1911 by a former suffragist activist, Dora Marsden, did not shy away from discussions of marriage reform, extramarital and nonmonogamous sex, and (male) homosexuality. From the perspective of the "freewoman," "spinsters" advocating male sexual restraint and purified sexual practices were not only politically misguided but personally repressed. As one correspondent to the *Freewoman* declared:

> it will be an unspeakable catastrophe if our richly complex Feminist movement with its possibilities of power and joy, falls under the domination of sexually deficient and disappointed women . . . [3]

Similarly acrimonious disputes over the role of sexuality in women's liberation and oppression have dominated debate among women in "second-wave" feminism of the late twentieth century. By the 1980s, these disputes had escalated into feminist "sex wars." One effect of organizing conversations around sex as a "war" of positions was the need to define neatly dichotomous and hostile camps. Typically positioned on the one side are "Radical Feminists," portrayed as unrelentingly hostile to sex, which

is seen as the source of women's oppression. On the other side, are "Sex Radical" feminists, who are portrayed in equally oversimplified terms as unvaryingly positive toward sex, which is understood as no more than a source of pleasure and power in women's lives.

The reality is far more complex. Feminist thinking on the subject of sex defies simple division into two coherent positions. Not only have many feminists argued in favor of a third camp[4] beyond the two polarized ones, but important differences of perspective exist within the two identified camps. Within so-called Radical Feminism, for instance, there exist at least two distinctive visions of sex. One of these perspectives selectively embraces some limited number of sexual practices as long as they are mutual and loving in their expression, while the other opposes all practices of sexuality because they are understood to be, invariably, expressions of male dominance over women. Similarly, within so-called Sex Radical feminism, distinctions can be made between those who understand sex to be inherently benign; those who see sex as potentially oppressive but only for those women who "choose" to embrace an identity as "victim";

those who view sex as neither inherently empowering nor oppressive but a contested terrain in which women must organize and demand their rights; and those who understand sex to be a cultural practice open to subversive performance and resignification. Within these debates over the meaning and function of sex, practices of prostitution serve as a central trope. The prostitute thus comes to function as both the most literal of sexual slaves and as the most subversive of sexual agents within a sexist social order.

Radical Feminism

Sociologist Steven Seidman argues that within American culture there exist two opposing perspectives on sexuality: "sexual romanticism" and "libertarianism." While libertarians, according to Seidman, believe sex to be benign whether as an expression of love or of pleasure, romanticists firmly tie sex to affection, intimacy, and love:

> Sex, say romanticists, is a way to express intimate feelings; it always implicates the core inner aspects of the self. It should never be approached casually or with an eye to mere erotic pleasure. . . . It should be gentle, caring, nurturing, respectful and entail reciprocal obligations.[5]

Within Seidman's system of classification, all feminists who oppose prostitution and pornography are relegated to the category of sexual romanticist. But, as Radical Feminist Karen Davis argues, "there are lots of good reasons to dislike objectified sex that do not reduce to a morality of love."[6] While some Radical Feminists do attack prostitution and pornography as corrupting practices undermining a natural foundation of "positive" sex, or

eros, based on love, other anti-prostitution feminists see commercial sex as only the most demystified form of sex, which is, by definition, oppressive to women. While the former position might be called a kind of pro-"positive" sex feminism, the latter is outspokenly anti-sex.

Pro-"Positive" Sex Feminism

For those feminists engaged in the recuperative project of attempting to uncover an eros free of the distortions of patriarchy, prostitution and pornography represent a useful foil. They serve as the antithesis of "positive" sexuality. Gloria Steinem, for example, defines the erotic as a "mutually pleasurable sexual expression . . . rooted in eros or passionate love, and thus in the idea of positive choice, free will, the yearning for a particular person." This she distinguishes from the "pornographic" which

> begins with a root meaning "prostitution" . . . thus letting us know that the subject is not mutual love, or love at all, but domination and violence against women. . . . It ends with a root meaning "writing about" . . . which puts still more distance between subject and object, and replaces a spontaneous yearning for closeness with objectification and a voyeur.[7]

From this perspective, then, sex can be divided between its "positive expression" in passionate love and its violent articulation in pornographic objectification.

In the hyperbolic terms of feminist writer Jean Bethke Elshtain,

> does not anonymous lovemaking, free from constraints, mimic rather than challenge the anonymous killing of war? . . . [We must] rethink whether the sexual liberation standard was from its

inception the generalization of a norm of adolescent male sexuality writ large onto the wider social fabric.[8]

As Elshtain's comments suggest, for feminist sexual romanticists, certain sexual practices are not only understood to be inherently bad, but also, and not coincidentally, gendered male. Robin Morgan, for instance, argues against a "male sexual style" which emphasizes "genital sexuality, objectification, promiscuity, emotional noninvolvement" in favor of a female-centered sexuality, which would place a "greater trust in love, sensuality, humor, tenderness, commitment."[9] Similarly, Dutch feminist Ariane Amsberg argues:

> It seems to me that prostitution is something that only men could have invented. Women need more of an emotional connection when they are sexually active. . . . For most people, or at least for most women, sex is absolutely about intimacy and a safe, loving relationship.[10]

When love, relationship, and mutual pleasure are the only appropriate context for sex, cash and contract cannot substitute as evidence of reciprocity. Kathleen Barry thus argues that positive sex "must be earned through trust and sharing. It follows then that sex cannot be purchased. . . ."[11] From this perspective, the practice of prostitution is not really sex at all, but an abuse of sex. This misrepresentation sold as sex through prostitution and pornography endangers the possibility of real, positive sexual experience. Commercial sexual culture is seen to be as contaminating as a virus. Kathleen Barry states:

> Pornography no longer describes only the sexual activities between prostitutes and their customers. Sexual liberation has brought into

the home many of the bizarre sexual activities that men have demanded with prostitutes. Pornography depicts not just what one can do with a whore but with one's lover, one's wife, and even one's daughter. Through pornography, time-honored distinctions of society are now blurring and the gap is quickly closing between love and violence, madonnas and whores.[12]

Prostitution, then, is seen to be increasingly the model for private sexuality even when there is no formal exchange of money for sex:

Public sexuality is institutionalized through the massive production and distribution of pornography and through the industrialization of prostitution which has the effect of reducing sex to an object and reducing women to sex {which} objectifies sex into a thing to be gotten, had or taken, disengages sex from its human experience, its dimensionality and places it in a marketing condition *whether in fact it is marketed or not.* . . . Public sexual exploitation increasingly is becoming the model for private sexual behavior.[13]

Commercial sex, therefore, can be held responsible for both literal and symbolic violence against women. In order to protect women and to preserve the possibility of positive sexual experience, prostitution and pornography must not only be abolished, but their contaminating effect on sexual fantasy and practice must be actively challenged.

This has led some pro-"positive" sex feminists to advocate a politics of cultural cleansing. At "The Sexual Liberals and the Attack on Feminism Conference,"[14] organized in 1987 by Radical Feminists, participants discussed whether it was possible to reclaim any aspect of sex for use by women:

Ultimately, {British author Sheila} Jeffreys believes that it is possible for lesbians to come up with a vision of egalitarian sexuality, one that doesn't have *all the residue* of heteropatriarchal society. She is doubtful, however, whether heterosexual relations can ever be *cleansed* to the point of equality. [15]

. . . Jeffreys was asked to elaborate on her earlier admission that she has had disturbing fantasies or has been aroused by pornographic material. In response, she commented on her efforts to *purge herself* of undesirable fantasies. She said she has given up fantasizing altogether; she took some time off from sex in order to try something *completely different.* . . . She suggested that giving up fantasies was a strategy to *cleanse the movement* of S/M.[16]

. . . The answer, according to {feminist sex therapist} Stock is to develop our own model. . . . We should continue to question sexuality in order to *detoxify* ourselves from this culture.[17]

For pro-"positive" sex feminists, then, sexuality may be able to be reclaimed from the patriarchy, but not in forms easily recognizable to us as sex. Because prostitution and pornography have already infiltrated our imaginations, women's fantasies and sexual activities must be cleansed of their residue. Pro-"positive" sex feminists advocate the abolition of practices of prostitution both in order to prevent further contamination of the erotic by the pornographic, and to free women from the burdens of sexual objectification by men. The objectification of women through the commodification of sex is understood to reinforce what Carole Pateman calls "male sex-right":

when women's bodies are on sale as commodities in the capitalist

market, the terms of the original {sexual} contract cannot be forgotten; the law of male sex-right is publicly affirmed, and men gain public acknowledgment as women's sexual masters—that is what is wrong with prostitution.[18]

Nancy Fraser, in a sympathetic critique of Pateman's argument, notes, however, that it is marriage and not prostitution that "establishes a long-term, hierarchical status relation whose terms are predetermined and unalterable, and whose roles are assigned according to sex." While a notion of male sex-right may well underlie the patriarchal meaning of sexual difference defining femininity as "subjection," the commodified version of that relationship through prostitution may offer a (limited) challenge to notions of boundless male dominance. The client or employer does not acquire unlimited command over the worker (except significantly, in cases of outright slavery). Thus, Fraser suggests, it is misleading to assimilate "commodification to command" because "even as the wage contract establishes workers as subject to the boss's command in the employment sphere, it simultaneously constitutes that sphere as a limited sphere."[19]

Anti-Sex Feminism

If, from the vantage point of romanticist feminism, a form of positive sexuality can be recovered through purification and selective abolition (of prostitution and pornography), from the perspective of other Radical Feminists, sex itself must be abolished. From the perspective of anti-sex feminists, there is nothing sexual to recover or reclaim because the very meaning of sex is male domination. Prostitution and pornography only reveal this message most clearly. Catharine MacKinnon, for example, argues that

> sexuality itself is a social construct, gendered to the ground. Male dominance here is not an artificial overlay upon an underlying inalterable substratum of uncorrupted essential sexual being.[20]

For this reason, MacKinnon dismisses romanticist feminism as liberal:

> The critical yet formally liberal view of Susan Griffin {*Pornography and Silence: Culture's Revenge Against Nature.* 1981} conceptualizes eroticism as natural and healthy but corrupted and confused by the "pornographic mind." Pornography distorts Eros, which preexists and persists, despite male culture's pornographic "revenge" upon it. Eros is, unaccountably, still there.[21]

Because sex is understood not to be "contaminated" but rather constituted by male domination, these feminists argue that the practice itself must be abandoned. Karen Davis argues that

> being "anti-sex" is not being against sexuality per se, merely against everything that has been organized as sex, everything one has been able to experience as sex within the constraints of our culture.[22]

One of the most explicit statements of this position has been articulated by the Southern Women's Writing Collective, who organized under the title "Women Against Sex." WAS advocates a strategy of "sex resistance":

> All sex acts subordinate women . . . all actions that are part of the practice of sexuality partake of the practice's political function or goal. . . . Thus all sex acts (and their depictions) mean the same thing, though some mean it more than others.[23]

Apparently, while sex always means male dominance, some forms of sexual practice—such as prostitution, s/m, or heterosexual penetration—are more clearly expressive of that dynamic than others (lesbian "vanilla" sex within the bonds of loving relationship, for example). Still, even the most apparently benign kinds of sex are still sex, and hence still an enactment of male supremacy.

From this perspective, it is not enough to reject some of the more apparently abusive sexual practices, it is also necessary to recognize that the language and symbolism of those acts are the building blocks for even that which women perceive to be their most authentic sexual selves. According to WAS, feminist sex resistance must involve resisting "patriarchy's attempt to make its work of subordinating women easier by 'consensually' constructing her desire in its own oppressive image."[24] Female desire must be recreated entirely outside the practices and symbols of contemporary culture. What desire would look like divorced from sex cannot be known:

> Any act which did not subordinate women would literally not be a sex act, but would be "something else." . . . The practice that could make this happen does not exist. In our feminist future, an act outwardly identical to a sex act might be informed by an entirely different practice. It might stand in a different relationship to conceptual and empirical male force. But the feminist future is where we want to go/be after the defeat of male supremacy—and that is to say, after dismantling the practice of sexuality.[25]

Sex, therefore, cannot be a tool for dismantling male supremacy because it is created by and for it, and is thus inextricably implicated in it. Sex, from this perspective, is "in" us but not "of" us. It is not ours to do with as we would, it does us. The only possible strategic response is opposition to sex:

> There is no way out on the inside of the practice of sexuality except out. . . . The function of this practice permits no true metamorphoses. [26]

Similarly, Andrea Dworkin insists that sex resists resignification:

> Experience is chosen for us, then imposed on us, especially in intercourse, *and so is its meaning.* . . . We have no freedom and no extravagance in the questions we can ask or the interpretations we can make.... Our bodies speak their language. Our minds think in it. The men are inside us through and through.[27]

Within the anti-sex framework, woman is constituted as and through sex. Thus, not only is sex synonymous with male supremacy and female objectification, but woman is synonymous with whore. Andrea Dworkin states:

> The metaphysics of male sexual domination is that all women are whores. This basic truth transcends all lesser truths in the male system . . .[28]

In the anti-sex invocation of "whore" (much like that of the romanticists), the prostitute is divorced from the notion of sex *worker* who negotiates a literal exchange of sex for money and is reduced to the position of sex *object* (that is, woman-as-sex, not women-does-sex). "Whore," like "woman," becomes a passive condition rather than a place of active engagement within the social and cultural order. Thus, Catharine MacKinnon insists ". . . men say all women are whores. We say men have the power to make this our fundamental condition."[29] Similarly, Kathleen Barry warns that "women exist as objects and as such will be taken if they don't give themselves."[30]

Women exist only as passive bodies because men have the power to make it so. Within anti-sex and romanticist feminist rhetoric, the prostitute becomes the symbol of women's abject powerlessness under conditions of male objectification and domination; they are simply objects in a marketplace.

> That is what prostitution is about: it is about bodies being exchanged on a market. . . . So what you have is a lot of bodies in Manila, a lot of bodies in Thailand, a lot of bodies in Saigon that have been used for prostitution. Now what do you do with them {after the U.S. troops withdraw from the region and no longer support the sex trade}? You don't send them home to mother. Prostitution doesn't work that way.[31]

Kathleen Barry thus explains the development of sex tourism in areas that once served as "rest and recreation" centers for American soldiers as strictly the result of traffickers' ingenuity. Women's need for continued employment plays no part; they are only "bodies that have been used for prostitution," soiled and thus no longer suitable to be sent home to mother.[32] Such language joins forces with the power it seeks to challenge. The dialectics of struggle disappear entirely into an apparently seamless system of male supremacy.[33] Male power is constantly reaffirmed even as it is denounced. In this way, anti-sex and romanticist feminist rhetoric tends to reproduce the very ideology it intends to destabilize.

By constantly reiterating that women are whores, and that whores are no more than objects, such feminists blind themselves to the fact that prostitutes, no less than any other worker, and no less than any other woman, engage in acts of negotiation, resistance, and subversion that belie their designation as passive objects. Anti-sex feminism, like pro-"positive" sex feminism, cannot accommodate this reality. Indeed, reality is understood to be identical to the image of it men would wish to impose. MacKinnon states:

> Gender is sexual. Pornography constitutes the meaning of that sexuality. Men treat women as who they see women as being. Pornography constructs who that is. *Men's power over women means that the way men see women defines who women can be.*[34]

Because the positions "inside" culture are defined as fixed, to act defiantly from within the sexual order by making subversive use of that culture is understood to be impossible. The only "radical" feminist act is one of opposition and resistance. The cultural order must be refused.

Sex Radical Feminism and the Meaning of Sex

Contemporary feminist sexual politics encompass positions beyond those of purification and resistance. Some feminists reject the distinction between "positive" and "perverted" sexuality and simultaneously insist on active engagement within the sexual order rather than the abolition of it. Steven Seidman categorizes these alternative positions as sexual "libertarianism." According to Seidman, while sexual romanticists assume that "certain sexual acts carry an intrinsic moral meaning," libertarians "frame sex as having multiple meanings . . . and {see it as} legitimate in multiple social settings."[35] Because libertarians resist the idea that sexual meaning is fixed, individuals (rather than the community) must determine whether an act is right or wrong for him or her. A libertarian notion of "consent" thus replaces a romanticist notion of "responsibility" as the ultimate measure of the ethics of any sexual activity. Seidman insists that this has the effect of individualizing the meaning of sex to the point where social structures such as gender inequality necessarily disappear from the account.[36]

Just as Seidman's category of sexual romanticism is too narrow to account for the divergent perspectives within Radical Feminism, so too is his designation libertarian inadequate to describe the diversity of positions within feminist Sex Radicalism. Among feminists broadly defined as Sex Radicals, a distinction can be drawn between those most closely aligned with the extreme individualism of libertarian ethics and politics, and those who explicitly situate sex (and the individuals enacting it) within structures of power and privilege.

Sexual Libertarianism

Sexual libertarianism offers a reversal of the image of sex presented in anti-sex feminism. Both insist that sex, as represented in prostitution and pornography, must be read as reality, and both conclude that the encoded message is one of power. Where these groups diverge is on the question of who holds that power. One of the most prominent voices of the libertarian perspective is Camille Paglia, whose uncompromising pronouncements on sex make her a fair match for such anti-sex feminists as Andrea Dworkin and Catharine MacKinnon. According to Paglia,

What you see in pornography and prostitution is the reality of sex. It is not a patriarchal distortion. It is the ultimate physical reality. So a feminist who claims to understand sexuality but cannot deal with pornography or topless clubs is no expert. She is a censor. She is a prude.[37]

While Dworkin and MacKinnon read messages of male power and female subjection in commercial sexual culture, Paglia sees the reverse:

Men are run ragged by female sexuality all their lives. From the beginning of his life to the end, no man ever fully commands any woman. It's an illusion. . . . That's what the strip clubs are about: not woman as victim, not woman as slave, but woman as goddess.[38]

Paglia insists that women's association with sex should be seen as her source of greatest power, not as the root of her oppression and abuse. Paglia thus intends not only to complicate the notion of women's sexual victimization by men, but to reverse it. It is men who are "run ragged" and feel powerless in the presence of women's sexuality:

The feminist line is, strippers and topless dancers are degraded, subordinated, and enslaved; they are victims, turned into objects by the display of their anatomy. But women are far from being victims—women *rule*; they are in total control. . . . The feminist analysis of prostitution says that men are using money as power over women. I'd say, yes, that's all that men *have*. The money is a confession of weakness. They have to buy women's attention. It's not a sign of power; it's a sign of weakness.[39]

If women rule sexually and enjoy total control in their encounters with men, then those who claim to be victims of male

sexual violence have only themselves to blame. In this way, sexual power is removed from any social or political context and instead becomes an attribute available to any individual alert enough to claim it.[40] Author bell hooks criticizes this libertarian feminist position for "embracing outmoded sexist visions of female sexual agency and pleasure." Such a politics, she argues, lacks imagination as it conceives of "sexual agency only by inverting the patriarchal standpoint and claiming it as their {women's} own."[41]

Hooks is not alone among contemporary feminists in rejecting both the radical individualism of libertarianism as well as the ubiquitous female sexual victimization of Radical Feminism. Many Sex Radical feminists explicitly situate sex within a culture of male domination; sex is understood to be constructed by this culture without being fully determined by it. Carole Vance, for example, suggests that

to focus only on pleasure and gratification ignores the patriarchal structure in which women act, yet to speak only of sexual violence and oppression ignores women's experience with sexual agency and choice and unwittingly increases the sexual terror and despair in which women live.[42]

Unlike libertarians, feminist Sex Radicals do not fully substitute an ethic of consent for one of responsibility. Social and political context beyond the individual continue to figure prominently in their interpretation and assessment of sex. For example, during her tenure as editor of the lesbian sex magazine, *On Our Backs*, Marcy Sheiner objected to photos in another erotic publication, *Future Sex*, on the grounds that they were both racist and sexist. Sheiner challenged these images

of sex tourism for glossing over a context of unequal power and privilege:

I'm the first to admit that these images and ideas generate sexual excitement in many people, even those who are ethically opposed to them. But is arousal potential the sole criteria for what goes into a sex magazine? . . . {this question} has plagued me since I penned and sold my first pornographic story several years ago. So while I champion freedom of expression, and continue to create sexual materials, I can't kid myself into believing there are black and white answers to the ethical questions raised during the course of my work.[43]

A similar tension was revealed in 1991 when Bobby Lilly, a leader of a mixed gender anti-censorship organization in California, CAL-ACT, reported on the struggles of sex workers and Sex Radical feminists to gain a voice within the largest American feminist organization, the National Organization for Women. A male reader returned the issue with the words "what irrelevant garbage" scrawled across the top. He also circled the words "Equal Rights Amendment" and "patriarchal" in the article, commenting that "this has nothing to do with the fight against censorship." Lilly, who "didn't know whether to laugh, cry, or spit," replied that as a feminist and a Sex Radical, her anti-censorship politics could never be gender-blind.[44] Sex Radical feminists and libertarians may both embrace a politics of sexual "free speech," but they diverge on the issue of whether an erotic ethic needs to extend beyond the formal question of consent.

In the early 1990s, a workshop on pornography was organized at the National Organization for Women's annual conference in New York. One presenter, a male academic, reported on the causal relationship he believed to exist between pornography and violence against women. After the presentation, an audience member approached him. "Isn't there some way," she asked, "to educate people about the difference between violence and consensual fantasies, something besides resorting to censorship? Maybe s/m photos could be captioned: 'This is a negotiated fantasy between two consenting adults.'" The man slowly shook his head. "I understand your concern. But while that might be enough for you or me, what about a group of Black teenagers at a newsstand on 42nd Street? They won't read or understand a message like that." Overhearing this exchange, I found myself wondering about the problematic alliances some women have made with "good" (White, professional) men out to protect the sisterhood from the "bad" (Black, poor) ones. But I was soon reminded that my own alliances can be no less embarrassing.

The group I was associated with at the conference, "Union Labia: Sex Workers and Sex Radical Feminists," had a number of male "supporters" attached to it. Some of them were fans of the various high profile porn stars in the delegation. The presence of these men made me acutely uncomfortable, but the pros simply treated them with the cursory courtesy reserved for johns. One man, however, received a more respectful sort of attention. He was a short, chubby, middle-aged fellow in a business suit. This man, I learned, was no average john; he was a journalist on assignment from Playboy magazine hoping to cover a catfight between sex workers and other now feminists.

Playboy had access to our group because the Playboy Foundation had contributed a small sum toward the airfare necessary to bring an international prostitution expert from the World Health Organization in Geneva to the meeting. In return, he was to see if there was a story to be had. I was profoundly ambivalent about his presence. While pornography may no longer be the declared enemy for feminists such as myself, Playboy's fondness for airbrushed "perfection" has never endeared them to me.

Throughout the conference, the Playboy reporter secreted himself away with one or another of the "Union Labia" members attempting, I assumed, to dig up dirt that wasn't being thrown. I managed to avoid him until the final afternoon. He opened our conversation with the offer of a marijuana cookie. Our alliance as outlaws thus cemented, I proceeded to give him my standard feminist critique of both the anti-pornography/anti-prostitution movement and of the male violence that inspires it. This is a familiar role for me in sex worker/sex radical settings where there are already many articulate voices asserting women's right to fuck convention by being sluts and whores.

Because I was talking to a Playboy, it felt especially satisfying to remind him that anti-porn feminists were responding to a very real state of emergency over women's sexual integrity and safety. "Still," I confided, "their insistence that people like me are the enemy is distressing, especially in this political moment when we so desperately need each other. We have to form a united front against the real and declared enemies." "Like who?" he asked. "Well, you know, like the President, the Supreme Court, the whole Reagan/Bush Right Wing." "Now, wait a minute," he interrupted, "what makes you think they're the enemy? I'm a contributor to the National Review myself. William Buckley is a personal friend. They've been very receptive to my articles defending free speech and pornography." I felt the room shift slightly, and it wasn't just the marijuana kicking in. The whole encounter reminded me that anti-pornography feminists have no monopoly on courting or tolerating the support of dubious allies to "advance the cause."

Sexual Subversion

Unlike sexual libertarians, feminist Sex Radicals generally accept romanticist and anti-sex feminists analyses of sex as deeply implicated in structures of inequality. But what distinguishes the Sex Radical perspective is the notion that sex is a terrain of struggle, not a fixed field of gender and power positions. Jana Sawicki explains:

> Neither wholly a source of domination nor of resistance, sexuality is also neither outside power nor wholly circumscribed by it. Instead, it is itself an arena of struggle. There are no inherently liberatory or repressive sexual practices, for any practice is co-optable and any is capable of becoming a source of resistance.[45]

Sex Radical feminists thus share with romanticist and anti-sex feminists a sense of outrage at the existing sexual order, but reject a politics of purification or abolition in favor of one of subversion from within sexual practice. This offers a vision of political struggle not predicated on a cleansing of culture or on a move outside of culture.

From this perspective, acts of apparent complicity may also be acts of subversive resistance. Just as a colonized people may make use of the language of the colonizer in transgressive ways,[46] women are understood to be able to subversively resignify sexual language and practices through using them in unintended ways. Pat Califia, for example, argues that lesbians can liberate a sexual vocabulary for their own use by seizing words previously used against them:

> Words that have been used in anti-sex, anti-lesbian ways can be coopted. By using these terms with pride, lesbians can liberate them and change their meaning. The word "dyke" has already been transformed this way.[47]

Daphne Marlatt has described this subversive relationship to the symbolic order in terms of being "an inhabitant of language, not master, nor even mistress . . . inside language she leaps for joy, shoving out the walls of taboo and propriety . . ."[48] Such attempts to redefine and reinhabit the sexual order are in part a response to the impossibility, of moving to a place outside of culture to create entirely anew. Teresa de Lauretis argues that

> paradoxically, the only way to position oneself outside of that discourse is to displace oneself within it—to refuse the question as formulated, or to answer deviously (though in its words), even to quote (but against the grain).[49]

In addition to the impossibility of moving to a place outside of culture, some feminists argue that a politics predicated on an abolition of the sexual order rather than engagement with it leaves women further impoverished. Betsy Warland, for example, acknowledges the shortcomings of sexual speech in describing women's experiences and desires, but urges women nonetheless to refuse to abandon it:

> the language itself does not reflect women's sensual experience. For most of us, however, it is our native tongue. The only language we have . . . so when we abandon words, it isn't a simple matter of

leaving them behind but rather a turning over of our power to those who keep them: speechlessness the consequence.[50]

Ntozake Shange wrestles with a similar concern in her decision to make use of sexual speech in her writing:

> One part of the exploitation of people of color—especially women—has been to rob us of any inner life, to rob us of our own sexuality and sensuality. . . . I hesitate to strip us of a concrete and vital language for sexual activities and desires and fantasies, because I don't think we can afford to lose too much more.[51]

But feminists like Shange who regard sexual language as a crucial resource for women are far from reverent in their uses of it:

> I'm taking words that men have used to make us dirty. I'm taking them to make us able to use them any way we choose . . . I can get myself in a big bind and never be able to write anything that is honest if I can't somehow uproot words or images that have been malignant and make them constructive for me.[52]

Pat Califia further argues that the meaning of sexual practice no less than sexual language is dependent on the context in which it is employed:

> No erotic act has an intrinsic meaning. A particular sexual activity may symbolize one thing in the majority culture, another thing to members of a sexual subculture. . . . The context within which an erotic act occurs can also alter its meaning.[53]

It is precisely this commitment to locating sex within a cultural and political context that distinguishes feminist Sex Radicals such as Califia from libertarians such as Paglia. While Paglia would generalize the ap-

parent control a performer has over a client in a strip club to assert that all women "are in total control" of sexual interactions with men, Califia would read the interaction and its meaning as context dependent.

Even in sub-cultural enactments of sex, dominant culture always remains important. Anne McClintock notes that within the "control frame of cash and fantasy" of commercial s/m, for example, men can "surrender" power to women while still maintaining control outside of that limited frame:

> In the private security of fantasy, men can indulge secretly and guiltily their knowledge of women's power, while enclosing female power in a fantasy land that lies far beyond the cities and towns of genuine feminist change.[54]

McClintock concludes that within the "magic circle" of subcultural sex, "social and personal contradictions can be deployed or negotiated, but need not be finally resolved, for the sources and ends of these paradoxes lie beyond the individual. . . ."[55] As sociologist Robert Connell concludes, a true "democracy of pleasure" requires an equalization of resources among and between men and women.[56]

While sexual libertarianism can ignore what lies beyond the individual, feminism cannot. Women are still disproportionately poor, overworked, and underpaid; women are still the deliberate targets of male sexual violence; women's bodies are still heavily regulated by state policies criminalizing subcultural sexual practices and restricting access to birth control and abortion; and women are still stigmatized and punished for sexual activity beyond the confines of monogamous heterosexual marriage. These realities co-determine women's experience of sex.

The key difference, then, between Sex Radical feminists and Radical Feminists does not rest on whether attention should be paid to the structures of gender inequality in which sex is constructed, enacted, and represented. Rather, the two perspectives differ in their assessments of whether the meaning and function of sex is fully determined by that sexist social order. While Radical Feminists insist that the sexual (mis)representations of patriarchy create "reality" because of the absolute power of men to make them function as such, feminist Sex Radicals understand sex to be a cultural tactic which can be used both to destabilize male power as well as to reinforce it. In much the same way, Michel de Certeau argues that culture

articulates conflicts and alternately legitimizes, displaces, or controls the superior force. It develops in an atmosphere of tensions, and often of violence {and} the tactics of consumption, the ingenious ways in which the weak make use of the strong, thus lend a political dimension to everyday practices.[57]

Practices of prostitution, like other forms of commodification and consumption, can be read in more complex ways than simply as a confirmation of male domination. They may also be seen as sites of ingenious resistance and cultural subversion. For this reason, Sex Radical feminists insist that the position of the prostitute cannot be reduced to one of a passive object used in a male sexual practice, but instead can be understood as a place of agency where the sex worker makes active use of the existing sexual order. Indeed, the Whore is often in-

voked by feminist Sex Radicals as a symbol of women's sexual autonomy and, as such, as a potential threat to patriarchal control over women's sexuality. Rebecca Kaplan suggests:

Women are usually called whores for being openly or highly sexual. Men who yell at women will often call them a "whore" and a "dyke" in the same breath. How is it that a woman can be simultaneously accused of having too much sex with men (whore) and too little sex with men (dyke)? This should make us realize that both of these terms condemn women's sexual autonomy. Whores and dykes are a threat to heteropatriarchy because both set their own rules for sex—rules which deny men the right to unlimited access to women's sexuality. Of course, prostitution can be critiqued like any other capitalist venture, but in a world in which a woman's body is so devalued, telling a man that he has to pay for access to it can be a radical act of self-determination.[58]

Pat Califia concurs:

The slut is, in Dworkin's parlance, male property—a victim of male violence—a woman who accepts male definition of her sexuality. Instead, I believe that she is someone men hate because she is potentially beyond their control. . . . A whore does not sell her body. She sells her time. So she has time that is not for sale, that belongs to no one but herself. Domesticated women don't dare put a price on their time.[59]

The slut, the dyke, and the whore are thus embraced by Sex Radicals as a potent symbolic challenge to confining notions of proper womanhood and conventional sexuality. Because Sex Radicals, like libertarians, embrace a vision of sex freed of the constraints of love, commitment, and convention, prostitution and

pornography are understood to be useful to enhance sexual exploration and diversity. While Kathleen Barry and other pro-"positive" sex feminists condemn prostitution for introducing "bizarre" pornographic practices into private sexual behavior, Pat Califia celebrates commercial sex for very similar reasons:

If you don't know that there's a whole group of people who engage in a particular sexual behavior, it makes it much more difficult to imagine yourself ever being able to do it. And porn is one of the commonest ways that people discover there are other folks out there who like to do cunnilingus, anal sex, gay sex, get tied up, have threesomes . . .[60]

Similarly, Lisa Duggan, Nan Hunter, and Carole Vance argue that

pornography carries many messages other than woman-hating: it advocates sexual adventure, sex outside of marriage, anonymous sex, group sex, voyeuristic sex, illegal sex, public sex. . . . Women's experience of pornography is not as universally victimizing as the {MacKinnon/Dworkin anti-pornography} ordinance would have it.[61]

Of course, Sex Radicals' invocation of prostitution and pornography as tools of liberation forged by undomesticated outlaw whores is as much of a rhetorical trope as the Radical Feminists depiction of commercial sex as realm of oppression populated by sexual slaves and exploited objects. Ira Levine, who has long worked in the adult film industry, reports, for example, that "outlaw" is not an identity all sex workers embrace:

It's amazing how in so many ways, many people in the porn industry have the same rather conventional values as people in any other industry. Do not assume that this is a bunch of wild bohemian personalities. We have our share of them, but we have an awful lot of people who struggle to lead conventional lives in spite of what they're doing. I think a lot of those people are missing out on the one real advantage of this job: the freedom of being a leper. After you've already done something loathsome to the majority of the population, you have a certain amount of latitude. I think it's a shame that these people feel an obligation to prove to everyone that they're really just perfectly normal people.[62]

Similarily, Carol Queen, a California sex worker and writer, notes that, far from being sexually enlightened, many prostitutes share the sexual prejudices of dominant culture:

Unlike many women working in the sex trades, I actually have a background in sex education. I want to think of the erotic desires of the people who come to me. I don't think of clients as kinky or perverted. I like it that they can come to me and say "I would like you to put your hand in my butt" or "I would like you to piss on me." One of the things that I know I am providing is a sexual safe space for people who haven't had that before. And I'm probably more safe for them than most prostitutes because I honor their desire. One piece of the puzzle of how to improve sex work is that sex workers could be trained in human sexuality, and other people could be assisted in developing both their own sex awareness and their communication skills.[63]

The reality of commercial sex (and the experiences of those performing erotic labor) is far more varied than either Radical or Sex Radical feminist rhetoric can express. Prostitution functions as an effective trope in these competing discourses of female sexuality, but the use of the sex worker as a symbol has also served to obscure the real complexity of her life.

Note: The notes for Reading 9 appear in the "Notes" section at the end of the book.

 Article Review Form at end of book.

Who benefits from the continued efforts to ban these abortion procedures?

The Partial-Birth Abortion Ban Act and the Undue Burden It Places on Women's Right to an Abortion

The controversy over D & E, dilatation and evacuation

Michelle Román

Currently pending before Congress are two bills, H.R. 1833[1] and S. 939[2]. If enacted, the bills will ban a later abortion procedure known as dilatation and evacuation ("D & E").[3] This procedure is actually one of the least used forms of late-term abortion because it is necessary only in situations where the woman's life or health is at risk.[4] This Summary examines the current controversy over the enactment of H.R. 1833/S. 939. It further examines the possible consequences that these bills will have on women seeking D & E as an abortion procedure if the bills are enacted into law.

The majority of abortions, in fact ninety-five percent of abortions, take place at or before the first trimester or early second trimester of pregnancy.[5] Fewer than 600 abortions per year are performed in the third trimester of pregnancy.[6] All abortions performed during the third trimester are the result of severe fetal abnormality or risk to the life of the pregnant woman.[7] Women seeking later abortions do so for these serious reasons. Some women learn, after numerous ultra-sounds, tests, and procedures that a devastating anomaly has been detected in the fetus at the twenty-eighth week of pregnancy or beyond.[8] Other women may be diagnosed with cancer or kidney failure late in pregnancy.[9] These women are faced with very difficult and painful decisions concerning the termination their very much wanted pregnancy.

For these women, D & E may be safer than other procedures because it reduces blood loss and prevents tearing the woman's cervix and uterus, leaving her able to become pregnant and give birth in the future.[10] Intact D & E is used only when other procedures, such as induced labor or vaginal delivery, would present higher risk to the woman's life, health, or future childbearing.[11] For example, cesarean section carries a much higher risk to a women's life and fertility than D & E.[12]

What Is the Medical Procedure for D & E?

D & E is a surgical procedure performed in some later abortions in which the fetus is removed intact.[13] The procedure is referred to as D & E, modified D & E, or

Women's Rights Law Reporter, The Partial-Birth Abortion Ban Act and the Undue Influence by Michelle Roman. Reprinted with permission.

Having (a) Sex: Gender, Sexuality, Reproduction **57**

D & X (dilatation and extraction).[14] Although a woman's cervix is dilated using a natural dilator called laminaria, her cervical opening is still not large enough for removal of the fetus without injury to the woman.[15] Thus, the doctor has to remove some fluid from the cranium of the fetus to bring the head out without causing tears or bleeding in the woman's cervix.[16]

Although anti-abortionists refer to this procedure as "partial-birth abortion", this term is a misconception about the procedure and it is used to mislead the public into believing that the fetus is alive until the end of the procedure.[17] The truth is that neurological fetal demise is induced before the procedure begins or early on in the procedure.[18] There are numerous benefits to this procedure. The intact fetus provides a compassionate ending to the tragedy of an untenable pregnancy.[19] Doctors are able to examine the fetus, advise the parents about future risks of pregnancy, and the woman, if she desires, is able to hold the fetus and grieve for its loss.[20] A case cited in a pamphlet by Religious Americans Speak Out[21] provides a compelling account of the agonizing decision a woman must face when confronted with such a situation. Coreen Costello explains that she

> found out when she was seven months pregnant that a lethal neuromuscular disease had left her much-wanted daughter unable to survive. Her little body had frozen and stiffened and was wedged against Coreen's cervix. Amniotic fluid had puddled and built up to dangerous toxic levels.
>
> Previously opposed to abortion, Coreen spent two and a half weeks consulting with doctors to find another option, but after ruling out induced labor and cesarean section, she and her husband decided that abortion was their

only real choice. [Afterward] my husband and I held her tight and sobbed. We stayed with her for hours. We memorized every inch of her tiny body. We prayed. We sang lullabies. She wasn't missing part of the brain. There was no hole from scissors. There was a needle hole covered with a regular band-aid on the back of her head. She looked peaceful . . . I had one of the safest, gentlest, and most compassionate ways of ending a pregnancy that had no hope.[22]

The Partial-Birth Abortion Ban Act of 1995

H.R. 1833/S 939 is designed to ban the use of a particular abortion method described in the bill as "partial-birth procedure."[23] "Partial-birth abortion" is defined as an "abortion in which the person performing the abortion partially vaginally delivers a living fetus before killing the fetus and completing the delivery."[24] A person, other than the pregnant woman, "in or affecting interstate or foreign commerce" who knowingly violates the ban is subject to fines and up to two years imprisonment.[25] Moreover, the bill creates a civil cause of action for monetary and statutory damages against those who violate the ban; and it can be maintained by the father, or the parents of a minor woman, even if the woman consents to the abortion.[26]

The bill provides an affirmative defense for physicians who violate the bill.[27] The defense must be proven by a preponderance of the evidence and the physician must reasonably believe that: (1) the partial-birth abortion was necessary to save the life of the woman upon whom it was performed; and (2) no other procedure would suffice for that purpose.[28]

Although the definition of partial-birth abortion is vague, it would essentially bar both D & E and D & X. For this reason, Kathryn Kolbert, Vice President of the Center for Reproductive Law & Policy, has testified before the committee assigned to hear opposition to H.R. 1833/S. 939.[29] First, Kolbert argues that the bill will place an undue burden on women seeking pre-viability abortions and post-viability abortions necessary to protect there lives or health.[30] Moreover, she argues that the fact that only a small number of women would be affected by the federal ban does not preclude a claim that it constitutes an undue burden.[31] Kolbert cites *Roe v. Wade*[32] and *Planned Parenthood v Casey*[33] to support her claim that the bill would impose an undue burden on women seeking pre-viability abortions limiting the physician's discretion to choose the most appropriate method of abortion based on the medical needs of his or her patient.[34] Moreover, she asserts that *Roe* found that women have a constitutional right to obtain post-viability abortion in cases where a woman's life and health are endangered and that the state may not make its interest in the fetus paramount to the women's or require a "trade-off" between a woman's health and fetal survival.[35] Kolbert asserts that banning specific abortion procedures would require this same trade-off of women's health.[36] The statute would prevent physicians from employing the safest abortion method available, thus prohibiting the physician from making the woman's health his/her paramount concern.

Second, Kolbert argues that there is no legitimate state interest to support the federal ban on abortion.[37] As to the State's interest in potential life, she asserts that as a previability restriction, the bill cannot be characterized as furthering the State's interest in potential life because it does nothing to affect a woman's decision whether to choose childbirth over abortion.[38] Nor does the bill purport to promote maternal health and safety.[39]

Lastly, Kolbert argues that the affirmative defense is inadequate and fails to protect women from severe health consequences.[40] The affirmative defense is only available to physicians who reasonably believed that the procedure used was the only procedure available to save the woman's life.[41] Thus, Kolbert asserts that other procedures are banned even in cases in which the physician believes that the use of any other method of abortion or childbirth would pose a significant risk to the woman's health.[42]

Finally, Kolbert urges the Committee to reject the bill as an unprecedented expansion of congressional regulation of health care.[43] She argues that this bill is an unconstitutional restriction on the reproductive rights of women, and is likely to be invalidated in the federal courts.[44] In fact, in October 1995 the U.S. District Court for the Southern District of Ohio[45] granted a preliminary injunction against enforcement of H.B. 135[46], a bill, very much like H.R. 1833, designed to ban particular methods of late abortions, essentially, banning dilation and extraction ("D & X").[47] The court found that H.B. 135's definition of a D & X procedure is impermissibly vague because it fails to provide physicians with fair warning as to what conduct is permitted, and as to what conduct will expose them to criminal and civil liability.[48] Moreover, the court found that by banning the safest and more widely available

method of late second-trimester abortion, Ohio placed a substantial obstacle in the path of women choosing abortions.[49]

Conclusion

Likewise, if H.R. 1833 is enacted, the bill will suffer from many of the same constitutional defects as Ohio H.B. 135. The bill will place an undue burden on women seeking late-term abortions and will deter physicians from offering their patients the best possible health care available. Thus, these bills must be rejected in Congress. The bill is unconstitutional and unduly interferes with a woman's right to an abortion.

1. H.R. 1833, 104th Cong., 2d. Sess (1995).
2. S. 939, 104th Cong., 2d. Sess. (1995).
3. *See infra* notes 13-16 and accompanying text: *see also* H.R. 1833; Religious Coalition for Reproductive Freedom. Religious Pro-Choice Americans Speak Out 1 (1996); The Center for Reproductive Law & Policy, Reproductive Freedom News 4 (Vol. 5 No. 8) (1996) [hereinafter The Center for Reproductive Law & Policy, Reproductive Freedom News]; The Center for Reproductive Law & Policy, Congressional Effort to Ban Abortion Method Unprecedented, Represents Direct Challenge to Roe v. Wade 1 (1995) [hereinafter The Center for Reproductive Law & Policy, Congressional Effort to Ban Abortion]; National Abortion Federation, Late Abortions: Questions and Answers 1 (1995).
4. *See* Religious Coalition for Reproductive Choice, *supra* note 3, at 1.
5. *See* National Abortion Federation, *supra* note 3. About 90% of these early abortions are in the first trimester. *Id.* Only a little over one half of one percent of abortions take place at or after 20 weeks gestation. *Id.*
6. *See id.*
7. *See* The Center for Reproductive Law & Policy, Congressional Effort to Ban Abortion, *supra* note 3, at 1.
8. *See* National Abortion Federation, *supra* note 3, at 2; Religious Coalition for Reproductive Choice, *supra* note 3.
9. *See* National Abortion Federation, *supra* note 3, at 2.
10. *See* Religious Coalition for Reproductive Choice. *supra* note 3, at 2.
11. *See id.*
12. *See id.*
13. *See* National Abortion Federation, *supra* note 3, at 3. Religious Coalition for Reproductive Choice, *supra* note 3, at 2.
14. *See* National Abortion Federation, *supra* note 3, at 3.
15. *See id.*
16. *See id.*
17. *See* Religious Coalition for Reproductive Choice, *supra* note 3, at 1.
18. See National Abortion Federation, *supra* note 3, at 6.
19. See Religious Coalition for Reproductive Choice, *supra* note 3, at 2.
20. *See id.*
21. *See id.* at 1.
22. *Id.*
23. *See generally* H.R. 1833
24. H.R. 1833 § 1531 (b) (1).
25. H.R. 1833 § 1531 (a).
26. *See* H.R. 1833 § 1531 (c) (1).
27. *See* H.R. 1833 § 1531 (a).
28. *See id.*
29. *See* The Center for Reproductive Law & Policy, Testimony of Kathryn Kolbert 1 (1995).
30. *See id.* at 4.
31. *See id.*
32. 410 U.S. 113 (1973) (holding that a woman has a constitutional right to an abortion).
33. 112 S. Ct. 2791 (1992) (holding that the state can not place an undue burden on women seeking an abortion).
34. *See* The Center for Reproductive Law & Policy, Testimony of Kathryn Kolbert, *supra* note 29, at 5.
35. *See id.* at 6; *see also Roe*, 410 U.S. at 121.
36. *See* The Center for Reproductive Law & Policy, Testimony of Kathryn Kolbert, *supra* note 29, at 6.
37. *See id.* at 8.
38. *See* The Center for Reproductive Law & Policy, Testimony of Kathryn Kolbert, *supra* note 29, at 8-9.
39. *See id.* at 9. She further asserts that by inhibiting the physician's and women's determination of which abortion method is in her best interest, the proposal undermines maternal health. *Id.*
40. *See id.*
41. *See id.*
42. *See id.*
43. *See* The Center for Reproductive Law & Policy, Testimony of Kathryn Kolbert, *supra* note 29, at 12.
44. *See id.*
45. *See* Women's Med. Prof'l Corp. v. Voinovich, 911 F. Supp. 1051 (S.D. Ohio 1995). The matter will now proceed on appeal to the U.S. Court of Appeals for the Sixth Circuit. *See* The Center for Reproductive Law & Policy, Reproductive Freedom in the Courts 1 (1996).
46. H.B. 135, 121st Gen., Ass., 1995 Ohio Sess. Law.
47. *See* The Center for Reproductive Law & Policy, Reproductive Freedom in the Courts, *supra* note 45, at 1.
48. *See id.*
49. *See id.*

 Article Review Form at end of book.

WiseGuide Wrap-Up

- While there are more than two sexes biologically, culturally we hold to the dual system of sex.

- Sexuality is a site of contestation between the genders for power.
- Gender roles are supported by biological arguments, as well as laws regarding sex and reproduction.

- Taking reproductive decisions out of the hands of women through law and social sanctions supports continued male dominance.

R.E.A.L. Sites

This provides a print preview of typical **coursewise** R.E.A.L. sites. (There are over 100 such sites at the **course links**™ site). The danger in printing URLs is that Web sites can change overnite. As we went to press, these sites were functional using the URLs provided. If you come across one that isn't, please let us know via email to: webmaster@coursewise.com. Use your Passport to access the most current list of R.E.A.L. sites at the **course links**™ site.

Site name: Historic Supreme Court Decisions
URL: http://supct. law.cornell. edu/supct/cases/topic.htm
Key topics: Health
Why is it R.E.A.L.? Using recent as well as previous case history to uncover the underlying arguments of this sensitive topic opens new avenues for understanding multiple positions.
Activity: After a full review of the cases posted online at this site on either abortion or birth control, write your own brief, arguing your own position. Ground your arguments using appropriate evidence to support your claim.

Site name: Coalition for Positive Sexuality
URL: http://www.positive.org
Key topics: Sexuality, Education
Why is it R.E.A.L.? This page is full of cutting edge information about sex, sexuality, and being a teenager. It has a BBS and multiple resources for young adults looking for information that was, at one point, nearly censored from the Internet, such as information about STDs and safe sex.
Activity: Sign up for the BBS; after reviewing the archives, post your own contribution to the BBS.

Site name: Gender and Sexuality
URL: http://eng.hss.cmu.edu/gender/
Key topics: Education, Sexuality
Why is it R.E.A.L.? This site publishes recent essays on a number of topics, including theoretical work on issues of sexuality and gender.
Activity: Choose two of the articles from the table of contents, and evaluate their thesis, language, and credibility.

Site name: RuPaul
URL http://rupaul. base.org
Key topics: Identity Politics, Stereotypes, Beauty Myth
Why is it R.E.A.L.? RuPaul—a male to female transexual—has reached mainstream status, with fewer sanctions than most other people who operate outside of gender norms.
Activity: After reviewing the RuPaul web site, write a brief essay describing your day as someone not of your biological sex or sexual orientation.

section 4

Key Points

- Children learn about gender roles through the toys they play with and the games they play. Gender role playing is more limited for girls than it is for boys.

- Globally, not all girls have access to formal schooling at the same levels as boys, for a variety of reasons, including the relative value of women's work outside of the home during adult life.

- Women's participation in math and science has been traced to the sometimes unintentional tracking of girls out of these fields, based on cultural assumptions of boys' and girls' innate abilities.

- Sports, classrooms, even household rules, are organized differently for boys than for girls, with boys benefiting from greater opportunities.

Playing Around: Gender Equity in School, at Play, and Growing Up

 Recent research has demonstrated that boys and girls have different educational experiences and opportunities. From early childhood through high school years, gender determines what toys children might play with, what interests they will be able to pursue, even their access to formal schooling. Girls play with toys that will teach them how to perform the tasks and play the roles of women, toys like Barbie, pretend make-up, and miniature kitchen centers. Boys also learn to behave appropriately through the toys and games they are directed to, which include a broader range of possibilities, from chemistry sets to footballs to action figures. Even on the playground, most girls' activities have traditionally been confined to more passive games, while most boys participate in competitive and physically challenging games.

In the classroom, assumptions about the relative abilities of boys and girls in relation to math and science are responsible for tracking girls away from these areas and into language arts and social studies, as areas in which they are perceived to excel. The years between the sixth and eighth grades are reported as critical years in this shift. While in the United States this problem has become a central concern for educators, parents, and employers, other problems persist in other political systems, where the proposition that girls should have the same level of formal schooling as boys is controversial, to say the least.

Hadden and London argue that, as the global economy changes, even though households resist educating girls for a number of reasons, the economic benefits and living standards are enhanced by higher educational levels for girls, in their essay "Educating Girls in the Third World." *USA Today Weekend Magazine* published a special issue detailing the different worlds that boys and girls inhabit in their high school years, including different curfews, who gets called on in class, and gender inequity in sports. Katha Pollitt traces the roots of the messages that boys and girls receive about gender roles through the toys they play with in "Why Boys Don't Play with Dolls." Suggestions for improved science education for both boys and girls, with an emphasis on ways to ensure girls' participation, are made by Katz-Stone in her editorial "Get Serious on Science."

Questions

Reading 11. What factors have influenced household decisions about the amount of schooling young girls have received in developing countries that are similar to ones that historically affected young girls' opportunities in the United States? What benefits are associated with equitable access to and opportunities in formal schooling for girls in developing countries?

Reading 12. What are the benefits of single-sex education? What are the negative aspects?

Reading 13. How does Pollitt assess the current field of arguments around biology as destiny and the social construction of gender roles?

Reading 14. Why is the inclusion of girls and women in scientific fields important?

What factors have influenced household decisions about the amount of schooling young girls have received in developing countries that are similar to ones that historically affected young girls' opportunities in the U.S.? What benefits are associated with equitable access to and opportunities in formal schooling for girls in developing countries?

Educating Girls in the Third World

The demographic, basic needs, and economic benefits

Kenneth Hadden*
and Bruce London**

*Department of Agricultural and Resource Economics, University of Connecticut, Storrs, CT 06268, U.S.A. ** Department of Sociology, Clark University, Worcester, MA 01601, U.S.A. Authors' names are listed alphabetically. All work was equally shared. This research was supported, in part, by a Small Grant from the Spencer Foundation of Chicago, IL to Professor London. This paper is Scientific Contribution # 1632 of the Storrs Agricultural Experiment Station, which provided support for Professor Hadden.

Abstract

Building on the widespread recent suggestion that the education of girls may well be one of the best investments that a less-developed country can make, this study presents the results of a series of quantitative, cross-national, panel regression analyses designed to assess the effects of a) level of girls' education (primary and secondary enrollment rates), and b) gender inequality in education (male-female enrollment ratios), on a wide range of demographic, social and economic development outcomes. Both the education of girls in and of itself, and the provision of equal access to education for boys and girls (i.e., gender equality in education) were found to have the following subsequent benefits for societies: lower crude birth rates, longer life expectancies, lower death rates of all sorts, improved basic needs provision, and more rapid rates of economic growth.

Introduction

Every United Nations sponsored report on international development since the late 1960s has stressed the importance of universal literacy and has urged an end to the widespread gender disparity in school enrolment (Rowley, 1993). These reports, including 1969's Pearson Report, the Brandt Report of 1987, and 1992's Agenda 21, were augmented by two influential reports issued during 1994. First *The Progress of Nations* (UNICEF, 1994:20) asserts:

> There is widespread agreement that the education of girls is one of the most important investments that any developing country can make in its own future. In the long term, almost every other aspect of progress, from nutrition to family planning, from child health to women's rights, is profoundly affected by whether or not a nation educates its girls.

These points were elaborated upon in the report on the U.N. Conference on Population and Development (United Nations, 1994:20-21):

> Since in all societies discrimination on the basis of sex often begins at the earliest stages of life, greater equality for the girl child is a necessary first step in ensuring that women realize their full potential and become equal partners in development. . . Investments made in the girl

Reprinted with permission from *International Journal of Comparative Sociology*.

child's health, nutrition and education, from infancy through adolescence, are critical.

Overall, the value of girl children to both their family and to society must be expanded beyond their definition as potential child-bearers and caretakers and reinforced through the adoption and implementation of educational and social policies that encourage their full participation in the development of the societies in which they live. . . . Beyond the achievement of the goal of universal primary education in all countries before the year 2015, all countries are urged to ensure the widest and earliest possible access by girls and women to secondary and higher levels of education. . .

The World Bank has also been making a concerted effort in recent years to spread the message that "educating girls quite possibly yields a higher rate of return that any other investment available in the developing world" (Summers, 1992:132; see also Schultz, 1993; Summers, 1994).

Over the past three decades there has been considerable growth in both primary and secondary school enrollments in the developing world. But as the foregoing comments clearly suggest, enrollment rates of girls continue to lag behind those of boys in most developing countries. While countries of East Asia and Latin America (excluding Bolivia, Guatemala and Haiti) are approaching parity in the primary and secondary school enrollments of boys and girls, the gender gap continues to be substantial in Africa, the Middle East and South Asia (Nuss and Majka, 1985; Herz et al., 1991; Bellew et al., 1995; Hill and King, 1993).

There are many reasons why girls are less apt than boys to be attending school. Since sons typi-cally are responsible for supporting parents in their old age, having educated sons is attractive to parents. The costs of education, both direct (e.g., school fees, books, uniforms, etc.) and opportunity (i.e., loss of household help and, in some cases, wages), are therefore more readily absorbed for sons than daughters. When we consider that the economic contributions of daughters to the household is much greater than sons in poor economies and that future economic opportunities are much more limited for females than males, it is not suprising that parents are more averse to girls' than boys' schooling. There is also generally much greater concern for the safety of daughters than sons, supported by patriarchal cultural traditions, which acts as a deterrent to sending daughters to school. Also, because girls ordinarily join their husband's family upon marriage and take with them the benefits of education, parents have little incentive to bear the costs of educating their daughters (Hill and King, 1993; Bellew et al., 1992; Herz et al., 1991). Finally, Clark (1992) has found that the investment and hiring practices of multinational corporations discourage high levels of education of women.

These constraints to female education operate almost exclusively at the household level. But many societies, too, have been unwilling to invest in educating girls. This is true in spite of increasing evidence from an accumulating body of research studies that there are great benefits" accruing to societies that do educate girls (for overviews, see Herz et al., 1991; Bellew et al., 1992). This literature, in fact, documents a wide array of "benefits" ranging from declines in fertility rates and improvements in health and mortal-ity rates to more general advances in both social and economic development. For example, the relationship between education and fertility has been studied extensively (Cochrane, 1979, 1983; Groff, 1979). Most studies focus on individual–level relations between the educational attainment of women (or sometimes literacy) and the numbers of children they have borne. While there is little dispute that the long-run impact of increasing female education in developing countries is lowered fertility (Leslie, et al., 1986; Datta, 1987; Sadik, 1990; Hyatt and Milne, 1992), the evidence concerning the short-term effect is mixed. Some research indicates that in the short-run fertility actually increases as education increases, while other studies show the short-run and long-run effects to be consistent. This ambiguity concerning immediate fertility effects of increasing education arises from the three major ways in which increased education of women affects their fertility. These may, but do not necessarily, counterbalance each other, producing the mixed short-term results. The fertility depressing effects of education arise because better educated women are more frequent and effective contraceptors and marry at older ages than less educated women. On the other hand, better educated women are less likely to breast feed their children or breast feed for only a short time, thus losing the natural contraceptive effect of prolonged lactation (cf., Jain, 1981; Gadalla et al., 1987).

There are also some ambiguities in aggregate-level or cross-national studies of the relationship between women's education and fertility (Mason, 1984). For example, using measures of women's absolute educational status (cross-sectional enrollment rates), Tsui and Bogue (1978), Mauldin and Berelson (1978), and Ward (1984) found only negligible effects of the education of women on fertility. But, using a measure of women's status relative to men (a male-female enrollment ratio), Menard (1985) found relative education to be a strong predictor of fertility. This insight, in conjunction with Caldwell's (1982) "Intergenerational Wealth-Flow Reversal Theory," informed London's (1992) recent cross-national analysis of gender inequalities in education and fertility (see also London and Hadden, 1989).

The crux of Caldwell's argument is that, in traditional economies, children are net producers of wealth and, therefore, wealth flows upward from children to parents. Under these circumstances, high fertility is economically rational. With the introduction of compulsory mass (i.e., both boys and girls) education, the direction of the flow of wealth is reversed. This occurs because school attendance reduces children's economic contributions, increases their costs, lengthens their dependence, and speeds up cultural and value change. Under these conditions, parents are motivated to have fewer children. Moreover, Caldwell (1982) is quite explicit about the import of women's education relative to men's. He asserts that "demographic change is unlikely if the movement towards mass schooling is confined largely to males" (Caldwell, 1982:305).

In this context, London (1992) opted to explicitly assess the effect of gender differences in education on fertility by examining a series of equations, each containing a different measure of education: (1) total primary school enrollment, (2) boys' primary school enrollment, (3) girls' pri-

mary-school enrollment, (4) male-female primary school enrollment ratio, (5) total secondary school enrollment, (6) boys' secondary school enrollment (7) girls' secondary school enrollment, and (8) male-female secondary school enrollment ratio. He found that the significant negative effect of total primary school enrollment actually masked a combined insignificant effect of the enrollments of boys with a strong effect from the enrollment of girls. The same "masking" effect was found in the equations on secondary enrollments. Moreover, the significant positive coefficients for both of the male-female enrollment ratios indicated that the lower girls' access to education is relative to that of boys, the slower the decline in fertility rates (London, 1992: 311). As you will see below, the present research is significantly informed by London's study. In fact, one of the primary objectives of this paper is to conduct a respecified quantitative, cross-national analysis of the relationship between education and fertility that builds upon London's method, while assessing the generality of the link between girls' education and fertility.

Of course, a decline in fertility is only one of the many hypothesized benefits of educating girls. It has also been suggested that there is a connection between reduced fertility and reduced child mortality among educated women. Under conditions of limited resources, fewer children means more resources for those children. They will be better fed and clothed, generally better cared for, and, therefore, healthier. In addition, better educated mothers will be more knowledgeable about health and safety risks and prevention, and about nutrition (McGuire and Popkin, 1990), all of which lower the mortality and im-

prove the health of their children. In this regard, Sadik (1990) estimates that child mortality is reduced seven to nine percent for every year of mothers' education. The relation between better educated mothers and healthier children, while not as thoroughly examined as the relationship with fertility, has been supported generally (Bellew et al., 1992; Herz et al., 1991; Hill and King, 1993) and in settings such as Gambia (Browne and Barrett, 1991), Nigeria (Boerma, 1987), and India (Raut, 1993).

Quite aside from the potential health and mortality benefits to infants and children provided by an educated mother, a broader question arises: Does the presence of educated females confer such benefits to the population generally? The second objective of the research reported in this paper is to assess the effects of educating girls on the life expectancy and mortality of the general population as well as on the mortality of infants and children.

In addition to the fertility, health, and mortality benefits of educating girls, some literature suggests that such education has enormous economic advantages as well. There is considerable support for the proposition that increasing the education of girls results in both greater labor force participation in adulthood and higher earnings (Bellew et al., 1992; Anderson, 1988; Psacharapoulos and Woodhall, 1985; Browne and Barrett, 1991; Boserup, 1986; Jazairy et al., 1992; Herz et al., 1991). The increased earnings and participation in the wage labor market by women generally translates into national per capita income growth, a common measure of economic development. In fact, one quantitative cross-national study explicitly analyzed "the impact of gender differences in education on economic growth from 1960 and 1985" (Benavot, 1989:14). Benavot (1989) compared the long-term effects of female versus male educational expansion at the primary and secondary levels in a panel model that used nations' logged per capita GNP, 1985 as the dependent variable, with logged per capita GNP, 1960 as the lagged dependent variable. His models for less-developed countries included a range of controls for export activity, fertility rates, and female labor force participation. Most crucially, he examined separate equations for male vs. female school enrollment rates. Specifically, one of his key equations included female primary and female secondary enrollments, the lagged dependent variable, and controls. The other key equation, for contrast, included male primary and secondary rates along with the same set of additional variables. He found (Benavot, 1989:26) that the primary education of both males and females had a strong positive effect on economic growth, and that the estimate of the effect of female education was higher than that for male education. At the secondary level the effect of the education of females was positive but not significant, while that of males was positive and significant.

Such "average" measures of economic development as GNP per capita, however, have been criticized because they provide no indication of the degree to which the benefits of development are distributed to the general population. Consequently, some attention is turning to measuring the determinants of the degree to which less-developed countries meet the "basic needs" of their population as an important di-

mension of "development" that is distinct from measures of strictly economic growth (cf. London and Williams, 1988).

Concern with basic needs provision or "social development" originated with development economists in the 1970s (e.g., Hicks 1979; Hicks & Streeten 1979; ILO 1977; Streeten 1979). By that time, it had become clear that economic growth in many nations did not lead to concomitant improvement in the living standards of most people. This was especially so in LDCs. In other words, there was a seeming contradiction between general economic growth and the specific distribution of social resources. This suggested that development should be measured in terms of "social output" rather than "economic output." "Such a focus supplements attention to *how much* is being produced, by attention to *what* is being produced, in *what ways,* for *whom* and with what *impact*" (Hicks and Streeten 1979:577). Thus, measuring basic needs is now seen as an important complement to the measurement of economic growth.

The most widely used measures of basic needs are (1) Morris' (1979) Physical Quality of Life Index (PQLI), a combination of measures of infant mortality at age one, literacy rates, and life expectancy, and (2) Estes' (1984) Index of Net Social Progress (INSP), a combination of 41 different indicators of the following dimensions: education progress, health status, women's status, defense effort, economic growth, demographic conditions, political stability, political participation, cultural diversity, and welfare effort (for details, see London and Williams, 1988:753). However, since the etiology of any given component of a basic needs index may be different from that of any

other component, London and Williams (1988:753-4) recommend that researchers examine as dependent variables several indicators "extracted" from each composite index (in addition to the indices themselves). This insight will influence the present research strategy (see below).

The final objective of this research, then, is to assess the effect of educating girls on both overall national economic growth rates and the general well-being (i.e., basic needs), of national populations. Actually, our concern with the three areas of fertility, health and mortality, and overall development is highly congruent with basic needs theory in that many of the same "dependent variables" are "shared" by both approaches. This insight, too, will influence the present research strategy (see below).

Rationale and Goals of the Research

This literature review suggests the need for additional, systematic study and documentation of the hypothesized multiple benefits of educating girls. This is the case for several reasons. The majority of studies to date are econometric, individual-level, case studies of particular populations. While suggestive, such studies cannot assess the degree to which their findings are generalizable. A quantitative, cross-national study of wide scope is thus recommended. However, those cross-national studies that have been published frequently contradict each other as a result of their widely divergent model specifications. A careful reconsideration of the most appropriate way to measure gender differences in education is also needed. In addition, the vast majority of studies focus on a single dependent variable—i.e., fertility *or* economic growth *or* something else. A single, carefully-specified study that simultaneously assesses the impact of girls' education on a wide range of outcomes (i.e., dependent variables) could prove to be informative. Finally, such a study would be most useful if informed by a uniform theoretical perspective. In this regard, we suggest that research on the hypothesized benefits of educating girls in the Third World would profit from the use of models and insights related to basic needs theory.

Actually, we are aware of one quantitative, cross-national study designed explicitly to simultaneously assess several of the hypothesized multiple benefits of educating girls. This study (Hill and King, 1993), an overview of women's education in developing countries, conducted multivariate analyses for more than 100 developing countries using pooled time-series data for quinquennial years from 1960-1985. A first equation estimated GNP, controlling for female gross enrollment rates, the gender gap in education (i.e., female enrollments as a percentage of male enrollments), capital stock (i.e., savings), size of the labor force, and world region. A second series of equations examined several indicators of "social well-being" (including life expectancy, infant and maternal mortality, and total fertility rates), controlling for female enrollment rates, the gender gap in education, predicted GNP, size, population per physician, and percent of population with safe water. Female education was found to be significantly associated with increased GNP and improved social well-being, while a large gender disparity significantly reduced

both GNP and social well-being. While the Hill and King (1993) study is very relevant to the present research, our own research will depart from it in several ways (see our rationale and discussion below).

Data are readily available on a wide range of population processes and social and economic development measures for a large number (usually 60–80) of nations. This will permit us to design and conduct our own quantitative cross-national analyses of many of the hypotheses implicit in the literature reviewed above. This study will develop both simple and complex panel regression models in order to assess the effect of the education of girls on a series of important dependent variables (see details below). The simple models will examine the effects of boys' vs. girls' primary and secondary education on change in each dependent variable between ca. 1965 and 1985, controlling for level of development. The more complex models will control for the effects of several additional independent variables (drawn from theory and research on basic needs) on the particular dependent variable under consideration.

These analyses could add considerably to our explicit knowledge of the many demonstrable benefits of the education of girls in the developing world. We all know *in theory* that women's education is an influential investment. And we know from econometric and case-study work that the education of girls can lead to substantial savings in individual countries. But to what extent are these findings generalizable to the Third World as a whole? What is the general "track record" of those less developed nations that have invested in girls' schooling as

compared to those that have not? And, how is this record reflected across a wide array of potentially very important "quality of life" or "basic needs" or "social well-being" outcomes, ranging, as noted above, from fertility and a variety of mortality rates, through life expectancies, to general economic and social development?

Data and Methods

The present research will build upon (respecify) existing studies in order to maximize the comparability of our results with those of previously-published works. Especially relevant in this regard are studies of basic needs provision by London and Williams (1988) and of Third World mortality by Wimberley (1990).

More specifically, in a modification of a study of the determinants of economic growth by Bornschier and Chase-Dunn (1985), London and Williams (1988) used panel regression analysis[1] to assess the effect of level of development (GNP per capita), foreign direct investment, gross domestic investment, investment dependence, and political protest on a range of dependent variables, including economic growth, the index of net social progress, life expectancy, and infant mortality. This study was couched explicitly in terms of basic needs theory. That is, all of the dependent variables (except economic growth) were conceived of as dimensions of basic needs, while the set of independent variables were construed to be "determinants of basic needs provision."

Wimberly (1990), in turn, used a very similar set of independent variables (dropping the measure of protest) to analyze variation in infant mortality and life expectancy in the context of basic needs theory. He also used panel models. One respecification of particular interest here was his inclusion in some equations of a control for secondary school enrollment rates. Arguing that high levels of education should increase economic growth, lessen income inequality, and, in turn, enhance life expectancy and reduce infant mortality, Wimberly (1990:79,82) found a significant negative effect of school enrollments on infant mortality.[2]

Using identical or similar data, we will merge several insights from these studies in order to pursue our current interest in assessing the effect of educating girls on a wide range of demographic, social, and economic development outcomes. These will include several of the dependent variables examined by London and Williams (1988) and Wimberley (1990), plus several dependent variables unique to this study. The dependent variables will include crude birth rate (1965 and 1984), life expectancy (1960 and 1983), crude death rate (1965 and 1984), child death rate (1965 and 1985), infant mortality rate (1960 and 1983), the index of net social progress (1970 and 1980), and the annual average growth rate of per capita GNP (1965-1984). For details on data sources and measurement, see London and Williams (1988:752-54 and 770-71) and the 1986 and 1987 *World Development Reports* of the World Bank. Note that all of the dependent variables are available for two time points, and are thus amenable to panel analyses, except for the measure of economic growth (which is an annual average growth rate).

Also in keeping with the earlier studies, common independent variables will include a lagged dependent variable (except in the case of GNP growth), level of development, foreign direct investment, and gross domestic investment[3] (i.e., the basic needs model). Then, instead of the summary measure of total secondary school enrollments used by Wimberley (1990), the main innovation or respecification of this study will be to examine, in a series of equations for each dependent variable, measures of (1) girls' primary school enrollments, (2) boys' primary school enrollments, (3) girls' secondary school enrollments, (4) boys' secondary school enrollments, and (5 and 6) measures of gender inequality (boys'/girls' enrollment ratios) in both primary and secondary school enrollments. This was the approach used by London (1992) in his study of fertility rates and it is similar to that used by Benavot (1989) in his study of economic development.

In other words, in addition to the constant set of independent variables, for each dependent variable, we compare the impact of educating girls versus that of educating boys. Moreover, these comparisons will be conducted for both primary and secondary education. And, the comparisons will be of two types: (1) equations identical in every respect except that one includes a measure of girls' enrollments while the other includes a measure of boys' enrollments, and (2) equations that "build in" comparison by incorporating measures of gender inequality instead of the boys' or girls' rates.

To establish an initial baseline for our analysis, we will first examine simple panel models of the effect of each of these measures of education on each dependent variable, controlling only for level of development (see Table 1). We will then compare these results with those from the more fully-specified models described above (see Table 2). Given that we will be examining a large number of equations (six "simple" and six "complex" equations for each of seven dependent variables = 84 equations),[4] and given that our main interest is in the various measures of education (that is, in the gender comparisons), Tables 1 and 2 will present only the coefficients for the education variables. In other words, each coefficient in the tables represents the education effect extracted from a larger equation. This focus on selected coefficients will enable us to highlight the contrast between girls' vs. boys' enrollments without using the time and space needed to present full equations.

Findings

Fertility: Table 1, which controls for country's level of development, shows that the larger the proportion of primary and secondary school age students who are actually in school, the greater is the subsequent reduction in the crude birth rate. Secondary school attendance has a somewhat stronger fertility reducing effect than primary attendance. These relationships hold for the education of both boys and girls, and are slightly stronger for girls' education than for boys'. But when, as is often the case, boys are disproportionately in school as compared with girls (i.e. gender inequality is high), the fertility reducing impact of education is attenuated. That is, the positive coefficients indicate that those countries with the highest level of gender inequality in primary and secondary education are also the countries which subsequently experienced the smallest fertility declines or even fertility increases.

Table 1 The Effects of (a) Girls' vs Boys' Enrollment Rates and (b) Gender Inequality in Education on Aspects of Demographic, Social, and Economic Development: Simple Models

	Crude Birth Rate	Life Expectancy	Crude Death Rate	Child Death Rate	Infant Mortality Rate	Overall Basic Needs	Economic Growth[a]
Girls' Primary Education	−.27**	.28**	−.26**	−.47**	−.46**	.15**	.33**
Boys' Primary Education	−.23**	.24**	−.27**	−.42**	−.18	.15**	.31**
Girls' Secondary Education	−.41**	.33**	−.24**	−.64**	−.62**	.23**	.38**
Boys' Secondary Education	−.34**	.21**	−.25**	−.52**	−.33**	.24**	.48**
Gender Inequality, Primary	.21**	−.19**	.08	.37**	.49**	−.08*	−.22**
Gender Inequality, Secondary	.24**	−.12*	−.00	.45**	.61**	−.04	−.14

[a]non-panel models
* B = 1.5 times the standard error of B
**B = 2 times the standard error of B

Thus, in order for the education of children to have the desired impact on fertility, both boys and girls must have equal access to primary and secondary schooling. Finally, when additional controls are introduced (Table 2), the relationships remain as just described.

Health and Mortality: The four dependent variables measuring mortality behave in essentially the same way. Both primary and secondary education, whether of boys or girls, have mortality reducing and, by implication, health enhancing effects. Girls' education has the strongest impact on the mortality of those over whom females usually have most direct responsibility—infants and children. Infant and child mortality rates experience the largest reductions in those countries where girls are most fully enrolled in school; and the effect is stronger for secondary enrollment, indicating that attending school beyond the primary level causes a cumulative benefit as far as infant and childhood mortality are concerned. The education of boys is also generally beneficial for infants (boys' secondary education, only) and children; but when boys are more fully enrolled in either primary or secondary school than

girls, then the reductions in infant and child mortality are lost or diminished. Or, to put it positively, in countries where both boys and girls have similar enrollment rates, infant and child mortality have the greatest subsequent reductions.

The effect of girls' primary and secondary enrollment on the general indicators of mortality—life expectancy and crude death rate—are weaker than for infant and child mortality, and more comparable to the effects of boys' enrollment. In all cases, however, higher enrollment rates have the effect of increasing life expectancy and reducing mortality generally. Actually, since (a) longer life expectancies and lower crude birth rates are, in part, functions of declines in (b) infant and child mortality, the effect of education on the former rates is mediated through its effect on the latter. Gender inequality in enrollment has no effect on the latter. Gender inequality in enrollment has no effect on the crude death rate, but does limit gains in life expectancy.

When we turn to Table 2, where additional controls are introduced, in almost every case the results described above continue to hold. One exception is that

boys' secondary enrollment, which has a significant negative effect on infant mortality in Table 1, ceases to be significant. In fact, boys' education has a significant effect on infant mortality in only one of four equations (i.e., boys' secondary education in the simple model/Table 1), and that effect disappears in the more fully-specified model. This is one instance in which the education of girls (rather than boys) has a particularly clear impact. Indeed, the effects of both types of gender inequality are particularly strong in the infant mortality equations, and they are nearly as strong in the child death rate equations. Once again, these findings suggest that the education of girls has the strongest subsequent impact on the health and mortality of those over whom adult females will have the most responsibility—their children.

Social and Economic Development: The importance of education for economic growth is borne out by Table 1. Countries which provide education for girls (and boys) later experience higher economic growth rates than countries which do not or which provide only limited educational access. The effect of secondary ed-

Table 2 The Effects of (a) Girls' vs Boys' Enrollment Rates and (b) Gender Inequality in Education on Aspects of Demographic, Social, and Economic Development: Complex Models

	Crude Birth Rate	Life Expectancy	Crude Death Rate	Child Death Rate	Infant Mortality Rate	Overall Basic Needs	Economic Growth[a]
Girls' Primary Education	−.25**	.30**	−.27**	−.47**	−.38**	.18**	.30**
Boys' Primary Education	−.22**	.24**	−.26**	−.43**	−.13	.19**	.27**
Girls' Secondary Education	−.45**	.39**	−.29**	−.74**	−.67**	.24**	.28**
Boys' Secondary Education	−.37**	.23**	−.27**	−.62**	−.22	.24**	.36**
Gender Inequality, Primary	.18**	−.22**	.09	.34**	.48**	−.09*	−.21*
Gender Inequality, Secondary	.24**	−.20*	−.02	.51**	.65**	−.06	−.14

[a]non-panel models
* B = 1.5 times the standard error of B
**B = 2 times the standard error of B

ucation, especially for boys, is somewhat stronger than the effect of primary education. Primary gender inequality has a modest adverse effect on economic growth, but secondary inequality has no significant impact.

Educating girls and boys has the effect of spreading the fruits of higher economic growth throughout the society in the form of improved overall basic needs provision. There is no difference between boys' and girls' enrollment in this regard, and secondary enrollment has only a slightly stronger effect on basic needs provision then primary enrollment does. Gender inequality in primary enrollments has a modest negative effect on basic needs provision, but gender inequality in secondary education has no effect on basic needs. Finally, Table 2 shows that the introduction of additional controls has virtually no effect on the results for either economic growth or basic needs provision. [5]

Conclusions

In sum, our analyses based on a large sample of Third World nations have shown that education in general, and the education of

girls in particular, have, as suggested by the extensive literature cited above, wide ranging beneficial effects on the demographic, social, and economic development patterns of nations. In societies with higher initial levels of girls' education, women subsequently have fewer children (i.e., lower crude birth rates) and healthier children (as evidenced by the lower infant mortality and child death rates). These initial gains seem also to be readily translated into a range of longer-term benefits that include longer life expectancies, declines in overall mortality rates, and improvements in both social and economic development rates. Also, for many of the comparisons examined, especially those regarding infant and child mortality, the specific effect of educating girls is stronger than that of educating boys. This insight regarding the special importance of educating girls is highlighted further in the gender inequality comparisons that point to the poor socioeconomic development performances of nations that provide more education for boys than for girls. The results of our analyses suggest, therefore, that all of the recent attention devoted to educating girls

by the United Nations and others is quite well-directed for the education of girls clearly contributes to both a nation's economic development and its ability to provide for the basic needs of its people.

Notes

1. In a panel regression analysis, the dependent variable, measured at a given point in time, is regressed on itself and the independent variables at an earlier time. This procedure yields an estimate of the effects of the independent variables on *change* in the dependent variable.

2. For a number of reasons, we will rely more heavily on a respecification of the London and Williams (1988) and Wimberley (1990) studies, than on the Hill and King (1993) study cited above. First, Hill and King use simple time lags between dependent and independent variables rather than panel analyses. Therefore, their study does not assess the effect of the independent variables on *change* in the dependent variables. They also include measures of level of women's education and gender gaps in education simultaneously in their equations, while omitting any separate equations for boys' education. This approach maximizes the potential for multicollinearity, and minimizes the ability to make multiple comparisons of the impact of education levels by gender on various outcomes. Finally, since their sets of independent variables are not based on sociological basic needs theory, they tend to focus on the

internal economic characteristics of nations, and to exclude potentially relevant international forces (i.e., foreign investment). It is important to note, however, that the existence of their study gives us another opportunity for "triangulation." Specifically, while Summers (1992) and London (1992) addressed similar questions with different data and methods, Hill and King (1993) and the present study will be using very similar data and methods (quantitative, cross-national analysis), but somewhat different model specifications. If both studies yield similar conclusions, our knowledge about the effects of educating girls will be greatly enhanced.

3. Given Firebaugh's (1992) recent critique of the measure of investment dependence used in these studies, we examined equations both with and without the measure. Its presence or absence has little impact on the various measures of education; coefficients remain similar in magnitude and level of significance. Tables 1 and 2 report the results of the equations that omitted the control for investment dependence.

4. Actually, we examined far more than 84 equations represented in our tables. Analyses were conducted, for example, both with and without the investment dependence measure. We also looked at some additional dependent variables, such as the PQLI, whose results were essentially redundant to those presented in the tables. Finally, we examined each equation for influential cases, and we took appropriate corrective procedures in the relatively few instances in which a case appeared to be excessively influential (see London (1992:315), for a brief discussion of the analysis of influential cases). In no instance did an ostensibly influential case alter the pattern of results or conclusions derived from the original equations.

5. While our focus of attention is clearly on the effect of the various measures of education (by gender) on the list of dependent variables, a word or two is in order regarding the effect of the other dependent variables. Patterns are quite consistent across large numbers of equations. For example, GNP per capita has significant coefficient in virtually every equation in which it appears. It is, as expected, negatively related to the various demographic rates, and positively related to all other dependent variables. Foreign direct investment is significantly and negatively related to the various mortality rates, is positively related on a consistent basis to economic growth, and has a significant positive effect on basic needs provision, in some equations. Gross domestic investment, on the other hand, only appears to have a recurring significant relationship (negative) to the various mortality rates. It does not produce significant coefficients for any of the other dependent variables. As suggested by Bornschier and Chase-Dunn (1985), and as adapted by London and Williams (1988), this set of independent variables may be interpreted as neoclassical economic indicators of economic growth and basic needs provision. Thus, our finding of a strong and recurring pattern of significant effects of a variety of education measures on our range of dependent variables suggests that education in general, and that of girls in particular (or, of girls relative to boys as well), has an important independent effect on demographic, economic, and social development net of the effect of predictors drawn from neoclassical economic theory.

Bibliography

Anderson, Lacelles
1988 "Rates of Return of Education for Females in El Salvador." *Social and Economic Studies*, 37:3, 279-287.

Bellew, Rosemary, Laura Raney, and K. Subearao 1992 "Educating Girls." *Finance and Development*, 29:1 (March), 54-56.

Benavot, Aaron
1989 "Education, Gender, and Economic Development: A Cross-National Study." *Sociology of Education*, 62 (January), 14-32.

Boerma, Ties
1987 "The Magnitude of the Maternal Mortality Problem in Sub-Saharan Africa." *Social Science Medicine*, 24:551-558.

Bornschier, Volker, and Christopher Chase-Dunn 1985 *Transnational Corporations and Underdevelopment*. Praeger.

Boserup, Ester
1986 *Woman's Role in Economic Development*, 2nd Edition. Aldershot, England: Gower.

Browne, Angela and Hazel Barrett
1991 "Female Education in Sub-Saharan Africa: The Key to Development?" *Comparative Education*, 27:3 (Oct.), 275-285.

Caldwell, John C.
1982 *Theory of Fertility Decline*. NY: Academic Press.

Clark, Roger
1992 "Multinational Corporate Investment and Women's Participation in Higher Education in Non-core Nations." *Sociology of Education*, 65:1 (Jan.), 37-47.

Cochrane, Susan
1979 *Fertility and Education: What Do We Really Know?* Washington, DC: World Bank.
1983 "Effects of Education and Urbanization on Fertility" in *Determinants of Fertility in Developing Countries*, R.A. Bulatao and R.D. Lee (Eds). Orlando, Fla: Academic Press.

Datta, R.C.
1987 "Women's Education, Family Size and Earnings." *Indian Journal of Social Work*, 48:3 (Oct.), 325-332.

Estes, Richard J.
1984 *The Social Progress of Nations*. Praeger.

Firebaugh, Glenn
1992 "Growth Effects of Foreign and Domestic Investment." *American Journal of Sociology* 98:105-30.

Gadalla, Saad, James McCarthy, and Neeraj Kax
1987 "The Determinants of Fertility in Rural Egypt." *Journal of Biosocial Science*, 19:2 (Apr.), 195-207.

Graff, Harvey J.
1979 "Literacy, Education and Fertility, Past and Present: A Critical Review." *Population and Development Review*, 5:105-140.

Herz, Barbara, K. Subbarao, Masooma Habih, and Laura Raney.
1991 *Letting Girls Learn: Promising Approaches in Primary and Secondary Education*, World Bank Discussion Papers, No. 133. Washington, DC: World Bank.

Hicks, Norman L.
1979 "Growth vs. Basic Needs: Is There a Trade-Off?" *World Development* 7:985-94.

Hicks, Norman L. and Paul P. Streeten
1979 "Indicators of Development: The Search for a Basic Needs Yardstick." *World Development* 7:567-80.

Hill, M. Anne and Elizabeth M. King
1993 "Women's Education in Developing Countries: An Overview." Chapter 1 in *Women's Education in Developing Countries*, Elizabeth M. King and M. Anne Hill

(Eds). Baltimore and London: The Johns Hopkins University Press.

Hyatt, D.E. and W.J. Milne
1993 " Determinants of Fertility in Urban and Rural Kenya: Estimates and a Simulation of The Impact of Education Policy." *Environment and Planning*, 25:3 (March), 371-382.

I.L.O. (International Labor Organization).
1977 *Employment, Growth and Basic Needs: A One-World Problem*. ILO.

Jain, Anrudh K.
1981 "The Effect of Female Education on Fertility: A Simple Explanation." *Demography*, 18:4 (Nov.), 577-595.

Jazairy, Idriss, Mohiuddin Alamoir, and Theresa Panuccio
1992 *The State of World Rural Poverty: An Inquiry into Its Causes and Consequences*. Published for the International Fund for Agricultural Development.

Leslie, Joanne, Margaret Lycette, and Mayra Buvinic
1988 "Weathering Economic Crises: The Crucial Role of Women in Health." Pp. 307-348 in *Health, Nutrition, and Economic Crises: Approaches to Policy in the Third World*, edited by David E. Bell and Michael R. Reich. Dover: Auburn House.

London, Bruce and Kenneth Hadden
1989 "The Spread of Education and Fertility Decline: A Thai Province Level Test of Caldwell's Wealth Flows Theory." *Rural Sociology* 54:1, 17-34.

London, Bruce and Bruce A. Williams
1988 "Multinational Corporate Penetration, Protest, and Basic Provision in Non-core Nations: A Cross National Analysis." *Social Forces* 66:747-73.

London, Bruce
1992 "School Enrollment Rates and Trends, Gender and Fertility." *Sociology of Education* 65 (Oct.), 306-316.

Mason, Karen O. 1984 *The Status of Women: A Review of its Relationships to Fertility and Mortality*. New York: Rockefeller Foundation.

Maudlin, W Parker and Bernard Berelson 1978 "Conditions of Fertility Decline in Developing Countries, 1965-75." *Studies in Family Planning*, 9:89-147.

McGuire, Judith S. and Barry M. Popkin
1990 "Helping Women Improve Nutrition in the Developing World: Beating the Zero Sum Game." World Bank Technical Paper No. 114, Washington, DC.

Menard, Scott
1985 "Inequality and Fertility." *Studies in Comparative International Development*, 20:83-97.

Morris, Morris David
1979 *Measuring the Condition of the World's Poor: The Physical Quality of Life Index*. Pergamon.

Nuss, Shirley and Lorraine Majka
1985 "Female Illiteracy and Education: Progress and Prospects for the Future." *International Journal of Contemporary Sociology*, 22:1-2 (Jan-April), 113-131.

Psacharapoulos, George and Maureen Woodhall
1985 *Education for Development*. NY: Oxford University Press.

Raut, Lakshmi
1993 "Per Capita Income Growth, Social Expenditures and Living Standards: Evidence from Rural India." *Journal of Asian Economics*, 4:1 (Spring), 59-76.

Rowley, John
1993 "Liberation and Change." *People and the Planet* 2:1, p. 3.

Sadik, Nafis
1990 *Investing in Women: The Focus of the '90's*. New York: United Nations Population Fund.

Schultz, T. Paul
1993 "Returns to Women's Education." Chapter 2 in *Women's Education in Developing Countries*, Elizabeth M. King and M. Anne Hill (Eds). Baltimore and London: The Johns Hopkins University Press.

Streeten, Paul P.
1979 "Basic Needs: Premises and Promises." *Journal of Policy Modeling* 1:136-46.

Summers, Lawrence
1992 "The Most Influential Investment." *Scientific American* (August), p. 132.
1994 *Investing in All the People: Educating Women in Developing Countries*. EDI Seminar Papers No. 45. Washington, DC: The World Bank.

Tsui, Amy Ong and Donald J. Bogue
1978 "Declining World Fertility: Trends, Causes, and Implications." *Population Bulletin* 33 (4) (whole issue).

UNICEF
1994 *The Progress of Nations*. NY: UNICEF House.

United Nations
1994 *Programs of Action of the United Nations International Conference on Population and Development*. NY: Post Conference Draft Report, Sept. 19, 1994.

Ward, Kathryn B.
1984 *Women in the World System: Its Impact on Status and Fertility*. New York: Praeger.

Wimberley, Dale W.
1990 "Investment Dependence and Alternative Explanations of Third World Mortality: A Cross National Study." *American Sociological Review* 55:75-91.

 Article Review Form at end of book.

What are the benefits of single sex education? What are the negative aspects?

The Great Divide

Teens and the gender gap

Gina Pera

Gina Pera, a writer based in San Diego, wrote much of last year's Teens & Race special issue.

The Difference Between Girls and Boys

Is there a gender gap? Yes, says 222,653 teens in grades 6–12 responding to USA WEEKEND's ninth annual teen write-in survey. Teens nationwide told us that gender bias shapes their lives daily, defining the boundaries of their relationships with parents, teachers—and each other.

The most dramatic finding concerned sexual harassment, which generated the most passionate response from students. Essay after essay described painful and embarrassing incidents. Less troubling but as telling was the revelation that parents continue to divide chores along traditional lines: Girls do the dishes, boys do the lawn.

Among the results from the survey, The Great Divide: Teens & the Gender Gap:

- **Sexual harassment is a daily reality.** Three out of four teens have experienced sexual

harassment (defined as anything from touching to being mooned). These findings are backed by a 1996 University of Michigan study which found that in public high schools 83 percent of girls and 60 percent of boys report having been sexually harassed.

Kevin Donahoe, 15, of Chatfield, Minn., who was a student editor of this special issue, says schools are starting to take action. "A starting pitcher on our baseball team called a girl a 'lezzie,' and they wouldn't let him play sports for two weeks, right during the tournament."

While huge numbers of teens say they have been sexually harassed—and more than half admit to dishing it out, according to the Michigan study—girls and boys generally react to it differently. Girls are almost twice as likely as boys to be upset by the experience, while boys are six times more likely than girls to be flattered.

- **Girls are more responsible.** Nearly 100 percent of girls say they behave more responsibly than boys; even 73 percent of boys agree. The vast majority of girls also believe they are given

more responsibility by parents, teachers and employers; 41 percent of boys concur.

"Boys can be just as responsible as girls," says Tia Mitchell, 17, of Louisville, who was also a student editor on this issue. "But society tells them they're supposed to goof off and have fun."

- **Teachers are stricter with boys.** Seventy-five percent of boys and 60 percent of girls say that when it comes to discipline, teachers are tougher on boys. Many experts agree, but they say boys are more disruptive in the classroom.

"A lot of this has to do with how we socialize boys and girls in society," says Pat O'Reilly, a developmental psychologist at the University of Cincinnati. "We rear boys to be Davy Crockett, but girls learn by the age of 5 that when an adult says something, they'd better listen."

- **Sex hurts girls' reputations more than boys'.** Teens are acutely aware of the age-old sexual double standard. In essay after essay, teens told us: When people find out that a boy and a girl have had sex, he is a "stud" but she is a "slut."

Only 22 percent of boys and 15 percent of girls say it hurts a boy's reputation, while 70 percent of boys and 87 percent of girls say a girl's reputation is damaged. Both sexes conclude: It's not fair, but that's the way it is.

- **Parents often divide chores along traditional lines.** In general, girls do more of the housework, and boys still do the outside chores. Six in 10 girls do laundry (vs. three in 10 boys), while nearly seven in 10 boys mow the lawn (vs. three in 10 girls). Perhaps some of this comes from the example set by parents. Nearly six in 10 of teens combined say Mom does more of the chores (less than 10 percent say Dad does more chores).

Still, even the most skeptical observers agree that, compared to 20 years ago, the gender gap has narrowed. USA WEEKEND's survey results indicate as much.

- The majority of teens support coed sports: 87 percent of girls and 61 percent of boys say girls should be allowed to play on boys' sports teams.

- More than half of teens say they expect a woman to be elected president in their lifetime.

- A whopping 84 percent of teens have been brought up to believe men and women have equal opportunities in society.

While non-scientific, the USA WEEKEND survey echoes other national studies on sex bias among teens and adults. A March Gallup Poll underscores the problem: 73 percent of adults say society favors men over women, and 64 percent say women don't experience job equality.

"Adolescents are the weather vanes of society. They reflect what's going on in the larger society," says Jim Garbarino, director of Cornell University's Family Life Development Center. "Kids are lagging behind because teachers and parents are lagging behind. Adults talk equality, but they aren't giving it everyday expression."

In My Opinion

"In general, adults treat girls more sensitively and more delicately. For example, I take out the garbage because it's a 'man's job.' Besides, let's say it really smells, which it mostly does. A girl will just drop it and say, "There's no way I'm touching that again." A boy won't really care; he'll just take it out."—*Leandro Figuereo, 13, Wanaque, N.J.*

In my school, there is a lot of name-calling back and forth between guys and girls. We need to sit down and talk about what we are [really] saying to one another. Listen to rap songs. Look at how TV portrays women. The struggle between the sexes is found there."—*Aisha Edwards, 16, Kansas City, Kan.*

"Both boys and girls suffer from stereotypes, but boys suffer from deeper, more socially unacceptable prejudices. Boys are seen as aggressive, immature and insensitive. Often, before even knowing a guy, a girl thinks of him as the "typical male"—a macho, unintelligent jerk. Males have a more difficult time beating such prejudices."—*Jamie Nicholas, 17, Machesney Park, Ill.*

"I find it interesting how different generations handle household chores. My father helps by telling

us to ask my mom if she needs help. When my brother lived with us, we always cleaned up after him. Now, when he and his wife visit, they talk about taking turns cleaning the bathroom. Imagine: My brother cleaning a toilet!"—*Amy Childs, 14, Woodlynne, N.J.*

It's Not Fair: Teachers Pick on Boys

When we asked students whether they experienced gender discrimination in school, we received an avalanche of essays. Most agreed, teachers are tougher on boys—though in their letters, some boys said they consider being called on in class "negative attention." Girls and boys generally disagreed, however, on who gets more positive attention in class. In their essays, some girls told us "positive attention" can mean being complimented on their clothing or hairstyle.

'Teachers favor girls'
Israel Saldana, age 18

Whitefield High School, Security, Colo.

"Teachers almost always call on the 'bright' girls, while the guys are left out. Teachers have a perception guys aren't that smart and don't care about school. Guys do have an interest, but most teachers don't take the time to see it.

"Girls ask a lot more questions than guys do. Problems that guys don't understand—like in math—they just figure they'll pick it up when they do their homework. Girls seem more anxious about getting it right, right away.

"Last year, the class valedictorian was a girl. Our National Honor Society was, basically, girls. Maybe these girls want to go to a better college. I usually get good grades, but I don't need to go to Yale or Princeton. I think the girls are aiming higher, because they want to prove they can do [as well] as boys."

'Teachers are pretty fair, but tougher on boys'

Lisa Savage, age 17

Tri-Valley High School, Downs, Ill.

"Teachers are pretty good about giving attention to both sexes. They are tougher on boys, but it's mainly because boys cause a lot of trouble. There are some guys who, if they tried, would be successful, but their attitude is, 'I'll do what I want to do.' I care about the consequences of what I do. Boys don't seem to.

"A lot of boys yell out the answers, and if they're wrong they don't seem to mind. They seem to have a shield against being embarrassed. I need to be more confident in my answers. Sometimes I've kept my mouth shut, even if I think I know the answer. But lots of times girls don't even get the chance to raise their hand or to be called on because the guys don't wait to be called on. Actually, the whole idea of girls having to be quiet and polite is a little irritating."

'Teachers expect more from girls'

C. J. Wallace, age 15

East Literature Magnet School, Nashville

"Teachers expect girls to work harder and do better just because we are girls. If a girl is very smart, it's nothing new. She's nothing special. But if a boy is smart, it's a great thing because it's not expected. This is unfair to both boys and girls.

"Certain boys are the class clowns, and teachers do pick on them more.

"In history class, some male teachers expect the boys to know about war and fighting. They usually do. They expect girls to know about different cultures and women's roles. But girls don't focus on just one topic that interests them. Girls focus more on learning. Period.

"Teachers also think boys are more physically fit and can do better at sports than girls. They ask girls to run errands, and they ask boys to move things. This tells girls that we're weak."

'Teachers call on boys more'

Steven Boyd, age 16

Moanalua High School, Honolulu

"Teachers do call on boys more, but it's usually because boys aren't paying attention. If it were a case of a boy and girl both raising their hands, teachers aren't more likely to call on one over the other.

"In the classroom, lots of things boys do—talking or making jokes—are just accepted. They do it to show off to the guys and attract the girls. In fact, girls will talk to those kinds of guys more often. It shouldn't happen; it's disrespectful to teachers.

"Girls also interact more with the teachers, such as helping on projects or just talking. Teachers trust the girls to get things done. If they ask a boy to do a favor, they don't get it done right away.

"Still, I've been trusted by teachers with certain projects, too. The thing is, you have to be quiet and attentive in class right from the start. As soon as you're rude, teachers turn away from you."

Interviews by Gina Pera

Statistic

Role Call: 75% of boys and 60% of girls say teachers are tougher on boys. 45% of boys say girls get more positive attention; girls, however, think it's equal.

Source: The Great Divide: Teens & the Gender Gap

In My Opinion

"Girls mature quicker and stuff, so [boys] will tend to just mess around when we're supposed to be listening and stuff. I guess it's just in our genes."—*Clayton Jackson, 12, Nixa, Mo.*

"An all-girl English class would be more challenging because I wouldn't be teased about being picked a lot. Also, if a girl has a crush on someone, she would worry about being embarrassed in front of him. Girls would feel freer to give their opinions with just girls."—*Stephanie Magsino, 13, New York City.*

"Since the third grade, I've been in the gifted program. In all that time, all my teachers seem to favor the females, plus all my teachers are females. Girls are usually very articulate, whereas I don't always feel confident that my answer is exactly right."—*Jeremy Longshore, 15, Panama City, Fla.*

"If a guy makes a joke, the teacher lets it go. Some teachers will even grin or laugh. And the class goes, 'That guy is so cool; he said this or that.' But if a girl does it, the teacher doesn't like you because you're not acting ladylike."—*Carissa Lenfert, 16, Memphis, Ind.*

What 222,653 Teens Said

The Great Divide: Teens & the Gender Gap survey ran in USA WEEKEND last spring and was taken by 222,653 students in grades 6 through 12. The non-scientific results reflect only the opinions of those teens who chose to respond. They were: 44% male, 56% female; 64% two-parent household, 17% single-parent household, 15% stepfamily household, 4% other arrangements; 27% grades 6–7, 36% grades 8–9, 37% grades 10–12; 99% attend co-ed school, 1% attend single-sex school; 77% white, 7% black, 6% Hispanic, 2% Asian, 2% Native American, 3% multiracial, 3% other.

1. If your school offered same-sex classes on certain subjects, would you want to take one?

	Boys	Girls
Yes	29%	41%
No	71%	59%

1a. If yes, which subjects would you most like to take with your own gender?

	Boys	Girls
English/literature	11%	13%
Math/science	17%	19%
Physical education	60%	61%
Computer science	10%	8%
Foreign languages	11%	12%
Social studies	9%	5%

2. In general, who gets more positive attention in the classroom?

	Boys	Girls
Boys	8%	14%
Girls	45%	28%
Both get same	47%	58%

3. In terms of discipline, teachers are generally tougher on:

	Boys	Girls
Boys	75%	60%
Girls	2%	6%
No real difference	23%	34%

4. Do you have some teachers who, in class, call on boys more often than girls?

	Boys	Girls
Yes	33%	42%
No	67%	58%

(Note: We didn't ask if girls are called on more often or if boys and girls are called on equally.)

5. Should girls have the opportunity to play on boys' sports teams?

	Boys	Girls
Yes	61%	87%
No	39%	13%

6. In a heated argument with a classmate, you are more likely to (choose one):

	Boys	Girls
Argue loudly	25%	33%
Hit the person	26%	7%
Walk away angry	13%	14%
Calmly walk away and try to resolve later	19%	20%
Talk it out right away	17%	26%

7. Have you ever cried at school?

	Boys	Girls
Yes	33%	72%
No	67%	28%

8. Percentage saying they have experienced the following at school:

	Boys	Girls
Comments, jokes, looks	56%	71%
Touches, grabs, pinches	33%	37%
Sexual rumors spread about self	19%	22%
Flashed or mooned	20%	13%
Called gay or lesbian	25%	16%
Forced to kiss or do something sexual	7%	2%
Shown sexual photos or notes	22%	15%
Seen sexual graffiti about self	8%	3%
None of the above	24%	19%

9. If you have experienced sexual harassment, how did it make you feel?

	Boys	Girls
Upset	30%	56%
Not upset at all	41%	23%
Flattered	19%	3%
Confused	10%	18%

(Note: The response depends on the form of sexual harassment experienced.)

10. Do you think that jokes and kidding around are sometimes misunderstood as sexual harassment?

	Boys	Girls
Yes	82%	83%
No	18%	17%

11. Percentage saying they perform these chores at home:

	Boys	Girls
Washing dishes	52%	72%
Taking out the trash	73%	37%
Mowing the lawn	67%	30%
Laundry	35%	59%

	Boys	Girls
Housecleaning	51%	70%
Caring for pets	55%	54%
Helping with dinner	39%	58%
Baby-sitting/ child care	27%	52%

12. If you live in a two-parent household, who does more chores?

	Boys	Girls
Mother/ stepmother	56%	60%
Father/ stepfather	5%	5%
Chores shared equally	39%	35%

13. In general, who has later curfews at home?

	Boys	Girls
Boys	47%	46%
Girls	11%	10%
Same for both	42%	44%

14. In general, who is given more responsibility (by parents, teachers, employers)?

	Boys	Girls
Boys	59%	18%
Girls	41%	82%

15. In general, who behaves more responsibly?

	Boys	Girls
Boys	27%	1%
Girls	73%	99%

16. In general, parents give more freedom to:

	Boys	Girls
Boys	43%	57%
Girls	21%	10%
Same for both	36%	33%

17. Have you been raised to believe that men and women have equal opportunities in society?

	Boys	Girls
Yes	85%	86%
No	15%	14%

18. In general, who has more career opportunities?

	Boys	Girls
Boys	82%	81%
Girls	18%	19%

19. Do you think that men and women are paid equally for equal work?

	Boys	Girls
Yes	48%	33%
No	52%	67%

(Note: Results do not conclude that either men or women are paid more.)

20. You worry more about:

	Boys	Girls
Finding a good job	72%	73%
Finding a good spouse	28%	27%

21. Do you think a female president will be elected in your lifetime?

	Boys	Girls
Yes	52%	58%
No	48%	42%

22. Do you expect your future spouse to work outside the home?

	Boys	Girls
Yes	80%	95%
No	20%	5%

23. If you have children, who will handle most of the child care?

	Boys	Girls
I'll do most of child care	4%	16%
Spouse will do most	17%	2%
We'll share equally	79%	82%

24a. When people find out that a boy has had sex, it hurts his reputation at school. Agree or disagree?

	Boys	Girls
Agree	22%	15%
Disagree	78%	85%

24b. When people find out that a girl has had sex, it hurts her reputation at school. Agree or disagree?

	Boys	Girls
Agree	70%	87%
Disagree	30%	13%

In My Opinion

"If boys aren't as responsible as girls are, why should they be given later curfews and so much opportunity to prove how irresponsible they are."—*Mary Mason, 14, Atlanta*

"In my family, males have greater advantages. I'm able to stay out later, date at an earlier age, and only have to do the outside work, whereas girls have all the inside chores."—*Jeff Holloway, 17, Petoskey, Mich.*

"I think girls are treated more strictly because there is so much crime, and parents are worried that girls won't be able to defend themselves. But against most bad things, boys can't either."—*Anna Podolanczuk, 15, Wall, N.J.*

A Day in the Life

By Myron B. Pitts

Day to day, how do boys and girls see their world? USA WEEKEND set out to answer that question by tagging along with busy Philadelphian Tarik Khan, 17, and fellow Central High School grads—twins Denise and Sabrina Holloway, 17; Troy Madres, 18; and Jocelyn Edathil, 17—plus senior John Rubin, 17. We provided a copy of our survey, The Great Divide: Teens & the Gender Gap, to get the discussion rolling.

Tuesday, 6:35 P.M.

Taking the Lead: Tarik, sporting shaving cream, tries to groom while organizing an evening outing. Even in school projects, "I'm usually the one who starts things." He says boys tend to parlay their aggression into leadership on projects.

8:05 P.M.

Girls keep pace: On South Street, the boys sometimes walk too far ahead. "Tarik, will you slow down, please?" says Denise, right. Later, they discuss women in sports and the military. All agree women should fly combat missions. "Women shouldn't play football," says Sabrina, second from right. Tarik generates excitement: "I think [female reporters] should not be allowed in a man's locker room. They talk about disgusting things in there." John, second from left, backs him, but no one else does.

8:20 P.M.

Group dynamics: The friends are upstairs at Jim's Steaks, a cheese steak joint on South Street. Troy, left, and John are poring over the gender survey, shooting out topics; the others wait. "Pick a topic, not the whole thing," Jocelyn, right, tells them. She and Sabrina begin talking about a science teacher with a "big ego" who they thought favored boys. Later, the talk turns to family dynamics. Jocelyn, part East Indian, says her mom, following custom, allows Jocelyn's dad to

eat first. "She'll eat with the kids, but not with my dad."

9:10 P.M.

Acting up in class: Denise sips a sweet "chocolate creamer" at the Supreme Bean Cafe. The group debates whether teachers call on boys more than girls. "Teachers call on guys to shut them up," Denise says. "The boys are acting up." She receives no disagreement.

10:30 P.M.

Boys change the rules: The teens leave the coffeehouse and walk along the South Street bridge. The girls buy strings of tacky beads from a vendor. What follows is a lesson in how boys like to color outside the lines. The girls put the beads around their necks; John and Troy interpret them as toys, sparking a game of "double dutch" jump-rope.

Wednesday, 8:30 A.M.

Beyond flirting: Tarik and the boys goof off on his talk show on public access station WPEB-FM. Tarik plays a rap song every 10 minutes or so, sandwiched by conversation. Denise and Sabrina are the "guests" Tarik interviews them about sexual harassment. "There were a couple guys in my old school who liked to be 'touchy,'" Denise says. "I didn't know what to do about it." Tarik says, "I think girls sometimes provoke it." A lot of girls, the way they respond" A friend finishes for him, adopting a "girlish" laugh: "Heeheehee."

An Experiment: Same-Sex Classes

By Pam Janis

When Wendy Ahern graduated from Franklin (Mass.) High School in June, she wished she

had done better academically. Her barrier to serious schoolwork, she says: boys. "The boys always goofed around and made class a circus," says Wendy, 18. "If I'd had all-girl classes, I wouldn't have worried what the boys would say or do when I said something in class."

Forty-one percent of all the girls responding to the USA WEEKEND survey, like Wendy, said they'd prefer all-girl classes in subjects such as gym and math. And 29 percent of boys said they would like all-boy classes—especially in gym. "Girls slow things down in my gym class," says Carl Anderson Jr., a 13-year-old ninth-grader in Chester, Pa. "An all-boys class would be more competitive."

He may one day get his chance: Single-sex classes are growing in popularity as school officials in about a dozen states experiment, hoping to narrow gaps in test scores between boys and girls in some subjects, such as math and science, and recognize social and developmental differences in others, such as gym.

The exact number of schools is not known, says Washington, D.C., education lawyer Deborah Brake, because they don't want to become targets of gender-equity lawsuits: They may be violating Title IX, the rule that federally funded schools must educate boys and girls equally. Exceptions are classes like human sexuality and contact sports, where privacy and safety are at stake. But, Brake says, many all-girl math and science classes are allowable as efforts to make up for past discrimination in traditionally male-dominated fields. (School officials first must prove with test scores, grades and other documentation that girls have lagged behind boys in a subject.)

In California and Maine, high schools teaching all-girl math classes survived legal inquiries by proving the classes filled remedial needs, opening the classes to boys (none signed up), and calling them classes for "under-represented students."

Patricia Vargas, 12, a seventh-grader at Hesperian Elementary School in San Lorenzo, Calif., wants to give all-girl classes a try: "Boys put down girls and make us feel stupid in class."

Of course, not all girls agree. "No way!" says Katie Luxa, a 15-year-old 10th-grader at Stadium High School in Tacoma, Wash. "I don't see people ignoring their work or flirting. The guys are joking around, but everyone is paying attention."

Statistic

Class division: 41% of girls and 29% of boys would like to take a same-sex class.

Source: The Great Divide: Teens & the Gender Gap

In My Opinion

"In health science, we talk about differences between boys and girls during puberty. The boys think it's funny, and the girls think it's serious. Girls would share their personal stories and talk more naturally in a class with just girls, because they're all going through the same things."— *Chavonda Pighet, 16, Rowland, N.C.*

"Girls don't usually cause trouble or get too goofy. If a class were all boys, we would probably get too rowdy and have to stay after school all the time. I wouldn't want all-boy classes—except for gym, because the girls are always late."—*Jonathan Charles, 12, Naperville, Ill.*

School Sports: Girls Take the Field

By Gina Pera

It's hard to imagine a girls' softball team bitterly dividing a small Nebraska town. But in U.S. cities big and small, gender battles are heating up on school athletic fields. Sometimes, the fight gets ugly.

The rhubarb in Minden, Neb., began in 1992 as Naomi Fritson's daughter entered high school. Fritson, who also has two sons, noticed boys had more opportunity than girls to play varsity sports. Other parents, while agreeing it was unfair, told Fritson, "You'll get used to it. It's only four years."

Instead, the farmer and part-time school-bus driver remembers thinking: "How can I expect my daughter to believe she can be whatever she wants to be when I let her go to school and hear 'No, you can't'?"

Four years later, Fritson has won her campaign to start a girls' varsity softball team—just as daughter Sarah Casper leaves for college. It took a class-action lawsuit, the first of four such suits in Nebraska. All were settled this summer by consent decree, with schools agreeing to start teams and provide facilities and equipment equal to those enjoyed by boys.

Fritson and parents in the other three towns spent years "jumping through hoops" set up by school boards, says Kristen Gallas, a Washington, D.C., lawyer who worked with the parents. "They started club teams to demonstrate interest [one even won a state championship]. They raised their own funds. Some even offered to fund the school

varsity team for three years." But the answer always came back "no."

"Some administrators said, 'This is the way it's always been,'" Gallas says. Others declared that football programs would suffer because of girls' softball.

"I thought I had all these friends," Sarah recalls, "and all of a sudden they wouldn't look at me."

After three frustrating years, Fritson—weary of obscene phone calls at 2 A.M. and feeling her job threatened—decided to sue. "When Naomi stood up," Gallas says, "the parents in the other towns joined her."

None had heard of Title IX, which forbids sex discrimination in federally funded schools. Yet ultimately, this law gave the schools incentive to settle.

The past decade's boom in coed teams for younger kids means more girls are playing sports. In 1971, just one girl in 27 participated in high school sports; in 1996, one girl in three plays.

More people now are questioning the traditional male emphasis in school sports. When USA WEEKEND asked teens if girls should be able to play on boys' teams, 61 percent of boys said yes (87 percent of girls agreed). After all, some pointed out, in some sports the boys' team is the only team.

Schools face some tough decisions, and many don't want to make them unless they're forced, says Mary Curtis, associate director of women's athletics at the University of Iowa. "Title IX was enacted in 1972, but most schools ignored it for 20 years," Curtis says.

As for Sarah, "I learned how standing up for something you believe in can cause lots of problems, and how things can get a whole lot worse before they get better. You see just how much people hate change."

Statistic

Fair play: 87% of girls and 61% of boys say girls should have the opportunity to play on boys' sports teams.

Source: The Great Divide: Teens & the Gender Gap

In My Opinion

"My school had only a boys' hockey team. Then one year a girl wanted to play and there was controversy! It turned out she be-came one of the most respected players. Now we have a girls' hockey team, [and] the cheerlead-ing squad is open to guys."
—*Joseph Botten, 16, Minneapolis*

"When we play volleyball in PE, the boys don't let the girls touch the ball. They think girls are too dumb to play sports. Rather than standing around, we talk. I would rather have a class by ourselves. That way, we could play."
—*Lilia Garcia, 12, El Paso*

"Guys get respect based on the fact that they are big and strong and can defend themselves. Girls get respect because of the way they act, their attitude or just little things like the way they dress. I know many girls who can beat me in sports."
—*David White, 14, Merritt Island, Fla.*

"Last year I signed up for football. I love just being part of a team, having fun, hitting people. At first, they gave me the wrong practice time. Some of my team-mates just didn't want me around."
—*Sandra McElroy, 14, Bossier City, La.*

 Article Review Form at end of book.

How does Pollitt assess the current field of arguments around biology as destiny and the social construction of gender roles?

Why Boys Don't Play With Dolls

Children get the message loud and clear. Can we change what they hear?

Katha Pollitt

Katha Pollitt is a poet and essayist.

It's 28 years since the founding of NOW, and boys still like trucks and girls still like dolls. Increasingly, we are told that the source of these robust preferences must lie outside society—in pre-natal hormonal influences, brain chemistry, genes—and that feminism has reached its natural limits. What else could possibly explain the love of preschool girls for party dresses or the desire of toddler boys to own more guns than Mark from Michigan.

True, recent studies claim to show small cognitive differences between the sexes: he gets around by orienting himself in space, she does it by remembering landmarks. Time will tell if any deserve the hoopla with which each is invariably greeted, over the protests of the researchers themselves. But even if the results hold up (and the history of such re-search is not encouraging), we don't need studies of self-differentiated brain activity in reading, say, to understand why boys and girls still seem so unalike.

The feminist movement has done much for some women, and something for every woman, but it has hardly turned America into a playground free of sex roles. It hasn't even got women to stop di-eting or men to stop interrupting them.

Instead of looking at kids to "prove" that differences in behav-ior by sex are innate, we can look at the ways we raise kids as an index to how unfinished the femi-nist revolution really is, and how tentatively it is embraced even by adults who fully expect their daughters to enter previously male-dominated professions and their sons to change diapers.

I'm at a children's birthday party. "I'm sorry," one mom silently mouths to the mother of the birthday girl, who has just torn open her present—Tropical Splash Barbie. Now, you can love Barbie or you can hate Barbie, and there are feminists in both camps. But *apologize* for Barbie? Inflict Barbie, against your own convic-tions, on the child of a friend you know will be none too pleased?

Every mother in that room had spent years becoming a per-son who had to be taken seriously, not least by herself. Even the most attractive, I'm willing to bet, had suffered over her body's failure to fit the impossible American ideal. Given all that, it seems crazy to transmit Barbie to the next gener-ation. Yet to reject her is to say that what Barbie represents—being sexy, thin, stylish—is unim-portant, which is obviously not true, and children know it's not true.

Women's looks matter terri-bly in this society, and so Barbie, however ambivalently, must be passed along. After all, there are worse toys. The Cut and Style Barbie styling head, for example, a grotesque object intended to encourage "hair play." The grown-ups who give that probably apologize, too.

How happy would most parents be to have a child who flouted sex conventions? I know a lot of women, feminists, who complain in a comical, eyeball-rolling way about their sons' passion for sports: the ruined weekends, obnoxious coaches, macho values. But they would not think of discouraging their sons from participating in this activity they find so foolish. Or do they? Their husbands are sports fans, too, and they like their husbands a lot.

Could it be that even sports-resistant moms see athletics as part of manliness? That if their sons wanted to spend the weekend writing up their diaries, or reading, or baking, they'd find it disturbing? Too antisocial? Too lonely? Too gay?

Theories of innate differences in behavior are appealing. They let parents off the hook—no small recommendation in a culture that holds moms, and sometimes even dads, responsible for their children's every misstep on the road to bliss and success.

They allow grown-ups to take the path of least resistance to the dominant culture, which always requires less psychic effort, even if it means more actual work: just ask the working mother who comes home exhausted and nonetheless finds it easier to pick up her son's socks than make him do it himself. They let families buy for their children, without *too* much guilt, the unbelievably sexist junk that the kids, who have been watching commercials since birth, understandably crave.

But the thing the theories do most of all is tell adults that the *adult* world—in which moms and dads still play by many of the old rules even as they question and fidget and chafe against them—is the way it's supposed to be. A girl with a doll and a boy with a truck "explain" why men are from Mars and women are from Venus, why wives do housework and husbands just don't understand.

The paradox is that the world of rigid and hierarchal sex roles evoked by determinist theories is already passing away. Three-year-olds may indeed insist that doctors are male and nurses female, even if their own mother is a physician. Six-year-olds know better. These days, something like half of all medical students are female, and male applications to nursing school are inching upward. When tomorrow's 3-year-olds play doctor, who's to say that they'll assign the roles?

With sex roles, as in every area of life, people aspire to what is possible, and conform to what is necessary. But these are not fixed, especially today. Biological determinism may reassure some adults about their present, but it is feminism, the ideology of flexible and converging sex roles, that fits our children's future, And the kids, somehow, know this.

That's why, if you look carefully, you'll find that for every kid who fits a stereotype, there's another who's breaking one down. Sometimes it's the same kid—the boy who skateboards *and* takes cooking in his after-school program; the girl who collects stuffed animals *and* A-pluses in science.

Feminists are often accused of imposing their "agenda" on children. Isn't that what adults always do, consciously and unconsciously? Kids aren't born religious, or polite, or kind, or able to remember where they put their sneakers. Inculcating these behaviors, and the values behind them, is a tremendous amount of work, involving many adults. We don't have a choice, really, about *whether* we should give our children messages about what it means to be male and female—they're bombarded with them from morning till night.

The question, as always, is what do we want those messages to be?

 **Article Review Form at end of book.**

Why is the inclusion of girls and women in scientific fields important?

Get Serious on Science

Continue to ignore it, and our kids will pay the price

Debora M. Katz-Stone

Dr. Debora M. Katz-Stone teaches physics at the U.S. Naval Academy in Annapolis, Md. These views are her own and do not necessarily represent the opinions of the U.S. Naval Academy.

Want to stop a conversation dead at a dinner party? Introduce yourself as a physics professor. People's eyes glaze over. They mumble, "That was the one class I *really* hated."

No one ever says, "Cool! Can you tell me what the universe is expanding into?" Lots of people tell me, "You don't *look* like a physicist." Meaning, of course, "but you're a *woman*."

With so few adults excited about science, it is no wonder people shy away from technological professions.

This is doubly true for women and minorities, who find so few role models in those fields. While women make up nearly half the U.S. labor force, fewer than 9% of engineers are women, and fewer than one-third of all computer specialists are women.

Overall, the number of people earning bachelor's degrees in physics is down 8% in the past five years. And the National Science Board reports that less than half the U.S. population even considers scientific research beneficial.

Why worry? Because most well-paying jobs today rely on some degree of technical knowledge, and by 2000 new entrants to the workforce will be predominantly women and minorities—the groups with the least science education.

"Our economic security will depend on how well we have educated, trained and incorporated these individuals into full participation," says Radcliffe College President Linda Wilson.

Our industrialized competitors have already figured out the importance of having a gender-balanced talent pool in the sciences. In a 1991 survey of 20 nations, for example, the United States tied for the lowest percentage (3%) of female faculty in physics.

To bridge the gender gap and ensure America's place at the cutting edge of technology, we need programs that encourage adults to value science as something exciting, vibrant, challenging, stimulating, and rewarding. Once we've sold parents on the importance of science, then they can sell it to their kids:

Read and talk science to your child. From the stories you read at bedtime to your conversation at the dinner table, parents and other close family members can play a role in shaping a child's life choices. Ask any male engineer why he chose his field and he'll say his family influenced him. Women in non-science roles say the same. But female engineers say they had to look beyond their family—either they were influenced by their teachers, the media or (perhaps most telling) by "no one."

Take an interest yourself. Many parents may take their children to the science museum or planetarium, but they see the trip as merely "something for the kids." We need parents to continue to enjoy and participate in science.

But we need other changes, too, that go beyond parents.

Set up science clubs. Not everyone who plays basketball on the weekends hopes to join the NBA; likewise, nonscientists can make scientific participation a serious—and fun—hobby.

Amateur astronomy groups, for example, exist in some communities, and they have fun by throwing "star parties"—taking out their telescopes and watching for supernova explosions or solar eclipses. Just recently many watched the Perseids meteor shower, which occurs every August.

So, such groups exist; there just aren't enough of them. And clubs such as these can be duplicated in other fields—archeology, for example—and members encouraged to bring along young people to instill in them the excitement of discovery.

Open the doors on research. Many universities and research laboratories which receive federal grants should be more accessible to the general public so people can see how their taxpayer dollars are being spent. These researchers

might offer community lectures or organize hands-on projects that allow the public—particularly the young—to participate in the research process.

One good example already in place is the NASA-Goddard Space Flight Center in Greenbelt, Md. It provides walking tours in which the public can see the NASA communications center and the Hubble Space Telescope Command Center. There is also a visitors' center where children and adults can have hands-on experience with computer-interactive exhibits as well as see some of the newest images of the universe.

Corporations can better promote science. The 3M Corp., based in St. Paul, Minn., has a program called "The Visiting Wizard." 3M scientists and engineers voluntarily go out in different settings—mostly to schools, but sometimes to adult groups, such as veterans—to generate interest in science.

One of the programs is cryogenics, which concerns the freezing of things. In these demonstrations the "wizards" show how liquid nitrogen works, freezing bananas and other foods

using the same technique McDonald's employs to "fresh freeze" a hamburger patty for shipment.

Bob Barton, the 3M chemist who created the program, says he is aware of only four or five other companies that have similar programs. That's not enough.

Establish gender-sensitive models. In order to increase the number of women and minorities in science and engineering, programs must be established to downplay gender stereotypes.

Take, for example, the American Association of Female Amateur Astronomers, whose mission is "to encourage, promote and support female amateur astronomers." Efforts like this ought to be replicated in other scientific fields.

We are a nation famous for its creativity. We can—and must—become the most scientifically literate adults on the planet. Telling our children to reach for the stars is not enough; we have to show them that the stars are indeed within their grasp.

 Article Review Form at end of book.

WiseGuide Wrap-Up

- Boys and girls grow up with different, and not necessarily equal, roles and opportunities.

- There is an inequitable distribution of education, formal and informal, for girls around the world, which materially affects their quality of life.

- The inadequate participation of women in math and science professions is directly related to their reduced opportunities in these subjects as they grow up.

R.E.A.L. Sites

This list provides a print preview of typical **coursewise** R.E.A.L. sites. (There are over 100 such sites at the **courselinks**™ site.) The danger of printing URLs is that Web sites can change overnight. As we went to press, these sites were functional using the URLs provided. If you come across one that isn't, please let us know via email to: webmaster@coursewise.com. Use your Passport to access the most current list of R.E.A.L. sites at the **courselinks**™ site.

Site name: Women's Educational Equity Act Resource Center: EQUITY ONLINE
URL: http://www.edc.org/WomensEquity/index.html
Key topics: Education, Discrimination
Why is it R.E.A.L.? The Women's Educational Equity Act is the U.S. government's primary structure for dealing with inequities in education. This site provides the most current information about government and nonprofit activities promoting gender inequity.
Activity: Read the information about Title IX; then do a survey of the resources offered to men's sports and women's sports on your own college campus or at your high school.

Site name: Bill Nye the Science Guy
URL: http://nyelabs.kcts.org
Key topics: Technology, Equity
Why is it R.E.A.L.? Bill Nye the Science Guy has developed a revolutionary program for children and science. He's almost the most popular science guy in kids' media right now.
Activity: Write a review of the success or failure of Nye's web site in encouraging gender equity for posting to a web site devoted to achieving equity for girls in education.

Site name: Gender Equity in Education
URL: http://www.cs.rice.edu/~mborrow/GenderEquity/geeqlist.html
Key topics: Discrimination
Why is it R.E.A.L.? This an active, up-to-date, comprehensive set of links for anyone interested in the issue of equity in education from many different perspectives.
Activity: Because there are so many links on this site, choose ten links, follow them, then write a brief report on the current state of affairs in education for girls based on the ten sites you have followed. Compare your results with those of others in the group who have followed different links.

Site name: Do's and Don'ts for Teachers When Teaching About Native American Peoples
URL: http://www.ableza.org/dodont.html
Key topics: Race, Discrimination, Education
Why is it R.E.A.L.? This site is a straightforward list of suggestions for helping teachers deal with prejudice and discrimination.
Activity: Using this site as a model, make a list of your own suggested do's and don'ts for teaching about women and girls.

section 5

Key Points

- Kinship groups are defined by cultures using blood kinship and legal contracts to determine moral and social obligations to the family group. The nuclear family, with father, mother, and birth children, is the traditional Western EuroAmerican family.

- Women occupy multiple positions within kinship groups. Alternative and non-nuclear groups offer different roles for women outside of those assigned to the wife and mother of the nuclear family.

- Technological changes compel cultural shifts in the roles assigned to women within kinship groups. The complications of artificial insemination, surrogate motherhood, in vitro fertilization, and the freezing of human eggs have rearranged the borders of motherhood.

- The heterosexual basis of the family is also defined by social and cultural systems.

Togetherness: Family and Community

 **WiseGuide Intro**

Just as the politics of reproductive rights have shaped contemporary discourse, so too has the cult of family values. What counts as family, how families operate, and the relative importance of family within larger cultural movements are all under scrutiny. In 1995, only 36 percent of households in the U.S. were comprised of a married couple with children (see *The State of Women in the World Atlas* 2nd ed., by Joni Seager, London: Penguin, 1997). The changing face of families has meant dramatic changes in women's lives, as well as in the constitution of the community.

The relationship between family and community is also marked by racial, class, sex, and cultural differences, as different groups define the family in distinct ways. As children grow up and as parents age, family relationships are altered. Also, new technologies transform the meaning of family and community. Women's places within these competing categories as daughters, sisters, mothers, aunts, grandmothers, friends, wives, and lovers complicate their understanding and deployment of femininity.

In "The Father Fixation," Judith Stacey responds to the backlash against single mothers in a straightforward rebuttal to groups which claim that children without fathers in the home are irreparably damaged. Mandava tells the story of resistance and reconciliation within a nuclear family, a process which has been complicated by cultural dislocation. Dorothy Allison remarks eloquently on poverty, family, and sexuality in "A Question of Class." In one of the few essays which explores the consequences of the common misapprehension of gender roles as well as family and community structures in an indigenous tribal group by outsiders, Cook-Lynn discusses the case of Marie Big Pipe. And Hartouni's essay on the case of Anna Johnson interrogates the implications of advances in reproductive technologies on the definition of family, and on the social relations in the community.

? Questions ?

Reading 15. What family structure has been identified through social science research as the most successful for the raising of children?

Reading 16. Which events have the most impact on Mandava as she moves through the stages of self-realization?

Reading 17. How is the stereotypical notion of family transformed by the "question of class"?

Reading 18. What systems does Cook-Lynn point to as complicit in the criminalization of childbearing Native American women?

Reading 19. In the final paragraph of her essay, Hartouni talks about the mapping of class, race, and gender power within the context of the cases at hand. What would that map look like in the case of Marie Big Pipe?

What family structure has been identified through social science research as the most successful for the raising of children?

The Father Fixation

Let's get real about American families

Judith Stacey

Judith Stacey is a professor of sociology and women's studies at UC-Davis. This article is adapted from her new book, In the Name of the Family: Rethinking Family Values in a Postmodern Age *(Beacon, 1996).*

As the electoral season hits full throttle, more and more voices are intoning the mantra of "family values." The Institute for American Values and its offshoot, the Council on Families in America, and other groups crusade on behalf of the supposed superiority of married-couple nuclear families, branding all other kinds of families second-rate—or worse. They are using the apparently objective language of social science to preach a sermon that we used to hear mainly in the fire-and-brimstone tones of the religious right. This quieted-down approach is having a major effect on Democratic Party and media rhetoric on family issues.

These groups pretend to speak for an overwhelming consensus of social scientists when they blame family "breakdown" —by which they mean primarily the rise of divorce and unwed parenting—for just about every social problem in the nation. David Blankenhorn, president of the Institute for American Values, for example, calls fatherlessness "the most harmful demographic trend of this generation." He writes that "it is the leading cause of declining child well-being in our society. It is also the engine driving our most urgent social problems from crime to adolescent pregnancy to child sexual abuse to domestic violence against women." The somewhat more temperate David Popenoe [see p. 68*] concedes that there are many sources of social decay but insists that "the evidence is now strong that the absence of fathers from the lives of children is one of the most important causes."

However well intentioned and appealing, most of the claims made by family values crusaders are blatantly false as well as destructive. As a sociologist, I can attest that there is absolutely no consensus among social scientists on family values, on the superior-

*Not included with this publication.

ity of the heterosexual nuclear family, or on the supposed evil effects of fatherlessness. In fact, the best research and the most careful, best-regarded researchers, among them Andrew Cherlin at Johns Hopkins University, confirm that the quality of our family relationships and resources is far more important than gender or structure. The claim that intact two-parent families are inherently superior rests exclusively on the misuse of statistics and on the most elementary social science sins—portraying correlations as though they were causes, ignoring mediating factors, and treating small, overlapping differences as gross and absolute.

Take, for example, the hysteria that the family values campaign has whipped up about the "doomsday" effects of divorce. Certainly, no sociologist—no reasonable adult I can think of— would argue that divorce is a meaningless or minor event for a family. No one among the many scholars of the family who share my views would deny that some divorces unfairly serve the inter-

UTNE Reader, Sept-Oct. 1996.

ests of one or both parents at the expense of their children. Still, the evidence resoundingly supports the idea that a high-conflict marriage injures children more than a divorce does. Instead of protecting children, the current assault on no-fault divorce endangers them by inviting more parental conflict, desertion, and fraud.

Moreover, research shows again and again that poverty and unemployment can more reliably predict who will marry, divorce, or commit or suffer domestic or social violence than can the best-tuned measure of values yet devised. A study conducted by University of California-Berkeley psychologist Ralph Catalano found, for example, that workers laid off from their jobs were six times more likely than employed workers to commit violent acts and that losing one's job was a better predictor of violence than gender, marital status, mental illness, or anything else. Those who really want to shore up marriages should fight for secure jobs and a living wage.

You don't need to be a social scientist to know that living with married biological parents offers children no magic shield against trouble. Indeed, a recent Kaiser Permanente study of youth and violence found that 68 percent of "youth highly exposed to health and safety threats" were living in two-parent households.

Poignantly, even in two-parent families, fathers were among the last people troubled teens said they would turn to for help: 44 percent said they would turn to their mothers for advice; 26 percent chose their friends; and only 10 percent picked their fathers.

Harping on the superiority of married biological parents and the evils of fatherlessness injures children and parents in a wide array of contemporary families, including the millions of children who live with gay or lesbian parents. Blankenhorn castigates lesbian couples who choose to have children for promoting "radical fatherlessness" and advocates restricting access to sperm banks and fertility services to married heterosexual couples. Popenoe claims that biological fathers make distinctive, irreplaceable contributions to their children's welfare.

Yet here the social science record is truly uniform. Nearly three decades of research finds gay and lesbian parents to be at least as successful as heterosexuals. Dozens of studies conclude that children reared by lesbian or gay parents have no greater gender or social difficulties than other children, except for the problems caused by homophobia and discrimination. Ironically, some of the worst risks these children suffer stem from our failure to legally recognize the actual two-parent

families in which many live. For example, a child whose lesbian birth mother dies often loses a second parent too, as Kristen Pearlman did in 1985 when a Florida court placed her in the custody of her grandparents rather than her surviving co-mother, Janine Ratcliffe, who had helped parent her since birth. Anyone who cares about the welfare of children should campaign to extend full marriage and custody rights to their parents rather than belittle them for lacking a father or mother.

It is time to face the irreversible historical fact that family diversity is here to stay. Of course, two good parents of whatever gender generally are better than one. But no one lives in a "general" family. Our unique, often imperfect, real families assume many shapes, sizes, and characters. Each type of family has strengths, vulnerabilities, and challenges, and each needs support and deserves respect. We can't coerce or preach people into successful marital or parenting relationships, but we can help them to succeed in the ones they form. What we need to promote instead of divisive, self-righteous family values are inclusive, democratic, and compassionate *social* values.

 Article Review Form at end of book.

Which events have the most impact on Mandava as she moves through the stages of self-realization?

Ghosts and Goddesses

Bhargavi C. Mandava

I remember walking into my dorm room at New York University on March 15, 1985. I had just been swaying to the gloomy music of Depeche Mode at the Beacon Theater. I saw the note on the floor from a roommate and even before reading it, I felt my stomach take a dive. It read, *Bhargavi, Your father is very sick. Call home.* I reached for the phone before I knew what I was doing and was met with what sounded like the cry of a wounded animal. It was my mother, and I knew before she uttered a coherent word that my father had died. She kept saying, "My life is over," in Telugu, our native tongue. I commanded her to stop talking such nonsense and assured her that I was on my way home. Everything was going to be fine. In truth, I felt the same way she did at that moment, but on instinct, I had taken over the reins my father once held so tightly. I hung up the phone and crumbled. I could never have known at the time how much my father's death would serve as a catalyst for my personal growth. My father's death accelerated my indepen-

dence as a woman, my discovery of my cultural roots and my reconnection with my mother, whom I had rejected. I guess in a way my mother was right when she said that her life was over. In a way it was, and a new life had begun for both of us.

The acrid white filled me with dizziness as I sleepwalked into the room where my father lay. I kept thinking he looked so real, so alive. He was just sleeping, wasn't he? As I walked closer, I saw his face. It was pulled taut on one side, and there was some dried blood near his lips. Quivering, I kissed my father on the cheek. There. Nothing. I kissed him some more. "Dad, I'm home now. It was wrong of me to move away from home and go to college. I knew it made you unhappy, but I did it anyway. Well, now I'm home. Okay? Dad? Dad, remember all those times you wanted me to kiss you good night and I ran away? And all those times I wouldn't sit on your lap because I felt funny? Well, here. See, I'm covering your face with kisses like I used to when I was a little girl. Why is nothing happening? You told me I was a princess, and princess kisses are magic, aren't they? Dad? Nana? I am so sorry."

The chain of events that followed was especially intense because no one wanted to talk about what he or she was feeling. My brother continued his studies in India, and I went back to NYU. My mother returned to working at the state mental hospital where she was a psychiatrist, but she resigned after a few months. My sister, unable to commute to the city because she didn't know how to drive, had to leave her job. It didn't help that my mother had inherited thousands of dollars in debts my father had racked up through his numerous failed business ventures. My sister defended my father as my mother bitterly denounced his deceptions. She had fully trusted my father and handed him all financial responsibilities. By telling my sister it was okay not to have a driver's license because he'd drive her everywhere, and by relieving my mother of such nuisances as balancing her checkbook, my father paved a path of dependence for both of them. At the end of that path, of course, was isolation.

Prior to my father's death, I had already had a taste of feeling trapped. I often found myself struggling to keep the peace between my siblings and my father, who would erupt in fits of violence. As the youngest, I was hit only twice in my life. I didn't understand why I was favored so much over my brother and sister, but I felt guilty about it. All three of us were pressured to become doctors. My brother and sister tried but failed to fulfill my parents' dream in this regard because their hearts were elsewhere. I exclaimed about my dislike of blood ever since I could talk. In the twelfth grade, when I announced I wanted to be a writer, they insisted I pursue broadcast journalism because "that's where the money is." I explored the option and decided I was much too shy for that field. Writing was what truly interested me.

My feelings of alienation were heightened by the fact that I wasn't allowed to date or even have male friends. My father made me account for all my time, including my social activities, which consisted of one weekly trip to the movies. My parents pressured my sister into an arranged marriage, which failed miserably, and talked about arranging one for me as well. Witnessing the horrible injustice of my sister's marriage in silence, I felt like an accomplice in burying my sister alive. I secretly vowed to run away if I was going to be forced into a marriage. Although at the time I had no idea what feminism encompassed, instinct prompted me to protect my rights: I was a woman, not a commodity to be bartered. I resisted the notion that female offspring were burdensome because parents had to "pay off" a groom and his family with an attractive dowry.

During high school, I saw the halls of my life lined with a lot of closed doors. By the time I decided on a college, I was lusting to break free from my isolation. Before I moved out, my sister had already filed for an annulment and my father had mellowed quite a bit—evidenced by the fact that he permitted me to go to NYU. Neither of my parents was happy that I was living in the city, but something made them respect my decision. Perhaps because of the failure of my sister's marriage, they realized that ruling with an iron fist was not working.

I was nonchalant about living on my own in the big city, which my parents dubbed a "jungle." Though I appeared to be confident and quite calm and quite calm about leaving home, inside I was anxious and frightened. But I wanted to dive into the sea of the city's vast opportunities, to make mistakes, to survive on my own. I turned up the music in my room and created worst-case scenarios: What if I wanted to date a white guy? What if I dropped out of college and was happy being manager of the local Burger King? What if I got pregnant? What if I got pregnant by a black guy? What if I wanted to have the baby? What if I wanted to have an abortion? What if I was a lesbian? Then what? I started to think about what my rights were not only as an individual, but as a woman. I started to forget about how my parents would react and started to think about how *I* would react. I was tired of adopting my parents' prejudices and judgments. Wanting to identify my struggle and fight my own battles steered me toward feminism. I was ready for another type of education.

My father took my moving out of the house pretty hard. He called me a lot and insisted I come home every weekend. I didn't mind doing so at first, but eventually the heavy loads of studying and club-hopping cut down my visits. By the winter of my first year, I had bopped down to Astor Place Haircutters and had my long hair cut into a tomboyish crop. I had never been allowed to cut my hair because long hair is very desirable in Indian culture. In my struggle to loosen the grip of a culture I could not comprehend at the time, I created a new persona. I was meeting people who knew nothing about me. I was in charge of telling my story, and I chose to forget all about my precollege life. This allowed me to distance myself from my family, its problems and my culture.

As a child, I was always embarrassed about the fact that I was Indian. I dreamed of having hair like the Breck girl—the *white* girl. Panic would flutter in my chest whenever a friend asked me over to her house, which wasn't often. I knew I'd have to reciprocate by extending an invitation to my house. In the event a friend was coming over, I would start brainwashing my mother and father into adapting their behavior for the occasion. "Please, please don't eat with your hands. And don't burp. Just say 'hello' and leave. Don't ask questions, and whatever you do, Dad, please don't walk around in your *lunghee*. It looks like a skirt." They'd always agree and nod their heads, and then something would happen. My mother would saunter into the living room wearing a sari and eating some curry with her hand or offer us her Indian version of an American food, such as curried meatballs. My friends would just stare and say something like, "Ewww! What is that?" Yes, meatballs. By then, my mother was convinced that in order to get a sufficient amount of protein in our diets, we had to start eating meat. We were doing our part to fit in to U.S. pop culture—my mom donned pantsuits, my father played the stock market and we kids became Big Mac-Coke-Twinkies junkies. This did not mean we converted to Christianity, although I will admit that, in my desperation to fit in, I wouldn't have thought it such a bad idea. Whenever my friends caught a glimpse of the clay statues of Hindu gods and goddesses sitting on the bureau in my parents' bedroom, I would pretend not to hear their questions. The fact is, I didn't fully understand myself what these bizarre-looking figurines were all about, but I was too embarrassed to admit I cared at that age.

I looked in the mirror at myself with short hair and didn't recognize the person I saw. I had begun to disappear. Without my father—the object of my defiance—my rebellion turned to confusion. Shortly after my father's death, my sister and mother both called me at college. They said that they needed me at home, that it was crucial for the family to stay together. They pleaded with me to come home. Before I had even fully processed their stunning request, I answered matter-of-factly: "No. I can't drop out of school. I'm sorry." That was the end of the conversation. From that day on, I was on my own. I knew I had to put myself through college. I was shocked at them for backing me into a wall like that, for being so selfish. I understand now that they were acting out of sheer fear. We were always taught to put familial welfare above our individual concerns. But family, which I was raised to depend on and trust, had fallen through. My father had left us all to fend for ourselves with little concern for our financial well-being. After his death, through a veneer of anger

and disappointment, I began to question the motives of all family members more carefully. This is not to say they were ill-intentioned, but each of us was playing with a different rule book. What was good for the family was not necessarily good for each of its members. After feeling guilty for so long about the unhappiness in my family, I finally refused to be suffocated under the weight of its seemingly endless catastrophes. The pinch of courage that had propelled me to leave home had grown considerably. With each passing day, I became stronger, more independent, and walked farther from home.

Healing was hindered by my hectic schedule, which I packed with classes, waitressing, campus work, studying and freelance music writing. I believed that strength meant forging ahead no matter what. I kept busy enough so I wouldn't have time to feel the pain. In a state of denial, I embarked on a rampage of drinking, shoplifting, staying out till all hours with other lost souls, listening to angry music and making myself unapproachable. This vexatious behavior stemmed from a variety of things: wanting to make the world pay for my father's death, a here-today-gone-tomorrow mindset, hypersensitivity to any inkling of racism, and my own insecurity. I was angry with my father not only for abandoning me, but also for promising me that he would always be around to take care of me. I felt cheated that he had been ripped away at such a young age—an age when he seemed to be relaxing his tyranny and allowing his benevolent side, which I had been privy to as a child, to blossom again.

Shortly after I was nabbed for shoplifting (I received only a warning), I began to realize that my anger was really self-directed.

I started to let my buzzed hair grow long again. It suddenly clicked that I had cut my hair to defy the cultural preference for long hair in India—to strip away my Indian identity—and not because I really liked the way I looked with short hair. When I arrived in the U.S. at the age of five, I almost immediately began a campaign to change my hair. I begged my mother to make my pin-straight hair curly. She reluctantly complied by slopping on the Dippity-Do. She laughed when I ended up looking like Shirley Temple with a wicked tan. Now, we laugh together at the incident. She is so happy that, at last, I no longer want to be the Breck girl.

A major impetus in my healing was the class "Hinduism, Buddhism, Taoism," in which I was enrolled at the time of my father's death. Originally, I took the class because I felt I could never honestly and properly respond when someone asked me what Hinduism is all about. Religion was never forced on me, although bits of divine mythology crept into my daily life. "Do you know why the goddesses are shown sitting on lotuses?" my mother might say. "No, Mom." "Because the lotus is a symbol of purity." I didn't understand the meanings of her stories because I had no context for them.

Seeing her children devour cheeseburgers, my mother would always demand to know, "Are you Indian or American?" None of us could ever answer. I had hidden my fear behind a veil of arrogance. Now, I wanted to know. I finally discovered that pinning down this beast of a cultural identity whirling inside of me was a key part of my struggle.

Although I was not yet openly communicating with my

mother, I started to flash back to times when she would start off her "when I was growing up" stories and I would tune her out with a quick nod. I began to realize that although we seemed worlds apart, filaments joined our warrior souls. Indian or American? I was becoming strong enough to handle the answer, and more important, to fight to hold on to and take pride in all that made me so different.

At the time of my father's death, our class was smack in the middle of the *Bhagavad-Gita* (*The Song of God* or *Celestial Song*), a Hindu scripture that addresses death, reincarnation and loyalty to family. I read and reread the small book. I cannot say I fully grasped the text at the time, but I found the answers to some of my questions. Explains the divine Sri Krishna to Arjuna, who was resisting going to war because he couldn't bear to kill family and friends in the process, "The truly wise mourn neither for the living nor for the dead. There was never a time when I did not exist, nor you, nor any of these kings. Nor is there any future where we shall cease to be. . . . That which is nonexistent can never come into being, and that which is, can never cease to be." The *Bhagavad-Gita* soothed me with its tranquil simplicity. I finally managed to smile, and by the end of that year I had begun on a labyrinthine path to solace.

Minoring in religion and delving into religious philosophy, I started to take pride in my Indian heritage during my final years in college. However, I never truly embraced the idea of being Hindu, perhaps because I also found truth in Buddhism, Zen Buddhism, mysticism and Taoism. Rather than labeling this a state of confusion, I now choose to see it as being in a state of

quest. In order to understand the soul, I had to locate it first, and mine was floating like a broken jigsaw puzzle in an ocean. I still hadn't determined what being an Indian American woman was all about. I was disjointed, loose, homeless. At the time, I couldn't even entertain the thought of worship, because it involved a degree of submission. After my father's death, I had just gotten a grasp of my life—or so I thought—and started seeing myself as an individual. I was wary of prematurely melting into the masses.

It wasn't until I journeyed back to India with my mother in 1991 that I really began to understand who I was and whence I sprang, culturally and religiously. Gradually, our relationship had become more fluid and natural. By the time I graduated we had learned to talk as peers—as women with common struggles. We shared stories about our disappointments, our victories and our unfulfilled dreams. It was the first time since elementary school that I showed my mother my writing. This trip, which was my mother's idea, revealed to me the palette of colors with which I am painting.

Traveling all over India, I was bombarded with images of goddesses, the stomach-turning plight of the poor, and the rich mythology of my people. I devoured it all ravenously, and my mother kept my plate piled high. I stared into the eyes of Parvati, the fierce goddess of courage after whom I was named, and felt an inextinguishable connection. Who was this woman who through numerous incarnations slayed demon after demon? Who was this woman who was as ravishing and gentle as she was brutal? "Parvati is the goddess of courage, creation and destruction; she is

whom I named you after," explained my mother for the nth time. But this time it was different. This time I was really listening.

As I stretched across the bed in a dank hotel room in Nasik, where my mother had taken me to be blessed by the spirit of the saint Shri Sai Baba of Shirdi, I remembered my first battle. Two sixth-graders pushed me down, snatched my Scotch-plaid lunch pail and books and threw them all over the street. Sobbing, I met my mother after a few blocks. She said she had gotten caught up watching *General Hospital* and had practically run to the school when she noticed what time it was. After a sweet treat, I hid any outward signs of injury. Inwardly, I felt that I had been attacked because I was dark and ugly. I guess my mother knew the effects such an incident could have on a child; she refused to keep quiet. The next day, she asked me to point out the two boys who had attacked me. I did, and she approached them. They ran in different directions. My mother ran after one, part of her sari trailing behind her in the wind, and caught him by the collar. She again asked me if this was one of the bullies. I nodded. Finger wagging in his face, she said with utter lucidity, "If you touch my daughter again, I'll kill you." I knew my mother wasn't capable of actually killing anyone, but at that moment, even I believed her. So much for Indian passivity. I was so proud to be her daughter. That day, my mother was as cool as Bugs Bunny (whom I idolized and mimicked as a child). Today, I know she was much cooler than that cartoon rabbit. She was a woman warrior in the image of Parvati. She was my defender and my life force. In those ten seconds, she gave me a taste of courage.

She showed me what a woman was capable of doing—standing up for herself and for what she believed to be just. Remembering this, I began to understand my connection to Parvati and to my mother.

I gazed across the hotel room at my mother, who was sleeping peacefully. Who was this woman? What made her wait an entire day in the rain to be blessed by a dead saint? What made her smile so broadly when our turn had finally arrived and we were shuffled past the white marble statue of Sai Baba of Shirdi? A disciple took the blanket my mother held out and draped it around Sai Baba's shoulders. He handed back the blanket and took our offering of flowers. And we were on our way. Outside, my mother gave me the blanket almost ecstatically and told me to take care of it. I promised her I would. Watching her, I realized a little more clearly what I had been striving for these past few years. I wanted something to believe in. I wanted the faith my mother had in God, in doing good deeds, and most important, the ability to believe in herself and her independence. I had been rejecting her because I perceived her as weak, helpless and trapped. On the contrary, my mother is a woman who made many sacrifices in order to become a doctor. She encountered discrimination and sexism in her predominantly male field. Some of her superiors gave her an especially heavy workload so she could "prove" her abilities. My mother held steadfastly to her dreams.

I started asking her a lot of questions about her childhood, and what I learned amazed me. My mother was a fiercely independent woman who got married to my father because of duty, not because she was spineless. She

was sad to leave her successful medical practice and start from scratch in America. She cried when she had to temporarily leave behind my brother and sister, eleven and twelve. Deep down in her soul, she knew the idea that there was something wrong with an unmarried woman was false. She was never thrilled with the idea of getting married herself because she felt it would interfere with her career plans. I believe the seeds of feminism were sown by her mother, as my mother was taught to persevere, excel, respect herself and demand equality not only between nationalities but also between the sexes. So, my mother's decision to honor some of her parents' wishes was a sign not of weakness, but of incredible courage and strength. She was going to stand by her husband and children even if that meant leaving her own dreams unfulfilled.

Almost seven years after my father died, I realized how much my mother and I were running from similar cultural expectations. We learned not to blame ourselves and somehow found our own answers. My mother realized that old beliefs had to change with the times after my sister's disastrous arranged marriage. Naturally, it is still somewhat difficult for her to accept certain things, such as the fact that at the age of twenty-eight, I'm still not married. She is all too familiar with the echoes of lost dreams, and she encourages me to pursue my hopes. I didn't want to be a doctor, and I wasn't going to major in broadcast journalism because "that's where the money is." I just wanted to be a writer. She grew to tolerate my decision because she recognized the spark in my eyes. It's the same spark that was in her eyes when as an adolescent she announced

that she wanted to be an artist. Her father growled, and she soon set her sights on medicine, an equally unusual career choice for a woman in her day. She knows now that my career choice is my decision. Whom my sister married should have been solely her decision. And it should have been my mother's decision when she married my father back in 1949, a year after India gained its independence.

My mother doesn't blame her parents. She knows that her individual strength was never discouraged, but rather misdirected. Her mother and father were devout Gandhians and fought to free the Indian people from British subjugation. She beams when she tells how her mother was pregnant with her when she was incarcerated for a peaceful protest against British rule. She stands proudly next to her mother, the warrior. And I stand proudly next to my mother, the warrior. Our mutual enemies of sexism and racism may have been different in appearance, but our sights were always fixed on freedom.

All along, I think my mother was unknowingly preparing me to fight for, explore and relish the freedoms that she was denied as a young woman who was quite ahead of her time. My mother raised me as her mother raised her—without a label for the progressive philosophy she lived. I have the advantage of viewing a "map" of feminism revealing where women have been, how far we have come and where we are going. I can link arms with other women and join feminist organizations that were not available to my mother. When my rights are violated, I can seek the support of sisters who will understand and give me strength when I feel weak. I have plenty of women to lean on.

Four years ago I became a vegetarian again. I am constantly pestering my mother for recipes of my favorite Indian dishes. Eating the food of my native land sits well with me. My body seems to digest more efficiently, and I have more energy. Interwoven with the recipes, my mother occasionally throws in a myth describing a battle fought by one of the Hindu goddesses. I find these goddesses—multihanded warriors who are loving, beautiful, revered and feared—inspirational. I marvel at the thought that at one time women embodied such power. I know that our fight is perpetual and that like the demons in Indian mythology, our oppressors are serpentine, slippery, faceless. Preparation for the battle is as crucial as the battle itself. There is no doubt in my mind that my mother prepared me well. Following her example, I could not be anything but a feminist, which, to me, means that I must do everything in my power to work with other women to abolish gender inequality.

My mother has dealt with her own conflicts, especially balancing her need for solitude with raising a family. A day before my father died, she expressed to him her desire to once again be alone as she had been before they married. She craved her freedom. As painful as it was for her to say and for him to hear, she stayed true to herself. Maybe it was the permission my father was waiting to hear to release him from this life. My mother is alone now, and she is rediscovering the fiery spirit that had been caged for decades—the goddess that had been silenced by a ghost. The woman who wanted to paint is finally painting. She is free to travel and garden. She is free to live. I thank her for kindling my spirit to seek out those freedoms.

My mother and I silently acknowledge that my father's death marked the beginning of our lives independent of family. As Hinduism asserts, death is not an ending, but a beginning. Currently, I am living the farthest I have ever lived from my mother, yet I feel the strongest, closest bond with her. Eager to live and learn, we are teaching each other about our individual cultures and perspectives. We don't always agree, but we listen. Oddly enough, the cultural void that blew us apart is the same entity that reunited us. Every time I hear another story, I understand a little more about the choices she made. Increasingly, I see that we are much more alike than different. As a surgeon who delivered babies, my mother spent much of her time handing out birth control and pregnancy prevention information to women in poverty-stricken areas of India. She had a thirst to educate other women, as I do. When I moved to Los Angeles, I became a counselor for a rape and battering hotline run by the L.A. Commission on Assaults Against Women. My mother and I discussed how important it is to answer the desire to connect with our sisters—to take action, participate and educate. I know now that before we are Indian, we are women—we are mother and daughter. That is our paramount bond, and all else strengthens that union. Finally, I can say that I am proud to be a woman, a warrior, myself.

Mandava, Bhargavi C. *Listen Up: Voices from the Next Feminist Generation.* Ed. Barbara Findlen. Seattle: Seal Press, 1995.

 Article Review Form at end of book.

How is the stereotypical notion of family transformed by the "question of class"?

A Question of Class

Dorothy Allison

The first time I heard, "They're different than us, don't value human life the way we do," I was in high school in Central Florida. The man speaking was an army recruiter talking to a bunch of boys, telling them what the army was really like, what they could expect overseas. A cold angry feeling swept over me. I had heard the work *they* pronounced in that same callous tone before. *They*, those people over there, those people who are not us, they die so easily, kill each other so casually. They are different. *We*, I thought. *Me*.

When I was six or eight back in Greenville, South Carolina, I had heard that same matter-of-fact tone of dismissal applied to me. "Don't you play with her. I don't want you talking to them." Me and my family, we had always been *they*. Who am I? I wondered, listening to that recruiter. Who are my people? We die so easily, disappear so completely—we/they, the poor and the queer. I pressed my bony white trash fists to my stubborn lesbian mouth. The rage was

a good feeling, stronger and purer than the shame that followed it, the fear and the sudden urge to run and hide, to deny, to pretend I did not know who I was and what the world would do to me.

My people were not remarkable. We were ordinary, but even so we were mythical. We were the *they* everyone talks about—the ungrateful poor. I grew up trying to run away from the fate that destroyed so many of the people I loved, and having learned the habit of hiding, I found I had also learned to hide from myself. I did not know who I was, only that I did not want to be *they*, the ones who are destroyed or dismissed to make the "real" people, the important people, feel safer. By the time I understood that I was queer, that habit of hiding was deeply set in me, so deeply that it was not a choice but an instinct. Hide, hide to survive, I thought, knowing that if I told the truth about my life, my family, my sexual desire, my history, I would move over into that unknown territory, the land of they, would never have the chance to name my own life, to understand it or claim it.

Why are you so afraid? my lovers and friends have asked me the many times I have suddenly seemed a stranger, someone who would not speak to them, would not do the things they believed I should do, simple things like applying for a job, or a grant, or some award they were sure I could acquire easily. Entitlement, I have told them, is a matter of feeling like we rather than they. You think you have a right to things, a place in the world, and it is so intrinsically a part of you that you cannot imagine people like me, people who seem to live in your world, who don't have it. I have explained what I know over and over, in every way I can, but I have never been able to make clear the degree of my fear, the extent to which I feel myself denied: not only that I am queer in a world that hates queers, but that I was born poor into a world that despises the poor. The need to make my world believable to people who have never experienced it is part of why I write fiction. I know that some things must be felt to be understood, that despair, for example, can never be adequately analyzed; it must be lived.

But if I can write a story that so draws the reader in that she imagines herself like my characters, feels their sense of fear and uncertainty, their hopes and terrors, then I have come closer to knowing myself as real, important as the very people I have always watched with awe.

I have known I was a lesbian since I was a teenager, and I have spent a good twenty years making peace with the effects of incest and physical abuse. But what may be the central fact of my life is that I was born in 1949 in Greenville, South Carolina, the bastard daughter of a white woman from a desperately poor family, a girl who had left the seventh grade the year before, worked as a waitress, and was just a month past fifteen when she had me. That fact, the inescapable impact of being born in a condition of poverty that this society finds shameful, contemptible, and somehow deserved, has had dominion over me to such an extent that I have spent my life trying to overcome or deny it. I have learned with great difficulty that the vast majority of people believe that poverty is a voluntary condition.

I have loved my family so stubbornly that every impulse to hold them in contempt has sparked in me a countersurge of pride—complicated and undercut by an urge to fit us into the acceptable myths and theories of both mainstream society and a lesbian-feminist reinterpretation. The choice becomes Steven Spielberg movies or Erskine Caldwell novels, the one valorizing and the other caricaturing, or the patriarchy as villain, trivializing the choices the men and women of my family have made. I have had to fight broad generalizations from every theoretical viewpoint.

Traditional feminist theory has had a limited understanding of class differences and of how sexuality and self are shaped by both desire and denial. The ideology implies that we are all sisters who should only turn our anger and suspicion on the world outside the lesbian community. It is easy to say that the patriarchy did it, that poverty and social contempt are products of the world of the fathers, and often I felt a need to collapse my sexual history into what I was willing to share of my class background, to pretend that my life both as a lesbian and as a working-class escapee was constructed by the patriarchy. Or conversely, to ignore how much my life was shaped by growing up poor and talk only about what incest did to my identity as a woman and as a lesbian. The difficulty is that I can't ascribe everything that has been problematic about my life simply and easily to the patriarchy, or to incest, or even to the invisible and much-denied class structure of our society.

In my lesbian-feminist collective we had long conversations about the mind/body split, the way we compartmentalize our lives to survive. For years I thought that that concept referred to the way I had separated my activist life from the passionate secret life in which I acted on my sexual desires. I was convinced that the fracture was fairly simple, that it would be healed when there was time and clarity to do so—at about the same point when I might begin to understand sex. I never imagined that it was not a split but a splintering, and I passed whole portions of my life—days, months, years—in pure directed progress, getting up every morning and setting to work, working so hard and so

continually that I avoided examining in any way what I knew about my life. Busywork became a trance state. I ignored who I really was and how I became that person, continued in that daily progress, became an automaton who was what she did.

I tried to become one with the lesbian-feminist community so as to feel real and valuable. I did not know that I was hiding, blending in for safety just as I had done in high school, in college. I did not recognize the impulse to forget. I believed that all those things I did not talk about, or even let myself think too much about, were not important, that none of them defined me. I had constructed a life, an identity in which I took pride, an alternative lesbian family in which I felt safe, and I did not realize that the fundamental me had almost disappeared.

It is surprising how easy it was to live that life. Everyone and everything cooperated with the process. Everything in our culture—books, television, movies, school, fashion—is presented as if it is being seen by one pair of eyes, shaped by one set of hands, heard by one pair of ears. Even if you know you are not part of that imaginary creature—if you like country music not symphonies, read books cynically, listen to the news unbelievingly, are lesbian not heterosexual, and surround yourself with your own small deviant community—you are still shaped by that hegemony, or your resistance to it. The only way I found to resist that homogenized view of the world was to make myself part of something larger than myself. As a feminist and a radical lesbian organizer, and later as a sex radical (which eventually became the term, along with pro-sex feminist, for those who were not anti-pornography but anti-censorship, those of us arguing for sexual diversity), the need to belong, to feel safe, was just as important for me as for any heterosexual, nonpolitical citizen, and sometimes even more important because the rest of my life was so embattled.

The first time I read the Jewish lesbian Irena Klepfisz's poems,* I experienced a frisson of recognition. It was not that my people had been "burned off the map" or murdered as hers had. No, we had been encouraged to destroy ourselves, made invisible because we did not fit the myths of the noble poor generated by the middle class. Even now, past forty and stubbornly proud of my family, I feel the draw of that mythology, that romanticized, edited version of the poor. I find myself looking back and wondering what was real, what was true. Within my family, so much was lied about, joked about, denied, or told with deliberate indirection, an undercurrent of humiliation or a brief pursed grimace that belied everything that had been said. What was real? The poverty depicted in books and movies was romantic, a backdrop for the story of how it was escaped.

The poverty portrayed by left-wing intellectuals was just as romantic, a platform for assailing the upper and middle classes, and from their perspective, the working-class hero was invariably male, righteously indignant, and inhumanly noble. The reality of self-hatred and violence was either absent or caricatured. The poverty I knew was dreary, deadening, shameful, the women powerful in ways not generally seen as heroic by the world outside the family.

*A Few Words in the Mother Tongue: Poems, Selected and New (Eighth Mountain Press: Portland, Oregon, 1990)

My family's lives were not on television, not in books, not even comic books. There was a myth of the poor in this country, but it did not include us, no matter how hard I tried to squeeze us in. There was an idea of the good poor—hard-working, ragged but clean, and intrinsically honorable. I understood that we were the bad poor: men who drank and couldn't keep a job; women, invariably pregnant before marriage, who quickly became worn, fat, and old from working too many hours and bearing too many children; and children with runny noses, watery eyes, and the wrong attitudes. My cousins quit school, stole cars, used drugs, and took dead-end jobs pumping gas or waiting tables. We were not noble, not grateful, not even hopeful. We knew ourselves despised. My family was ashamed of being poor, of feeling hopeless. What was there to work for, to save money for, to fight for or struggle against? We had generations before us to teach us that nothing ever changed, and that those who did try to escape failed.

My mama had eleven brothers and sisters, of whom I can name only six. No one is left alive to tell me the names of the others. It was my grandmother who told me about my real daddy, a shiftless pretty man who was supposed to have married, had six children, and sold cut-rate life insurance to poor Black people. My mama married when I was a year old, but her husband died just after my little sister was born a year later.

When I was five, Mama married the man she lived with until she died. Within the first year of their marriage Mama miscarried, and while we waited out in the hospital parking lot, my stepfather

molested me for the first time, something he continued to do until I was past thirteen. When I was eight or so, Mama took us away to a motel after my stepfather beat me so badly it caused a family scandal, but we returned after two weeks. Mama told me that she really had no choice: she could not support us alone. When I was eleven I told one of my cousins that my stepfather was molesting me. Mama packed up my sisters and me and took us away for a few days, but again, my stepfather swore he would stop, and again we went back after a few weeks. I stopped talking for a while, and I have only vague memories of the next two years.

My stepfather worked as a route salesman, my mama as a waitress, laundry worker, cook, or fruit packer. I could never understand, since they both worked so hard and such long hours, how we never had enough money, but it was also true of my mama's brothers and sisters who worked hard in the mills or the furnace industry. In fact, my parents did better than anyone else in the family. But eventually my stepfather was fired and we hit bottom—nightmarish months of marshals at the door, repossessed furniture, and rubber checks. My parents worked out a scheme so that it appeared my stepfather had abandoned us, but instead he went down to Florida, got a new job, and rented us a house. He returned with a U-Haul trailer in the dead of night, packed us up, and moved us south.

The night we left South Carolina for Florida, my mama leaned over the backseat of her old Pontiac and promised us girls, "It'll be better there." I don't know if we believed her, but I remember crossing Georgia in the early morning, watching the red clay hills and swaying grey blankets of moss recede through the back window. I kept looking at the trailer behind us, ridiculously small to contain everything we owned. Mama had packed nothing that wasn't fully paid off, which meant she had only two things of worth: her washing and sewing machines, both of them tied securely to the trailer walls. Throughout the trip I fantasized an accident that would burst that trailer, scattering old clothes and cracked dishes on the tarmac.

I was only thirteen. I wanted us to start over completely, to begin again as new people with nothing of the past left over. I wanted to run away from who we had been seen to be, who we had been. That desire is one I have seen in other members of my family. It is the first thing I think of when trouble comes—the geographic solution. Change your name, leave town, disappear, make yourself over. What hides behind that impulse is the conviction that the life you have lived, the person you are, is valueless, better off abandoned, that running away is easier than trying to change things, that change itself is not possible. Sometimes I think it is this conviction—more seductive than alcohol or violence, more subtle than sexual hatred or gender injustice—that has dominated my life and made real change so painful and difficult.

Moving to Central Florida did not fix our lives. It did not stop my stepfather's violence, heal my shame, or make my mother happy. Once there, our lives became controlled by my mother's illness and medical bills. She had a hysterectomy when I was about eight and endured a series of hospitalizations for ulcers and a chronic back problem. Through most of my adolescence

she superstitiously refused to allow anyone to mention the word *cancer*. When she was not sick, Mama and my stepfather went on working, struggling to pay off what seemed an insurmountable load of debts.

By the time I was fourteen, my sisters and I had found ways to discourage most of our stepfather's sexual advances. We were not close, but we united against him. Our efforts were helped along when he was referred to a psychotherapist after he lost his temper at work, and was prescribed drugs that made him sullen but less violent. We were growing up quickly, my sisters moving toward dropping out of school while I got good grades and took every scholarship exam I could find. I was the first person in my family to graduate from high school, and the fact that I went on to college was nothing short of astonishing.

We all imagine our lives are normal, and I did not know my life was not everyone's. It was in Central Florida that I began to realize just how different we were. The people we met there had not been shaped by the rigid class structure that dominated the South Carolina Piedmont. The first time I looked around my junior high classroom and realized I did not know who those people were—not only as individuals but as categories, who their people were and how they saw themselves—I also realized that they did not know me. In Greenville, everyone knew my family, knew we were trash, and that meant we were supposed to be poor, supposed to have grim low-paid jobs, have babies in our teens, and never finish school. But Central Florida in the 1960s was full of runaways and immigrants, and our mostly white working-class

suburban school sorted us out not by income and family background but by intelligence and aptitude tests. Suddenly I was boosted into the college-bound track, and while there was plenty of contempt for my inept social skills, pitiful wardrobe, and slow drawling accent, there was also something I had never experienced before: a protective anonymity, and a kind of grudging respect and curiosity about who I might become. Because they did not see poverty and hopelessness as a foregone conclusion for my life, I could begin to imagine other futures for myself.

In that new country, we were unknown. The myth of the poor settled over us and glamorized us. I saw it in the eyes of my teachers, the Lion's Club representative who paid for my new glasses, and the lady from the Junior League who told me about the scholarship I had won. Better, far better, to be one of the mythical poor than to be part of the *they* I had known before. I also experienced a new level of fear, a fear of losing what had never before been imaginable. Don't let me lose this chance, I prayed, and lived in terror that I might suddenly be seen again as what I knew myself to be.

As an adolescent I thought that my family's escape from South Carolina played like a bad movie. We fled the way runaway serfs might have done, with the sheriff who would have arrested my stepfather the imagined border guard. I am certain that if we had remained in South Carolina, I would have been trapped by my family's heritage of poverty, jail, and illegitimate children—that even being smart, stubborn, and a lesbian would have made no difference.

My grandmother died when I was twenty, and after Mama

went home for the funeral, I had a series of dreams in which we still lived up in Greenville, just down the road from where Granny died. In the dreams I had two children and only one eye, lived in a trailer, and worked at the textile mill. Most of my time was taken up with deciding when I would finally kill my children and myself. The dreams were so vivid, I became convinced they were about the life I was meant to have had, and I began to work even harder to put as much distance as I could between my family and me. I copied the dress, mannerisms, attitudes, and ambitions of the girls I met in college, changing or hiding my own tastes, interests, and desires. I kept my lesbianism a secret, forming a relationship with an effeminate male friend that served to shelter and disguise us both. I explained to friends that I went home so rarely because my stepfather and I fought too much for me to be comfortable in his house. But that was only part of the reason I avoided home, the easiest reason. The truth was that I feared the person I might become in my mama's house, the woman of my dreams—hateful, violent, and hopeless.

It is hard to explain how deliberately and thoroughly I ran away from my own life. I did not forget where I came from, but I gritted my teeth and hid it. When I could not get enough scholarship money to pay for graduate school, I spent a year of rage working as a salad girl, substitute teacher, and maid. I finally managed to find a job by agreeing to take any city assignment where the Social Security Administration needed a clerk. Once I had a job and my own place far away from anyone in my family, I became sexually and politically active, joining the Women's Center sup-

port staff and falling in love with a series of middle-class women who thought my accent and stories thoroughly charming. The stories I told about my family, about South Carolina, about being poor itself, were all lies, carefully edited to seem droll or funny. I knew damn well that no one would want to hear the truth about poverty, the hopelessness and fear, the feeling that nothing I did would ever make any difference and the raging resentment that burned beneath my jokes. Even when my lovers and I formed an alternative lesbian family, sharing what we could of our resources, I kept the truth about my background and who I knew myself to be a carefully obscured mystery. I worked as hard as I could to make myself a new person, an emotionally healthy radical lesbian activist, and I believed completely that by remaking myself I was helping to remake the world.

For a decade, I did not go home for more than a few days at a time.

When in the 1980s I ran into the concept of feminist sexuality, I genuinely did not know what it meant. Though I was, and am, a feminist, and committed to claiming the right to act on my sexual desires without tailoring my lust to a sex-fearing society, demands that I explain or justify my sexual fantasies have left me at a loss. How does anyone explain sexual need?

The Sex Wars are over, I've been told, and it always makes me want to ask who won. But my sense of humor may be a little obscure to women who have never felt threatened by the way most lesbians use and mean the words *pervert* and *queer*. I use the word queer to mean more than lesbian. Since I first used it in 1980 I have

always meant it to imply that I am not only a lesbian but a transgressive lesbian—femme, masochistic, as sexually aggressive as the women I seek out, and as pornographic in my imagination and sexual activities as the heterosexual hegemony has ever believed.

My aunt Dot used to joke, "There are two or three things I know for sure, but never the same things and I'm never as sure as I'd like." What I know for sure is that class, gender, sexual preference, and prejudice—racial, ethnic, and religious—form an intricate lattice that restricts and shapes our lives, and that resistance to hatred is not a simple act. Claiming your identity in the cauldron of hatred and resistance to hatred is infinitely complicated, and worse, almost unexplainable.

I know that I have been hated as a lesbian both by "society" and by the intimate world of my extended family, but I have also been hated or held in contempt (which is in some ways more debilitating and slippery than hatred) by lesbians for behavior and sexual practices shaped in large part by class. My sexual identity is intimately constructed by my class and regional background, and much of the hatred directed at my sexual preferences is class hatred—however much people, feminists in particular, like to pretend this is not a factor. The kind of woman I am attracted to is invariably the kind of woman who embarrasses respectably middle-class, politically aware lesbian feminists. My sexual ideal is butch, exhibitionistic, physically aggressive, smarter than she wants you to know, and proud of being called a pervert. Most often she is working class, with an aura of danger and an ironic sense of humor. There is a lot of contemporary lip service paid to sexual tolerance, but the fact that my sexuality is constructed within, and by, a butch/femme and leather fetishism is widely viewed with distaste or outright hatred.

For most of my life I have been presumed to be misguided, damaged by incest and childhood physical abuse, or deliberately indulging in hateful and retrograde sexual practices out of a selfish concentration on my own sexual satisfaction. I have been expected to abandon my desires, to become the normalized woman who flirts with fetishization, who plays with gender roles and treats the historical categories of deviant desire with humor or gentle contempt but never takes any of it so seriously as to claim a sexual identity based on these categories. It was hard enough for me to shake off demands when they were made by straight society. It was appalling when I found the same demands made by other lesbians.

One of the strengths I derive from my class background is that I am accustomed to contempt. I know that I have no chance of becoming what my detractors expect of me, and I believe that even the attempt to please them will only further engage their contempt, and my own self-contempt as well. Nonetheless, the relationship between the life I have lived and the way that life is seen by strangers has constantly invited a kind of self-mythologizing fantasy. It has always been tempting for me to play off of the stereotypes and misconceptions of mainstream culture, rather than describe a difficult and sometimes painful reality.

I am trying to understand how we internalize the myths of our society even as we resist them. I have felt a powerful temptation to write about my family as a kind of morality tale, with us as the heroes and middle and upper classes as the villains. It would be within the romantic myth, for example, to pretend that we were the kind of noble Southern whites portrayed in the movies, mill workers for generations until driven out by alcoholism and a family propensity for rebellion and union talk. But that would be a lie. The truth is that no one in my family ever joined a union.

Taken to its limits, the myth of the poor would make my family over into union organizers or people broken by the failure of the unions. As far as my family was concerned union organizers, like preachers, were of a different class, suspect and hated however much they might be admired for what they were supposed to be trying to achieve. Nominally Southern Baptist, no one in my family actually paid much attention to preachers, and only little children went to Sunday school. Serious belief in anything—any political ideology, any religious system, or any theory of life's meaning and purpose—was seen as unrealistic. It was an attitude that bothered me a lot when I started reading the socially conscious novels I found in the paperback racks when I was eleven or so. I particularly loved Sinclair Lewis's novels and wanted to imagine my own family as part of the working man's struggle.

"We were not joiners," my aunt Dot told me with a grin when I asked her about the union. My cousin Butch laughed at that, told me the union charged dues, and said, "Hell, we can't even be persuaded to toss money in the collection plate. An't gonna give it to no union man." It shamed me that the only thing my family wholeheartedly believed in was luck and the waywardness of fate. They held the dogged conviction that the admirable and wise thing to do was keep a sense of humor, never whine or cower, and trust that luck might someday turn as good as it had been bad—and with just as much reason. Becoming a political activist with an almost religious fervor was the thing I did that most outraged my family and the Southern working-class community they were part of.

Similarly, it was not my sexuality, my lesbianism, that my family saw as most rebellious; for most of my life, no one but my mama took my sexual preference very seriously. It was the way I thought about work, ambition, and self-respect. They were waitresses, laundry workers, counter girls. I was the one who went to work as a maid, something I never told any of them. They would have been angry if they had known. Work was just work for them, necessary. You did what you had to do to survive. They did not so much believe in taking pride in doing your job as in stubbornly enduring hard work and hard times. At the same time, they held that there were some forms of work, including maid's work, that were only for Black people, not white, and while I did not share that belief, I knew how intrinsic it was to the way my family saw the world. Sometimes I felt as if I straddled cultures and belonged on neither side. I would grind my teeth at what I knew was my family's unquestioning racism while continuing to respect their pragmatic endurance. But more and more as I grew older, what I felt was a deep estrangement from their view of the world, and gradually a sense of shame that would have been completely incomprehensible to them.

"Long as there's lunch counters, you can always find work," I was told by my mother and my aunts. Then they'd add, "I can get me a little extra with a smile." It was obvious there was supposed to be nothing shameful about it, that needy smile across a lunch counter, that rueful grin when you didn't have rent, or the half-provocative, half-pleading way my mama could cajole the man at the store to give her a little credit. But I hated it, hated the need for it and the shame that would follow every time I did it myself. It was begging, as far as I was concerned, a quasi-prostitution that I despised even while I continued to rely on it. After all, I needed the money.

"Just use that smile," my girl cousins used to joke, and I hated what I knew they meant. After college, when I began to support myself and study feminist theory, I became more contemptuous rather than more understanding of the women in my family. I told myself that prostitution is a skilled profession and my cousins were never more than amateurs. There was a certain truth in this, though like all cruel judgments rendered from the outside, it ignored the conditions that made it true. The women in my family, my mother included, had sugar daddies, not johns, men who slipped them money because they needed it so badly. From their point of view they were nice to those men because the men were nice to them, and it was never so direct or crass an arrangement that they would set a price on their favors. Nor would they have described what they did as prostitution. Nothing made them angrier than the suggestion that the men who helped them out did it just for their favors. They worked for a living, they swore, but this was different.

I always wondered if my mother hated her sugar daddy, or if not him then her need for what he offered her, but it did not seem to me in memory that she had. He was an old man, half-crippled, hesitant and needy, and he treated my mama with enormous consideration and, yes, respect. The relationship between them was painful, and since she and my stepfather could not earn enough to support the family, Mama could not refuse her sugar daddy's money. At the same time the man made no assumptions about that money buying anything Mama was not already offering. The truth was, I think, that she genuinely liked him, and only partly because he treated her so well.

Even now, I am not sure whether there was a sexual exchange between them. Mama was a pretty woman, and she was kind to him, a kindness he obviously did not get from anyone else in his life. Moreover, he took extreme care not to cause her any problems with my stepfather. As a teenager, with a teenager's contempt for moral failings and sexual complexity of any kind, I had been convinced that Mama's relationship with that old man was contemptible. Also, that I would never do such a thing. But the first time a lover of mine gave me money and I took it, everything in my head shifted. The amount was not much to her, but it was a lot to me and I needed it. While I could not refuse it, I hated myself for taking it and I hated her for giving it. Worse, she had much less grace about my need than my mama's sugar daddy had displayed toward her. All that bitter contempt I felt for my needy cousins and aunts raged through me and burned out the love. I ended the relationship quickly, unable to forgive myself for selling what I believed should only be offered freely—not sex but love itself.

When the women in my family talked about how hard they worked, the men would spit to the side and shake their heads. Men took real jobs—harsh, dangerous, physically daunting work. They went to jail, not just the cold-eyed, careless boys who scared me with their brutal hands, but their gentler, softer brothers. It was another family thing, what people expected of my mama's people, mine. "His daddy's that one was sent off to jail in Georgia, and his uncle's another. Like as not, he's just the same," you'd hear people say of boys so young they still had their milk teeth. We were always driving down to the county farm to see somebody, some uncle, cousin, or nameless male relation. Shaven-headed, sullen, and stunned, they wept on Mama's shoulder or begged my aunts to help. "I didn't do nothing, Mama," they'd say, and it might have been true, but if even we didn't believe them, who would? No one told the truth, not even about how their lives were destroyed.

One of my favorite cousins went to jail when I was eight years old, for breaking into pay phones with another boy. The other boy was returned to the custody of his parents. My cousin was sent to the boys' facility at the county farm. After three months, my mama took us down there to visit, carrying a big basket of fried chicken, cold cornbread, and potato salad. Along with a hundred others we sat out on the lawn with my cousin and watched him eat like he hadn't had a full meal in the whole three months. I stared at his near-bald head and his ears marked with fine blue scars from the carelessly handled razor. People were laughing, music was playing, and a tall, lazy, uniformed man walked past us chewing on toothpicks and watching us all closely. My cousin kept his head down, his face hard with hatred, only looking back at the guard when he turned away.

"Sons-a-bitches," he whispered, and my mama shushed him. We all sat still when the guard turned back to us. There was a long moment of quiet, and then that man let his face relax into a big wide grin.

"Uh-huh," he said. That was all he said. Then he turned and walked away. None of us spoke. None of us ate. He went back inside soon after, and we left. When we got back to the car, my mama sat there for a while crying quietly. The next week my cousin was reported for fighting and had his stay extended by six months.

My cousin was fifteen. He never went back to school, and after jail he couldn't join the army. When he finally did come home we never talked, never had to. I knew without asking that the guard had had his little revenge, knew too that my cousin would break into another phone booth as soon as he could, but do it sober and not get caught. I knew without asking the source of his rage, the way he felt about clean, well-dressed, contemptuous people who looked at him like his life wasn't as important as a dog's. I knew because I felt it too. That guard had looked at me and Mama with the same expression he used on my cousin. We were trash. We were the ones they built the county farm to house and break. The boy who was sent home was the son of a deacon in the church, the man who managed the hardware store.

As much as I hated that man, and his boy, there was a way in which I also hated my cousin. He should have known better, I told myself, should have known the risk he ran. He should have been more careful. As I grew older and started living on my own, it was a litany I used against myself even more angrily than I used it against my cousin. I knew who I was, knew that the most important thing I had to do was protect myself and hide my despised identity, blend into the myth of both the good poor and the reasonable lesbian. When I became a feminist activist, that litany went on reverberating in my head, but by then it had become a groundnote, something so deep and omnipresent I no longer heard it, even when everything I did was set to its cadence.

By 1975 I was earning a meager living as a photographer's assistant in Tallahassee, Florida. But the real work of my life was my lesbian-feminist activism, the work I did with the local women's center and the committee to found a women's studies program at Florida State University. Part of my role, as I saw it, was to be a kind of evangelical lesbian feminist, and to help develop a political analysis of this woman-hating society. I did not talk about class, except to give lip service to how we all needed to think about it, the same way I thought we all needed to think about racism. I was a determined person, living in a lesbian collective—all of us young and white and serious—studying each new book that purported to address feminist issues, driven by what I saw as a need to revolutionize the world.

Years later it's difficult to convey just how reasonable my life seemed to me at that time. I was not flippant, not consciously condescending, not casual about how tough a struggle remaking social relations would be, but like so many women of my generation, I believed absolutely that I could make a difference with my life, and I was willing to give my life for the chance to make that difference. I expected hard times, long slow periods of self-sacrifice and grinding work, expected to be hated and attacked in public, to have to set aside personal desire, lovers, and family in order to be part of something greater and more important than my individual concerns. At the same time, I was working ferociously to take my desires, my sexuality, my needs as a woman and a lesbian more seriously. I believed I was making the personal political revolution with my life every moment, whether I was scrubbing the floor of the childcare center, setting up a new budget for the women's lecture series at the university, editing the local feminist magazine, or starting a women's bookstore. That I was constantly exhausted and had no health insurance, did hours of dreary unpaid work and still sneaked out of the collective to date butch women my housemates thought retrograde and sexist never interfered with my sense of total commitment to the feminist revolution. I was not living in a closet; I had compartmentalized my own mind to such an extent that I never questioned why I did what I did. And I never admitted what lay behind all my feminist convictions—a class-constructed distrust of change, a secret fear that someday I would be found out for who I really was, found out and thrown out. If I had not been raised to give my life away, would I have made such an effective, self-sacrificing revolutionary?

The narrowly focused concentration of a revolutionary shifted only when I began to write again. The idea of writing stories seemed frivolous when there was so much work to be done, but everything changed when I found myself confronting emotions and ideas that could not be explained away or postponed until after the revolution. The way it happened was simple and unexpected. One week I was asked to speak to two completely different groups: an Episcopalian Sunday school class and a juvenile detention center. The Episcopalians were all white, well-dressed, highly articulate, nominally polite, and obsessed with getting me to tell them (without their having to ask directly) just what it was that two women did together in bed. The delinquents were all women, 80 percent Black and Hispanic, wearing green uniform dresses or blue jeans and workshirts, profane, rude, fearless, witty, and just as determined to get me to talk about what it was that two women did together in bed.

I tried to have fun with the Episcopalians, teasing them about their fears and insecurities, and being as bluntly honest as I could about my sexual practices. The Sunday school teacher, a man who had assured me of his liberal inclinations, kept blushing and stammering as the questions about my growing up and coming out became more detailed. I stepped out into the sunshine when the meeting was over, angry at the contemptuous attitude implied by all their questioning, and though I did not know why, so deeply depressed I couldn't even cry.

The delinquents were another story. Shameless, they had

me blushing within the first few minutes, yelling out questions that were part curiosity and partly a way of boasting about what they already knew. "You butch or femme?" "You ever fuck boys?" "You ever want to?" "You want to have children?" "What's your girlfriend like?" I finally broke up when one very tall, confident girl leaned way over and called out, "Hey, girlfriend! I'm getting out of here next weekend. What you doing that night?" I laughed so hard I almost choked. I laughed until we were all howling and giggling together. Even getting frisked as I left didn't ruin my mood. I was still grinning when I climbed into the waterbed with my lover that night, grinning right up to the moment when she wrapped her arms around me and I burst into tears.

That I night I understood, suddenly, everything that had happened to my cousins and me, understood it from a wholly new and agonizing perspective, one that made clear how brutal I had been to both my family and myself. I grasped all over again how we had been robbed and dismissed, and why I had worked so hard not to think about it. I had learned as a child that what could not be changed had to go unspoken, and worse, that those who cannot change their own lives have every reason to be ashamed of that fact and to hide it. I had accepted that shame and believed in it, but why? What had I or my cousins done to deserve the contempt directed at us? Why had I always believed us contemptible by nature? I wanted to talk to someone about all the things I was thinking that night, but I could not. Among the women I knew there was no one who would have understood what I

was thinking, no other working-class woman in the women's collective where I was living. I began to suspect that we shared no common language to speak those bitter truths.

In the days that followed I found myself remembering that afternoon long ago at the county farm, that feeling of being the animal in the zoo, the thing looked at and laughed at and used by the real people who watched us. For all his liberal convictions, that Sunday school teacher had looked at me with the eyes of my cousin's long-ago guard. I felt thrown back into my childhood, into all the fears I had tried to escape. Once again I felt myself at the mercy of the important people who knew how to dress and talk, and would always be given the benefit of the doubt, while my family and I would not.

I experienced an outrage so old I could not have traced all the ways it shaped my life. I realized again that some are given no quarter, no chance, that all their courage, humor, and love for each other is just a joke to the ones who make the rules, and I hated the rule-makers. Finally, I recognized that part of my grief came from the fact that I no longer knew who I was or where I belonged. I had run away from my family, refused to go home to visit, and tried in every way to make myself a new person. How could I be working class with a college degree? As a lesbian activist? I thought about the guards at the detention center. They had not stared at me with the same picture-window emptiness they turned on the girls who came to hear me, girls who were closer to the life I had been meant to live than I could bear to examine. The contempt in their eyes was contempt for me as a lesbian, different and the same, but still contempt.

While I raged, my girlfriend held me and comforted me and tried to get me to explain what was hurting me so bad, but I could not. She had told me so often about her awkward relationship with her own family, the father who ran his own business and still sent her checks every other month. She knew almost nothing about my family, only the jokes and careful stories I had given her. I felt so alone and at risk lying in her arms that I could not have explained anything at all. I thought about those girls in the detention center and the stories they told in brutal shorthand about their sisters, brothers, cousins, and lovers. I thought about their one-note references to those they had lost, never mentioning the loss of their own hopes, their own futures, the bent and painful shape of their lives when they would finally get free. Cried-out and dry-eyed, I lay watching my sleeping girlfriend and thinking about what I had not been able to say to her. After a few hours I got up and made some notes for a poem I wanted to write, a bare, painful litany of loss shaped as a conversation between two women, one who cannot understand the other, and one who cannot tell all she knows.

It took me a long time to take that poem from a raw lyric of outage and grief to a piece of fiction that explained to me something I had never let myself see up close before—the whole process of running away, of closing up inside yourself, of hiding. It has taken me most of my life to understand that, to see how and why those of us who are born poor and different are so driven to give ourselves

away or lose ourselves, but most of all, simply to disappear as the people we really are. By the time that poem became the story "River of Names,"* I had made the decision to reverse that process: to claim my family, my true history, and to tell the truth not only about who I was but about the temptation to lie.

By the time I taught myself the basics of storytelling on the page, I knew there was only one story that would haunt me until I understood how to tell it—the complicated, painful story of how my mama had, and had not, saved me as a girl. Writing *Bastard Out of Carolina*** became, ultimately, the way to claim my family's pride and tragedy, and the embattled sexuality I had fashioned on a base of violence and abuse.

The compartmentalized life I had created burst open in the late 1970s after I began to write what I really thought about my family. I lost patience with my fear of what the women I worked with, mostly lesbians, thought of who I slept with and what we did together. When schisms developed within my community; when I was no longer able to hide within the regular dyke network; when I could not continue to justify my life by constant political activism or distract myself by sleeping around; when my sexual promiscuity, butch/femme orientation, and exploration of sadomasochistic sex became part of what was driving me out of my community of choice—I went home again. I went home to my mother and my sisters, to visit, talk, argue, and begin to understand.

Trash (Firebrand Books: Ithaca, New York, 1988)
**Dutton: New York, 1992

Once home I saw that as far as my family was concerned, lesbians were lesbians whether they wore suitcoats or leather jackets. Moreover, in all that time when I had not made peace with myself, my family had managed to make a kind of peace with me. My girlfriends were treated like slightly odd versions of my sisters' husbands, while I was simply the daughter who had always been difficult but was still a part of their lives. The result was that I started trying to confront what had made me unable really to talk to my sisters for so many years. I discovered that they no longer knew who I was either, and it took time and lots of listening to each other to rediscover my sense of family, and my love for them.

It is only as the child of my class and my unique family background that I have been able to put together what is for me a meaningful politics, to regain a sense of why I believe in activism, why self-revelation is so important for lesbians. There is no all-purpose feminist analysis that explains the complicated ways our sexuality and core identity are shaped, the way we see ourselves as parts of both our birth families and the extended family of friends and lovers we invariably create within the lesbian community. For me, the bottom line has simply become the need to resist that omnipresent fear, that urge to hide and disappear, to disguise my life, my desires, and the truth about how little any of us understand—even as we try to make the world a more just and human place. Most of all, I have tried to understand the politics of *they*, why human beings fear and stigmatize the different while secretly dreading that they might be one of the different themselves. Class, race, sexuality, gender—and all the other categories by which we categorize and dismiss each other—need to be excavated from the inside.

The horror of class stratification, racism, and prejudice is that some people begin to believe that the security of their families and communities depends on the oppression of others, that for some to have good lives there must be others whose lives are truncated and brutal. It is a belief that dominates this culture. It is what makes the poor whites of the South so determinedly racist and the middle class so contemptuous of the poor. It is a myth that allows some to imagine that they build their lives on the ruin of others, a secret core of shame for the middle class, a goad and a spur to the marginal working class, and cause enough for the homeless and poor to feel no constraints on hatred or violence. The power of the myth is made even more apparent when we examine how, within the lesbian and feminist communities where we have addressed considerable attention to the politics of marginalization, there is still so much exclusion and fear, many of us who do not feel safe.

I grew up poor, hated, the victim of physical, emotional, and sexual violence, and I know that suffering does not ennoble. It destroys. To resist destruction, self-hatred, or lifelong hopelessness, we have to throw off the conditioning of being despised, the fear of becoming the *they* that is talked about so dismissively, to refuse lying myths and easy moralities, to see ourselves as human, flawed, and extraordinary. All of us—extaordinary.

An earlier version of this essay appeared in *Sisters, Sexperts, Queers*, edited by Arlene Stein (Penguin/Plume: New York, 1993).

 Article Review Form at end of book.

What systems does Cook-Lynn point to as complicit in the criminalization of childbearing Native American women?

The Big Pipe Case

"It is true," says an old Dakota legend, "that women have always had a very hard time. Their richness and joy is in having many children and numerous relatives."

Elizabeth Cook-Lynn

What mainstream America may know about Sioux Indians is that they name Civil War captains "Dances with Wolves." What social scientists and politicians know stems from their relentless gathering of dismal statistics concerning poverty, alcoholism, early death, and fetal alcohol syndrome in tribal childbearing.[1] Probably one of the things that the American public most needs to know is that the enforced movement toward modernity for Indians is embedded in a legal world which can best be described as a confusing and vast folly emerging from the nineteenth-century Major Crimes Act, and that for no one has this folly been more profoundly dangerous than for the women of the tribes, who were, literally and figuratively, stripped of their authority in tribal life.

The modern attack on the civil and tribal rights of Indian women of childbearing age on reservation homelands suggests that life for them is not only "hard," as the legend says, but that modern change has often resulted in staggering, violent,

misogynistic practices previously unknown to the tribes. As alcohol and native women have interacted with the imported legal system of the white man, the once-honored women of tribal societies have become scapegoats for the failed system. As the U.S. government has taken legal charge of Indian lives, the results of its work in a specific, exemplary case are worth contemplating.

In 1989, a grand jury issued an indictment of a teenage, alcoholic Indian mother in South Dakota who, denied abortion services, gave birth to her third infant. It was charged that the Indian mother neglected and "assaulted her with intent to commit serious bodily injury" by breastfeeding the infant while under the influence, thereby committing a felony.[2]

The court, without a jury trial, sentenced her to almost four years in a federal penitentiary at Lexington, Kentucky. Shortly thereafter, the tribal court terminated her parental rights to this child and two previous children. The court believes it has "done the right thing."

"Do not forget," admonished the U.S. Attorney for South

Dakota at that time, Philip Hogen, "a lot of caring people got involved. They investigated the conditions in the home. They went to the authorities and they got that child out of there and she is now in foster care. And Sadie Big Pipe (not her real name) who will soon be two years old, is going to live. . . . I hope that you are not going to forget that there were courageous, caring people involved here, and that they did exactly the right thing."

The early details of the entire episode might, for some, seem to bear out Mr. Hogen's position. When tribal police were called to the Big Pipe home at Lower Brule that spring day, they saw a nearly starved infant and a drunken mother. They went to the tribal judge and, with the help of social workers, the Community Health Representative (CHR) and others removed the nursing child from the home and took her to the only hospital in the area, some twenty miles off the reservation in Chamberlain, South Dakota.

The child had a bad diaper rash, virus-caused ulcers on her legs, and an alcohol level in her blood measured at .02. The infant, then nine weeks old, weighed 5 pounds and 4 ounces. While no infant should ever ingest alcohol, many medical assessments on this level suggest that it is, perhaps, not in every case "medically consequential."

The mother's blood-alcohol levels, on the other hand, measured at different intervals over the next two weeks as she was incarcerated and released, were .10, .12 and .30 (.10 being legally intoxicated and unable to drive a car). These levels suggest that the mother's condition was worsening, and many medical persons believe them to be dangerous. Some say that at a level of .25 some people lose consciousness, and at .50 death may occur. Yet, Marie Big Pipe was never hospitalized, nor was she sent to a detoxification center during this entire episode.

Within days, the South Dakota State Department of Social Services took custody of the child. The action was called a "rescue" in formal reports. Because Marie Big Pipe was indigent, the federal courts appointed an attorney for her and then released her on condition that she "refrain from the use of alcohol" and "enroll in an out-patient alcohol treatment center." Ten days later, the court revoked the release when Marie was arrested on charges of intoxication in violation of the bond.

Another ten days passed before a hearing was scheduled, during which time the court stated that the teenaged mother "[had] a serious history of alcohol abuse and [was] unable to control her use of alcohol without an inpatient treatment program; that currently there [were] no inpatient facilities capable of providing placement; and that she [was] unlikely to abide by any terms and conditions of release to assure her court appearance." The court ordered that she be held in custody and that a jury trial be scheduled for two weeks later.

Marie's attorney from Chamberlain, the second lawyer on the case, who was appointed by the court when the previously appointed lawyer from Gregory, several hours' drive away from the reservation, withdrew, filed a futile motion to dismiss. His argument was that the heart of the matter was the legal definition of "assault with intent to commit serious bodily injury" as only involving beatings and did not apply to nursing babies and their alcoholic mothers. Basically, he said, the issue was whether her actions constituted "neglect," a misdemeanor; or assault with "intent" to commit serious bodily injury," a felony.

Black's Law Dictionary defines assault as "any willful attempt or threat to inflict injury upon the person of another when coupled with an apparent present ability to do so, and any intentional display of force such as would give the victim reason to fear or expect immediate bodily harm . . . an assault may be committed without actually touching, or striking, or doing bodily harm, to the person of another." Neglect, as defined in *Black's*, "may mean to omit, fail or forbear to do a thing which can be done, but it may also import an absence of care or attention in the doing or omission of a given act. And it may mean a designed refusal or unwillingness to perform one's duty."

The U.S. Attorney in his opposition to the motion to dismiss argued that Marie's "decision not to care for the baby is an intentional act of omission which is sufficient under the circumstances of this case to constitute an assault." He went on to say that "her act of giving the infant alco-holic beverages or allowing alcohol to enter the baby's system is sufficient to constitute an assault against the child." The motion to dismiss was denied. Marie's health problems were criminalized, her parental actions defined as crimes, and her family forever destroyed.

A jury was never impaneled, and five months later a federal judge quietly sent Marie Big Pipe to the Kentucky prison for nearly four years. There was no outcry—not from the attorney who handled her case, nor from the Indian community of relatives and friends, nor from Marie herself.

Twisted History Declares Women a Threat

The principal effects of overt federal legal action to condemn Indian parenthood and take Indian children away from Indian parents have been the subject of controversy in native communities for a century, during which time Indian children were routinely snatched from dysfunctional tribal families by state agencies and other concerned parties. Finally, in defense of themselves, the tribes fought for the 1978 Indian Child Welfare Act, saw it passed, and convinced themselves that help was on its way. The irony of the usurpation of this legislation in specific cases such as Marie Big Pipe's is a cruel one. No matter what the tribes assert in theory, they are faced with a paternalizing federal mandate.

One of the convincing arguments against criminalizing an Indian parent's action and terminating forever the rights of recalcitrant parents was articulated in the mid-1970s by Ramona Bennett, chairwoman of the Puyallup Tribe of Washington State:

The alienations of Indian children from their parents can become a serious mental health problem. If you lose your child you are dead; you are never going to get rehabilitated or you are never going to get well. If there are problems, once the children are gone, the whole family unit is never going to get well.

If this is true, who will help Marie Big Pipe get well? If she does not get well, what is the future for any of us?

To suggest that an ill parent (an alcoholic parent) should be made a criminal and that her children should be forever removed from her presence, violates one of the principles of Chairwoman Bennett's brilliant and useful discussion, twenty years ago, on the welfare of Indian children. The effort to get tribal jurisdiction over tribal children was not made so that objectionable parents, particularly mothers, could forever be banished from tribal life through criminalization and incarceration.

Every Indian parent will tell you that the welfare of tribal children is dependent upon the welfare of tribal parents, not the state or federal government. Foster care, placement, termination of parental rights, preadoptive placement, and adoptive placement, while now in the hands of the tribal officials since the passage of Indian Child Welfare Act in 1978, were never meant to become instruments destructive to families. How has this all happened? Why? Who is responsible?

A Little Background

From about 1944 through 1964, the United States government, using its powers of eminent domain, seized thousands of acres of Lakota/Dakota, treaty-protected reservation lands in the northern plains to bring domestic electricity and agricultural irrigation to the region. In the process, Indian communities (including the Lower Brule reservation, which is the home of Marie Big Pipe and her relatives) were destroyed by flooding. As if nothing could stop the mid-century rush for hydropower, communities of the Missouri River tribes of the Sioux were uprooted and moved, and it has taken decades to even begin to heal the wounds. Traditional governing groups steeped in long-sustained cultural values were fragmented, economic systems and reservation infrastructures were destroyed, as they had been in the late 1800s. Churches, cemeteries, governmental, medical, and educational facilities were flooded out, moved out, and never replaced.

The South Dakota Indian reservations called Crow Creek and Lower Brule, across the river from each other, the smallest groups of the Sioux Nation and the setting for events in this article, were particularly devastated. As the physical landscape was torn apart, so was the fabric of the social and cultural life of the tribes. *Termination* was the word which described the federal policy toward these communities and these people.

Accompanying the physical devastation on the reservations was the backlash of paternalism, racism, and misogyny by the nearby white populations and the federal government, which now claimed supremacy and domination over these reservation lands and resources. Decades later, the Sioux Nation and most other native communities are still fighting an undeclared war for their sovereign rights against an ineffectual and stifling paternalistic bureaucracy. And Sioux women, exemplars of their own tribal histories, are subjected to an incapacitating colonial tyranny.

There is evidence that women, thought by the tribes to be the backbone of native society and the bearers of sacred children and repositors of cultural values, are now thought to pose a significant threat to tribal survival. Indeed, the intrusive federal government now interprets the law on Indian reservations in ways which sanction indicting alcoholic, childbearing Indian woman as though they alone are responsible for the fragmentation of the social fabric of Indian lives. As infants with fetal alcohol syndrome (FAS) and fetal alcohol effect (FAE) are born in increasing numbers, it is said that womens' recalcitrant behavior (consuming alcohol and other drugs during pregnancy and nursing) needs to be legally criminalized by the federal system to make it a felony for a woman to commit such acts.

The collaboration of tribal, federal, and state law-enforcement agencies in recent times, particularly, has done little to support Indian values or put any value on the Indian family. In fact, many Indian women's groups believe it does the opposite by solidifying non-Indian values and perpetuating the separation of family. What the imposed laws have finally done is to declare that what used to be a tribal societal problem, that is, a failure to protect women and children from harm, is now solely a woman's failure, a woman's despair, a woman's fault, a woman's crime. Young Indian women, many with minimal education and weakened familial support systems, have been subjected to closer scrutiny by social services and the court system than ever before. They have become objects of scorn, singled out for a particular kind of punishment dictated by their alcoholism, drug use, and promiscuity. They are seen as a root cause of the rise in infant mortality, abuse, and fetal deformity.

The white man's law and the tribe's adoption of Anglo government have removed the traditional forms of punishment and control for criminal acts. As tribal police, court systems, state social service agencies, and Christian conservatives replace traditional tribal ideas and systems of control, the legal focus on the young childbearing Indian woman as culprit and criminal has been of major concern to women's groups.

In prior days, while childbearing was considered women's business, it was not thought to be separated from the natural and ethical responsibilities of males. Therefore, men who caused stress in the community or risk to the survival of the tribe by dishonoring women were held accountable by the people. They could not carry the sacred pipe, nor could they hold positions of status. They were often physically attacked by the woman's male relatives and driven from tribal life. These particular controls in tribal society often no longer apply. In many tribal communities, such men who are known to degrade women and abandon children, now hold positions of power, even sometimes sitting at the tribal council tables. They are directors of tribal programs, and they often participate unmolested in sacred ceremonies. Many others who may not purposefully or intentionally degrade women often remain silent about the atrocities and hypocrisies they see in their communities. In the process of their public lives they assist in transferring to women the responsibility for the social ills of the tribes.

Such contradictions may occur, some suggest, because the historical influence of Christian religions and Anglo law in native communities has made it possible for individuals to abandon longheld views concerning marriage patterns and tribal arrangements for childbearing and parental responsibilities. Interracial marriages and illicit sexual relationships, denied the sanction of the tribes and families, often ignore the particular responsibilities prescribed for both males and females in traditional societies. Failures in these duties were dealt swift and severe punishment, but seldom was male honor in matters of marriage and sex abandoned as routinely as it is today. Young women, while held accountable for their actions, were seldom the only ones condemned in matters of this kind, as they are today.

If the Marie Big Pipe case is any indication of law enforcement and justice on the reservation, it is a sad portrayal of the failure of the system and the subsequent loss of a woman's human and civil rights, and obviously of her treaty rights as well. The complex issue of Indian sovereignty, that is, the "power of self-governance and the inherent right to control their internal affairs," while beyond the scope of this article, is as much a subject of this discussion as is a woman's right to protection by the law.

Federal Authority Criminalizes the Disease of Alcoholism

In South Dakota two sovereign entities have criminal jurisdiction over crimes committed on reservations: the Indian nation and the federal government. Who has jurisdiction depends on various factors, such as the severity or degree of the crime, the location, who committed the crime, and against whom.

Indian jurisdiction has been steadily eroded by Congress through the Major Crimes Act (18 U.S.C. 1153), which transferred jurisdiction over major crimes committed on reservations to the federal government. This act was passed by Congress in 1885 as a result of public reaction to the Supreme Court's holding that federal courts lacked jurisdiction over a Sioux Indian who had already been punished by his tribe (the Sicangu) for the killing of another Indian (the now famous exparte Crow Dog case). The Act is now seen by many as a major incursion into traditional tribal powers.

Fourteen enumerated crimes (originally there were only seven) are now under the provision of this federal jurisdiction. The charge of assault, the definition of which has been broadened and redefined through the appeals process, is now used by the courts and social agencies on reservations to redefine a woman's health issues in terms of criminal behavior.

If such federal litigation as has been allowed in the Big Pipe case occurs because of the federal government's notion of its own superiority, it may also be the function of a deep-seated misogyny that white feminists say is at the core of American society. In either case, it pits mother against child in a way that is unbearable to thinking American Indians. Yet, almost everybody is too stunned by the rising statistics of bitter violence in Indian communities, substance abuse, divorce, family violence, murder, crimes of brother against brother, cruelty toward women and the elderly, child abuse and neglect, and wife-beating, to defy the idea that making criminals out of young, childbearing Indian women and applying for federal funds to build "shelters" are viable solutions.

In such an outrageously dangerous world, it is thought, there has to be someone to blame. Quickly, easily, thoughtlessly, the blame is directed toward a defenseless victim who is said to be victimizing others, and Marie Big Pipe becomes everyone's target. This is nothing new in America, known for its culture of quick and easy solutions, but it is something new to many Indians whose societies have often cherished the idea that for the weak, the young, the aged, ill and orphaned, there has been a special tribal care-taking obligation.

Indian America knows that Marie Big Pipe, ill and weak, too young to help herself, was neither to blame nor blameless. More than anything, Indian America knows that *she, too, is its daughter, neither criminal nor saint.*

The Big Pipe case is one of thousands in America today, many of which occur on reservations, that represents an outrageous violation of human rights for those who come from tribal societies in which the child is a sacred gift and motherhood a cultural ideal, to be protected as the quintessential survival mechanism of an ethical society. It makes a mockery of the 1948 Universal Declaration of Human Rights which states that "Motherhood and Childhood (not just childhood) are entitled to special care and assistance."

America Defends Itself against Marie Big Pipe

It is interesting to note that U.S. federal attorneys have discretion in which cases they will try, that they pick and choose the cases which will justify their time and purpose. It is probably no accident that federal authorities, with either the acquiescence of or a directive from tribal authorities, decided upon the criminality of Marie Big Pipe's actions for reasons well articulated in the early findings. The child abuse or neglect charge could have been brought by the tribal authorities, because it is still within their jurisdiction to prosecute misdemeanor charges, but it was rejected in favor of the federal "assault resulting in serious bodily harm" charge available from the federal arsenal of legal remedies.

This decision-making process probably deserves further discussion, which should center upon whether the law provides appropriate remedy to Indian communities beset with poverty, social ills, inadequate education, health, housing, and legal facilities, to say nothing of constant harassment concerning jurisdictional issues from federal, state, and county governments. (In South Dakota, the tribes confront steady efforts by the courts to overturn settled law in everything from hunting to casino gaming issues, often with the blessing of the state and federal legislators.)

For whom should the law provide extraordinary protection under these particular conditions, and what is the role to be played by the courts? Unfortunately, tribal courts have no jurisdiction over many offenses committed on their homelands. Even when they

do have jurisdictional decisions to make, however, they often fail to rise to the occasion.

In the Big Pipe case, former U.S. Attorney Phil Hogen says, "There is no ideal federal statute for this kind of offense or crime of omission, though it was, of course, a classic case of child abuse/neglect. The assault resulting in serious bodily injury is the charge that most nearly fit."

Most nearly fit? This is a clear failure of the courts and the lawyers in Indian Country to take to a jury not only a challenge to the feminization of the "assault" charge which some believe has been the result of more than a decade of conservative, right-wing thinking, but also a challenge to any argument over whether alcoholism is a crime or a disease. If alcoholism is a disease rather than a crime, as defined by the federal government (and by the American Medical Association since 1956), why didn't this case reflect that description? While there is no question Marie's infant was not receiving love and care and nourishment from her mother, whose responsibility it was to see that she came to no harm, there is no evidence that this neglectful, ill, addicted mother could be described as incorrigible, nor genetically defective, evil, vengeful, nor criminally violent for the purpose of domination or control, nor any of the other more egregious or radical definitions of criminality. Even a doctor's deposition, presented in her defense, indicated that there was no evidence of "malicious, evil intent" on her part.

The Indian Public Health facility, the institution in charge of health care for her people, and to which she turned for help, provides some assistance in birth control but denies access to abortion services and probably fails in its counseling of young women of childbearing age. At this time, there is little or no sex education in most federal and tribal schools.

Needless to say, the oppressive Christian religious presences on reservations, the churches, the schools (which exert considerable influence in Indian communities), the dismissal of traditional native female guidance and medical advice by existing, reservation-based institutions—all these combined to stifle Marie Big Pipe's natural inclination to do what she knew was best for her in this instance.

Drinking heavily at the time, depressed, apathetic, and in serious ill health, she knew she wanted an abortion but did not have the confidence, the personal knowledge, nor the financial means to seek out abortion services on her own. Medical practitioners know that when a woman's *choice* to bear children is removed in cases like this, suicide can be the next logical step. Alcohol may have been Marie's method of suicide or, at the very least, self-obliteration if one wants to make a case for willful behavior. Abortion services, including counseling on options, are legally outlawed in reservation hospitals, and there are no hospital facilities at all on the Crow Creek and Lower Brule Sioux reservations, an area of several hundred thousand acres.

There is only one abortion clinic in South Dakota, located in Sioux Falls, several hours' drive from the Lower Brule reservation. Its physician, Dr. Buck Williams, OB/GYN, has appeared on national television saying he fears for his life as the result of threats from antiabortion factions in the state. Dr. Williams says he wears a bulletproof vest and carries a gun. Pro-lifers in the state have threatened to "cut off my fingers," he has said.

Interviews with Marie reveal a troubled young woman burdened by inadequate education and unable to make choices (her schooling at a local Catholic boarding school was ended at seventh grade). Her mention of the sexual abuse and repeated rapes she endured over a long period of her young life at home and at the boarding school were never taken seriously by any of her mostly male interviewers.

Not taking any of these matters under advisement, handling the case as though it were without context, failing to take the responsibility to alleviate the suffering of both victims in this case, the United States' denial of the motion to dismiss argued that Marie Big Pipe's "decision not to care for the baby was an intentional act of omission, which is sufficient under the circumstances of this case to constitute an assault. Furthermore, her act of giving the infant alcoholic beverages or allowing alcohol to enter the baby's system is sufficient to constitute an assault against the child."

It argued further that Marie's actions "were more than neglect. She intentionally decided to starve the child so that she would not be around to further 'mess up her life.'"

This argument was based upon a narrative written by a white male agent of the FBI who interrogated her months after she was arrested. This interview, conducted in the presence of a white female social worker from the South Dakota Department of Social Services in Pierre, was in the eyes of the judge particularly damning. The FBI agent wrote,

Big Pipe stated that she felt that Sadie was the source of all her problems. She did not want to have her and tried everything she could think of to induce an abortion while she was carrying her. She continued to drink all during the pregnancy, she would do situps, and jump up and down in an effort to induce an abortion. She even investigated having a surgical abortion performed but was unable to find any agency that would pay for it so she did not have it done. She still wanted to have an abortion performed on herself after the three-month limit but could find no one to help or to pay for it. She felt that the pregnancy "screwed up" her good life with her new boyfriend. He would not accept the pregnancy or the baby since it would not be his. Even after the baby was born, she didn't want it and could barely bring herself to touch it or care for it. It made her mad and angry because she had "messed up [her] life." Her older daughter didn't like her either and did not want her around. Marie cares a great deal for this older daughter's feelings and felt bad for her being against the baby but understood how she felt, she had ruined her life, too.

The government, in its prosecution of Marie Big Pipe, referred to a newspaper article from July, 1989, which reported a mother in New York who abandoned her baby in the woods and was charged with first-degree assault and first-degree reckless endangerment. The government pressed this parallel, though its speciousness was readily apparent since Marie had not abandoned her baby. Indeed, Marie said she tried not to nurse the infant while she was under the influence of alcohol but the infant refused to take the bottle with its prepared formula. Because a jury was not impaneled to hear the discussion of all relevant inquiry, and the question of "intent" was never fully explored, the case clearly was stacked against the defendant.

By the end of five months of local incarceration, Marie's will to continue her "not guilty" stance had worn down completely. She finally signed a statement which her lawyer claims she had written and understood:

> My attorney has explained my . . . rights . . . and explained the facts of this incident and what impact they will have upon a jury. He also explained that whether I assaulted my daughter by neglecting her is a unique case and presents a fairly significant factual issue for the jury. Even if I [sic] would lose this case by a jury verdict, the issue of assault by neglect presents a strong appealable issue.
>
> My attorney has further explained that this will not be an easy case to win, because of the emotional impact of a malnourished child.
>
> I have decided to plead guilty to the charge lodged against me. I do so with the understanding that I waive my right to appeal the issue of assault/neglect and all other constitutional rights I have. I chose to plead guilty because of the possibility of a jury conviction, the trauma of a jury trial, and the desire to avoid having this entire matter aired to the court.

In subsequent writings that seem particularly poignant and naive, Marie said her counsel "would urge that any sentence I receive will be served in the Springfield Correction Institution in Springfield, South Dakota." She also said that she wanted to get her baby back and take care of her. The honorable Chief Judge of the U.S. District Court, Donald J. Porter, would have none of it, of course, and sentenced her to "hard time."

Marie Big Pipe is home now, after more than two years in a federal prison. She is on probation until 1996. Her grandmother says, "She done her time and she just wants to put it behind her." Many people connected with the case refuse to discuss it publicly.

Damaged Tribal Families

One of the pragmatic realities for contemporary Indians in the defense of themselves is that, too often, lawyers who are supposedly defending them on their homelands, overwhelmed with the complexity surrounding issues of jurisdiction and structure, just "carry the brief," or plea bargain the cases before them. These lawyers rarely vigorously defend their clients by establishing precedents which might prove useful to the development of a civilized legal system on Indian homelands in America.

By simply plea bargaining in this case, Marie Big Pipe's lawyer failed to persuade her that they should proceed with a jury trial, or look at the legal issues this case presented. He says he responded in accordance with "his client's wishes" and did not take it to a jury because, he says, his client was reluctant to have the matter aired before the jury.

This rationale seems unconvincing, since we have here a woman with a minimal education who relied on her attorney. He should have taken this case to the jury and called for a reassessment of the new legal definitions by which the illnesses of Indian women and their loss of human and reproductive rights continue to be criminalized. As is generally true of Indians with court-appointed attorneys, Marie just didn't get good legal advice. Her quick and painful legal history, then, and the inglorious and corrupt history of the white man's law as it has been applied to indigenous peoples, are inextricably tied.

In the sense that justice is rarely separated from political and legislative processes, neither is it separate from the national ideologies which are expressed therein. Today's politics of the war upon women everywhere (I refer you not only to older works like Brownmiller's *Against Our Wills,* but also the new work on the Hill/Thomas case, *Strange Justice*) and the suppression of Indian women's rights—reproductive rights in particular—is not unconnected to the suppression of the rights of the indigenes historically. The historical fear that federal power will somehow suffer and that America will suffer damage if tribal government and courts reflect tribal cultural ideals which suggest that *Lakota womanhood is sacred* seems to prevail.

Law is not beyond context, and no one can ignore the effects of historical oppression. Some believe it all seemed to happen quickly and inadvertently. In 1885, a rider to an Indian General Appropriations Act, which seemed to some to be just an unimportant paragraph, soon became the basis for the oppressive Major Crimes Act mentioned earlier in this article. My view of it all is much more cynical because of the consequences. This quick and inadvertent action divested the tribes of virtually any legal and moral jurisdiction over their lives, and it was the beginning of a fearsome justice on Indian lands. It became the law's answer to the political questions posed by "vanishing American" theories resulting in assimilation and genocide. It became the major political tool used in the destruction of long-standing, humane Native American ethical and legal systems.

It is argued by some Native American scholars that the responsibilities inherent in ethical childbearing issues were always in the hands of women, never in legal nor in male societies. Today, on Indian reservations, you can find women's organizations fighting to regain the reproductive rights that they say were once theirs in sympathetic and comforting tribal societies. Responsible men and women of the tribes are working toward developing culturally based systems through which their social lives may be improved. Their antagonists, however, the paternalistically driven federal institutions which have for so long fought for power over tribal infrastructures, are still in place,

The principal effect of the nineteenth-century, white-male-sponsored Major Crimes Act was to permit prosecution of Indians by reference to selected federal criminal statutes applicable on federal reservations. Seven crimes were originally covered. To make sure that no illegal acts escaped punishment, however, the U. S. Congress, only four years after assuming that jurisdiction, passed the Assimilative Crimes Act in 1889, which allowed the government to take on cases for the states. This act includes the following language:

> Whoever is guilty of an act or omission which although not made punishable by any enactment of Congress, would be punishable if committed or omitted within the jurisdiction of State, Territory, Possession, or District in which such place is situated . . . shall be guilty of a like offense and subject to a like punishment.

What this has meant in Indian country is that when local, state, and regional laws cannot apply, the federal government can "assimilate" them, in other words, assume control, and this often results in making state criminal laws applicable on Indian land, in violation of cultural belief systems or anything else. It is, perhaps, redundant to say that all of this congressional activity was undertaken in violation of the 1868 treaty between the Sioux Nation and the United States, which defends as one its principles the upholding of trivial sovereignty.

By a series of amendments, then, and through case law, the former list of seven major crimes has been expanded to the present fourteen: murder, manslaughter, kidnapping, rape, carnal knowledge by a man of any female not his wife or sixteen years of age, assault with the intent to commit rape, incest, assault with the intent to commit murder, assault with a dangerous weapon, assault resulting in serious bodily harm, arson, burglary, robbery, and larceny.

All of these crimes have been removed over the years from tribal jurisdiction by white American politicians and lawyers, the U. S. Congress, and the courts. These imponderable forces have often conspired with malice aforethought, in my view, to colonize and suppress a sovereign nation of people, and even now, with this distortion of American democracy exposed, everyone, lawyers and victims alike, continues to turn away.

The expanded definitions of *assault, abuse,* and *neglect* are used now to punish childbearing Indian women suffering from alcoholism as a result of that historical jurisdictional *fait accompli* before the turn of the century when Indians had absolutely no access to the U. S. courts.

In spite of these new definitions, which must be deplored, there is still the question of a jury trial. What happened to the idea of "a jury of your peers" as a facet of justice on Indian reservations? In the Big Pipe case, held in the Ninth District, a jury trial might have made a difference not only for Marie but for all of us. In one of its lucid moments in 1973 the Supreme Court rendered a decision (*Keeble v. United States,* 412 USA 204) which said that an Indian is entitled to an *instruction on a lesser included offense* because he or she is entitled to be tried "in the same manner" as a non-Indian under 18 USCA x 3242. While this is not a perfect solution to sovereignty issues, an argument to a jury of her "peers" might have been convincing and might have given the courts a chance to make distinctions between criminal actions and health issues. This maneuver might have put matters back in community hands where native belief systems could have been a part of the solution mechanism. Without the protection of a jury trial, a judge (*always* white and male in South Dakota) may simply refuse to consider other objections and responses.

If Marie had been tried and convicted of "simple assault," she would have been subject to a $500 fine and six months in tribal jail. Under other, more humane, systems of justice, she might even have undergone extensive medical treatment. She might have been appropriately assisted toward rehabilitation, and her family might have remained intact, her parental rights sustained. Tribal courts are, today, taking these matters under legal discussion, suggesting that the usurpation of tribal court authority in these cases is unconstitutional and that the infusion of massive federal funds into the tribal court systems for training and education would strengthen the integrity of their own communities.

Even with a jury trial, however, as juries are now constituted, there is no assurance that Marie would have been treated fairly. It appears that Indians in positions of power on reservations (mostly male) are themselves Christian religious leaders holding rigid, fundamentalist views, or they are police and social workers trained to defend the status quo, educated in the long-standing and destructive theories of race and law perpetuated in American educational systems. They often "go with the flow," say the lawyers and others who deal with these juries and tribal power systems. They vote with the majority when they vote. They often, as do most Americans, and midwesterners in general, have simplistic attitudes toward complex social and legal problems. Be that as it may, the impact of removing moral and legal jurisdiction from tribal control and placing it in the hands of "exterior," or "white men's," legal and legislative systems has been a disaster.

Most Indian individuals caught up in criminal charges learn that the legal system to which they are subjected is illogical, inconsistent, counterproductive and, often, anti-Indian and racist. Speeding and driving under the influence of alcohol on the reservation roads, for example, may get you arrested by the tribal police, or the state patrol, or a county sheriff, or no one at all, depending upon which of the latest jurisdictional battles has been won or lost. But one thing can be predicted: If you are a childbearing Indian woman, you will merit the special attention of the federal court system.

In fantasies of a perfect world, idealized models exist in which justice never fails, and people always get what they deserve. The reality is that for all of us in this world, and for American Indians in particular, there is a complex mixture of social, political, institutional, experiential, and personal factors from which courts pick and choose, lawyers argue, and judges rule.

There is, clearly, much work to be done by both whites and Indians before justice can prevail. Only one thing, say tribal leaders, scholars, and politicians, can rid Indians of this chaotic and destructive legal situation: a clear recognition of the sovereign nature of America's Indian nations—which means, in practical terms, land reform, cultural revitalization, and the legal, financial, educational, and economic control of our own resources. Most of all, it means the reform of a colonial system of law long despised by the people. The U. S. Congress, its president, and its courts are beginning to understand the need for true home rule on Indian lands, but no one should believe that the antagonists aren't still in place.

 **Article Review Form at end of book.**

In the final paragraph of this essay, Hartouni talks about the mapping of class, race, and gender power within the context of the cases at hand. How would that map look in the case of Marie Big Pipe?

Breached Birth

Anna Johnson and the reproduction of raced bodies

Valerie Hartouni

I

On September 19, 1990, Anna Johnson, a black single parent of one, gave birth to a six-pound, ten-ounce, white baby boy in Santa Ana, California. Two days later, she surrendered custody of the boy to his genetic parents, Mark and Crispina Calvert, in order to avoid his temporary placement in a foster home while Orange County Superior Court Judge Richard N. Parslow Jr. reviewed Johnson's suit for parental rights and custody. The Calverts had contracted with Johnson the previous year to bring to term their in vitro fertilized embryo. In exchange for ten thousand dollars, Johnson agreed to be surgically impregnated with the Calvert zygote and to deliver the infant with whom she shared no genetic link once she was herself delivered. Claiming, however, that she had bonded with the fetus in the latter months of pregnancy and that the Calverts had, in any event, breached their contract both by defaulting on a prearranged pay-

ment schedule and by not caring adequately for her or the fetus—actions that, Johnson's lawyers maintained, constituted "fetal neglect"—Johnson sued for custody. "The child is not genetically mine, but I have more feelings for him than his natural parents do," she charged in a *Los Angeles Times* interview several months before the October delivery date. "If they are distant and uncaring now, what are they going to be like when he comes?"[1]

Maintaining that they had done even more for Johnson than they had been required to do by contract—they had "dr[iven] her to her doctor's appointments, g[iven] her money, brought her food, and asked how she was doing"—the Calverts contended that if anyone had been victimized financially or emotionally by this alternative reproductive arrangement it was they, not Johnson.[2] By their account, Johnson had acted in an increasingly unpredictable and exploitative manner; she demanded, for example, that they accelerate their payments on the ten thousand dollars owed her, which they did,

and then threatened to keep the baby if they failed to produce the remaining balance. In their view, it was individual greed rather than maternal need that had motivated Johnson to sue for custody.

Circumstantially damning in this regard was not only the frequency with which Johnson had begun to appear on the popular talk-show circuit, but the public revelation, shortly after she filed suit, that she was facing two felony counts for welfare fraud.[3] Having allegedly failed to report her income fully for a ten-month period in 1989, Johnson was said to have received excess food stamps and AFDC benefits amounting to approximately five thousand dollars in overpayment. Although this was certainly not "the crime of the century," as Johnson's lawyer pejoratively characterized the district attorney's earnest prosecution of the case,[4] during the Reagan/Bush years welfare fraud had come to exercise a decidedly devastating hold on the national imagination and was both represented and regarded as the crime of the decade. Indeed, within Reagan's America, the always black, always urban, supposedly lazy welfare-dependent single mother or "welfare queen" functioned as a condensed symbol, deployed to "explain" not only the deeper pathology in black family life, but the destruction of the American way of life.[5]

Although the felony charges against Johnson clearly worked to discredit her testimony—lawyers for the Calverts lost little time in pointing out the wide shadow of doubt these charges cast on her integrity and the authenticity of her claims—in the end, I want to argue, it was largely irrelevant whether and in what sense they were actually true. Occupying and occupied by the category "black woman," Johnson entered the public discourse an already densely scripted figure whose deviance, whatever its particular form, was etched in flesh. Situated within a racially stratified society in which color is always already constituted and read through a received, if ever shifting, stockpile of commonplace images, Johnson entered the public discourse in terms whose meanings were narrowly circumscribed historically, symbolically, and politically, terms that rendered the integrity and authenticity of her speech already suspect.

In this respect, "her" story preceded and prefigured her. Set in postindustrial urban black America, reinforced by the visual terrain of popular culture and the discursive terrains of law and medicine, and iterated throughout the 1980s in the register of epidemic, this story had to do with the defrauding of social service agencies; with the long-term social and financial costs of "mentally and emotionally deficient" children perinatally exposed to crack cocaine; with the undoing of black masculinity and, as the

media derisively depicted it, the "impending extinction" of the African American male;[6] with teenage promiscuity, pregnancy, illegitimacy, and the reproduction of a state-dependent and delinquent underclass; with child abuse and neglect, the erosion of family life, family values, and what the New York Times referred to as "one of the strongest forces in nature," the maternal instinct, through drug addiction, welfare addiction, and crime.[7] This story bore little relationship to the story Johnson herself would attempt to tell the court and was clearly irrelevant to her bid for custody. It was also and obviously partial: notwithstanding popular portrayals to the contrary, the majority of drug addicts in the United States are not black, but white and middle-class, and the rise in "illegitimate" births, said to have reached epidemic proportions during the decade among black women and teenagers, was rather among white women and teens.[8] Nevertheless, as part of the "cathected set of narratives signaled by the category 'black woman,' "[9] the tale of urban disorder and social decay would combine with an appeal to things genetic and natural to dominate the custody hearings. Not explicitly articulated, but both present and pervasive, it would be utilized not only to image the difference between truth and appearance, but to render Johnson's attachment to the white baby she had borne implausible and, thus, coldly calculating and confused.

II

As in the case of Baby M, the challenge for the Orange County Superior Court when custody hearings over Baby Boy Johnson

were convened on October 9, 1990, was to restabilize conventional understanding of motherhood and family and thereby recontain the proliferation of meanings, identities, and relationships generated by the panoply of new reproductive practices and, in particular, the practice of gestational surrogacy. This the court would do in the process of making a twofold determination—determining, on one hand, whether gestational surrogacy was a form of baby selling (and therefore illegal) and determining, on the other, whether and to what extent a gestational surrogate had claims over a child to whom she had given birth but to whom she bore no genetic connection. In either case, the pivotal question was the same: Was the genetic difference a difference that make a difference?

Anna Johnson maintained that it did not. As one of her attorneys plainly put the matter in court, "Genetics means crap in determining parental rights," and his claim was not without considerable grounding in legal, medical, and popular practice. For example, while fashioned in a pretechnobaby age and concerned primarily with paternity and adoption, California's 1975 National Uniform Parenting Act presumptively regards the "birth mother" as the "natural mother."[10] The policy statement on surrogacy issued by the American College of Obstetricians and Gynecologists similarly endorses treating the birth tie as the natural tie.[11] And then there is the reproductive discourse of the decade—a largely reactionary, biologically reductive, and often contradictory set of narratives—elaborated in the distinct but clearly related arenas of abortion and infertility, shaped by the newly imaged, newly "discovered" fetal "person" and directed toward refiguring maternal drives and desires, or what, in a postliberation era and through the lens of this "discovery," appeared to have become recklessly and grossly "disfigured."

Both abortion and infertility discourse constitute "maternal nature" in and through gestation; indeed, gestation is regarded as precisely what activates or brings fully into play women's essential maternal core. This "core" or collection of drives and desires was represented throughout the decade of the 1980s and within the context of both discourses as being undeniably present in all women, even if it was also dormant in some and disturbed, displace, or frustrated in others. Its assumed existence, as we have seen elsewhere in this book, not only contributed to the construction of abortion as an especially heinous crime against nature, an act of self-mutilation as well as murder, but also lent legitimacy and urgency to the development of new techniques and technologies for treating involuntary childlessness—a condition that would necessarily have to include *all* childlessness, whether chosen or not, as it certainly appeared to do by the decade's end.

Consider by way of example the report that appeared in the *New England Journal of Medicine*— the same week, ironically, that Judge Parslow handed down his decision in *Johnson v. Calvert*— announcing the development of innovative new techniques that would allow postmenopausal women to "reset their biological clocks" and "become mothers." The segment of the female population most fully and publicly featured as beneficiaries of these new techniques was not the 10 percent who had stopped ovulating in their thirties.[12] Rather, it was women who had "chosen" less traditional career paths and subsequently felt both loss and remorse—women, in other words, whose regret seemed to confirm, emotionally, what infertility spoken in the register of epidemic seemed to confirm biologically and scientifically; that however seductive professional life and ambition might initially appear, the ultimate end and reward of womanhood is motherhood. Here, as in much of the decade's discourse, anatomy and destiny were linked inextricably, even while the biologically uncompromising terms of that destiny could now be altered. That these women would be, as Anna Johnson was, genetic strangers to the embryos they would carry and the children they would later bear and rear hardly bore mention in the popular press; indeed, the question of genetic connection was virtually nonexistent as such.[13] The privileged story was the maternal story, gestationally rather than genetically spun and spoken.

If postmenopausal therapies in particular and infertility discourse more generally presuppose (and produce) a maternal nature that emerges in and through gestation, abortion discourse similarly assumes such a nature, although one that seems clearly to have gone awry given the prevalence of abortion: just as some animals kill their offspring when they are disturbed or in some way confused, so too were women killing theirs, "in restless agitation against a natural order."[14] A variety of explanations circulated throughout the decade as to the how and why of this disturbance, but shared among them was the sense, kindled by a 1983 study by noted bioethicist Joseph Fletcher and physician Mark Evans that appeared in the *New England Journal of Medicine,* that the problem lay in arousing repressed maternal drives or inciting recognition with respect to the true nature of fetal life and women's responsibility toward it.

In their study—itself based, as we saw in chapter 2, on only two unrelated interviews— Fletcher and Evans argue that early ultrasound imaging of the fetal form can be used, in effect, as a remedial aid to stimulate maternal feelings in women who are equivocal about taking their pregnancies to term. According to Fletcher and Evans, viewing the fetus in utero appears to produce a "shock" of recognition in pregnant women who have been unable or unwilling otherwise to perceive the fetus as a separate and vulnerable living entity that belongs to and is dependent upon them alone. This sense of recognition and, by implication, responsibility, in their view, constitutes the stuff of maternal bonding, "the fundamental element in the later parent-child bond." Once this sense of recognition is aroused, they argue, women are more likely "to resolve 'ambivalent' pregnancies in favor of the fetus."[15]

Fletcher and Evans's speculations about the potential use of early ultrasound testing to cultivate maternal nature and thus promote pregnancy—their "visual bonding theory," as Rosalind Petchesky has referred to it—captured the imagination of prolife activists and communities alike: it inspired the production of *The Silent Scream* by the National Right-to-Life Committee,[16] intensified the mass circulation of fetal images in the latter years of the decade, and fostered legislative as well as judicial efforts to force pregnant women to view their fetuses prior to aborting them. Their speculations also prompted the practice among some obstetricians of incorporating ultrasound imaging at each monthly prenatal visit for the purpose of "helping [a] woman bond to her baby."[17] Finally, Fletcher and Evans's "visual bonding theory" could be deployed—although it was not—to account for the "shock" of recognition and growing emotional attachment Anna Johnson claimed to have experienced toward the fetus she was gestating sometime after it quickened.

Recognizing that imaging practices produce the "fetus as baby" even as they appear only to reveal it as such, and keeping in mind as well the extraordinarily thin and narrow scope of Fletcher and Evans's "study," its pronatal agenda, and the larger political agenda it legitimated and was legitimated by, Anna Johnson could nevertheless be read through the lens of their study and the set of assumptions that ground it, indeed, the same lens and assumptions through which courts and legislatures throughout the land in the 1980s appeared both eager and poised to read millions of women, whether pregnant or only potentially so. She could be read as a woman initially "in denial," as a woman in whom maternal nature had been repressed, or as a woman whose initial sense of detachment from and ambivalence toward the fetus she was carrying was resolved "favorably" with the aid of monthly ultrasound testing, even though such testing was performed throughout her difficult pregnancy in order to track fetal growth rather than to facilitate "bonding."

The point here is that the way in which Anna Johnson was positioned and the terms in which she was read together reflect a subtle but significant shift in registers, a shift that can be seen and sharpened through a series of questions. In other words, if Johnson underwent precisely the kind of "conversion experience" during her pregnancy described and inscribed throughout the decade in dominant reproductive discourse as appropriately maternal and natural; if gestation aroused in her what postmenopausal therapies, among other reproductive interventions, assume to be and address as a deep, biologically rooted sense of maternal desire *regardless of genetic ties*; if her experience of herself, her pregnancy, and her relationship to the fetus she carried changed, as it typically does for women, once the fetus had quickened, what exactly did both the Superior and Supreme Courts of California, as well as the popular media, find so puzzling about her claim of having bonded with the child she produced and her bid for custody based on it? If "bonding" is regarded as something that happens universally and naturally; if the exception is considered that instance when a woman does not develop an attachment to the fetus she is carrying rather than when she does, indeed, if a woman's lack of maternal attachment is what is typically considered the stuff of scandal and deviance, what rendered Johnson's claim so remarkably queer, unfathomable, deviant, or unusual—in fact, so specious—as to inspire Superior Court Judge Richard Parslow to pathologize it as criminal, as a potential instrument for future emotional and financial extortion, and to dismiss it as groundless?[18]

Ostensibly, the issue from the court's point of view was Johnson's veracity—or, perhaps more accurately, her apparent lack of it. As Judge Parslow observed in his decision, "One of the problems with bonding is that it always involves credibility issues. If the only evidence is someone say[ing] 'I felt strongly towards the child, I bonded with the child,' you've got to take their word for it."[19] This the judge was clearly unwilling to do, noting that there was "substantial evidence in the record that [Johnson] never bonded with th[e child she gestated] until she filed her lawsuit, if then."[20] Giving birth was not in itself a constitutive sign of maternity. While acknowledging her gestational contribution—she provided " a place to carry the child" and was its "host"—the court went on to characterize Johnson's maternal attachment as provisional and, therefore, secondary. In Judge Parslow's words:

Anna's relationship to the child is analogous to that of a foster parent, providing care, protection, and nurture during the period of time that the natural mother, Crispina Calvert, was unable to care for the child. . . . A foster parent provides care always understanding that the day may come when the mother of the child will once again be able to take the child and you have to give the child to the mother when she's met whatever conditions she has had to meet to have the child returned to her and walk away and live with it. That's the way it works. That's the way its worked for a long time.[21]

According to the judge, Johnson was neither conned nor coerced by the Calverts, but knowingly and willingly entered into a business agreement with them that circumscribed her relationship with the child she had consented to produce. This knowledge, he argued, the knowledge that "the baby would be exclusively the Calverts' when it was born," precluded the possibility of her having developed the deep, strong, meaningful, and abiding bond with it that she claimed to have developed. Invoking the testimony of Dr. Justin David Call, a child psychiatrist and pediatrician at the University of California, Irvine, and expert witness for the Calverts, Judge Parslow went on to distinguish Johnson's gestational attachment as primarily social rather than biological or natural. Bonds of the sort she insisted had formed, true maternal bonds, were likely to occur, he argued, only within the sanctity of a proper family unit, among "married mothers with husbands whose babies they carry."[22] Outside of this context, such bonding, in his view, was a matter of chance or choice:

People that are married and get pregnant and plan for a child, that contributes to the mother's feelings toward the child she is carrying. And, in a situation, [Dr. Call] said, where the plan is from day one that the child is the genetic child of another couple but it's going to be given to that couple to raise exclusively when it's born means that there is less likelihood and should be less likelihood psychologically of a person carrying the child bonding with the child.[23]

Finally, the judge contended (again invoking Call's testimony) that, even in the unlikely event that Anna Johnson had, as she claimed, bonded with the fetus while gestating it, there was no clear indication, "no evidence whatsoever," that the fetus had bonded with her.[24]

As the court read the facts before it, who and what the fetus was and would become—its indi-vidual physiological and psychological identity—had more or less been settled genetically.[25] This, in its view, not only rendered the child the Calverts' product and property, but established between the child and the Calverts a bond that was both innate and indivisible—indeed, a bond that the court speculated would, were it severed, reduce the child, Christopher, to a state of genealogical confusion, imperil the development of his sense of self-hood, and eventually compel him later in life to seek out the deeper roots of his identity, his original family or place of natural origin. In the view of the court, the search for such origins or the desire to know the where, who, and how of our existence is itself a "built-in," natural, human instinct or drive, concretely expressed in the formation of families and, on a somewhat grander scale, the very science of genetics.[26] Insisting that a "three parent, two-mom claim was a situation ripe for crazy-making," Judge Parslow found that genetic connection alone both made and sustained a family unit and that gestation itself was merely an incidental in this case, a contractual moment in the constitution of that unit. Describing Mark and Crispina Calvert as a couple who had sought only to realize their most precious possession, their genetic heritage, a couple who between them could produce an embryo, but simply "ha[d] no place to carry it," the judge awarded exclusive custody of the boy to them, his genetic, biological, natural, and thus "real" parents, while relegating Anna Johnson to the status of surrogate carrier. That both of the "natural" parents had come by their "natural" parenthood in the most "unnatural" of fashions was apparently beside the point from the perspective of the bench. Speaking strictly in the register of the natural, the register that the court itself deployed, Anna Johnson's activities were considerably "more natural" than those the Calverts themselves performed. Nevertheless, in the interest of avoiding future psychological confusion and of consolidating this newly made yet "natural" family, further contact between Johnson and the child was terminated.

III

No one except Anna Johnson herself can say why she has waged this unseemly struggle.[27]

Judge Parslow asserted that of the many issues he was called upon to disentangle in the case before him, race was not among them, and the print media apparently agreed, noting that race itself had "played no discernible role" in either the proceedings or the decision. Notwithstanding "the public prejudice," as William Steiner, court-appointed guardian for the baby, reported it, "that Anna [was] a dumb welfare mother trying to rip off the Calverts," in the estimation of the press, the only moment of obvious racial impropriety during the hearings was a remark made by Mark Calvert characterizing the custody battle as "our blackest nightmare."[28] While recognized as tactless, this comment was nevertheless excused as an indiscretion born of rage and frustration. The Calverts, after all, were themselves an interracial, hence self-evidently tolerant, couple—although not exactly brown, Crispina Calvert, a Filipina, was not exactly white either. To the degree that anyone was identified as having a "problem" with race, that person, ironically, was Johnson. As lawyers for the Calverts attempted to present the matter, Johnson had been motivated to sue for custody not, as she claimed, because of "maternal instincts" that had "just come out naturally," but rather, they implied, because she fetishized whiteness. "Have you ever told anyone that you always wanted to have a white baby?" they inquired over the objections of her attorney. "Considering that I'm half white myself," she replied, "no."[29]

Despite posttrial assessments to the contrary, the proceedings as well as the decision in *Johnson v. Calvert* clearly worked to safeguard the prerogatives of race and class privilege—indeed, both worked, as Johnson's lawyer succinctly put it, to ensure that the white baby was given to the white couple.[30] What invites and requires closer scrutiny is *how:* What constellation of assumptions makes plausible the suggestion that the dark-skinned Johnson was simply lost in a dream of whiteness—so lost in a struggle to achieve whiteness that she misled and entrapped a couple whose infertility rendered them desperate and vulnerable, indeed, so lost that she failed to see clearly who she was and to whom the white baby she had "hosted" belonged even though the answer had been scientifically established with DNA tests and was, for many at least, visibly apparent? As Crispina Calvert asserted repeatedly in court and to the press, "He looks just like us."

Likewise, what narratives were at play and took flesh to facilitate the many curious inversions in this case? How did the judge, the Calverts, and the media, for example, escape what Johnson apparently could not, a preoccupation with race that courted pathology? What permit-ted the struggle she waged to be dismissed as "unseemly" when, typically, "foster mothers who grow attached to their charges and try to keep them are regarded with much popular sympathy and sometimes even succeed"?[31] And, speaking still of inversion, how did Johnson rather than the Calverts come to be positioned as exploitative and parasitic, when the Calverts paid Johnson what amounted to approximately $1.54 an hour—well below the minimum wage—to satisfy their genetic yearnings and gestate their zygote? Who exactly was the instrument of whom? Finally, what set of stories grounded the court's confidence, and apparently the public's at well, that they could read Johnson's "true" desires even if she herself denied or refused to speak them? What makes credible and coherent their conclusion that her custody challenge was duplicitous at best, evidence not of a change of heart or mind but of a failed moral character? And what evidence, other than her word, could Johnson have produced that would have qualified as such and substantiated her claim?

I suggested earlier that, as a black woman, Johnson entered the public discourse a densely scripted figure, positioned in and by a crude, if commonplace, set of racial caricatures and cultural narratives about "the way black women are." In the context of the court's allegedly neutral and neutralizing practice of "racial non-recognition"—a practice that holds that "race" exists apart from the social and historical meanings that construct it, that assumes that one can acknowledge color without also reading it and that thus works to privilege precisely what it ostensibly prevents—both enjoyed unrestrained circulation, setting and circumscribing the terms in which her account could be rendered and heard.[32] Consider the felony charges of welfare fraud that were leveled in advance of the custody hearings and that haunted them throughout even though the infraction they alleged was shown later to have been the result of a bureaucratic mix-up of the sort for which state and federal agencies are legendary. These charges functioned to ignite, reinforce, and affix to the figure of Johnson "a constellation of ideas, images, and fears [already in circulation] about black women, the black family, economics, and cultural well-being."[33] They established as fact larger fictions of skin, or what Johnson's color already suggested could be assumed: *that she had been on welfare,* had, therefore, engaged in a form of "undeserved theft," and was, therefore, predisposed to ripping people off. The fact of welfare commingled with skin signified, among other things, moral depravity, lack of veracity, and capacity for deception.[34] It marked her as someone capable of deceiving the Calverts and exploiting their procreative yearnings in a coldly calculating fashion, for gain—indeed, as someone who lied rather than simply changed her mind.

If economic dependence, and the moral depravity it supposedly reflects, rendered Johnson's claim of having bonded with the white baby she had borne implausible, a related and equally powerful set of narratives having to do with the absent or arrested character of black maternal nature called into question her very ability to bond. Although these narratives have varied historically, they have figured black women's bodies and lives in one form or another since slavery, and share the assumption that black women are not only or simply maternally deficient: black women, while fertile, are rather "natally dead."[35]

The recitation of ostensibly high rates of illegitimate births, devastating images of babies perinatally exposed to crack or AIDS, equally arresting images of inner-city street slaughter, court-ordered implantation of the contraceptive Norplant to protect the current *and unconceived children* of women charged with "bad parenting"— these stories and others that circulated during the 1980s worked in conjunction with and as part of the dominant reproductive discourse of the decade to suggest that although black women can and do "breed" children, "they" neither possess nor display the instinctual drives necessary for mothering them.[36] As the court maintained with respect to Johnson—giving birth is not in itself proof of maternity—so too with respect to black women within the culture at large. In contrast to the maternally dormant and repressed white bodies depicted in abortion discourse or the maternally desperate and frustrated ones of infertility, the reproductive black body was figured within the decade's dominant discourse primarily in the coextensive if contradictory registers of absence and excess—as natally dead and thus dangerous, as boundlessly fertile and in need of containment. When black women fail so consistently to develop instinctual attachments to their own genetic offspring, the likelihood that one could or would develop bonds of the sort Johnson claimed to have formed with a genetically unrelated infant is remote. Indeed, it is, as the court's reading of Johnson through the medium and saturated meaning of skin clearly found it, unfathomable.

IV

Throughout this essay, I have been suggesting that the racialized meanings of skin set the terms in which the larger issues raised in the Anna Johnson case were addressed and settled. Color bears meaning and bears particular histories of meaning. Both enjoyed unrestrained circulation throughout the proceedings, indeed, both were clearly constitutive in shaping the particular way in which the court restabilized conventional understandings of parenthood and family disturbed by the practice of gestational surrogacy and the proliferation of relationships and identities accompanying it.

Having said this, I want also to suggest that the outcome of the case would not have been significantly different had Anna Johnson been white. Had Johnson been white, the central issues of race, class, and gender would clearly have been figured differently, and this difference might have recast the question of "extortion," for example, or resculpted the issue of veracity, or shifted the terms that informed the court's reasoning with respect to the child's "best interest." The outcome of the case, however, would have remained the same. The challenge before the court was to contain what signified as excess within the context of conventional understandings of parent and family or (re)naturalize and (re)authorize extant forms of life against other possible forms and formations. Containing excess or reauthoring and authorizing the familar is precisely what Judge Parslow's decision accomplished through the deployment of genetics, and it is also what his ruling would have sought to accomplish had the gestational surrogate been white. New reproductive practices and processes

may force open the possibility of refiguring conventional cultural categories, identities, and relations: Judge Parslow "might have decided that while Johnson could not be considered a legal parent, she had a lesser right to share responsibility for and participate in the child's life."[37] But, as we have seen throughout this book, such practices and processes also work, not surprisingly, to foreclose this possibility, "to reproduce and enhance existing relations of power."[38] The court's findings in this case as well as the New Jersey court's findings in the case of Baby M worked to preserve the "natural" family (even as they also produced it) against "crazy-making" alternatives. And out of both conflicts the "natural" family emerged as a biologically rooted, racially closed, heterosexual, middle-class unit.

If the Baby M case intensifies our attention to how biological facts are deployed to facilitate the parasitical workings of class prerogative and male prerogative both shaped by particular imperatives about race in the construction of the "natural" family, the case of Anna J. allows us to track the parasitical workings and production of race shaped by class and gender. Although mapping the production and operation of class, race, and gender power in the context of rulings on such cases will not, in itself, interrupt this power, such a mapping can nevertheless serve the more modest but critical end of demystifying how such power works—and in that end lies a political beginning.

Note: The notes for Reading 19 are in the "Notes" section at the end of the book.

 Article Review Form at end of book.

WiseGuide Wrap-Up

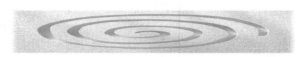

- Family structures are defined culturally, and women participate in those structures as members of a gendered category.

- Race and class inflect patterns of women's roles in families.

- Heterosexual partnerships are the basis for the current definition of what constitutes family.

- Technology breaks apart existing links between family structures and community relations.

R.E.A.L. Sites

This list provides a print preview of typical **coursewise** R.E.A.L. sites. (There are over 100 such sites at the **courselinks**™ site.) The danger in printing URLs is that Web sites can change overnight. As we went to press, these sites were functional using the URLs provided. If you come across one that isn't, please let us know via email to: webmaster@coursewise.com. Use your Passport to access the most current list of R.E.A.L. sites at the **courselinks**™ site.

Site name: The Family Violence Prevention Fund
URL: http://www.igc.org/fund/
Key topics: Violence Against Women, Families
Why is it R.E.A.L.? This site is maintained by one of the most active nonprofit organizations working against domestic violence.
Activity: After reviewing this site, based on the statistics, stories, and reports, develop a plan of action for your college campus which would address issues of violence against the women students on your campus. Include this plan in your own web site on domestic violence and its effects on families.

Site name: Feminist Majority Foundation
URL: http://www.feminist.org/
Key topics: Community, Feminism, Technology
Why is it R.E.A.L.? This site is the most comprehensive site on the Internet for women's issues.
Activity: Send an e-mail through the feedback page of this site, discussing the ways in which this site operates as a community of feminists in cyberspace, and whether or not you think it succeeds. Include information about yourself and feedback on what works and what doesn't work in building a feminist community. You will need to review the entire site first.

Site name: Sol's Pages: An 11-Year-Old Girl Speaks Out About Her Lesbian Family
URL: http://www.geocities.com/WestHollywood/Heights/6502/index.html #TableofContents
Key topics: Families, Gay and Lesbian, Discrimination
Why is it R.E.A.L.? This ten-year-old girl is currently participating in a number of activities around the discrimination against gay and lesbian parents and their children. Her site is a personal story, but it is also a record of larger social attitudes and public legislative battles for equality.
Activity: Do a web search for other sites that deal with the subject of lesbian and gay families. Build your own web site using the results of your search as a set of links about lesbian and gay families. Include a brief abstract about each link, as well as an introductory and concluding set of remarks about the discrimination faced by gay and lesbian families.

section 6

Key Points

- Women's contributions and participation in technology, agriculture, and health care issues are often invisible.

- New developments in these areas sometimes negatively impact women's lives.

- Technology and the environment are linked through global economics. These links are inflected by gender in both traditional and unexpected ways.

- As social systems become more globally interdependent, opportunities arise for coalitions between different groups of women. Labor exploitation, erasure, violence, and disease become sites of resistance to male dominance.

Techno-eco-nomics: Technology, Eco-Feminism, Global Economies, Women's Health

 **WiseGuide Intro**

This section covers several developing issues for women. Advancements in technology, ecological concerns, and increasing globalization affect all women within their local community groups, even as changes in these areas are occurring on a global level. As noted in Sections 3 and 5, technology has fundamentally altered human reproduction. The computer has invaded multiple levels of worldwide social systems, all the while perpetuating masculine control over and with this critical tool of late twentieth century political economies. As technology moves forward, the devastation of the earth's environment threatens to undermine technological potential. These two seemingly competing developments are linked through the movements of governments and corporations toward a globalized economy. While these would, on the surface, seem to be more than "just women's issues" (a troubling assertion about anything), these new arenas go directly to the heart of women's lives, now and in the future, and will have a direct impact on their health and their participation in the new global economy.

Women use reproductive technologies, while men invent and refine them. Women input data into computers, while men read and manipulate that data. Women earn pennies to build computers, in the process being exposed to dangerous environmental hazards, while men reap enormous profits from bargain labor and sparse environmental controls. The use of women's bodies, without their complete participation and representation in the process of development and without their full partnership in the final rewards of technology—improved health care, environmental protection, and the accumulation of capital—is a replication of male dominance and female subordination.

In these essays, a pattern emerges of the erasure of women. Sadie Plant's essay demonstrates that, even as women have been part of the computer revolution in important ways, their participation has been forgotten. In "The Real Number-One Killer," Cool exposes the research and treatment of a more deadly killer for women than breast cancer. The *Harvard Women's Health Watch* provides details about new studies of postmenopausal women, lifestyle links to cancer and cardiovascular disease, and ethnic differences at the onset of menopause. Enloe looks beyond U.S. borders to uncover the circulation of women's bodies in the multinational labor pool in "The Globetrotting Sneaker," while Nathan reveals the hidden world behind that female labor pool as one full of violence, but one in which women participate as more than victims. Shiva exposes the erasure of women's participation in agriculture in "GATT, Agriculture and Third World Women." Finally, Bunch and Fried in "Beijing '95" suggest strategies from the Fourth World Conference on Women for making global progress for women's rights.

Questions

Reading 20. Who is Ada Lovelace and how does she fit into our ideas of computers as "masculine" tools?

Reading 21. Why do more women believe they are at greater risk for breast cancer than for heart disease?

Reading 22. Which health concerns are more likely to be addressed in research on women's bodies?

Reading 23. Nike responds to increases in labor costs in any given country by moving its factories to new countries with lower wages. How does Nike justify these moves?

Reading 24. How does the violence perpetuated against the young women working in the maquilas benefit the corporations contracting with the maquilas?

Reading 25. What does the indigenous farmers' loss of ownership of genetic material as Intellectual Property Rights to transnational corporations mean to the lives of women in developing countries?

Reading 26. Given the labor exploitation of transnational corporations such as Nike and the loss of control of local resources that global treaties like GATT herald, what impact will coalitions around human rights as women's rights have on global economies?

Who is Ada Lovelace and how does she fit into our ideas of computers as "masculine" tools?

Zeros and Ones

Digital women and the new technoculture

Sadie Plant

In 1833, a teenage girl met a machine which she came to regard "as a friend." It was a futuristic device which seemed to have dropped into her world at least a century before its time.

Later to be known as Ada Lovelace, she was then Ada Byron, the only child of Annabella, a mathematician who had herself been dubbed Princess of Parallelograms by her husband, Lord Byron. The machine was the Difference Engine, a calculating system on which the engineer Charles Babbage had been working for many years. "We both went to see the thinking machine (for such it seems) last Monday," Annabella wrote in her diary. To the amazement of its onlookers, it "raised several Nos. to the 2nd & 3rd powers, and extracted the root of a quadratic Equation." While most of the audience gazed in astonishment at the machine, Ada "young as she was, understood its working, and saw the great beauty of the invention."

When Babbage had begun work on the Difference Engine, he was interested in the possibility of "making machinery to compute arithmetical tables." Although he struggled to persuade the British government to fund his work, he had no doubt about the feasibility and the value of such a machine. Isolating common mathematical differences between tabulated numbers, Babbage was convinced that this "method of differences supplied a general principle by which *all* tables might be computed through limited intervals, by one uniform process." By 1822 he had made a small but functional machine, and "in the year 1833, an event of great importance in the history of the engine occurred. Mr. Babbage had directed a portion of it, consisting of sixteen figures, to be put together. It was capable of calculating tables having two or three orders of differences, and, to some extent, of forming other tables. The action of this portion completely justified the expectations raised, and gave a most satisfactory assurance of its final success."

Shortly after this part of his machine went on public display, Babbage was struck by the thought that the Difference Engine, still incomplete, had already superseded itself. "Having, in the meanwhile, naturally speculated upon the general principles on which machinery for calculation might be constructed, *a principle of an entirely new kind* occurred to him, the power of which over the most complicated arithmetical operations seemed nearly unbounded. On reexamining his drawings . . . the new principle appeared to be limited only by the extent of the mechanism it might require." If the simplicity of the mechanisms which allowed the Difference Engine to perform addition could be extended to thousands rather than hundreds of components, a machine could be built which would "execute more rapidly the calculations for which the *Difference* Engine was intended; or, that the *Difference* Engine would itself be superseded by a far simpler mode of construction." The government officials who had funded Babbage's work on the first machine were not pleased to learn that it was now to be abandoned in favor of a new set of mechanical processes which "were essentially different from those of the Difference Engine." While Babbage did his best to persuade them that the "fact of a new superseding an old machine, in a very few years, is one of constant occurrence in our manufactories;

and instances might be pointed out in which the advance of invention has been so rapid, and the demand for machinery so great, that half-finished machines have been thrown aside as useless before their completion." Babbage's decision to proceed with his new machine was also his break with the bodies which had funded his previous work. Babbage lost the support of the state, but he had already gained assistance of a very different kind.

"You are a brave man," Ada told Babbage, "to give yourself wholly up to Fairy-Guidance!—I advise you to allow yourself to be unresistingly bewitched . . ." No one, she added, "knows what almost *awful* energy & power lie yet undeveloped in that *wiry* little system of mine."

In 1842 Louis Menabrea, an Italian military engineer, had deposited his *Sketch of the Analytical Engine Invented by Charles Babbage* in the Bibliothèque Universelle de Génève. Shortly after its appearance, Babbage later wrote, the "Countess of Lovelace informed me that she had translated the memoir of Menabrea." Enormously impressed by this work, Babbage invited her to join him in the development of the machine. "I asked why she had not herself written an original paper on a subject with which she was so intimately acquainted? To this Lady Lovelace replied that the thought had not occurred to her. I then suggested that she should add some notes to Menabrea's

> "A strong-minded woman! Much like her mother, eh? Wears green spectacles and writes learned books . . . She wants to upset the universe, and play dice with the hemispheres. Women *never* know when to stop . . ."
> **William Gibson and Bruce Sterling, *The Difference Engine***

memoir; an idea which was immediately adopted."

Babbage and Ada developed an intense relationship. "We discussed together the various illustrations that might be introduced," wrote Babbage. "I suggested several, but the selection was entirely her own. So also was the algebraic working out of the different problems, except, indeed, that relating to the numbers of Bernoulli, which I had offered to do to save Lady Lovelace the trouble. This she sent back to me for an amendment, having detected a grave mistake which I had made in the process."

Babbage's mathematical errors, and many of his attitudes, greatly irritated Ada. While his tendency to blame other bodies for the slow progress of his work was sometimes well founded, when he insisted on prefacing the publication of the memoir and her notes with a complaint about the attitude of the British authorities to his work, Ada refused to endorse him. "I never *can* or *will* support you in acting on principles which I consider not only wrong in themselves, but suicidal." She declared Babbage "one of the most impracticable, selfish, & intemperate persons one can have to do with," and laid down several severe conditions for the continuation of their collaboration. "Can you," she asked, with undisguised impatience, "undertake to give your mind *wholly and undividedly*, as a primary object that no engagement is to interfere with, to the consider-

ation of all those matters in which I shall at times require your intellectual *assistance & supervision*, & can you promise not to *slur & hurry* things over; or to mislay & allow confusion & mistakes to enter into documents &c?"

Ada was, she said, "very much *afraid* as yet of exciting the powers I *know I have over others*, & the *evidence* of which I have certainly been *most unwilling to admit*, in fact for a long time considered quite fanciful and absurd . . . I therefore carefully refrain from all attempts *intentionally* to exercise unusual powers." Perhaps this was why her work was simply attributed to A.A.L. "It is not my wish to *proclaim* who has written it," she wrote. These were just a few afterthoughts, a mere commentary on someone else's work. But Ada did want them to bear some name: "I rather wish to append anything that may tend hereafter to *individualize it & identify it*, with other productions of the said A.A.L." And for all her apparent modesty, Ada knew how important her notes really were. "To say the truth, I am rather *amazed* at them; & cannot help being struck quite *malgré moi*, with the really masterly nature of the style, & its Superiority to that of the Memoir itself." Her work was indeed vastly more influential—and three times longer—than the text to which they were supposed to be mere adjuncts. A hundred years before the hardware had been built, Ada had produced the first example of what was later called computer programming.

 Article Review Form at end of book.

Why do more women believe they are at greater risk for breast cancer than for heart disease?

The Real Number-One Killer

Let's scratch everything you've assumed about heart disease and get something straight. It's the number-one killer of women (breast cancer is number three), it affects men and women differently, and it's not limited to senior citizens. One more thing. It's the choices you make today—what you eat, whether you smoke, how you handle stress—that determine your risk. Nicotine patch, anyone?

Lisa Collier Cool

On her 40th birthday, Lori Morray woke with an ache in her chest. Indigestion, she thought. Too many cigarettes. When that pain persisted into the afternoon, though, she dropped in to see her doctor, who dismissed it as stress and sent her on her way. Worse by that evening—tired, and with a throbbing, laborlike pain in her chest—she skipped her birthday festivities and headed to the emergency room, where doctors hooked her up to an electrocardiogram, popped nitroglycerin under her tongue and informed her, to her utter amazement, that she was having a heart attack.

Without realizing it, Morray was a prime candidate for such a catastrophe, with a family history of the disease (her mother), a pack-a-day habit, a few extra

pounds to lose and an aversion to exercise. "I just didn't know enough to pay attention," she says. Neither, apparently, did her doctor. Which brings us to the crux of the issue: Most of us, physicians included, don't know much about heart disease in women. (For years, the medical community simply extrapolated what they knew about the disease in men.) A pity—some would say an outrage—because heart disease is the leading cause of death for women, and this is a case in which ignorance can kill.

The good news for Morray is that she survived her heart attack despite the obstacles she encountered in getting care (she's since given up cigarettes, taken up walking and dropped a few pounds). The good news for all women is that research is beginning to yield surprising new insight into the vagaries of the

female heart, much of which sheds light on the reasons heart disease is such an unrecognized problem among women, and on what they can do to reduce their risks and get better treatment. Here, some of the most unexpected new findings:

Heart disease is more likely to kill you than breast cancer is.

Some 52 percent of women think they're more likely to die of breast cancer than of heart disease, according to a 1997 *New York Times*/CBS News Poll on women's health issues. The real ratio? Only 3 percent of women are likely to succumb to breast cancer, while 30 percent are expected to meet their end via heart disease, says Elsa-Grace Giardina, M.D., director of the Center for

Courtesy of Harper's Bazaar.

Women's Health at Columbia-Presbyterian Medical Center in New York City. (Breast cancer is actually the *third* leading cause of death in women, the second being lung cancer.) The perception discrepancy has a lot to do with the emotional nature of breast cancer and the thoroughness with which breast-cancer advocates have educated women about the importance of mammograms and self-exams, say heart researchers. Somehow the word that heart disease is the more likely killer has been lost in the din.

As a result women who will nag their cigarette-smoking, fatty-food eating, sedentary husbands (the stereotypical heart-attack candidates) about changing their ways aren't necessarily likely to heed their own advice. Thirty-five percent of adult women in this country are overweight, 24.8 percent smoke, and 62 percent don't exercise regularly. And though the risk of a heart attack is highest for women after menopause, it's early health habits that ultimately determine your risk, says Marla Mendelson, M.D., who chaired the American Heart Association of Chicago's 1997 conference on cardiovascular disease in women. "Waiting until menopause to do something is *way* too late."

Chest pain may not be the first sign of a heart attack.

The typical symptoms for women tend *not* to be the classic elephant-sitting-on-your-chest, pain-down-your-left-arm kinds men describe. Instead women tend to experience a wide range of sensations, including an uneasy feeling in the chest, shortness of breath, fatigue,

dizziness or fainting, fluttering heartbeat, swelling in the ankles or lower legs and nausea. The tricky aspect of all this, of course, is that there are a number of reasons you might feel any one of these symptoms, from a stomach bug to skipping lunch. One indication that something more serious may be afoot is if your symptoms appear or get worse with exercise, or anytime the heart's under stress, says Elizabeth Ross, M.D., a cardiologist at Washington Hospital Center in Washington, DC, and author of *Healing the Female Heart* (Simon & Schuster). "I've seen patients who had warning signs, in that they got 'indigestion' every time they played tennis or worked out," she says. "They didn't realize it was cardiac pain."

Your doctor may know less about your heart than you do.

That's a *slight* exaggeration—but it's not too far off the mark. Only 39 percent of primary-care physicians (the ones you're most likely to call in a crisis) surveyed in a 1996 Gallup poll said that they were well trained in the specificities of heart disease in women. About two thirds mistakenly believed that the warning signs for a heart attack are the same for men and women, and 90 percent had no idea what the significant female symptoms might be. Worse yet, only 50 percent knew that the leading health threat for women is heart disease. Dismal as this sounds, it's an improvement over the 1995 survey, in which only 11 percent of physicians were considered well trained.

Basically there's less than a 50-50 chance that your doctor is

up to speed on your heart, which means that a little medical knowledge on your part might very well save your life. Consider the case of a 24-year-old emergency medical technician who, suspecting that the chest pain she was having was heart related, insisted on a full workup when she went to the emergency room. It turned out not only that she'd had a heart attack but also that two of her arteries were so badly clogged that she needed bypass surgery. "If she hadn't demanded tests, she'd probably have been one of those cases of sudden cardiac death you read about, where someone drops dead playing basketball or jogging," say Giardina, who later became the young woman's doctor.

Most of us aren't routinely screened for heart risks.

Nearly 60 percent of the women polled for a recent *Prevention* magazine survey said their doctors had never discussed heart disease with them, and 50 percent said their cholesterol—the level of which can indicate risk—is not regularly checked by their doctors. To make sure that you and your physician are doing everything possible to lower your risk for heart disease, cardiologists recommend having all three cholesterols (high-density lipoprotein, low-density lipoprotein and triglycerides) measured; getting your blood pressure taken (if it's over 140/90, you're at risk); and having your blood sugar checked. Poorly controlled diabetes—a disorder that's much more prevalent than people realize—is a major risk factor for heart disease in young women.

A woman's symptoms are often brushed off as psychosomatic.

When women see their doctors about palpitations, they're frequently told the problem is in their head, not their heart, according to a new study by Allegheny University of the Health Sciences, in Philadelphia. Of the 98 people surveyed—all of whom had arrhythmias serious enough to require surgery—35 percent of the women, versus 4 percent of the men, said they'd originally been misdiagnosed with anxiety; half of the misdiagnosed women had been given powerful antianxiety medication they didn't need. It's a shame, says Beverly Hills cardiologist Debra R. Judelson, M.D., president of the American Medical Women's Association, because though not all arrhythmias need medical attention, some that do may be easily treatable with a new procedure called radiofrequency ablation, which can be performed under local anesthesia in a three-hour hospital procedure. "But," says Judelson, "I continue to see women who have been told by *many* doctors that their problem is just anxiety."

The treadmill stress test isn't effective for women.

Since the treadmill test is based on the typical male build, heart function and response to exercise, women's results have to be "translated," which leaves a lot of room for error. The treadmill test fails to identify as many as 70 percent of women with cardiac disorders, according to a recent study. On the flip side, up to 40 percent of women with healthy hearts get false-positive results, which means that they risk being sent for needless and invasive follow-up tests. The solution, according to another recent study, appears to be use of an imaging test (such as echocardiography, in which an ultrasound is used to visualize the heart in motion) in *addition* to the treadmill. The results of the combination have been deemed 80 percent accurate.

Men may have more heart attacks, but women are more likely to die from them.

Roughly 987,000 men age 29 and over have heart attacks each year, compared with 513,000 women in the same age group, according to estimates from the Framingham Heart Study. The catch is that almost as many women as men (about 250,000) die from them. Why the deadly gender gap? As in the case of Lori Morray, women underestimate their risk for heart disease and delay getting medical treatment for their symptoms; then they're unable to get treatment, because many of the doctors they consult first don't recognize the problem. By the time they do go to the hospital, it's often too late for lifesaving therapies like clot busters, which can stop damage to the heart if given within a few hours of the attack. What's more, many doctors don't take women's heart attacks as seriously even when they know what's going on. Women are only a third as likely to receive balloon angioplasty or bypass surgery as equally ill men, which might explain why 44 percent of women but only 27 percent of men die within a year of having a heart attack.

Folic acid helps keep your heart healthy.

As if there weren't enough heart hazards to worry about already, researchers have recently identified a brand-new enemy: the amino acid homocysteine, a by-product of protein breakdown. The more of it you have in your bloodstream, the greater your odds of developing plaqued arteries, and thus having a heart attack. "High homocysteine levels may be responsible for the deaths from heart disease of up to 35,000 women in the U.S. each year," says Shirley A.A. Beresford, professor of epidemiology at the University of Washington in Seattle. The same researchers who identified homocysteine have also found that the B-vitamin folic acid helps convert it into other, harmless by-products, and that a deficiency of folic acid ups your risk of high levels of homocysteine in the blood. You can get the vitamin via supplements or by eating foods such as citrus fruits, beans or leafy greens. Don't take more than 400 micrograms, however, since there's concern that very high levels can mask a vitamin B-12 deficiency.

Anger is almost as bad for you as smoking and not exercising.

The sterotype of the driven, hostile, type A personality as the classic heart-attack candidate is only partly right, according to new research. It turns out that being ambitious won't kill you, but anger might. "Angry, hostile individuals tend to have higher blood pressure, which is a major risk factor for a heart attack," explains Roxanne A. Rodney, M.D., associate director of nuclear cardiology at Columbia University. "When people get mad, they produce a surge of catecholamines—stress hormones—that increase heart rate and blood pressure and, over time, can damage coronary arteries and increase the likelihood of developing blood clots, precursors to both heart attacks and strokes." Even if you don't have hypertension to begin with, says Rodney, flying into a rage on a regular basis can take its toll.

The fight-or-flight reaction to stress can hurt you.

It's not stress per se that makes us vulnerable to illness, but how we react to it. "If stress stimulates you to achieve your goals, it's an extremely positive force," says Elizabeth Ross. "But if you bottle it up so that you get anxious, depressed or chronically frustrated, it's dangerous." In addition to being an emotional drain, these negative emotions can actually cause blood vessels to constrict, cutting down blood flow to the heart. Being stressed out doubled the risk that the hearts of a group of patients (who had clogged arteries to begin with) participating in a recent Duke University Medical Center study wouldn't get enough blood flow, while chilling out significantly improved it. One of the key warning signs that stress may be getting the best of you is something heart experts refer to as vital exhaustion: feeling mentally and physically depleted first thing in the morning.

Resources: For more information or to order the book *The Silent Epidemic: The Truth About Women and Heart Disease*, call the American Heart Association at 800-AHA-USA1, or visit its Web site, http://www.americanheart.org. The National Heart, Lung, and Blood Institute offers several low-cost publications, including the *Healthy Heart Handbook for Women* ($5.50). To order it or to get a complete publication list, write to the NHLBI Information Center, P.O. Box 30105, Bethesda, MD 20824-0105, or call 800-575-WELL. You can also read up on the topic for free via the NHLBI Web site, at http://www.nhlbi.nih.gov/nhlbi/nhlbi.htm.

 Article Review Form at end of book.

Which health concerns are more likely to be addressed in research on women's bodies?

Women's Health Studies

The gender gap in medical research is closing. It has been since 1990, when the Office of Research on Women's Health was established at the National Institutes of Health to address the underrepresentation of women in medical studies. Since then, women in such investigations have increased not only in number, but also in diversity. Postmenopausal women, once all but ignored in scientific investigations, have become the focus of several new projects, and efforts to include African-American, Asian, and Hispanic women have expanded. These studies should provide information to guide us in reducing our risks of heart disease, cancer, osteoporosis, and other degenerative diseases. They generally take one of two forms—observational or interventional investigations.

Observational studies are designed to reveal possible associations between physical characteristics or health habits and disease. They usually include large numbers of people who are followed for several years. The participants may answer periodic questionnaires and may also be tracked through hospital records, tumor registries or death records.

Interventional studies are designed to determine the effects of specific treatments, diets, or health practices. Controlled trials are considered the gold standard of interventional studies. In these investigations, participants are randomly assigned to groups and each group follows a certain treatment, with at least one of the groups receiving a placebo or no treatment at all. At the end of the study, the results in each of the groups are compared.

The following studies are the first major investigations to deal exclusively with health issues of women at mid-life and beyond.

- *The Women's Health Initiative.* The largest study of women to date, the WHI includes both observational and interventional components. Researchers at 40 centers around the country are studying 160,000 healthy, postmenopausal women who were between the ages of 50 and 79 when they enrolled.

  In the Observational Study, 100,000 women will undergo a physical examination upon entry and again after 3 years. Every year, the participants will complete questionnaires on their health habits.

The remaining 60,000 women are being enrolled in one or more of three controlled trials—the Dietary Modification (DM) Study, the Hormone Replacement Therapy (HRT) Study, or the Calcium and Vitamin D Supplementation (CaD) Study. The DM is designed to determine whether a low-fat diet reduces the risk of breast and colorectal cancer. The CaD study will test the effects of taking calcium and vitamin D supplements on osteoporosis risk.

The HRT Study should help to determine whether postmenopausal hormone supplementation actually lowers the risk of heart disease and osteoporosis and increases the risk of breast cancer, as some observational studies have indicated. It may also help to resolve the question of estrogen's effect on mental acuity and on the risk of developing Alzheimer's disease: women over age 65 will take annual examinations to test memory and reasoning. To enroll in this study, call 1-800-54-WOMEN.

- *The Nurses' Health Study.* This ongoing observational study, conducted by researchers at Brigham and Women's

Hospital, Harvard Medical School, and Harvard School of Public Health, was inaugurated in 1976, when 120,000 women between the ages of 30 and 55 were enrolled. They are asked to fill out extensive questionnaires about their health and lifestyles every two years. By changing the questions asked, the researchers are able to examine the relationship between different lifestyle factors and medical outcomes. The more than 100 reports emanating from this study have provided the foundation for additional research into women's health risks. These reports have, among other things, indicated that there are health benefits in regular exercise, diets high in fruits and vegetables, and maintaining a lean body mass. They have suggested that oral contraceptive use does not increase the risk of cardiovascular disease, that postmenopausal replacement therapy with estrogen alone is

linked with an increased risk of endometrial cancer, that drinking alcohol increases the risk of breast cancer, that the risk of gallstones rises with obesity, that suntanning increases the likelihood of melanoma, and that aspirin, estrogen, and exercise may reduce the risk of colon cancer.

The participants in the Nurses' Study are now between 50 and 75. Not only have their answers changed with age—more have suffered heart attacks, osteoporosis or cancer—but the questions have, too. The next round of inquiry is designed to obtain information on the psychosocial factors, such as stress, anxiety, social isolation and mood changes, that may influence health and longevity.

- *Study of Women's Health Across the Nation* (SWAN). This observational investigation, sponsored by the National Institute on Aging, is underway at seven medical centers in the United States. Researchers are selecting 3,200 women between the ages of 42 and 52, whom they will track for about five years. The project will focus on the physical and psychological differences among African-American, Hispanic, Asian-American, and Caucasian women during menopause.

The researchers will look at body composition, bone density, hormone levels, cardiovascular function, and menstrual bleeding. They will also consider psychosocial influences, such as sexuality, interpersonal relationships, commitment toward work, social values, and attitudes toward aging. Lifestyle factors—diet, exercise, smoking, and alcohol consumption—will also be included.

 Article Review Form at end of book.

Nike responds to increases in labor costs in any given country by moving its factories to new countries with lower wages. How does Nike justify these moves?

The Globetrotting Sneaker

Cynthia Enloe

Cynthia Enloe is a professor of government at Clark University. Her most recent book is "The Morning After: Sexual Politics at the End of the Cold War" (University of California Press).

Four years after the fall of the Berlin Wall marked the end of the Cold War, Reebok, one of the fastest growing companies in United States history, decided that the time had come to make its mark in Russia. Thus it was with considerable fanfare that Reebok's executives opened their first store in downtown Moscow in July 1993. A week after the grand opening, store managers described sales as well above expectations.

Reebok's opening in Moscow was the perfect post-Cold War scenario: commercial rivalry replacing military posturing; consumerist tastes homogenizing heretofore hostile peoples; capital and managerial expertise flowing freely across newly porous state borders. Russians suddenly had the "freedom" to spend money on U.S. cultural icons like athletic footwear, items priced above and beyond daily subsistence: at the end of 1993, the average Russian earned the equivalent of $40 a

month. Shoes on display were in the $100 range. Almost 60 percent of single parents, most of whom were women, were living in poverty. Yet in Moscow and Kiev, shoe promoters had begun targeting children, persuading them to pressure their mothers to spend money on stylish, Western sneakers. And as far as strategy goes, athletic shoe giants have, you might say, a good track record. In the U.S. many inner-city boys who see basketball as a "ticket out of the ghetto" have become convinced that certain brand-name shoes will give them an edge.

But no matter where sneakers are bought or sold, the potency of their advertising imagery has made it easy to ignore this mundane fact: Shaquille O'Neal's Reeboks are stitched by someone; Michael Jordans' Nikes are stitched by someone; so are your roommate's, so are your grandmother's. Those someones are women, mostly Asian women who are supposed to believe that their "opportunity" to make sneakers for U.S. companies is a sign of their country's progress—just as a Russian woman's chance to spend two month's salary on a pair of shoes for her child allegedly symbolizes the new Russia.

As the global economy expands, sneaker executives are looking to pay women workers less and less, even though the shoes that they produce are capturing an ever-growing share of the footwear market. By the end of 1993, sales in the U.S. alone had reached $11.6 billion. Nike, the largest supplier of athletic footwear in the world, posted a record $298 million profit for 1993—earnings that had nearly tripled in five years. And sneaker companies continue to refine their strategies for "global competitiveness"—hiring supposedly docile women to make their shoes, changing designs as quickly as we fickle customers change our tastes, and shifting factories from country to country as trade barriers rise and fall.

The logic of it all is really quite simple; yet trade agreements such as the North American Free Trade Agreement (NAFTA) and the General Agreement of Tariffs and Trade (GATT) are, of course, talked about in a jargon that alienates us, as if they were technical matters fit only for economists and diplomats. The bottom line is that all companies operating overseas depend on trade agreements made between their own governments and the regimes ruling the countries in which they want to make or sell their products. Korean, Indonesian, and other women workers around the world know this better than anyone. They are tackling trade politics because they have learned from hard experience that the trade deals their governments sign do little to improve the lives of workers. Guarantees of fair, healthy labor practices, of the rights to speak freely and to organize independently, will usually be left out of trade pacts—and women will suffer. The recent passage of both NAFTA and GATT ensures that a growing number of private companies will now be competing across borders without restriction [see page 137]. The result? Big business will step up efforts to pit working women in industrialized countries against much lower-paid working women in "developing" countries, perpetuating the misleading notion that they are inevitable rivals in the global job market.

All the "New World Order" really means to corporate giants like athletic shoemakers is that they now have the green light to accelerate long-standing industry practices. In the early 1980s, the field marshals commanding Reebok and Nike, which are both U.S.-based, decided to manufacture most of their sneakers in South Korea and Taiwan, hiring local women. L.A. Gear, Adidas, Fila, and Asics quickly followed their lead. In short time, the coastal city of Pusan, South Korea, became the "sneaker capital of the world." Between 1982 and 1989 the U.S. lost 58,500 footwear jobs to cities like Pusan, which attracted sneaker executives because its location facilitated international transport. More to

the point, South Korea's military government had an interest in suppressing labor organizing, and it had a comfortable military alliance with the U.S. Korean women also seemed accepting of Confucian philosophy, which measured a woman's morality by her willingness to work hard for her family's well-being and to acquiesce to her father's and husband's dictates. With their sense of patriotic duty, Korean women seemed the ideal labor force for export-oriented factories.

U.S. and European sneaker company executives were also attracted by the ready supply of eager Korean male entrepreneurs with whom they could make profitable arrangements. This fact was central to Nike's strategy in particular. When they moved their production sites to Asia to lower labor costs, the executives of the Oregon-based company decided to reduce their corporate responsibilities further. Instead of owning factories outright, a more efficient strategy would be to subcontract the manufacturing to wholly foreign-owned—in this case, South Korean—companies. Let them be responsible for workers' health and safety. Let them ne-

gotiate with newly emergent unions. Nike would retain control over those parts of sneaker production that gave its officials the greatest professional satisfaction and the ultimate word on the product: design and marketing. Although Nike was following in the footsteps of garment and textile manufacturers, it set the trend for the rest of the athletic footwear industry.

But at the same time, women workers were developing their own strategies. As the South Korean pro-democracy movement grew throughout the 1980s, increasing numbers of women rejected traditional notions of feminine duty. Women began organizing in response to the dangerous working conditions, daily humiliations, and low pay built into their work. Such resistance was profoundly threatening to the government, given the fact that South Korea's emergence as an industrialized "tiger" had depended on women accepting their "role" in growing industries like sneaker manu-

Hourly Wages in Athletic Footwear Factories

$7.38-7.94

$2.02-2.27

$ .65-.74

$ .10-.14
China

$ .16-.20
Indonesia

Thailand

S. Korea

U.S.

Figures are estimates based on 1993 data from the International Textile, Garment, and Leather Workers Federation; International Labor Organization; and the U.S. Bureau of Labor Statistics.

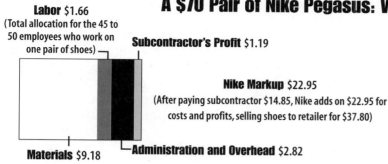

A $70 Pair of Nike Pegasus: Where the Money Goes

Labor $1.66
(Total allocation for the 45 to 50 employees who work on one pair of shoes)

Subcontractor's Profit $1.19

Nike Markup $22.95
(After paying subcontractor $14.85, Nike adds on $22.95 for costs and profits, selling shoes to retailer for $37.80)

Retail Markup $32.20
(Retailer adds on $32.20 for costs and profits, selling shoes for $70)

Materials $9.18

Administration and Overhead $2.82

Source: Nike, Inc.

facture. If women re-imagined their lives as daughters, as wives, as workers, as citizens, it wouldn't just rattle their employers; it would shake the very foundations of the whole political system.

At the first sign of trouble, factory managers called in government riot police to break up employees' meetings. Troops sexually assaulted women workers, stripping, fondling, and raping them "as a control mechanism for suppressing women's engagement in the labor movement," reported Jeong-Lim Nam of Hyosung Women's University in Taegu. It didn't work. It didn't work because the feminist activists in groups like the Korean Women Workers Association (KWWA) helped women understand and deal with the assaults. The KWWA held consciousness-raising sessions in which notions of feminine duty and respectability were tackled along with wages and benefits. They organized independently of the male-led labor unions to ensure that their issues would be taken seriously, in labor negotiations and in the pro-democracy movement as a whole.

The result was that women were at meetings with management, making sure that in addition to issues like long hours and low pay, sexual assault at the

hands of managers and health care were on the table. Their activism paid off: in addition to winning the right to organize women's unions, their earnings grew. In 1980, South Korean women in manufacturing jobs earned 45 percent of the wages of their male counterparts; by 1990, they were earning more than 50 percent. Modest though it was, the pay increase was concrete progress, given that the gap between women's and men's manufacturing wages in Japan, Singapore, and Sri Lanka actually *widened* during the 1980s. Last but certainly not least, women's organizing was credited with playing a major role in toppling the country's military regime and forcing open elections in 1987.

Without that special kind of workplace control that only an authoritarian government could offer, sneaker executives knew that it was time to move. In Nike's case, its famous advertising slogan—"Just Do It"—proved truer to its corporate philosophy than its women's "empowerment" ad campaign, designed to rally women's athletic (and consumer) spirit. In response to South Korean women workers' newfound activist self-confidence, the sneaker company and its subcontractors began shutting down a

number of their South Korean factories in the late 1980s and early 1990s. After bargaining with government officials in nearby China and Indonesia, many Nike subcontractors set up shop in those countries, while some went to Thailand. China's government remains nominally Communist; Indonesia's ruling generals are staunchly anti-Communist. But both are governed by authoritarian regimes who share the belief that if women can be kept hard at work, low paid, and unorganized, they can serve as a magnet for foreign investors.

Where does all this leave South Korean women—or any woman who is threatened with a factory closure if she demands decent working conditions and a fair wage? They face the dilemma confronted by thousands of women from dozens of countries. The risk of job loss is especially acute in relatively mobile industries; it's easier for a sneaker, garment, or electronics manufacturer to pick up and move than it is for an automaker or a steel producer. In the case of South Korea, poor women had moved from rural villages into the cities searching for jobs to support not only themselves, but parents and siblings. The exodus of manufacturing jobs has forced more women into the growing "entertainment" industry. The kinds of bars and massage parlors offering sexual services that had mushroomed around U.S. military bases during the Cold War have been opening up across the country.

But the reality is that women throughout Asia are organizing, knowing full well the risks involved. Theirs is a long-term view; they are taking direct aim at companies' nomadic advantage, by building links among workers in countries targeted for "development" by multinational corporations. Through sustained grassroots efforts, women are developing the skills and confidence that will make it increasingly difficult to keep their labor cheap. Many are looking to the United Nations conference on women in Beijing, China, this September, as a rare opportunity to expand their cross-border strategizing.

The Beijing conference will also provide an important opportunity to call world attention to the hypocrisy of the governments and corporations doing business in China. Numerous athletic shoe companies followed Nike in setting up manufacturing sites throughout the country. This included Reebok—a company claiming its share of responsibility for ridding the world of "injustice, poverty, and other ills that gnaw away at the social fabric," according to a statement of corporate principles.

Since 1988, Reebok has been giving out annual human rights awards to dissidents from around the world. But it wasn't until 1992 that the company adopted its own "human rights production standards"—after labor advocates made it known that the quality of life in factories run by its subcontractors was just as dismal as that at most other athletic shoe suppliers in Asia. Reebok's code of conduct, for example, includes a pledge to "seek" those subcontractors who respect workers' rights to organize. The only problem is that independent trade unions are banned in China. Reebok has chosen to ignore that fact, even though Chinese dissidents have been the recipients of the company's own human rights awards. As for working conditions, Reebok now says it sends its own inspectors to production sites a couple of times a year. But they have easily "missed" what subcontractors are trying to hide—like 400 young women workers locked at night into an overcrowded dormitory near a Reebok-contracted factory in the town of Zhuhai, as reported last August in the *Asian Wall Street Journal Weekly*.

Nike's cofounder and CEO Philip Knight has said that he would like the world to think of Nike as "a company with a soul that recognizes the value of human beings." Nike, like Reebok, says it sends in inspectors from time to time to check up on work conditions at its factories; in Indonesia, those factories are run largely by South Korean subcontractors. But according to Donald Katz in a recent book on the company, Nike spokesman Dave Taylor told an in-house newsletter that the factories are "[the sub-contractors'] business to run." For the most part, the company relies on regular reports from subcontractors regarding its "Memorandum of Understanding," which managers must sign, promising to impose "local government standards" for wages, working conditions, treatment of workers, and benefits.

In April, the minimum wage in the Indonesian capital of Jakarta will be $1.89 *a day*—among the highest in a country where the minimum wage varies by region. And managers are required to pay only 75 percent of the wage directly; the remainder can be withheld for "benefits." By now, Nike has a well-honed response to growing criticism of its low-cost labor strategy. Such wages should not be seen as exploitative, says Nike, but rather as the first rung on the ladder of economic opportunity that Nike has extended to workers with few options. Otherwise, they'd be out "harvesting coconut meat in the tropical sun," wrote Nike spokesman Dusty Kidd, in a letter to the *Utne Reader*. The all-is-relative response craftily shifts attention away from reality: Nike didn't move to Indonesia to help Indonesians; it moved to ensure that its profit margin continues to grow. And that is pretty much guaranteed in a country where "local standards" for wages rarely take a worker over the poverty line. A 1991 survey by the International Labor Organization (ILO) found that 88 percent of women working at the Jakarta minimum wage at the time— slightly less than a dollar a day— were malnourished.

A women named Riyanti might have been among the workers surveyed by the ILO. Interviewed by the Boston *Globe* in 1991, she told the reporter who

Reebok inspectors have "missed" what subcontractors hide—like 400 women locked into a dorm at night.

How GATT Puts Hard-Won Victories at Risk

Mary McGinn

The bigger the economy gets, say free trade proponents, the higher incomes around the world will rise and the lower prices will fall. A global market means global prosperity. But in the case of the General Agreement on Tariffs and Trade (GATT), bigger appears better only for the heads of big business. The 125-nation trade deal, which the U.S. ratified in late 1994, dramatically expands corporate rights at the expense of workers, consumers, and the environment.

Under GATT, tariffs—essentially taxes on imported goods—will be reduced by as much as 36 percent over the next decade. As with the North American Free Trade Agreement (NAFTA), which took effect in early 1994, tariff reductions open domestic markets to foreign competition. Lower tariffs also make it cheaper for manufacturers in industrialized countries to set up shop in countries where labor costs less. Such changes have meant accelerated job loss in the U.S. during NAFTA's first year, particularly in the garment industry, where women workers are the majority. And as a result of GATT, the Amalgamated Clothing and Textile Workers Union estimates that upward of a half million textile and garment jobs are at risk. Women also make up the majority of workers in other vulnerable industries, such as food processing and data entry.

A reduction in tariffs also means the world's largest tax break for multinational corporations, resulting in sizable revenue losses for governments. In the U.S., Congress is proposing several ways to make up for the estimated $13.9 billion that will be lost, such as cuts in an already underfunded federal pension program. While Republicans and Democrats alike cry for a reduction of the federal deficit, GATT only puts the U.S. further in the hole.

But GATT's most insidious feature is that it makes it much easier for corporations to push for "deregulation" —the scrapping of any national, state, or even local law that places restraints on their business practices. Such restraints can be environmental laws like a ban on asbestos, limits on the use of child labor, a mandatory minimum wage—or even affirmative action and pay equity policies. Antidiscrimination measures benefiting women and other disadvantaged groups may be considered unfair restraints on a company's right to hire whom it wants, for the hours it wants, at the right price. In essence, free trade agreements level the corporate playing field by pushing labor, health, and environmental standards to the lowest common denominator.

The European Union, for example, has made it clear that it has a problem with the U.S.'s new law requiring all food manufacturers to list complete nutritional content on labels. Under GATT, the union can now lodge a complaint with the new World Trade Organization (WTO), a lofty name for a body administered by three non-elected regulators. These "trade experts" will consider complaints submitted by any GATT member-country that views a particular law in another country as an obstacle to free trade. So the European Union can argue that because most European food manufacturers aren't required to label their foods as specified under U.S. law, the law serves to keep European goods off U.S. shelves. Instead of adopting its own consumer protection laws, the European Union will most likely appeal to the WTO to have the U.S. law modified, or even overturned. If the U.S. refuses, it will be charged steep fines, unless it can convince a majority of GATT member-countries to override the WTO decision. Keep in mind that WTO tribunals are closed to the public and press. As consumer advocate Ralph Nader has written, the WTO mandate is a "staggering rejection of our due process and democratic procedures."

Unfortunately, most U.S. women's advocacy groups took no position on GATT. But clearly, all women have a lot to lose: expanded freedom for multinational corporations jeopardizes social justice everywhere.

Mary McGinn is the North American regional coordinator for Transnationals Information Exchange and the international coordinator of "Labor Notes."

---

had asked about her long hours and low pay: "I'm happy working here. . . . I can make money and I can make friends." But in fact, the reporter discovered that Riyanti had already joined her coworkers in two strikes, the first to force one of Nike's Korean subcontractors to accept a new women's union and the second to compel managers to pay at least the minimum wage. That Riyanti appeared less than forthcoming about her activities isn't surprising. Many Indonesian factories have military men posted in their front offices who find no fault with managers who tape women's mouths shut to keep them from talking among themselves. They and their superiors have a political reach that extends far beyond the barracks. Indonesia has all the makings for a political explosion, especially since the gap between rich and poor is widening into a chasm. It is in this setting that the government has tried to crack down on any independent labor organizing—a policy that Nike has helped to implement. Referring to a recent strike in a Nike-contracted factory, Tony Nava, Nike representative in Indonesia, told the

Playing women off against each other is essential to international trade politics.

Chicago *Tribune* in November 1994 that the "troublemakers" had been fired. When asked about Nike policy on the issue, spokesman Keith Peters struck a conciliatory note: "If the government were to allow and encourage independent labor organizing, we would be happy to support it."

Indonesian workers' efforts to create unions independent of governmental control were a surprise to shoe companies. Although their moves from South Korea have been immensely profitable [see chart, page 134], they do not have the sort of immunity from activism that they had expected. In May 1993, the murder of a female labor activist outside Surabaya set off a storm of local and international protest. Even the U.S. State Department was forced to take note in its 1993 worldwide human rights report, describing a system similar to that which generated South Korea's boom 20 years earlier: severely restricted union organizing, security forces used to break up strikes, low wages for men, lower wages for women—complete with government rhetoric celebrating women's contribution to national development.

Yet when President Clinton visited Indonesia last November, he made only a token effort to address the country's human rights

problem. Instead, he touted the benefits of free trade, sounding indeed more enlightened, more in tune with the spirit of the post-Cold War era than do those defenders of protectionist trading policies who coat their rhetoric with "America first" chauvinism. But "free trade" as actually being practiced today is hardly *free* for any workers—in the U.S. or abroad—who have to accept the Indonesian, Chinese, or Korean workplace model as the price of keeping their jobs.

The not-so-new plot of the international trade story has been "divide and rule." If women workers and their government in one country can see that a sneaker company will pick up and leave if their labor demands prove more costly than those in a neighbor country, then women workers will tend to see their neighbors not as regional sisters, but as competitors who can steal their precarious livelihoods. Playing women off against each other is, of course, old hat. Yet it is as essential to international trade politics as is the fine print in GATT.

But women workers allied through networks like the Hong Kong-based Committee for Asian Women are developing their own post-Cold War foreign policy, which means addressing women's

needs: how to convince fathers and husbands that a woman going out to organizing meetings at night is not sexually promiscuous; how to develop workplace agendas that respond to family needs; how to work with male unionists who push women's demands to the bottom of their lists; how to build a global movement.

These women refuse to stand in awe of the corporate power of the Nike or Reebok or Adidas executive. Growing numbers of Asian women today have concluded that trade politics have to be understood by women on their own terms. They will be coming to Beijing this September ready to engage with women from other regions to link the politics of consumerism with the politics of manufacturing. If women in Russia and Eastern Europe can challenge Americanized consumerism, if Asian activists can solidify their alliances, and if U.S. women can join with them by taking on trade politics—the post-Cold War sneaker may be a less comfortable fit in the 1990s.

This article draws from the work of South Korean scholars Hyun Sook Kim, Seung-kyung Kim, Katharine Moon, Seungsook Moon, and Jeong-Lim Nam.

 **Article Review Form at end of book.**

How does the violence perpetuated against the young women working in the maquilas benefit the corporations contracting with the maquilas?

Death Comes to the *Maquilas*

A border story

Nineteen victims in the Juárez area constitute the biggest mass sex-murder case in Mexican History—with young women working the factories made easy prey.

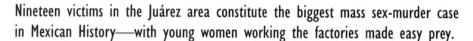

Debbie Nathan

Debbie Nathan, an El Paso–based writer, is the author of Women and Other Aliens: Essays from the U.S.-Mexico Border *(Cinco Puntos), and co-author, with Michael Snedeker, of* Satan's Silence: Ritual Abuse and the Making of a Modern American Witch-Hunt *(Basic).*

On a scorching day in August 1995 in Ciudad Juárez, Mexico, a trash picker combing an illegal dump site discovered the half-naked corpse of a young woman. Police eventually identified her as Elizabeth Castro, a 17-year-old from a poor neighborhood who had last been seen alive downtown a few days earlier. Since then in the same desert area—just a few miles south of El Paso, Texas—eleven more female bodies have been found. Most were adolescents as young as 14. All were slender and dark-skinned, with shoulder-length hair. Many bodies are too decomposed to determine the cause of death, but the better-preserved victims were

raped and strangled or stabbed. Most were partly unclothed, with their underpants torn. Some had their wrists bound; on some, a breast was mutilated or severed. Of the victims police have identified, all came from impoverished families. Last spring, seven more bodies turned up in another desolate part of town. Again, they were half-naked, bound and mutilated. They had slim figures and longish hair, and the identifiable ones were poor.

These nineteen victims constitute the biggest mass sex-murder case in Mexican history, and the nation is horrified. In Juárez, everyone has responded—from a conservative mayor embarrassed by the violence, to women's activists, who have played it up to bolster campaigns against more common forms of sexual assault. Several suspects have been arrested, yet in the public mind the murders remain a mystery. Partly this is due to police corruption and ineptitude.

But more deeply, the continuing whodunit reflects a lack of understanding of how sexuality and violence intertwined for the victims, whose lives and deaths centered around their work on the global assembly line.

Many of the dead young women had jobs in *maquiladoras*— or *maquilas,* as they're popularly known—transnational assembly plants that have blanketed Mexico's northern border since the mid-sixties, displacing jobs from the United States and recycling them for wages that currently equal about $23 a week in take-home pay. Some 170,000 Juárez residents have jobs in the plants. Half are female, and most are so young (as young as 14, even though Mexican law says they must be 16) that inside the factories and outside, they are still called *muchachas*—girls.

Six days a week, thousands of them leave their shantytown neighborhoods, cram into aging buses, transfer downtown and eventually reach vast industrial parks. There they put in forty-eight-hour weeks soldering electronics boards, plugging wires into car dashboards, binding surgical gowns and sorting millions of cosmetics discount coupons mailed by North Americans to P.O. boxes in El Paso. The work they do is highly repetitive and requires little training. Their labor is easily replaceable, and turnover is astronomical, often 100 percent a year or more.

These are the girls of what author Jeremy Seabrook calls the "Cities of the South"—those sprawling new enclaves of Third World capitalist glitz, surrounded by slums full of workers who feed the local neon and the consumer appetites of the North. Navigating this territory, factory girls are subject to unprecedented sexual harassment and violence, of which serial killing is only the most horrific extreme. It has always been risky for women to move through cities on their own, and in Juárez, everyone acknowledges the connection between work and danger. But few talk about work and pleasure; few recognize that when *maquila* girls' shifts end, they are loosed to sample freedoms their mothers never imagined.

Miles from their neighborhoods and with paycheck in hand, they have access to urban diversions that their brothers always had but that "proper" girls used to be denied: public nightlife, friendship based on affinity rather than kin and, most momentously, sex. According to University of Chicago sociologist Leslie Salzinger, who has worked on Juárez assembly lines, even girls who still live at home with their parents enjoy these pleasures.

Indeed, Salzinger says, many girls have told her that they take *maquila* jobs not for survival but for independence: to buy clothes with their own money and to get out of their houses and socialize. (Affluent kids do this at school, but for the working class, education is a luxury. Mexico guarantees public schooling only to sixth grade.)

So poor teens go to work. But unlike their older North American sisters, who dress for the assembly line in no-nonsense T-shirts and sneakers, most *maquila* girls don miniskirts, heels and gobs of lipstick and eye shadow. Their flashiness is hardly incidental to their jobs. Instead, it is a fundamental feature of those *maquilas* that make a priority of hiring females: the reinforcement and updating of a rigid version of "womanhood."

The process begins even when a girl is still looking for a job. *Se Solicita Muno de Obra Feminina*—Female Labor Wanted—blare the newspaper want ads. Managers say that females have more nimble fingers, deal better with boredom, and are "more docile"—i.e., less inclined to engage in disruptive behavior, including union organizing. When *maquilas* first came to the border, men were virtually excluded as line workers. Labor shortages have since led to their hiring, but in many plants women still predominate, particularly in electronic assembly.

While gentle hands and natures are a plus for transnational exploitation, fecundity is a minus. Typically, *maquilas* will hire women only after they've taken a pregnancy test (this is implicitly illegal, according to Mexican labor law) that comes out negative. In many plants, management inspects workers' sanitary napkins for monthly menstrual flow.

Meanwhile, in-plant health services are sparse except for generous provision of birth-control pills.

There are also discriminatory job classifications. At an electronics plant Salzinger worked in, stuffing computer boards is a task exclusively assigned to women; cabinet assembly and screen installation are reserved for men because the company deems this "heavy" work. Meanwhile, almost all technicians, supervisors and managers—who make the most money—are men.

Identification numbers distinguish men from women. So does work clothing, with women assigned light blue smocks and men navy. Women are monitored more rigorously than men, by Mexican supervisors who pace the assembly lines, staring, flirting and asking for dates. The foreign manager also walks the lines and chats up his favorites. Invariably they are the youngest, prettiest girls, and under their smocks, they are usually dressed to the nines. These girls are groomed for annual industrywide "Señorita Maquiladora" beauty contests, complete with evening gown and swimsuit competitions.

This sexualization of factory life, as Salzinger calls it, creates a dense web of intrigue. Dating, boyfriends, clothing and gossip about whom the manager has the hots for are constant sources of conversation and palpable tension. Indeed, sexualization allies workers with management and alienates them from one another. It also makes horribly tedious, draining work bearable, as the *maquila* becomes a fantasy world.

Not surprisingly, eros overflows the plants, especially on weekends after work. Instead of going straight home then, many employees stop at a strip of downtown bars with names like Alive, La Tuna and Noa Noa. Several clubs advertise free admission for girls, as well as "Most Daring Bra" and "Wet String Bikini" contests with prizes of $30 to $45—more than a week's pay on the assembly line. Others feature Chippendale-style male striptease dancers. All provide huge sound systems, and dance floors are packed with couples doing everything from disco slamming to *la quebradita,* which mixes the two-step with pelvis grinding, techno-tango gyrations.

Prostitutes do business in some bars, and in more casual fashion, so do many *maquila* girls. This is hardly novel for industrial workers in Dickensian circumstances. A century ago, New York City's factory girls were roaming dance halls and amusement parks, picking up unknown young men and trading sexual favors for romance and the "treats"—like clothing and entertainment — they couldn't afford.

Activists see this as the spectacular tip of an iceberg of sexual assault against border women; some mention the *maquilas'* complicity.

In Juárez, police investigating the first serial murder wave determined that several victims had frequented the downtown bars. A break in the case came when a teenager revealed that she had met a man at one and gone home with him, where he tried to rape her and told her she would end up like the women in the dump. He was arrested, and after his picture appeared in the news, witnesses told police they'd seen him with some of the girls later found in the desert.

The suspect, jailed since October 1995, is Sharif Abdel Latif Sharif. A 50-year-old Egyptian, he has lived most of the past two decades in the United States. "Give me a fucking break!" Sharif snorts in English, to the delight of Juárez reporters. He indignantly denies any connection to the corpses in the dump, but Sharif also says he has come to know "all the prostitutes downtown" since he moved to Juárez two years ago. Before that, he racked up an extensive record for violent sexual assault in the United States, including six years in a Florida prison for savagely beating and raping a woman. Following another charge in 1993, Sharif fled Midland, Texas. He had been working there as a chemist, and he beat his rap by helping his employer set up operations across the border. He relocated to Juárez and settled in a posh neighborhood.

With his athletic build, olive skin and dapper mustache, Sharif looks like a Spanish-language soap opera star—the kind who plays the rich, handsome father. Police say Sharif befriended his victims in the downtown bars, then cruised their workplaces or bus stops, offering them rides in his shiny white Grand Marquis. *Maquila* workers tell me it's common to accept such propositions, even from strangers, to save car fare and the dreary bus trip home. And for girls whose families and friends can barely afford seventies junkers, tooling around in a late-model vehicle is a thrill, especially with an attractive man.

Witnesses also saw some victims chatting or taking rides from young Mexican men dressed in cowboy hats and boots; this led investigators to suspect that Sharif had accomplices. It took a long time to figure all this out, though, because the victims' parents had no idea their daughters frequented bars, and their friends were loath to admit it. In Mexico, the thinking goes, good girls don't go to bars or watch male strippers or display their bras for money. And they would never think of leading *la doble vida*—the double life of assembly work by day and casual prostitution by night.

Parents who harbor these beliefs are clinging to memories of their youth, when poor but decent Mexican daughters were still cloistered until marriage. Understandably, they are comforted by industry's characterization of the *maquila* as a chaste, surrogate "home" for their daughters. But U.S. organizers seem equally naïve. A few summers ago, when I helped with a solidarity tour for North American union women who'd lost their jobs to transnational flight, one guest expressed dismay at the girls' makeup and high heels: "They sure don't look like they're working," she huffed. "They don't even look poor."

Disapproving of girls' involvement with night life and sex constitutes "hypocritical moralizing," says Esther Chávez. An accountant in her 50s, she is spokeswoman for Juárez's Coalition of Non-Governmental Women's Organizations, which does groundbreaking work to combat sexual and domestic violence. Like Chávez, some coalition leaders are affluent. Some are former *maquila* workers who were blacklisted for trying to unionize, but who continue their organizing efforts from outside the plants. Others are human rights advocates who've spent years protesting police brutality and torture.

Chávez and other activists understand casual prostitution as a response to poverty, and they see the serial killings as the spectacular tip of an iceberg of sexual assault against border women. In October alone, there were thirty-two reported cases of rape and molestation. According to Chávez, Juárez logs the highest rate of these crimes in Mexico, and authorities think they are a mere twentieth of the total. Only a fifth go to prosecution. Most victims are 18 or younger.

Many coalition activists attribute the high sexual assault statistics to gender inequality, and some mention the *maquila* industry's complicity in fostering it. However, coalition organizers focus far more narrowly. Even before the first of the mass murders surfaced two years ago, Juárez feminists were petitioning the city and state administrations for kiosks where the public could report sexual assaults and for a woman-staffed sex-crimes unit in the district attorney's office.

It's easy to see how a crime as revolting as serial murder could inspire a law-and-order approach. That's what has happened in Juárez, particularly since the second group of bodies—many of them freshly dead—began turning up last spring, after Sharif had been locked up for months. The populace was terrified, and the women's coalition sprang into action. It organized marches, held press conferences and sent the United Nations a report describing the killings as a violation of women's human rights.

Feminists weren't the only ones pressing for a resolution to the case. Juárez police answer to a mayor and a state governor who are members of the Catholic-based, conservative National Action Party. The PAN has gained power in Juárez and other northern Mexican cities recently, but the infamous and powerful PRI— the Institutional Revolutionary Party—is constantly looking for ways to discredit its rival. By spring, the local PRI was noisily mocking PAN leaders' failure to protect the city's women. To make matters worse, the PANista Attorney General failed to win even one murder indictment against Sharif; a judge ruled there wasn't enough material evidence.

Finally, late one Saturday night in April, a phalanx of police surrounded several *maquila*-worker bars and arrested more than 100 people, including dozens of underage girls. Police now claim that nine young men, members of a gang called the Rebels, committed the murders along with Sharif. Most wear cowboy clothes; some worked as male strippers and musicians in the bars, where they are said to have done a brisk business in illegal drugs, bootleg liquor and pimping. The police allege that they were paid by Sharif to recruit and kill victims—even after he was jailed, when he calculated that new corpses would make him look innocent.

A rich foreign boss, a crew of native-born male supervisors, a high-turnover supply of females. Is this a true-crime scenario or a *maquila*-saturated city's freaked-out, global-assembly-line fantasy: mass production as mass murder? Serial killers are popularly portrayed as lone, Ripper-style offenders, but multiple murderers may actually account for as many as a fifth of all cases, according to Penn State history professor Philip Jenkins.

A Sharif & Co.–type enterprise is thus imaginable, and there are indications that some of the accused may have been involved.

One purported Rebels member was seen visiting Sharif in jail. Tests done on another's car supposedly have found blood. The gang's so-called leader, a beefy 26-year-old who police say is nicknamed "The Devil," was seen at a bar with a victim, and authorities say bite marks on her corpse match his dentition. At least two women have reported that they were kidnapped and/or raped by gang members but managed to escape.

On the other hand, the case is seriously flawed. The biggest problem is the inability of the police to identify most of the dead women so they can investigate possible connections. Speculation is that these Jane Does were newcomers to the city: poor girls who journeyed north to work in the *maquilas* or cross to the United States. Artists' sketches of facial reconstructions appear in the papers, along with itemizations of victims' clothing that constitute inventories of the globalized textile market these girls both worked and consumed in. ("Lee jeans size 3M, Hanes panties," reads one list. To the sad bemusement of garment-worker organizers, police surmised that another victim was Central American because a label in her clothing said "Made in Honduras.")

More disturbing is that in addition to the nineteen bodies associated with the serial murders, the women's coalition recently tallied old press items and police records and discovered that fifty-three other raped and murdered female corpses have been found scattered about Juárez in the past three years. Are their deaths related? Are there other sex murderers?

Even the "hard evidence" is fraught with problems. Mexican police have claimed they found blood and semen in suspects' cars, but authorities in El Paso, where the vehicles were sent for testing, have denied detecting body fluids. A representative of the Mexican Human Rights Commission reports that suspects were arrested without warrants, denied lawyers and injured during questioning; defendants say the police beat them, stuck their heads into toilets, held pistols to their heads and threatened to kill them unless they confessed. Bar habitués report being kidnapped by cops and subjected to the same treatment to force them to incriminate suspects. The human rights commission finds these claims credible since Mexican police are notorious for using Inquisition-style methods. (The police insist the Rebels were freely confessing until the human rights representative gave them legal advice. At a recent indictment hearing, a judge agreed—and finally charged Sharif with the murder of Elizabeth Castro, the teenager whose corpse started the case.)

Feminists like Chávez wonder uneasily whether they've opened a Pandora's box of false accusations and sexist moralizing. But they're reluctant to criticize the investigation. One reason for the activists' silence is their reluctance to fuel PRI squabbles with the PAN. More significant is that their outcry about the murders has finally achieved gains from the government, including the woman-staffed sex-crimes unit in the district attorney's office and discussions about opening a state-run battered women's shelter. So activists who were once vocal critics of police brutality—including against women *maquila* workers trying to unionize—are now quiet.

Left in the lurch, *maquila* girls have their own opinions. Some are common-sensically skeptical: "I don't believe the police," one factory worker comments. "They keep contradicting themselves." Others are frighteningly ignorant about sex murderers: "The young men they've accused can't be guilty," opines another, heavily made-up young woman, "because they're poor and the killer is probably rich." There are wild conspiracy theories in which the killers are military or police or organ traffickers. And of course, that they are foreign *maquila* managers—because, as another worker notes, "they know so much about the victims' habits."

Managers do know the girls, at least better than labor unionists and feminists do. Organizers need to catch up. They might start by campaigning to abolish discriminatory hiring, job classifications and everything else based on M and F—including the pregnancy tests. They could work with women's advocates to organize mother-daughter classes in sexuality and self-defense. Such actions would recognize young *maquila* women's right to equality, dignity and pleasure. They would also help sever the link between murderous sexual assault and the more insidious—and far more widespread—violence of work on the global assembly line.

 Article Review Form at end of book.

What does the indigenous farmers' loss of ownership of genetic material as Intellectual Property Rights to transnational corporations mean to the lives of women in developing countries?

GATT,*
Agriculture and
Third World
Women

Vandana Shiva

Agriculture and related activities are the most important source of livelihood for Third World women. Free trade in agriculture as construed in GATT terms aims to create freedom for transnational corporations (TNCs) to invest, produce and trade in agricultural commodities without restriction, regulation or responsibility. This freedom for agribusiness is based on the denial of freedom to rural women to produce, process and consume food according to the local environmental, economic and cultural needs. What GATT aims to achieve is the replacement of women and other subsistence producers by TNCs as the main providers of food. Behind the obfuscation of such terms as 'market access', 'domestic support', 'sanitary and phytosanitary measures' and 'intellectual property rights' in the final draft of the GATT agreement, is a raw restructuring of power around food: taking it away from people and concentrat-

ing it in the hands of a handful of agro-industrial interests. The conflict is not between farmers of the North and those of the South, but between small farmers everywhere and multinationals. It is no surprise that the bulk of US, Japanese and European farmers are also opposed to the proposed GATT reforms, because these reforms are meant to drive the mass of small farmers out of business.

In the Third World, most small farmers are women, even though their role has remained invisible and has been neglected in official agriculture development programmes. By focusing on international trade in food, GATT policies are aimed at further marginalizing the household and domestic food economies in which women play a significant role. Further, since GATT is a self-executing treaty, it will automatically lead to the setting up of a Multilateral Trade Organization (MTO) which, with World Bank and IMF, will form the centre of world governance.

Women and Food Production

The negative impact of GATT will be greater on Third World women because they play a major role in food production and processing, even though this fact has remained invisible and neglected.

In India, agriculture employs 70 per cent of the working population, and about 84 percent of all economically active women.[1] For example, in the tribal economy of Orissa—shifting cultivation (*bogodo*)—women spend 105.4 days per year on agricultural operations compared to men's 59.11 days.[2]

According to Vir Singh's assessment in the Indian Himalaya, a pair of bullocks work for 1,064 hours, a man for 1,212 hours and a woman for 3,485 hours a year on a one hectare farm: a woman works longer than men and farm animals combined![3]

K. Saradamoni's study of women agricultural labourers and cultivators in three rice growing states—Kerala, Tamilnadu and

*General Agreement on Tariffs and Trade

From Vandana Shiva, "GATT, Agriculture and Third World Women" in Ecofeminism, eds. M. Miles and V. S. Shiva, 1993. Reprinted by permission of Zed Books, Ltd., London.

West Bengal—shows that both groups of women make crucial contributions to production and processing.[4] Joan Mencher's studies in the Palghat region of Kerala reveal that outside ploughing, which is exclusively men's work, women have a predominant role in all other processes. On the basis of this study, it is estimated that more than two-thirds of the labour input is female.[5]

Bhati and Singh in a study of the gender division of labour in hill agriculture in Himachal Pradesh show that overall women contribute 61 per cent of the total labour on farms.[6] A detailed study by Jain and Chand in three villages each in Rajasthan and West Bengal, covering 127 households over 12 months, highlights the fact that women in the age group 19-70 spend longer hours than do men in a variety of activities.[7]

Women's work and livelihoods in subsistence agriculture, for example, are based on multiple use and management of biomass for fodder, fertilizer, food and fuel. The collection of fodder from the forest is part of the process of transferring fertility for crop production and managing soil and water stability. The work of the women engaged in such activity tends to be discounted and made invisible for all sectors.[8]

When these allied activities which are ecologically and economically critical are taken into account, agriculture is revealed as the major occupation of 'working' women in rural India. The majority of women in India are not simply 'housewives', but farmers.[9]

Displacing Small Farmers

GATT policies that encourage free export and import of agricultural products translate into policies for the destruction of small farmers' local food production capacities. By locating food in the domain of international trade, these policies dislocate its production in the household and community. Policies being imposed under 'market access' and 'domestic support' on the agriculture agreement are basically policies that allow TNCs to displace the small producer. Under 'market access'[10] countries are forced to allow free import of food grain and remove all restrictions on imports and exports. 'Market access' is thus an instrument for the conversion of the Third World's subsistence production of food into a 'market' for TNCs. Similarly, by relating domestic policy to international markets through clauses on domestic support, GATT facilitates the shifting of subsidies from poor producers and consumers to big agribusiness.

This has been India's experience under World Bank/IMF Structural Adjustment which forced the government to reduce domestic support and to import wheat. During 1992, as a result of the structural adjustment, there was a difference of Rs. 80 between market price and government procurement price of wheat. Enough wheat was produced in the country, but government policy, distorted by structural adjustment, failed to procure it. Using this artificially created scarcity, and under World Bank pressure for import liberalization of food grain, the Indian government bought 2.5 million tonnes of wheat in 1992 at the cost of Rs. 4,800 crore (one crore = one hundred million) in hard currency.

The structural adjustment programme prescribed that food subsidies which provided cheap food for public distribution, be removed; simultaneously, the Bank recommended liberalization of farm imports. The net result has been not the removal of food subsidies, but their redistribution; the beneficiaries are no longer India's poor but powerful transnational corporations in the US.

In 1991, India *exported* 672,000 tonnes of wheat at the cost of over Rs. 178 crore. Under the pressure of import liberalization and structural adjustment, however, India *imported* 2.5 million tonnes of wheat in 1992. Of this, one million tonnes was from the US, which gives a $30 per tonne subsidy to its exporters. Despite the US subsidy, the cost of imported wheat after adding transport and handling charges was higher than would have been the subsidy the government paid to Indian farmers—this amounted to Rs. 260 per quintal (one quintal = 100 kg) of wheat, but imported wheat from North America costs Rs. 560 per quintal. Indian farmers' movements are therefore demanding that, rather than import wheat and subsidize multinational corporations (thereby draining foreign exchange and increasing debt), the government should raise the domestic support prices.

Neither fertilizer decontrol nor import liberalization have reduced the burden on the Indian exchequer. Public spending and foreign exchange expenditure have actually increased under the structural adjustment programme, although this is supposed to reduce both. The aim seems to be destabilization instead of stabilization of the economy, leaving India with no option but further dependence on the World Bank and TNCs. According to an ex-US Agricultural Secretary, 'the idea that developing countries should feed themselves is an anachronism from a bygone era. They could better ensure their food security by relying on US agricultural products which are available, in most cases, at a lower cost.'

However, US foodgrain is cheaper not because it is produced more efficiently at less cost but because despite high costs of production, US corporations and the US government can subsidize and fix prices.

In a letter to *Time* magazine, Senator Rudy Boschwitz, a spokesman of the Reagan farm policy, stated quite clearly that US farm policy was aimed at putting Third World food exporters out of business. He wrote: 'If we do not lower our farm prices to discourage these countries now, our worldwide competitive position will continue to slide and be much more difficult to regain. This discouragement should be one of the foremost goals of our agricultural policy.'[11]

Lowering food prices in the US is achieved by precisely those measures such as subsidies, which the World Bank, IMF and GATT want removed in Third World countries through their conditionalities. Thus in 1986, the US spent almost $10 billion to subsidize corn and wheat exports for which it received only $4.2 billion. While the World Bank uses arguments of cost effectiveness to dismantle public food distribution systems and remove food subsidies in the Third World, the US builds its food monopoly through totally subsidized and *cost ineffective* programmes.

Thus, the US lowered world prices of rice from around eight dollars to less than four dollars per hundredweight, not by reducing production costs, but by providing an export subsidy of $17 per hundredweight. This totally artificial price is nearly $80 per tonne below Third World costs of production, and approximately $140 per ton below the US production costs.[12]

The result is an overt attack on the survival of Third World farmers and Third World economies. The effect of the 50 per cent reduction in world rice prices by the US Farm Policy was so severely damaging to the four million Thai rice farmers that they were forced to demonstrate against the US Farm Bill at the US Embassy in Bangkok.

The dumping of subsidized surpluses brings business to food TNCs, but starvation to Third World peasants. During 1986, the US and the EC were selling wheat surpluses in West African countries, such as Mali and Burkina Faso, at prices as low as $60 per tonne—around one-third lower than equivalent production, transport and marketing costs for locally produced cereals such as sorghum. This was facilitated by direct and indirect subsidies and export prices.[13] Subsidized TNCs are thus pitted against Third World peasants who earn less from their produce as cheap imports depress the price of staples and are finally forced to leave agriculture when earnings fall below subsistence.

Food imports were forced upon Costa Rica through the World Bank's structural adjustment programme, which led to a ten per cent a year increase in imports and a sharp decline in the local production of staples. The Philippines has had a similar experience: from a position of near self-sufficiency in the mid-1980s, by 1990 the Philippines was importing some 600,000 tons of rice annually, equivalent to some 16 per cent of national consumption.[14]

The displacement of small farmers is a deliberate policy of GATT. The draft agreement has clauses for 'structural adjustment' for 'producer retirement' and 'resource retirement' which is merely a convoluted way of stating that farmers and their resources should be treated as surplus and dispensed with through 'programmes designed to remove land or other resources, including livestock, from marketable agricultural production.'[15] This includes violent mechanisms such as wasteful slaughter of livestock.

The models of agricultural production introduced by TNCs therefore necessitate the displacement of small farmers and their treatment as a 'surplus' population. The small peasants who produce for themselves will be threatened, because worldwide, World Bank structural adjustment loans have supported processes which are conducive to small farmers mortgaging their land and their consequent displacement. In addition, austerity measures and the liberalization of the banking sector mean that agricultural credit to small farmers is squeezed, and farm inputs and transport costs increase. Privatization of banks, and development of agribusiness also mean that land, the farmers' most important asset will pass into the hands of corporate agribusiness and banks. This process has already taken place in the US where farm debt rose from $120 billion in the early 1970s to $225 billion in the early 1980s. Farm population dropped by 30 per cent between 1950 and 1960 and a further 26 per cent between 1960 and 1970 as small farmers were thrown off their land. Since 1981, 600,000 small farmers have been driven off their land.[16] IMF/World Bank/GATT prescriptions aim at applying those same policies to Indian agriculture. Imagine the consequences if 50 per cent of Indian farmers and peasants were alienated from their land over the coming years! It cannot be argued that they can seek industrial employment because there, too, an 'exit' policy is under operation.

The displacement of women and other small peasants' from agricultural production will also have a serious impact on food consumption since peasants' access to food is through participation in its production. As TNCs dump subsidized surpluses on the Third World, peasants are driven out of food production into famine.

A conservative assessment of the impact of so-called liberalization on food consumption indicates that in India, by the year 2000, there will be 5.6 per cent more hungry people than would have been the case if free trade in agriculture was not introduced. Free trade will lead to 26.2 per cent reduction in human consumption of agricultural produce.[17] The growth of free trade thus implies the growth of hunger.

The growth of TNC profits takes place at the cost of people's food needs being met. Since women have been responsible for food production and provisioning, the decline in food availability has direct impact on them. Control over food is thus increasingly taken out of the hands of Third World women and put in the hands of Northern TNCs. The concentration of marketers, trade and power in the hands of a few TNCs makes competition by small farmers in the Third World impossible. US grain exports account for 76 per cent of world agricultural

trade. In 1921, 36 firms accounted for 85 per cent of US wheat exports. By the end of the 1970s just six companies: Cargill, Continental Grain, Luis Dreyfus, Bunge, Andre & Co and Mitsui/Cook exported 85 per cent of all US wheat, 95 per cent of its corn, 80 per cent of its sorghum. These same companies were handling 90 per cent of the EC's trade in wheat and corn, and 90 per cent of Australia's sorghum exports. Between them, Cargill, the largest private corporation in the US, and Continental Grain, the third largest, control 25 per cent of the market.[18]

When the corporate interest has been damaged the US government has retaliated politically. The threat posed to developing country food policy sovereignty in the Uruguay Round has been strengthened by the case of Nigeria—formerly sub-Sahara's largest wheat importer. In 1988, the Nigerian government imposed a ban on wheat imports; these had depressed domestic food prices and reduced the production of domestic staples such as cassava, yams and millet. The wheat campaign by Cargill Corporation (formerly Nigeria's main wheat supplier), has threatened trade sanctions against Nigerian textiles. It has also warned that a GATT settlement on agricultural trade liberalization will be applied to demand the restoration of free market access for US wheat. Clauses on cross retaliation in GATT are aimed at such disciplining. That this freedom will rob Nigerian farmers of freedom to produce their own staples is of little concern to Cargill or the US.[19] The recent import of wheat in India portends a similar vulnerability for that country. Cheap imports will not only push farmers out of agricultural pro-

duction, they will also add to India's foreign debts and balance of payment position, because food is being imported instead of locally produced. Given the cosy relationship between government and corporations it is of little surprise the 'free trade' as interpreted on GATT platforms allows TNCs to regulate prices, again demonstrating that 'free trade' for corporations is based on the denial of freedom and autonomy to Third World governments and people.

Besides manipulating prices, TNCs also control exports and imports through the manipulation of food safety standards. The Dunkel draft clearly states that sanitary and phytosanitary measures will be 'harmonized' in order to minimize their negative effects on trade. The draft also states that standards will be set by international agencies such as Codex Alimentarius, Dupont, Chevron, Monsanto, Merck, American Gnanud, Mitsubishi, Shell or advisors to Codex, which are strongly influenced by TNCs. In addition, according to the draft, 'contracting parties shall ensure that sanitary and phytosanitary measures based on scientific principles are not maintained against available scientific evidence'. Together, these principles mean that GATT can apply standards to regulate import and export for the convenience of TNCs. On such criteria, tailored to fit TNCs' interests, genetically-engineered organisms introduced by TNCs can be treated as 'safe', and organic food exported by the Third World can be treated as 'unsafe'.[20]

The removal of state controls over agriculture at the national level through GATT does not mean an absence of control over Third World farmers. But instead of being controlled by Third World governments, Third World farmers' fate is under the control of international bureaucracies (the IMF, World Bank and the MTO) which serve TNC interests. This does not imply any measure of freedom for farmers, but new and less accountable forms of control and regulation. Freedom at the small farmer level can be based only on freedom from state as well as transnational corporate sector control.

Intellectual Property Rights and Ownership of Seeds

Intellectual Property Rights (IPR) are another instrument in the GATT agreement which will dispossess rural women of their power, control, and knowledge. IPRs in GATT and other international platforms aim to take seed out of peasant women's custody and make it the private property of TNCs. By adding 'trade related' to IPRs, GATT has forced issues of the ownership of genetic resources and life forms on to the agenda of international trade through TRIPs.

At the conceptual level, Trade-Related Intellectual Property Rights (TRIPs) are restrictive, being by definition weighted in favour of transnational corporations, and against citizens in general, and particularly Third World peasants and forest-dwellers. People everywhere innovate and create. In fact, the poorest have to be the most innovative, since they have to create their means of survival while it is daily threatened. Women have been important innovators and protectors of seeds and genetic resources.

Limitations to the ownership of intellectual property rights, as construed in the trade negotiations, operate on a number of levels. The first is the shift from common to private rights: the preamble of the TRIPs agreement states that intellectual property rights are recognized only as private rights. This excludes all kinds of knowledge, ideas, and innovations that take place in the 'intellectual commons', in villages among farmers, in forests among tribals and even in universities among scientists. TRIPs is therefore a mechanism to privatize the intellectual commons and de-intellectualize civil society, so that in effect, the mind becomes a corporate monopoly.

The second limitation is that intellectual property rights are recognized only when knowledge and innovation generate profits, not when they meet social needs. According to Article 27.1,[21] to be recognized as an IPR, innovation must be capable of industrial application. Only profits and capital accumulation are recognized as viable uses of creativity. Under corporate control and the 'deindustrialization' of small-scale informal sector production, the social good is discounted.

The most significant limitation of IPRs is achieved by way of the prefix 'trade-related'. Most innovation by women is for domestic, local and public use, not for international trade; MNCs innovate for the sole purpose of increasing their share in global markets and international trade; and TRIPs in GATT will only enforce MNCs' rights to monopolize all production, distribution and profits at the cost of all citizens and small producers worldwide.

Article 27 on patentable matter is a clear indication that national decisions made on grounds of public interest are overruled. Article 27(1) states that 'patents shall be available for any inventions, whether products or processes, in all fields of technology, provided that they are new, involve an inventive step, and are capable of industrial application.' This nullifies the exclusions built into national patent laws for the protection of the public and the national interest. For example, in the Patent Act of India, 1970, methods of agriculture and horticulture were excluded, were not patentable, whereas the TRIPs text includes these as patentable. Under the Indian Patent Act, only process patents can be granted to food, medicines, drugs and chemical products, but under the MTO, the Third World will have to grant product patents also in this area. Article 27 calls for a review of the scope of patentability and subject matter of patents four years after signing the text. Within an MTO with no democratic structure, however, such a review will only be used by MNCs to expand the domain of their monopoly control. The worldwide movement against patents on life has rejected TRIPs in GATT, while Sustainable Agriculture Movements and biodiversity conservation movements have expressed concern about the universalization of patent regimes. Article 27(3) states that 'parties shall provide for the protection of plant varieties either by patents or by an effective *in generis* system or by any combination thereof.'[22]

Under the impact of this enforcement, farmers will not be allowed to save their own seed. The International Convention of the Union for the Protection of New Varieties of Plants (UPOV) had maintained farmers' rights to save seed, but in a March 1991 amendment this clause was removed. The new clause in UPOV (and TRIPs) can be used to enforce royalty payments on farmers if they save their own seed. With the stronger intellectual property rights regime being conceived under MTO, the transfer of extra funds as royalty payments from the poor to the rich countries would exacerbate the current Third World debt crisis tenfold. This is ironical, since most plant diversity originates in the Third World, and seeds and plant materials that today are under the control of the industrialized world, were originally taken freely from the farmers to whom they will now be sold back as patented material. As a result, seed companies will reap monopoly profits, while the genius of Third World farmers will go unrewarded and they will be banned from saving and using their own seeds.

IPRs in the area of seeds and plant material are in any case not easy to demarcate, since the genetic resources used by multinational corporations for claiming patents are the product of centuries of innovation and selection by Third World farmers, especially women. The UN Food and Agriculture Organization (FAO) has recognized these contributions in the form of 'Farmers' Rights'; and the Biodiversity Convention signed at the 1992 Earth Summit also recognizes them, and accepts the need to make IPRs subservient to the objectives of biodiversity conservation.

The TRIPs text, however, biased as it is in favour of acknowledging only MNC rights, goes against these agreements reached on other international platforms. The negative impact on farmers and other Third World citizens will be increased due to the extension of the working and the terms of the patent, and the reversal of the burden of proof. Article 34 of the draft text reverses the burden of proof in the area of process

patents. In normal law, the accused is innocent unless proven guilty. Under the reversal in the MTO regime, however, it is the accused who must demonstrate their innocence; if they cannot do so, then they are deemed guilty of having infringed upon the right of the patent holder.[23]

In the area of agriculture this can have absurd and highly unjust consequences. MNCs are now taking out broad patents on plant varieties, covering ownership of traits and characteristics. With the reversal of the burden of proof clauses, it becomes legally possible for a corporation to accuse the farmers who originally contributed the seeds with a particular trait, of patent infringement. There is no clause in TRIPs to offer protection to farmers in such cases.

When this situation is combined with possibilities of cross-retaliation that the MTO will institutionalize, MNCs will have a very powerful tool to subsume all agriculture and all production under their monopoly control. This monopolization of the entire economy is the main motive for setting up an MTO with a TRIPs council.

The Third World has consistently maintained that IPRs have no place in international trade negotiations, furthermore, the relevance of applying IPRs to agriculture—biodiversity and biotechnology in particular—is a seriously contested issue. These are debates that need to evolve and be resolved democratically in order to protect people's health, and their environmental rights. To set up an MTO with the central issue of IPRs still unresolved, implies that only MNCs have rights, citizens have none. This regime is based not on free trade but corporations' freedom to engage in re-

strictive business practices thus providing a scenario for a global command economy based on coercion and non-accountable power.

Seeds will be at the centre of this conflict. Patented seed varieties linked to agrochemicals and agroprocessing are central to the creation of new dependencies. The New Seed Policy has already allowed the entry of multinationals in the seed sector; Trade Related Investments Measures (TRIMs) in GATT will make such investment even freer. TNCs, as we have noted, will thus take farmers' seeds, process them, and sell them back as patented varieties.

In India, the pharmaceutical giant, Sandoz (India), has entered into an agreement with Northup King of the US, subsidiary of its multinational parent company, and with the Dutch vegetable king, Zaaduine. ITC is tying up with Pacific Seeds, a subsidiary of Australia's Continental Grains; the US seed giant Cargill has tied up with Gill and Company, retaining a controlling interest in the company. Two other US companies, Sedtec International and Dehlgien, have entered into agreements with Maharashtra Hybrid and Nath Seed Company, respectively. Pioneer Hibred has started an Indian subsidiary Pioneer Seed Company. Apart from these, Hindustan Lever is negotiating with a Belgian firm, while Hoechst, Ciba-Geigy are reportedly moving in with other tie-ups.[24]

In addition to loss of control over genetic resources is a new threat of loss of control over ownership of land. As banks become privatized and contract farming is introduced, the farmer will risk losing his/her land. Protection of rights to land, water and genetic resources are central to the freedom of farmers. GATT, however, defines legal protection only in terms of the interests of the corporate sector and freedom of TNCs. Whose rights to resources need protection from the viewpoint of sustainability and justice? This question will move centre stage as farmers' and environmental movements begin to address the emerging control over natural resources by global interests for global profits.

Local control over natural resources is an essential precondition for farmers' freedom. But free trade which, as we have seen, implies a relocation of control over natural resources for farmers and Third World governments to global institutions has serious environmental consequences.

Corporations use land, water and genetic resources in non-renewable, non-sustainable ways, being mainly concerned to maximize profits rather than to conserve local resources. Local laws and regulations for limiting environmental degradation will be treated as barriers to free trade. Local communities' democratic decisions on resource conservation are thus excluded by GATT. The GATT draft by Dunkel requires that central governments adopt measures to ensure that state governments comply with GATT rules, which further reduces farmers' influence in decision-making. Thus farmers' organizations will be weakened, as will state legislators and parliament: all power will be concentrated in the hands of GATT and TNCs.

TNCs vs Freedom for Subsistence Producers

The freedom that transnational corporations are claiming through intellectual property rights protection in the GATT agreement on TRIPs is the freedom that European colonizers have claimed since 1492 when Columbus set precedence in treating the license to conquer non-European people as a *natural right* of European men. The land titles issued by the Pope through European kings and queens were the first patents. Charters and patents issued to merchant adventurers were authorizations to 'discover, find, search out and view such remote heathen and barbarous lands, countries and territories not actually possessed of any Christian prince or people.'[25] The colonizers' freedom was built on slavery and subjugation of the people with original rights to the land. This violent take-over was rendered 'natural' by defining the colonized people into nature, thus denying them their humanity and freedom.

Locke's treatise on property[26] effectually legitimized this same process of theft and robbery during the enclosure movement in Europe. Locke clearly articulates capitalism's freedom to build on the freedom to steal; he states that property is created by removing resources from nature through mixing with labour. But this 'labour' is not physical labour, but labour in its 'spiritual' form as manifested in the control of capital. According to Locke, only capital can add value to appropriated nature, and hence only those who own capital have the natural right to own natural resources; a right that supersedes the common rights of others with prior claims. Capital is thus defined as a source of freedom, but this freedom is based on the denial of freedom to the land, forests, rivers and biodiversity that capital claims as its own. Because property obtained through privatization of commons is equated with freedom, those commoners laying claim to it are perceived to be depriving the owner of capital of freedom. Thus peasants and tribals who demand the return of their rights and access to resources are regarded as thieves.

Within the ambit of IPRs, the Lockean concept of property merges with the Cartesian concept of knowledge, to give shape to a perverted world which appears 'natural' in the eyes of capitalist patriarchy. During the scientific revolution, Descartes fashioned a new intellectual world order in which mind and body were deemed to be totally separate, and only the male, European mind was considered capable of complete intellectual transcendence of the body. Intellectual and manual labour were thus pronounced to be 'unrelated', even though all human labour, however simple, requires a degree of unity of 'head and hand'. But capitalist patriarchy denies the 'head', the mind, to women and Third World peoples. The application of IPRs to agriculture is the ultimate denial of the intellectual creativity and contribution of Third World peasants, women and men who have saved and used seed over millennia.

The implication of a worldview that assumes the possession of an intellect to be limited to only one class of human beings is that they are entitled to claim all products of intellectual labour as their private property, even when they have appropriated it from others—the Third World. Intellectual property rights and patents on life are the ultimate expression of capitalist patriarchy's impulse to control all that is living and free.

GATT is the platform where capitalist patriarchy's notion of freedom as the unrestrained right of men with economic power to own, control and destroy life is articulated as 'free-trade'. But for the Third World, and for women, freedom has different meanings. In what seems the remote domain of international trade, these different means of freedom are a focus of contest and conflict. Free trade in food and agriculture is the concrete location of the most fundamental ethical and economic issues of human existence of the present times. It is here that Third World women have a unique contribution to make, because in their daily lives they embody the three colonizations on which modern patriarchy is based; the colonization of nature, of women and of the Third World.

Notes

1. National Sample Survey, 38th Round, Report No. 341.
2. Fernandes, Walter, and Geeta Menon, 'Tribal Women and Forest Economy', Indian Social Institute, New Delhi, 1987.
3. Singh, Vir, 'Hills of Hardship', *The Hindustan Times Weekly*, 18 January 1987.
4. Saradamoni, K., 'Labour, Land and Rice Production: Women's Involvement in their States', *Economic and Political Weekly*, 22(17) 1987.
5. Mencher, Joan, 'Women's Work and Poverty: Women's Contribution to Household Maintenance in Two Regions of South India', in Droyer, D. and J. Bruce (eds) *A Home Divided: Women and Income Control in the Third World*, Stanford University Press, Stanford, 1987.
6. Bhati, J. B. and D. V. Singh, 'Women's Contribution to Agricultural Economy in Hill Regions of North West India', *Economic and Political Weekly*, Vol. 22, No. 17, 1987.
7. Jain, Devaki and Malini Chand Seth, 'Domestic Work: Its Implication for Enumeration of Workers', in Saradamoni (ed.) *Women, Work and Society*, Indian Statistical Institute, Delhi 1985.
8. Shiva, Vandana, *Staying Alive. Women, Ecology and Survival*. Kali, New Delhi, 1988 and Zed Books, 1990, London.
9. Shiva, Vandana, 'Women's Knowledge and Work in Mountain Agriculture'. Paper presented at Conference on Women in Mountain Development, ICIMOD, Kathmandu, 1988.
10. Draft Final Agreement on GATT, GATT Secretariat, Geneva, December 1991.
11. Shiva, Vandana, 'Structural Reforms and Agriculture', *Observer*, November 1992.
12. Ritchie, Mark and Kevin Ristau, 'Crisis by Design: A Brief Review of U.S. Farm Policy', League of Rural Voters Education Project, Minneapolis, 1987.
13. Watkins, Kevin, 'GATT and the Third World' in *Race and Class*, 'The New Conquistadors', Vol. 34, No. 1, July-September 1992.
14. Ibid.
15. GATT Draft Agreement
16. Ritchie, Mark and Kevin Ristau, op cit.
17. Frohberg, K., G. Fischer and K. Parikh, 'Would Developing Countries Benefit from Agricultural Trade Liberalisation in OECD Countries' in Goldin, I. and Knudsen Odin (eds) *Agricultural Trade Liberalisation—Implications for Developing Countries*. OECD, Paris, 1990.
18. Morgan, Dan, *Merchants of Grain*. New York, Viking, 1979.
19. Ritchie, Mark, 'GATT, Agriculture and the Environment, the US Double Zero Plan,' *Ecologist* Vol. 20, No. 6, November-December 1990.
20. Lang, Tim, 'Food Fit for the World? How the GATT Food Trade Talks Challenge Public Health, the Environment and the Citizen', Sustainable Agriculture, Food and the Environment (SAFE) Alliance, London, March 1992.
21. Draft Agreement, GATT.
22. Ibid.
23. Ibid.
24. 'Seeds—A Hard Row to Hoe', *India Today*, 15 February 1989.
25. Kadir, Djelal, *Columbus and the Ends of the Earth*. University of California Press, 1992, p. 90.
26. Locke, John, Peter Caslett (ed) *Two Treaties of Government*. Cambridge University Press, 1967.

 Article Review Form at end of book.

Given the labor exploitation of transnational corporations like Nike, and the loss of control of local resources that global treaties like GATT herald, what impact will coalitions around human rights as women's rights have on global economies?

Beijing '95

Moving women's human rights from margin to center

Charlotte Bunch

Center for Women's Global Leadership, Douglass College, and Bloustein School of Planning and Public Policy, Rutgers, The State University of New Jersey

Susana Fried

Center for Women's Global Leadership, Douglass College, and Departments of Political Science and Urban Development, Rutgers, The State University of New Jersey

The Fourth World Conference on Women in Beijing established clearly that women are a global force for the twenty-first century and that women's human rights are central to women's leadership for the future. Women's rights as human rights permeated debates and delegates' speeches at the official UN intergovernmental conference as well as at the parallel Non-Governmental Organization (NGO) Forum held some thirty miles away in Huairou, where it was a palpable presence in many sessions. The combined effect of these activities was a groundswell of support for making the entire Platform an affirmation of the human rights of women, including women's rights to education, health, and freedom from violence, as well as to the exercise of citizenship in all its manifestations. Previous UN women's conferences were seen as primarily about women and development or even women's rights, but not about the concept of human rights as it applies to women.

This report assesses the Beijing Declaration and Platform for Action, which came out of the governmental conference, focusing on its implications for women's human rights advocacy. The conference was mandated to produce a consensus "platform" that would implement the goals set forth in the "Forward-Looking Strategies" from the 1985 Nairobi World Conference on Women and advance the 1995 conference theme of "Action for Equality, Development, and Peace." More than four thousand NGO delegates accredited to the governmental conference worked to influence the document's articulation of the conditions faced by women worldwide as well as the content of the strategies proposed.

In the context of such international UN meetings, controversies over language are debates about the direction of governmental policy. If the agreements that result from these meetings are to be meaningful beyond the moment, attention must be paid to the details of the compromises, as well as to the subtextual disputes they represent. These documents address several aspects of international debates over gender roles, including (1) ways in which feminist language and concepts are beginning to inform public policy, (2) instances in which these concepts are deployed to undermine feminist goals, (3) cases in which the links between feminist theoretical analyses and political practices are weak, and (4) spaces where the political attention of women's movements must be focused in a more concerted fashion.

An important caveat to be made about documents that come out of UN conferences is that they are consensus based, which means that often the lowest common denominator prevails, and, therefore, weak language may emerge from the most contentious and passionate debates. Nevertheless, getting reluctant governments even to agree to weak text when it represents an advancement over their prior positions can be important. Further, these documents and programs of action do not have the status of international law. Instead, they carry political and moral weight as policy guidelines for the UN, governments, and other international organizations. To use these documents effectively, they must be approached as statements of best intentions and commitments to which organized groups can seek to hold governments and the UN accountable.

Overall, the Beijing Platform for Action is a positive affirmation of women's human rights in many areas. It demands the economic and political empowerment of women and calls for more active intervention by governments on behalf of women's equality. The successes that women achieved in this process have been long in the making. They grow out of many decades of women's organizing generally, and specifically out of twenty years of attention to women at the UN, and four years of women's explicit and increasing participation as an organized force in UN intergovernmental conferences addressing major global concerns, such as the environment (Rio de Janeiro, 1992), human rights (Vienna, 1993), population and development (Cairo, 1994), and social development (Copenhagen, 1995). This has resulted in increasingly sophisticated lobbying of governmental delegates by women whose efforts are based on years of working to build international feminist strategies

around common concerns, such as reproductive rights and violence against women. Networking among women prior to the Beijing conference produced effective cross-cultural alliances and led to significant collaboration between women on government delegations, in the UN and in NGO caucuses.

The Platform for Action outlines action for the human rights of women in twelve interrelated critical areas, from poverty and education to violence and the media. In spite of concerted attempts by religious fundamentalists and secular conservatives to narrow the reach of human rights, women's rights are framed throughout the Platform as indivisible, universal, and inalienable human rights. Such an understanding can be transformed into human rights practices—reaffirming women's rights to literacy, food, and housing, along with their rights to freedom of association and speech and to live free of violence, enslavement, or torture.

Yet, while the Platform clearly moves in the direction of advancing women's rights as human rights, it also reflects contentious debate about women's role in society and the construction of gender. The subtext to the Platform was the ongoing controversy about feminism and gender roles. For instance, one of the hottest debates in the final preparatory meeting was over the use of the term *gender* in the draft Platform. The Vatican and a few states argued against using *gender* at all unless it was explicitly tied to the "natural" biological roles of the sexes. When its efforts failed, the Holy See noted in its final statement to the conference that its members understood the term *gender* to be "grounded in biological sexual identity, male or female.

. . . The Holy See thus excludes dubious interpretations based on world views which assert that sexual identity can be adopted indefinitely to suit new and different purposes."[1]

Some major controversies illustrate what women gained and the limitations of the Platform for Action. For example, in the contested area of sexual rights, many thought governments would not accept this language, and the phrase *sexual rights* per se was rejected. However, these boundaries were expanded in the health section of the Platform, which states in paragraph 97 that "the human rights of women include their right to have control over and decide freely and responsibly on matters related to their sexuality, including sexual and reproductive health, free of coercion, discrimination and violence." Similarly, explicit support for the rights of lesbians and the term *sexual orientation* were excluded from the Platform in final late-night negotiations. Nevertheless, the door was opened with this first open discussion of the issue in the UN, which also exposed the virulence of homophobia among those who manipulate it to oppose women's rights generally. At least some governments in each region of the world supported the need to include sexual orientation as deserving of protection from discrimination, and a number stated that their interpretation of the prohibition against discrimination on the basis of "other" status in several human rights treaties applies to lesbians and gays.

Another major debate centered on the term *universal* and the use of religion and culture to limit

[1]United Nations, *UN Report of the Fourth World Conference on Women* (New York: United Nations, 1995), 165.

women's human rights. Women sought to maintain the 1993 Vienna World Conference on Human Rights recognition that women's human rights are universal, inalienable, indivisible, and interdependent. The Vatican, some Islamist governments, and a few other states overtly attempted unsuccessfully to limit the extent of universal application of women's human rights. However, they used this debate to claim that there is a feminist imperialism that reflects disrespect for religion and culture, an overzealous individualism, and an effort to impose Western values that destroy the family and local communities. Nineteen states entered reservations to text in the Platform that was not in conformity with Islamic law or traditional religious interpretations, particularly references to reproductive health and rights, inheritance, sexuality, and abortion. This is not a new debate, but women need to learn better how to argue for universality of rights without implying homogenization, especially around religion and culture, which can be positive for some women.

Human rights is not a static concept; it has varying meanings depending on a range of political, intellectual, and cultural traditions. Often in international organizing women speak of "culture" and national sovereignty in debates over human rights only as negative influences because they are so often used as excuses to deny women's rights. However, culture is constructed in many ways and exists not only as hege-

monic culture but also as alternative cultures, oppositional cultures, and cultures of resistance. Women must create a more nuanced conversation that can address the tension between calls for recognizing the universality of women's human rights and the respect for and nurturance of local cultures and oppositional strategies. This entails women's defining the terms of debate and of culture themselves rather than letting the debate be defined by others.

The movement for women's human rights has sought to be a partial answer to this tension. In contrast to organizing that emphasizes categories of difference or identity, which were also well represented at the NGO Forum and government conference, efforts around women's human rights take as their reason for coming together the construction of a common political goal, based on a set of norms or justice, however problematic that may be, rather than a commonality of experience. The coalitions that emerge, then, are politically constructed, rather than determined on the basis of biology, geography, culture, ethnicity, and so on. The potential of such coalitions could be seen at the NGO Forum and in many of the global issue caucuses that lobbied together across geographical lines for more feminist language in the Platform for Action.

This incorporation of women's human rights language and concepts by governments and organizations from all parts of the world and in all manner of ways

indicates more than a rhetorical gesture. It represents a shift in analysis that moves beyond single-issue politics or identity-based organizing and enhances women's capacity to build global alliances based on collective political goals and a common agenda. Moreover, because human rights is a language that has legitimacy among many individuals and governments, the appeal to human rights agreements and international norms can fortify women's organizing.

However, realization of the potential we viewed in Beijing requires vigorous leadership and a willingness to engage in open and often difficult political dialogue across many differences that tend to divide women. It also demands that women become politically active in local communities, in national political contests, and in international debates in the effort to reshape the terms of debate for the twenty-first century. The Beijing Platform for Action can be a vital tool in this process as it provides an affirmation of women's rights as human rights and outlines many of the actions necessary to realize women's empowerment. But how far the Platform and the concept of women's human rights will take women depends on whether women are able to use them to further their efforts to influence policy and action at all levels from the global to the local.

 Article Review Form at end of book.

WiseGuide Wrap-Up

- Technology, ecology, and the global economy are linked by and to women's issues.

- Women's health concerns, such as menopause, have been ignored in the past, and the unique characteristics of women's responses to nongender specific problems have been invisible, because men have been both the primary researchers and the primary research subjects.

- Human rights provides a possible space for women to form effective global coalitions.

R.E.A.L. Sites

This list provides a print preview of typical **coursewise** R.E.A.L. sites. (There are over 100 such sites at the **courselinks**™ site.) The danger in printing URLs is that Web sites can change overnight. As we went to press, these sites were functional using the URLs provided. If you come across one that isn't, please let us know via email to: webmaster@coursewise.com. Use your Passport to access the most current list of R.E.A.L. sites at the **courselinks**™ site.

Site name: University Health Quarterly—Breast Cancer
URL: http://www.umdnj.edu/univhosp/d163.html
Key topics: Breast Cancer, Health
Why is it R.E.A.L.? Breast cancer is on the rise, and women are increasingly aware of the risks, as well as of their options for detection and treatment. This site offers a community-based review of the most recent advice about breast cancer.
Activity: After reading the material on this page, click on the UHQ Articles link and look at the other material published by this major research hospital. Evaluate the amount of material that addresses women's health issues. Review the article "Affairs of the Heart" for information that would be helpful to women patients, in light of the article "The Real Number-One Killer."

Site name: Eve Online
URL: http://www.envirolink.org/orgs/eve/issues/issues.html
Key topics: Eco-Feminism, Global Economics, Feminist Theory
Why is it R.E.A.L.? This site includes links to other environmental activist sites, as well as a number of pages about current issues and actions in the eco-feminist community.
Activity: Using a world map and the WebCrawler search engine, pinpoint five strategic global locations for eco-feminist groups to target. These locations should be places where both environmental concerns and gender issues are at stake.

Site name: The Ethnic Woman International
URL: http://www.thefuturesite.com/ethnic/index.html
Key topics: Feminist Theory, Race, Difference
Why is it R.E.A.L.? The Ethnic Woman International develops its own materials, as well as linking site visitors to current global conditions for ethnic women.
Activity: After reviewing the articles and links at this site, click on the survey button on the home page and submit your answers to the two questions. Print out your response and compare your ideas for topics with those of others in your class.

Site name: Women's Studies: Stereotypes and Expected Behaviors
URL: http://www.socialstudies.com/mar/gender2.html
Key topics: Stereotypes, Feminist Theory
Why is it R.E.A.L.? This site uses online technology to provide historical groundwork for an understanding of gender stereotyping.
Activity: After completing all of the activities on this site, including reading the linked materials, assess its interest and impact for high school students.

section

7

Key Points

Key Points

- Patriarchy is a socially constructed system, which benefits men at the expense of women.

- Female infanticide, dietary restrictions, stereotypes, and other restrictions are deployed only against female bodies as a way to control and contain women.

- Feminist movements, or women's movements, combine theoretical positions with real practices to gain equal rights for all women and to ensure equal participation of women in all social systems.

Good Girls/Bad GRRRLS: Feminism and Patriarchy

WiseGuide Intro

Patriarchy is the system of gender relations in which men exercise control over women's bodies through legal, social, and religious sanctions and practices. Property, names, and kinship ties are passed from generation to generation through the father. Benefits accrue to male bodies at the expense of female bodies.

Feminism is a set of theories and practices developed in response to the continued exclusion of women from the public sphere and the ongoing violence and discrimination against women in the private sphere. Women who marched, protested, and spoke out against the injustices of patriarchy have historically been marked out as bad girls and have suffered painful sanctions, such as jail, loss of their children, and complete separation from economic and social safety nets. When it was illegal for women to own property, have money of their own, and to vote, men benefited from the free labor of women in the home, and no competition from women for jobs.

Shirley Geok-lin Lim's powerful poem "Pantoun for Chinese Women" describes the painful reality of female infanticide, a practice which marks girls as undesirable. Social norms for women that restrict access to food or enforce strict adherence to a standardized body type are both accepted and resisted in "What Bengali Widows Cannot Eat" and "Over Dinner." Susan Faludi exposes the hypocrisy of women claiming to be feminists who actually work against the best interests of women in general in "I'm Not a Feminist but I Play One on TV." And, finally, Gerda Lerner, a pioneer in women's history, offers a brief history of the development of patriarchy, undercutting the myth that male dominance is just "the way things are supposed to be."

Questions

Reading 27. What does "a child with two mouths" mean?

Reading 28. Why is a Bengali widow required to deny herself food?

Reading 29. What differences in constructions of femininity do Fine and Macpherson hear from the young women participating in this conversation?

Reading 30. Why do the women who claim to be feminists but, according to Faludi, really aren't, get so much media attention?

Reading 31. Along with women in general, what other groups have struggled for access to the power of naming, which is the power of the patriarchy?

What does "a child with two mouths" mean?

Pantoun for Chinese Women

Shirley Geok-lin Lim

At present, the phenomena of butchering, drowning, and leaving to die female infants have been very serious.'
(The People's Daily, Peking, March 3rd, 1983)

They say a child with two mouths is no good.
In the slippery wet, a hollow space,
Smooth, gumming, echoing wide for food.
No wonder my man is not here at his place.

In the slippery wet, a hollow space,
A slit narrowly sheathed within its hood.
No wonder my man is not here at his place:
He is digging for the dragon jar of soot.

That slit narrowly sheathed within its hood!
His mother, squatting, coughs by the fire's blaze
While he digs for the dragon jar of soot.
We had saved ashes for a hundred days.

His mother, squatting, coughs by the fire's blaze.
The child kicks against me mewing like a flute.
We had saved ashes for a hundred days,
Knowing, if the time came, that we would.

The child kicks against me crying like a flute
Through its two weak mouths. His mother prays
Knowing when the time comes, that we would,
For broken clay is never set in glaze.

Through her two weak mouths his mother prays.
She will not pluck the rooster nor serve its blood,
For broken clay is never set in glaze:
Women are made of river sand and wood.

She will not pluck the rooster nor serve its blood.
My husband frowns, pretending in his haste
Women are made of river sand and wood.
Milk soaks the bedding. I cannot bear the waste.

My husband frowns, pretending in his haste.
Oh clean the girl, dress her in ashy soot!
Milk soaks our bedding, I cannot bear the waste.
They say a child with two mouths is no good.

 Article Review Form at end of book.

Why is a Bengali widow required to deny herself food?

What Bengali Widows Cannot Eat

Chitrita Banerji

My father died at the beginning of a particularly radiant and colourful spring. Spring in Bengal is teasing and elusive, secret yet palpable, waiting to be discovered. The crimson and scarlet of *palash* and *shimul* flowers post the season's banners on high trees. Compared to the scented flowers of the summer and monsoon—jasmine, *beli, chameli, kamini,* gardenias, all of which are white—these scentless spring flowers are utterly assertive with the one asset they have: colour. My father, who was a retiring, unassuming man, took great pleasure in their flaunting, shameless reds. When I arrived in Calcutta for his funeral, I was comforted by the sight of the flowers in full bloom along the road from the airport.

That first evening back home, my mother and I sat out on our roof, talking. As darkness obscured all colours, the breeze became gusty, laden with unsettling scents from out-of-season potted flowers on neighbouring roofs.

My mother had always been dynamic, forceful, efficient: the

family's principal breadwinner for nearly thirty years, she had risen above personal anxiety and ignored social disapproval to allow me, alone, young and unmarried, to pursue my studies in the United States. Yet overnight, she had been transformed into the archetypal Bengali widow—meek, faltering, hollow-cheeked, sunken-eyed, the woman in white from whose life all colour and pleasure must evaporate.

During the thirteen days of mourning that precede the Hindu rituals of *shraddha* (last rites) and the subsequent *niyambhanga* (literally, the breaking of rules), all members of the bereaved family live ascetically on one main meal a day of rice and vegetables cooked together in an earthen pot with no spices except sea salt, and no oil, only a touch of ghee. The sanction against oil embraces its cosmetic use too, and for me, the roughness of my mother's parched skin and hair made her colourless appearance excruciating. But what disturbed me most was the eagerness with which she seemed to be embracing the trappings of bereavement. Under the curious, observant and critical

eyes of female relatives, neighbours and visitors, she appeared to be mortifying her flesh almost joyfully, as if those thirteen days were a preparation for the future. As if it is utterly logical for a woman to lose her self and plunge into a life of ritual suffering once her husband is dead.

Hindu tradition in Bengal holds that the widow must strive for purity through deprivation. In contrast with the bride, who is dressed in red and, if her family's means permit, decked out in gold jewellery, the widow, regardless of her wealth and status, is drained of colour. Immediately after her husband's death, other women wash the *sindur*, a vermilion powder announcing married status, from the parting in the widow's hair. All jewellery is removed, and she exchanges her coloured or patterned sari for the permanent, unvarying uniform of the *thaan*, borderless yards of blank white cotton. Thus transformed, she remains, for the rest of her life, the pallid symbol of misfortune, the ghostly twin of the western bride, dressed in virginal white, drifting down the aisle towards happiness.

Chitrita Banerji is the author of *Life and Food in Bengal* (1991) and *Bengali Cooking: Seasons and Festivals* (1997). She is also the editor of an environmental magazine, *Conservation Matters*, published by the Conservation Law Foundation of New England. Reprinted with permission.

As recently as fifty years ago, widows were also forced to shave their heads as part of a socially prescribed move towards androgyny. Both of my grandfather's sisters were widowed in their twenties: my childhood memories of them are of two nearly identical creatures wrapped in shroud-like white who emerged from their village a couple of times a year and came to visit us in the city. Whenever the *thaan* covering their heads slipped, I would be overcome with an urge to rub my hands over their prickly scalps that resembled the spherical, yellow, white-bristled flowers of the *kadam* tree in our garden.

Until the Hindu Widow Remarriage Act was passed in 1856, widows were forbidden to marry for a second time. But for more than a hundred years after the act became law, it did not translate into any kind of widespread social reality (unlike the 1829 edict abolishing the burning of widows on the same pyre as their dead husbands—the infamous practice of suttee). Rural Bengali households were full of widows who were no more than children, because barely pubescent girls often found themselves married to men old enough to be their fathers.

It was not until the morning before the actual *shraddha* ceremony that I was forced to confront the cruellest of the rules imposed on the widow by the Sanskrit *shastras*, the body of rules and rituals of Hindu life to which have been added innumerable folk beliefs. One of my aunts took me aside and asked if my mother had made up her mind to give up eating fish and meat—*amish*, non-vegetarian food, forbidden for widows. With a sinking heart, I realized that the image of the

widow had taken such a hold of my mother that she was only too likely to embrace a vegetarian diet—all the more so because she had always loved fish and had been renowned for the way she cooked it. If I said nothing, she would never again touch those wonders of the Bengali kitchen—*shorshe-ilish, maacher jhol, galda chingrir, malaikari, lauchingri, doi-maach, maacher kalia*. It was an unbearable thought.

The vegetarian stricture is not considered a hardship in most regions of India where the majority, particularly the Brahmins and some of the upper castes, have always been vegetarians. But Bengal is blessed with innumerable rivers criss-crossing a fertile delta, and it is famed for its rice and its fish. Even Brahmins have lapsed in Bengal by giving in to the regional taste for fish, which plays a central part in both the diet and the culinary imagination of the country. Fish, in its ubiquity, symbolism and variety, becomes, for the Bengali widow, the finest instrument of torture.

Several other items are forbidden to widows simply because of their associations with *amish*. *Puishak*, for instance, a spinach-like leafy green often cooked with small shrimps or the fried head of a *hilsa* fish, is disallowed. So are onion and garlic, which were eschewed by most Hindus until the last century because of their association with meat-loving Muslims. They are further supposed to have lust-inducing properties, making them doubly unsuitable for widows. Lentils, a good source of protein in the absence of meat, are also taboo—a stricture which might stem from the widespread practice of spicing them with chopped onion.

Social historians have speculated that these dietary restrictions served a more sinister and worldly function than simply that of moving a widow towards a state of purity: they would also lead to malnutrition, thus reducing her lifespan. A widow often has property, and her death would inevitably benefit someone—her sons, her siblings, her husband's family. And in the case of a young widow, the sooner she could be dispatched to the next world, the less the risk of any moral transgression and ensuing scandal.

My grandmother lived the last twenty-seven of her eighty-two years as a widow, obeying every stricture imposed by rules and custom. The memory of her bleak, pinched, white-robed widowhood intensified my determination to prevent my mother from embracing a similar fate. I particularly remember a scene from my early teens. I was the only child living with an extended family of parents, uncles and aunts—and my grandmother. It had been a punishingly hot and dry summer. During the day, the asphalt on the streets would melt, holding on to my sandals as I walked. Night brought sweat-drenched sleeplessness and the absorbing itchiness of prickly heat. Relief would come only with the eagerly awaited monsoon.

The rains came early one morning—dark, violent, lightning-streaked, fragrant and beautiful. The cook rushed to the market and came back with a big *hilsa* fish which was cut up and fried, the crispy, flavourful pieces served at lunchtime with *khichuri*, rice and dhal cooked together. This is the traditional way to celebrate the arrival of the monsoon. Though I knew my grandmother did not eat fish, I was amazed on this occasion to see that she did not touch either the *khichuri* or the battered slices of aubergine or the fried potatoes. These were vegetarian items, and I had seen her eat them before on other wet and chilly days. This time, she ate, in her usual solitary spot, *luchis*, a kind of fried bread, that looked stale, along with some equally unappetizing cold cooked vegetables.

Why? I asked in outrage. And my mother explained that this was because of a rare coincidence: the rains had arrived on the first day of Ambubachi, the three-day period in the Bengali month of Asharh that, according to the almanac, marks the beginning of the rainy season. The ancients visualized this as the period of the earth's receptive fertility, when the summer sun vanishes, the skies open and mingle with the parched land to produce a red or brown fluid flow of earth and water, nature's manifestation of menstruating femininity. How right then for widows to suffer more than usual at such a time. They were not allowed to cook during the three-day period, and, although they were allowed to eat some foods that had been prepared in advance, boiled rice was absolutely forbidden. Since nature rarely conforms to the calculations of the almanac, I had never noticed these Ambubachi strictures being observed on the long-awaited rainy day.

The almanac was an absolute necessity for conforming to the standards of ritual purity, and my grandmother consulted it assiduously. On the day before Ambubachi started, she would prepare enough *luchis* and vegetables for three midday meals. Sweet yogurt and fruit, mixed with *chira*—dried, flattened rice—were also permissible. That first

night of monsoon, newly aware of the sanctions of Ambubachi, I went to look for my grandmother around dinner time. All she ate was a small portion of *kheer*, milk that had been boiled down to nearly solid proportions, and some pieces of mango. I had hoped she would at least be permitted one of her favourite evening meals—warm milk mixed with crushed mango pulp. But no. Milk cannot be heated, for the widow's food must not receive the touch of fire during Ambubachi. The *kheer*, a traditional way of preserving milk, had been prepared for her the day before.

It is true that despite deprivations, household drudgery and the imposition of many fasts, widows sometimes live to a great age, and the gifted cooks among them have contributed greatly to the range, originality and subtlety of Hindu vegetarian cooking in Bengal. A nineteenth-century food writer once said that it was impossible to taste the full glory of vegetarian food unless your own wife became a widow. And Bengali literature is full of references to elderly widows whose magic touch can transform the most mundane or bitter of vegetables to nectar, whose subtlety with spices cannot be reproduced by other hands.

But however glorious these concoctions, no married woman envies the widow's fate. And until recently, most widows remained imprisoned within the austere bounds of their imposed diets. Even if they were consumed with temptation or resentment, fear of discovery and public censure were enough to inhibit them.

I knew the power of public opinion as I watched my mother during the day of the *shraddha*. My aunt, who had been widowed when fairly young, had been bold

enough, with the encouragement of her three daughters, to continue eating fish. But I knew that my mother and many of her cronies would find it far less acceptable for a woman in her seventies not to give up *amish* in her widowhood. As one who lived abroad, in America, I also knew that my opinion was unlikely to carry much weight. But I was determined that she should not be deprived of fish, and with the support of my aunt and cousins I prepared to fight.

The crucial day of the *niyambhanga*, the third day after the *shraddha*, came. On this day, members of the bereaved family invite all their relatives to lunch, and an elaborate meal is served, representing the transition between the austerity of mourning and normal life—for everyone except the widow. Since we wanted to invite many people who were not relatives, we arranged to have two catered meals, lunch and dinner, the latter for friends and neighbours. My mother seemed to recover some of her former energy that day, supervising everything with efficiency, attending to all the guests. But she hardly touched any food. After the last guest had left, and the caterers had packed up their equipment, leaving enough food to last us for two or three days, I asked her to sit down and eat dinner with me. For the first time since my father's death, the two of us were absolutely alone in the house. I told her I would serve the food; I would be the grown-up now.

She smiled and sat down at the table. I helped her to rice and dhal, then to two of the vegetable dishes. She held up her hand then. No more. I was not to go on to the fish. Silently, we ate. She asked for a little more rice and vegetables. I complied, then lifted a piece of *rui* fish and held it over her plate. Utter panic filled her eyes, and she shot anxious glances around the room. She told me, vehemently, to eat the fish myself.

It was that panic-stricken look around her own house, where she was alone with me, her daughter, that filled me with rage. I was determined to vanquish the oppressive force of ancient belief, reinforced by whatever model of virtue she had inherited from my grandmother. We argued for what seemed like hours, my voice rising, she asking me to be quiet for fear of the neighbours, until finally I declared that I would never touch any *amish* myself as long as she refused to eat fish. The mother who could not bear the thought of her child's deprivation eventually prevailed, though the woman still quaked with fear of sin and retribution.

I have won a small victory, but I have lost the bigger battle. My mother's enjoyment of food, particularly of fish, as well as her joyful exuberance in the kitchen where her labours produced such memorable creations, have vanished. Sometimes, as I sit and look at her, I see a procession of silent women in white going back through the centuries. They live as household drudges, slaves in the kitchen and the field; they are ostracized even in their own homes during weddings or other happy ceremonies—their very presence considered an invitation to misfortune.

In the dim corners they inhabit, they try to contain their hunger. Several times a year, they fast and pray and prepare spreads for priests and Brahmins, all in the hope of escaping widowhood in the next life. On the eleventh day of each moon, they deny themselves food and water and shed tears over their blameful fate, while women with husbands make a joyous ritual out of eating rice and fish. Their anguish and anger secreted in the resinous chamber of fear, these white-clad women make their wasteful progress towards death.

 Article Review Form at end of book.

What differences in constructions of femininity do Fine and Macpherson hear from the young women participating in this conversation?

Over Dinner

Feminism and adolescent female bodies

Michelle Fine and Pat Macpherson

Michelle Fine is Professor of Psychology at the Graduate Center of the City University of New York. Pat Macpherson, a teacher of English at the Germantown Friends School in Philadelphia for thirteen years, is now a freelance writer.

> The experience of being women can create an illusory unity, for it is not the experience of being woman but the meanings attached to gender, race, class, and age at various historical moments . . . that [are] of strategic significance.
>
> Chandra Mohanty
> "Feminist Encounters"
> Copyright 1 (1987), p. 39

When we invited four teenagers—Shermika, Damalleaux, Janet, and Sophie—for a series of two dinners to talk with us about being young women in the 1990s, we could not see our own assumptions about female adolescence much more clearly than we saw theirs. By the end of the first dinner, however, we could recognize how old we were, how dated the academic literature is, how powerful feminism had been in shaping their lives and the meanings they made of them, and yet how inadequately their feminism dealt with key issues of identity and peer relations.

Only when we started to write could we see the inadequacies of our feminism to understand the issues of female adolescence they struggled to communicate. In this space of our incredulity, between our comprehension of their meanings and our *in*comprehension of how they could call themselves feminist, we are now able to see the configuration of our own fantasies of feminism for female adolescents. The re-vision that is central to feminist process gets very tricky when applied to adolescence, because our own unsatisfactory pasts return as the "before" picture, demanding that the "after" picture of current adolescent females measure all the gains of the women's movement. Our longing is for psychic as well as political completion. Michael Payne describes the fantasy of the Other: "What I desire—and therefore lack—is in the other culture, the other race, the other gender"[1]—the other generation, in our case. In the case of these four young women, to our disbelief, the desired Other is "one of the guys."

We grew convinced that we needed to construct an essay about these young women's interpretations of the discourses of adolescence, femininity, and feminism in their peer cultures. Barbara Hudson explains the incompatibility of femininity and adolescence:

> [F]emininity and adolescence as discourses [are] subversive of each other. All of our images of the adolescent—the restless, searching teen; the Hamlet figure; the sower of wild oats and tester of growing powers—these are masculine figures. . . . If adolescence is characterized by masculine constructs, then any attempt by girls to satisfy society's demands of them qua adolescents is bound to involve them in displaying notably a lack of maturity but also a lack of femininity.[2]

Adolescence for these four young women was about the adventures of males and the constraints on

Michelle Fine and Pat Macpherson, "Over Dinner: Feminism and Adolescent Female Bodies," in Sari Knopp Biklen and Diane Pollard, eds., *Gender and Education, Ninety-second Yearbook of the National Society for the Study of Education, Part 1* (Chicago: University of Chicago Press, 1993), pp. 126–154.

females, so their version of feminism unselfconsciously rejected femininity and embraced the benign version of masculinity that allowed them to be "one of the guys." They fantasized the safe place of adolescence to be among guys who overlook their (female) gender out of respect for their (unfeminine) independence, intelligence, and integrity. For them, femininity meant the taming of adolescent passions, outrage, and intelligence. Feminism was a flight from "other girls" as unworthy and untrustworthy. Their version of feminism was about equal access to being like men.

When we scoured the literature on adolescent females and their bodies, we concluded that the very construction of the topic is positioned largely from white, middle-class, nondisabled, heterosexual adult women's perspectives. The concerns of white elite women are represented as *the* concerns of this age cohort. Eating disorders are defined within the contours of what *elite* women suffer (e.g., anorexia and bulimia) and less so what nonelite women experience (e.g., overeating, obesity). The literature on sexual harassment is constructed from *our* age perspective—that unwanted sexual attention is and should be constituted as a crime—and not from the complicated perspectives of young women involved. The literature on disability is saturated with images produced by *nondisabled* researchers of self-pitying or embarrassed "victims" of biology, and is rarely filled with voices of resistant, critical, and powerfully "flaunting" adolescents who refuse to wear prostheses, delight in the passions of their bodies, and are outraged by the social and family discrimination they experience.[3]

We found that women of all ages, according to this literature, are allegedly scripted to be "good women," and that they have, in compliance, smothered their passions, appetites, and outrage. When sexually harassed, they tell "his stories."[4] To please the lingering internalized "him," they suffer in body image and indulge in eating disorders.[5] And to satisfy social demands for "attractiveness," women with and without disabilities transform and mutilate their bodies.[6]

We presumed initially that the three arenas of adolescence in which young women would most passionately struggle with gendered power would include eating, sexuality, and outrage. And so we turned to see what the literature said, and to unpack how race, class, disability, and sexuality played within each of these arenas. In brief, we saw in this literature a polarizing: (1) eating disorders appear to be a question studied among elite white women in their anticipated tensions of career *vs.* mother identities; (2) sexuality is examined disproportionately as problematic for girls who are black and underprivileged, with motherhood as their primary identity posed as "the problem"; and (3) young women's political "outrage" simply does not exist as a category for feminist intellectual analysis. The literature on adolescent women had thoroughly extricated these categories of analysis from women's lives. So, in our text we decided to rely instead upon the frames that these young women offered as they narrated their own lives, and on the interpretations we could generate through culture and class.

Our method was quite simple, feminist, and, ironically, anti-

eating disorder. We invited the six of us to talk together over pizza and soda, while Sam—Michelle's four-year-old—circled the table. We talked for hours, two nights two months apart, and together stretched to create conversations about common differences; about the spaces in which we could delight together as six women; the moments in which they bonded together as four young women who enjoy football, hit their boyfriends, and can't trust other girls—"Not ever!"; and, too, the arenas in which the race, class, and cultural distances in the room stretched too far for these age peers to weave any common sense of womanhood. Collectively, we created a context that Shermika and Sophie spontaneously considered "the space where I feel most safe." We were together, chatting, listening, hearing, laughing a lot, and truly interested in understanding our connections and differences, contoured always along the fault lines of age, class, race and culture, bodies, experiences, and politics.

But we each delighted in this context differently. For Michelle and Pat, it was a space in which we could pose feminist intellectual questions from our generation—questions about sexuality, power, victimization, and politics—which the young women then turned on their heads. For Shermika (African-American, age 15) it was a place for public performance, to say outrageous things, admit embarrassing moments, "practice" ways of being female in public discourse, and see how we would react. For Damalleaux (African-American, age 14) it was a place to "not be shy" even though the group was integrated by race, a combination that had historically made her uncomfortable. For

Sophie ("WASP," age 17), it was a "safe place" where, perhaps for the first time, she was not the only self-proclaimed feminist in a room full of peers. And for Janet (Korean-American, age 17), like other occasions in which she was the only Asian-American among whites and blacks, it was a time to test her assimilated "sense of belonging," always at the margins. In negotiating gender, race, ethnicity, and class as critical feminist agents, these four women successfully betrayed the academic literature, written by so many of us only twenty years older. Our writings have been persistently committed to public representations of women's victimization and structural assaults, and have consequently ignored, indeed misrepresented, *how well young women talk as subjects,* passionate about and relishing in their capacities to move between nexuses of power and powerlessness. That is to say, feminist scholars have forgotten to take notice of how firmly young women resist—alone and sometimes together.

The four young women began their conversation within this space of gendered resistance. Shermika complained, "Boys think girls cannot do *anything,*" to which Sophie added, "So we have to harass them." Shermika explained, "[Guys think] long as they're takin' care of 'em [girls will] do anything they want. And if I'm in a relationship, I'm gonna take care of you just as much as you take care of me. You can't say 'I did this'—No: 'We did this'. . . . Guys think you're not nothin'—anything—without them." Janet sneered, "Ego." Shermika recruited her friend into this conversation by saying, "Damalleaux *rule* her boyfriend (Shermika's brother)." Damalleaux announced

her governing principle, "Boys—they try to take advantage of you. . . . As far as I'm concerned, I won't let a boy own me." Janet provided an example of the "emotionally messed up guys" she encounters: "I didn't want to take care of him. I didn't want to constantly explain things to him. . . . I want to coexist with them and not be like their mother. . . . It happened to me twice." And Sophie explained: "I'm really assertive with guys [who say sexist stuff]. If they have to be shot down I'll shoot them down. They have to know their place." The four expressed their feminism here as resistance to male domination in their peer relations. They applied the same principle in discussing how they saw careers and marriage. When Michelle asked about men in their future plans, Shermika laid it out in material terms: "I imagine bein' in my *own* house in *my name.* And then get married. So my husband can get out of *my house.*" Sophie chimed in, "Seriously?" and Shermika nodded, "Yes, *very important.* So I won't end up one of them battered women we were talkin' about. I'm not going to have no man beatin' on me." Sophie offered her version: "You have to like, be independent. You have to establish yourself as your own person before some guy takes you—I mean—." Janet asserted her standard of independence: "I wouldn't follow a guy to college." Their feminism asserted women's independence from men's power to dominate and direct.

Class and cultural differences entered the conversations with their examples of domination and resistance. Shermika's example of guys materially "takin' care" of girls to establish dominance, and Damalleaux's re-

sistance to male "ownership" reflected the practice of gift-giving as ownership, a norm of their local sexual politics.[7] Damalleaux explained that *respect* could interrupt this dominance structure: "How much respect a guy has for you—especially in front of his friends. . . . If a boy finds out you don't care how they treat you, and you don't have respect for your*self* . . . they won't have respect for you." Damalleaux turned to Shermika and said, "You try to teach me." Shermika's talk was full of lessons learned from her mother, and examples of their closeness. "My mom and me like this, 'cause she understands." Not talking "*leads* to problems. My mom tells me so much about life."

Sophie and Janet defined their resistance within their "professional class," peopled by "individuals," not relationships, who suffer from the dilemmas of "independence," typically explained in terms of psychology. Their isolation from their mothers and female friends enabled them to frame their stories alone, as one-on-one battles across the lines of gender and generations.

Ways of Talking: On Cultures of Womanhood

Herein lies a cautionary tale for feminists who insist that underneath or beyond the differences among women there must be some shared identity—as if commonality were a metaphysical given, as if a shared viewpoint were not a difficult political achievement. . . . Western feminist theory has in effect . . . [demanded that] Afro-American, Asian-American or Latin-American women separate their "woman's voice" from their racial or ethnic voice without also requiring white women to distinguish being a "woman" from being white. This double standard implies that while on the one hand there is a seamless web of whiteness and womanness, on the other hand, blackness and womanness, say, or Indianness and womanness, are discrete and separable elements of identity. If . . . I believe that the woman in every woman is a woman just like me, and if I also assume that there is no difference between being white and being a woman, then seeing another woman "as a woman" will involve me seeing her as fundamentally like the woman I am. In other words, the womanness underneath the black woman's skin is a white woman's, and deep down inside the latina woman is an Anglo woman waiting to burst through the obscuring cultural shroud. As Barbara Omolade has said, "Black women are not white women with color."[8]

At this moment in social history, when the tensions of race, class, and gender could not be in more dramatic relief, social anxieties load onto the bodies of adolescent women.[9] Struggles for social control attach to these unclaimed territories, evident in public debates over teen pregnancy, adolescent promiscuity, parental consent for contraception and abortion, date rapes and stories of sexual harassment, as well as in women's personal narratives of starving themselves or bingeing and purging toward thinness. For each of these social "controversies," there is, however, a contest of wills, a set of negotiations. Young women are engaged with questions of "being female"; that is, who will control, and to what extent can they control, their own bodies?

Threaded through our conversations at the dining room table, culture and class helped to construct at least two distinct versions of womanhood. It became clear that the elite women, for instance, constructed an interior sense of womanhood out of oppositional relation with white men. They positioned white men as the power group White Men.[10] And they positioned themselves in an ongoing, critical, hierarchical struggle with these men. Sophie, for example, often defined her feminism in relation to white boys; instead of "reinforcing guys all the time, I *bust* on guys. Because if you don't bust 'em they'll get ahead. You have to keep 'em in their place."

It was quite another thing to hear the sense of womanhood constructed horizontally—still in struggle—by African-American women, situated with or near African-American men. Given the assault on black men by the broader culture, it was clear that any announced sense of female superiority would be seen as "castrating," and unreconcilable with cross-gender alliances against racism.[11] So the construction of black womanhood was far less dichotomized and oppositional toward men, and far richer in a sense of connection to community.[12] In the context of being "deprived," then, of the traditional (oppositional to White Men) feminine socialization, women of color, like women with disabilities, may construct womanhoods less deeply repulsed by the traditional accoutrements of femininity, less oppositional to the cardboard White Male, and less assured that gender survives as the primary or exclusive category of social identity.

Among these four, then, we heard two quite distinct construc-

tions of "being female." From the African-American women, both living in relatively impoverished circumstances, we heard a "womanhood" of fluid connections among women within and across generations; maturity conceived of as an extension of self with others; a taken-for-granted integration of body and mind; a comfortable practice of using public talk as a place to "work out" concerns, constraints, and choices; and a nourishing, anchored sense of *home* and *community*. bell hooks describes home as the site of nurturance and identity, *positive in its resistance* to racist ideologies of black inferiority.

> Despite the brutal reality of racial apartheid, of domination, one's homeplace was the one site where one could freely confront the issue of humanization, where one could resist. Black women resisted by making homes where all black people could strive to be subjects, not objects, where we could be affirmed in our minds and our hearts despite poverty, hardship, and deprivation, where we could restore to ourselves the dignity denied us on the outside in the public world.[13]

As the words of Damalleaux and Shermika reveal to us, however, the drawback of this centeredness in community is its fragility, its contingent sense of the future, terrors of what's "across the border," and the lack of resources or supports for planned upward mobility.

Indeed, when we discussed future plans, Shermika "joked" she'd be a custodian or bag lady. She "joked" she'd like to be dead, to see what the other world was like. She said she'd like to come back as a bird. "Not a pigeon, I hope," said Sophie. "Dove or peacock," Shermika decided, "something nobody be kickin' around all the time." Shermika finally confided in an uncharacteristic whisper that she'd like to be a lawyer, even the D.A. (the district attorney). What Shermika can be, could be, would like to be, and will be constitutes the terrain of Shermika's and Damalleaux's dilemma. Shermika doesn't worry that education would defeminize her, or that her parents expect something more or different from her career than she does. She quite simply and realistically doubts she'll be able to get all the way to D.A.

Nevertheless, Damalleaux and Shermika, on the other hand, expressed the connections with and respect for mothers found in Gloria Joseph and Jill Lewis's African-American daughters, "A decisive 94.5 percent expressed respect for their mothers in terms of strength, honesty, ability to overcome difficulties, and ability to survive."[14] Shermika's many examples of respect for her mother and Damalleaux's mother calling her "my first girl" suggest "the centrality of mothers in their daughters' lives."[15] In their stories, active female sexuality and motherhood are everywhere "embodied," while "career" is a distant and indistinct dream, marginal, foreign, and threateningly isolated.

In contrast, from the two privileged women, both living in relatively elite circumstances, we heard a "womanhood" struggling for positive definition and safe boundaries; a sharp splitting of body and mind; maturity as a dividing of self from family and school to find individual identity; an obsessive commitment to using privacy—in body, thought, and conversation—as the only way to "work out" one's problems; all nourishing a highly individualized, privatized, and competitive

sense of home and community as sites which they would ultimately leave, unfettered, to launch "autonomous" lives as independent women. Materially and imaginatively these two women recognized an almost uninterruptable trajectory for future plans. Their "womanhood" was built on the sense of *self as exception,* "achievement" meritocratically determining how "exceptional" each individual can prove herself (away) from the group. Self-as-exception, for women, involves "transcending" gender. Rachel Hare-Mustin describes the illusion of gender-neutral choices:

> The liberal/humanist tradition of our epoch assumes that the meanings of our lives reflect individual experience and individual subjectivity. This tradition has idealized individual identity and self-fulfillment and shown a lack of concern about power. Liberalism masks male privilege and dominance by holding that every (undergendered) individual is free. The individual has been regarded as responsible for his or her fate and the basic social order has been regarded as equitable. Liberal humanism implies free choice when individuals are not free of coercion by the social order.[16]

The invisibility of women's "coercion by the social order" came out most clearly in Janet's and Sophie's relationships with their working mothers. They did not analyze their mothers' lives for power.

Sophie said, "My mom doesn't like her job but she has to work so I can go to college." Janet and Sophie said they were afraid of becoming their mothers, unhappy and overworked in jobs they hate, their workloads doubled with domestic responsibilities. "I fear I might be like her. I want to be independent of her,"

white middle-class women said of their mothers in the research of Joseph and Lewis.[17] Janet and Sophie said they didn't talk much, or very honestly, to their mothers, and didn't feel they could ever do enough to gain their mothers' approval. Janet said, "My mother [says] I really have to go to college . . . be a doctor or lawyer. . . . That's her main goal . . . job security. Then she wants me to get married and have a nice family, preferably Catholic. . . . Mom's got my life mapped out." Ambition and career "embody" this mother-daughter relationship, in a sense, while the daughter's problems with sexuality and power and with the mother *as woman*, are absent in the relationship Janet describes.

When discussing whom they would tell if they had a problem, Shermika immediately said "my mom" and Damalleaux said, "I tell Shermika almost everything before I tell my mother." Sophie and Janet agreed only in the negative. It would not be their mothers: "Don't talk to my mom."

Janet: I can't tell my mother anything. If I told her something she would ground me for an entire century.

Sophie: Once you tell them one thing, they want to hear more, and they *pry.* I keep my home life and school—social—life so separate.

Janet: I'll be noncommittal or I won't tell her the truth. I'll just tell her what she wants to hear.

Sophie: I wish I could talk to my mom. It'd be great if I could.

Shermika: It's the wrong thing to do [not talking], though. . . . It always *leads* to problems. My mom tells me so much about life.

Janet said her mother stares at her complexion [her acne] and says, "You're not going to get married, you're not going to have a boyfriend." "I get so mad at her," Janet said. She tells her mother either "I'm leaving, I'm leaving" or "Stop it! Stop it!" Later, when Pat asked whether self-respect was learned from the mother, Janet said her self-respect had "nothing to do with my mother. I used to hate myself, partly because of my mother. But not anymore. My mother's opinion just doesn't matter to me." Sophie said,

My mother ... nitpicks. ... I'm sure it was like her mom [who] never approved anything about her. I get self-respect from my mom because she wants me to respect myself. ... I don't think she respects herself enough. I respect her more than she respects herself. Her mother belittled her so much.

Later Sophie said, "I have the feeling that no matter what I do, it's not enough." Janet said her mother makes her and her sister feel like her mother's "racehorses":

My mom *lives* through her kids. Two daughters: two *chances.* My sister wants to be an actress and my parents hate that [dykey] way she looks. ... My mom: "You're just not *feminine* enough!" I'm just like, "Mom, grow up!" ... She compares her daughters to everyone else's. [One example is] a straight-A student on top of all her chores ... I know there's things in her personality that are part of myself. ... We're just like racehorses. ... "My daughter has three wonderful children and a husband who makes a million dollars a year."

For Janet and Sophie, their mothers were supports you get over, central to the life these daughters wished to escape, and to revise, in their own futures. Within their liberal discourse of free choice, the inequalities of

power determining their mothers' misery were invisible to them, and their own exceptional futures were also unquestioned.

The Body: Boundaries and Connections

Over our dinners we created a democracy of feminist differences. That is, all four, as an age/gender cohort, introduced us to the female body in play with gendered politics. These young women consistently recast *our* prioritizing of sex at the center of feminist politics into *their* collective critique of gender politics. Using a language that analyzed dominance and power, they refused to separate sex from other power relations. Perhaps even more deeply Foucauldian than we assumed ourselves to be, they deconstructed our voyeurism with examples of sexuality as only one embodied site through which gendered politics operate. All four shared a distrust of men: "They think they have power." But they also distrusted female solidarity: "They back stab you all the time." Their examples overturned our notions of sisterhood by showing us that both young women and young men proficiently police the borders, and tenets, of masculinity and femininity among today's teens. They are often reminded of their bodies as a public site (gone right or wrong), commented on and monitored by others, both males and females. But as often, they reminded us, they forcefully reclaim their bodies by talking back, and by talking feminist. "It'd be harder not to talk," Sophie thought. "It'd be harder to sit and swallow whatever people are saying."

Resonating with much of feminist literature, when these

four young women spoke of their bodies, it was clear that they found themselves sitting centrally at the nexus of race, class, and gender politics. *Gender* determines that the young women are subject to external surveillance and responsible for internal body management, and it is their gender that makes them feel vulnerable to male sexual threat and assault. *Culture and class* determine how, that is, determine the norms of body and the codes of surveillance, management, threat, assault, and resistance available to them.

Susan Bordo writes about body management as a text for control in the middle class.[18] Reflecting both elite material status and a pure, interior soul, this fetish of body management, operated by the "normalizing machinery of power," produces a desire to control flesh otherwise out of control, as it positions individuals within an elite class location. The tight svelte body reflects material and moral comfort, while the loose sagging body falls to the "lumpen." Bordo's cultural analysis of the representations and experiences of women's bodies and women's revulsion at sagging fat captures and yet too narrowly homogenizes what the four young women reported.

Each of the four, as Bordo would argue, was meticulously concerned with her body as the site for cataloguing both her own and others' "list" of her inadequacies. Indeed, each body had become the space within which she would receive unsolicited advice about having "too many pimples," "being too chocolate," "looking chubby," "becoming too thin," "looking like a boy," or in the case of a sister, dressing "very butch." The fetish to control, however, was experienced in ways deeply marked by class and race. While the elite women were familiar with, if not obsessed by, eating disorders now fashionable among their status peers, the African-American women were quite literally bewildered at the image of a young woman bingeing on food, and then purging. Therein lies a serious problematic in white feminist literature where class and culture practices are coded exclusively as *gender*, reinforcing hegemonic definitions of (white) womanhood, while obscuring class/culture contours of the body.

For these women, the female body not only signified a site of interior management vis-à-vis male attention or neglect. It was also a site for gendered politics enacted through sexual violence. Celia Kitzinger, in an analysis of how 2000 young women and men frame their personal experiences with "unfairness," found that 24 percent of interviewed girls spontaneously volunteered instances of body-centered unfairness, including sexual harassment, rape, and/or abuse.[19] So, too, stories of violence were offered by all four of the young women, each particular to her social context:

Damalleaux: When I got my first boyfriend [he] pressured me to have sex with him. That's why I didn't never go over his house.

Sophie: I feel safe nowhere.

Shermika: When he pulled a gun on me, I said, "This is over."

Janet: I know it's unlikely, but I am terrified of someday being date-raped. It's always been something I've been afraid of.

For Janet, violence is imagined as possible because of the stories of her friends. For Sophie, violence is encountered as harassment on the street. For Damalleaux and Shermika, vio-

lence is encountered or threatened in relations with boyfriends.

Michelle: Is there any place where guys have more power than you?

Damalleaux: In bed.

Shermika: In the street. In the store, when he has all the money.

Damalleaux: And all the guys can beat girls. But I don't think it's true.

Michelle: Are you ever afraid that the hitting will get bad?

Shermika: Yeah, that's why I don't do so much hitting.

Damalleaux: When I go out with a boy I hit him a lot to see if he's going to do anything. . . . You hit me once, I don't want anything to do with you.

Shermika: Sometimes you can get raped with words, though. You feel so slimy. . . . The guy at the newspaper stand, I speak to him every morning. Then one day he said, "How old is you? I can't wait till you 16." And I told my mom, and she came [with me and told him off]. He lost respect. He didn't give me none. And that day I felt bad, what was I, bein' too loose? . . . You just can't help feelin' like that [slimy].

Liz Kelly offers this definition of sexual violence: Sexual violence includes any physical, visual, verbal or sexual act that is experienced by the woman or girl, at the time or later, as a threat, invasion, or assault that has the effect of degrading or hurting her and/or takes away her ability to control intimate contact.[20]

We found that the impression and/or experience of surviving male violence was indeed central. But class and race influenced its expression by the four young women. These fears and experiences were deeply traumatic to all the women, and yet the African-American women more frequently and more pub-

licly, if uncomfortably, related them in the context of conversation. For the elite women the assaults and fears were more privatized and so left relatively unanalyzed, unchallenged, and in critical ways "buried." For example, Janet's story of a friend's date-rape contrasts radically with Shermika's stories of male violence and female resistance.

Janet: That happened to one of my friends.

Sophie: A date rape?

Janet: Sort of . . . He'd been pressuring her for a long time, and she's just "no no no no." She's at this party, her [girl] friend says, "Why don't you just do it?" and she says, "Because I don't *want* to." . . . She was drunk, puking. She fell asleep, and the next thing she knows she wakes up and he's on top of her and she's not really happy about it but she didn't do anything about it so she just let it happen. And . . . she was upset about it, she was really angry about it, but there was nothing she could *do* about it? [Janet's voice rises into a kind of question mark.] It didn't really bother her, but after that she totally knew who her friends were.

Sophie: She could've done something about it.

Janet: I guess we didn't talk about how she really really felt about it. She seemed really comfortable with it after it. She was upset for a while. After she . . .

Sophie: There's no way she was *comfortable* with it.

Janet: She's dealt with it in a way. She's gotten to the point where it doesn't really make her cry to talk about it.

Earlier in the conversation Sophie complained that the popular crowd got drunk at parties and had one-night stands. Somewhat defensive, Janet said aside to Sophie, "Hey, *I've* done that."

Janet's story of the rape included Janet's anger at the girl's girlfriend: "Her *friend* was the hostess of the party and gave her the condoms and told her to go do it." Betrayal by the girlfriend and the boyfriend, a rape Janet calls "sort of" a date-rape, in a party situation Janet has been in many times, anger and helplessness, talking about it finally without tears: this worst-case scenario of women's sexuality and powerlessness is "dealt with" by *not* "talk[ing] about how she really felt about it." Janet's story was about the social and interior limits on one girl's control, before and after "sex" she didn't want.

In sharp contrast, Shermika offered a story of embodied resistance and resistance through public talk. Michelle asked, "Have you ever been in a relationship where you felt you were being forced to do what you didn't want to do?" Shermika's answer was immediate and emphatic, "Yeah, I quit 'em." She followed with a story about what happened when she "quit" the boyfriend who was getting possessive:

Shermika: I almost got killed. Some guy pulled a gun on me. . . . He put the gun *to my head*. I said, "You'd better kill me cause if you don't I'm gonna kill you." Then he dropped the gun. . . . I kicked him where it hurts. . . . hard, he had to go to the hospital. I was scared.

Janet: What happened? Have you ever seen him again?

Shermika: I see him every day.

Michelle: Did you call the cops?

Shermika: Yeah. He had to stay in jail [2 weeks] till I decided not to press charges. . . . Don't nobody around my way playin' like that with them guns.

Shermika's examples of male threat and violence all show her and her mother talking back, striking back, or disarming the man. The woman is embodied as her own best protector. Shermika followed up her first story (which stunned her audience into awed silence) with a second, another jealous boyfriend:

He told me if I went with anybody else he'd kill me. And he pulled a knife on me . . . "Stab me. Either way, you ain't gonna have me."

Later she told a story about her mother:

My stepfather and my mother were fightin'—it's the only time they ever fought. And he stepped back and hit my momma with all his might. And he thought she was gonna give up. She stepped back and hit *him* with all *her* might—and he fell asleep. She knocked the mess outta him. He never hit her again.

And another about herself, with her mother as model:

A guy tried to beat me with a belt, and I grabbed it and let him see how it felt to get beat with that belt. My mom wouldn't even take that.

The scars of actual and/or anticipated sexual violence were clear for each of the young women, and always culturally specific as encounter and resistance in the telling.

As with the violence of gender, the violence of racism on the female body was painfully voiced by the three women of color. Fears of attending a white prep school "where they'll ignore me," stories of fleeing an integrated school after three weeks and retrospective outbursts of anger at being "the only woman of color in my class!" showed a kind of agora-phobia which kept Shermika and Damalleaux in their wholly black communities, and, inversely, created in Janet deep assimilative wishes to disappear into the white suburbs. For Janet the "white church" in her elite suburban neighborhood—not the Korean church her parents attend—was the "safest place" she could imagine.

For Damalleaux and Shermika, the neighborhood and its school are clearly the only safe places. Damalleaux reported that she had lasted three weeks at an integrated school, "It was O.K. but I didn't feel right. I didn't know anybody. I don't like introducing myself to people, I'm too shy . . . I came back to the neighborhood school."

Shermika was offered a scholarship to go to a fancy private school in a white suburb. When discussing what scares us about the future, Shermika admitted she fears "being neglected. Not fitting in. One time I'm goin' in and nobody likes me." When Michelle asked if that was her fear about the prep school, Shermika said, "Not as far as the people. But I don't like travelling. And I'm not staying on the campus. . . . I ain't stayin' away from home, though." By the time of our second interview, Shermika had convinced her mother to delay her going to prep school, from mid-year until the next fall. Shermika said she feared she would not be able to keep her grades up in the new school. Shermika's reliance on nonstandard English meant she would have to manage a major cultural shift both academically and socially. Her only envy of Sophie and Janet's school was what she called it's "socializing" function, which taught them "how to get along, socialize, fit in, knowin' the right thing to say and do." Shermika said that when she has a job she wants to stay in her neighborhood "where it all happenin' [not] where you won't fit in." Racial identity, segregation, and racism combine to reinforce the boundaries of Shermika's and Damalleaux's lives and futures, by defining where and who is "safe."

Shermika evidently decided our dinner table was a "safe" enough place to explore our own racial (and maybe racist) differences. Shermika asked Janet, "Are you Chinese?" and Janet said, "No, Korean," and launched into a story about Japanese racism, including the sale of "Sambo" dolls in Japan, and then a story about the 4,000-year-old hatred of Koreans for the Japanese. Shermika responded, "Well, I don't understand that. I mean, I'm supposed to hate somebody white because somebody I know was a slave?" Then Shermika put race and racism right on our dinner table:

Shermika: I walk into a store and Chinese people be starin' at me. [Shermika was mistaking Korean for Chinese for the third time.]

Janet: My *mother* does that. I hate that, my *mother* does it. [Her mother runs a dry cleaner shop.] And I'm just like, "Mom, STOP it."

Damalleaux: I leave [the store].

Janet: How do you feel when you're the only minority in a room?

Damalleaux: I don't care.

Shermika: I make a joke out of it. I feel like a zebra.

Unlike Janet's experience, the assaultive nature of Shermika's and Damalleaux's encounters with the white world had given them little encouragement to isolate themselves among a white majority. Shermika said her "darkness" meant she "looked like a clown" when they put on make-up for her local TV interview about the scholarship program she's in, then her pride and excitement about the video of herself on TV was clouded by family jokes about her dark skin making her "invisible" to the camera. Shermika reported plenty of harassment about her dark skin, from girlfriends and boyfriends, even those as dark as herself. "Choc-late!" was the common, hated term, and Shermika was troubled by its implied racial hierarchy and self-hatred. Atypically, she had no easy "come-back" for that one.

Race in Sophie's (WASP) experience is about being privileged, and feeling harassed for her blonde and blue-eyed good looks. Janet, for instance, annoys Sophie by calling her the "Aryan Goddess." Sophie is harassed on public transportation on her daily commute, where she is in the minority as a white woman. (Janet, in contrast, drives from suburb to school.) Sophie became exasperated in our interview when she felt targeted for white racism, and said she didn't "notice" race half as often as race identified her in public situations in which she is made to represent WASPhood or white womanhood.

Just as these women co-created for us a shared, if negotiated, sense of body politics, they separated along culture lines in their expressed reliance on social connections and surveillance of bodily borders. The African-American women, for instance, detailed deeply textured and relational lives. They not only care for many, but many also care for them. They give much to others, and receive much in return, but don't call it volunteer or charity work—simply "what I do." When they receive favors (from mothers and boyfriends), they feel neither "guilty" nor "obligated." Held in a complex web of reciprocal relations, they contribute, easily assured that "what goes around comes around." They resonate to ideas found in the writing of Robinson and Ward:

> Nobles' conception of "the extended self" is seen in the value structure of many black families. Willie argues that many African-American children are encouraged to employ their own personal achievements as a means to resist racism.[21] The importance of hard work and communalism is viewed threefold: as a personal responsibility, as an intergenerational commitment to family, and as a tie to the larger collective. A resistant strategy of liberation, in keeping with African-American traditional values, ties individual achievement to collective struggle. We maintain that in the service of personal and cultural liberation, African-American adolescent girls must resist an individualism that sees the self as disconnected from others in the black community and, as it is culturally and psychologically dysfunctional, she must resist those who might advocate her isolation and separation from traditional African-American cultural practices, values, and beliefs.[22]

The elite women, in contrast, deployed a language of bodily integrity, patroled borders, social charity, obligation, and guilt. As for any favors of gifts or time from mothers and boyfriends, they felt a need to "pay back." Bearing often quite deeply hostile feelings toward their mothers, they nevertheless both feel obligated to repay her sacrifices by fulfilling her expectations, often a professional career in return for a gigantic tuition bill. As vigilantly, they monitor their social and bodily boundaries for what and how much comes in and leaves: food, drink, drugs, exercise, money, sacrifices, and gifts. And they give back to community in the form of "charity." They live their connections almost contractually.

Related to these contrasting forms of body-in-relation, these two groups performed quite differently within our *public talk*. That is, they parted sharply in terms of how they hibernated in privacy, and how they revealed themselves through public talk. In numerous instances the white and Korean teens deferred to a "cultured privacy" in which "personal problems" were rarely aired, "personal grievances" were typically suffocated, "personal disagreements" were usually revealed "behind our backs." They often withheld juicy details of life, safe only in diaries or other private writings. Their bodies absorbed, carried, and embodied their "private troubles." These elite girls made it quite clear that their strategies for survival were interior, personal, and usually not shared. The costs of "privilege," as they revealed them, were in the internalizing, personalizing, and depoliticizing of gender dilemmas. Research makes evident these costs in anorexia, bulimia, depression, "talking behind each other's back," and even the "secrets" of rape or abuse survival stories. Socialized out of using public talk to practice varied forms of womanhood, while these women recognized collective gender power struggles, they retreated from women, and they embodied their resistance alone, through feminist individualism.

The individualism from which modern feminism was born has much to answer for but much in which to take pride. Individualism has decisively repudiated previous notions of hierarchy and particularism to declare the possibility of freedom for all. In so doing, it transformed slavery from one unfree condition among many into freedom's antithesis—thereby insisting that the subordination of one person to any other is morally and politically unacceptable. But the gradual extension of individualism and the gradual abolition of the remaining forms of social and political bondage have come trailing after two dangerous notions: that individual freedom could—indeed must—be absolute, and that social role and personal identity must be coterminous.

Following the principles of individualism, modern western societies have determined that the persistence of slavery in any form violates the fundamental principle of a just society. But in grounding the justification in absolute individual right, they have unleashed the specter of a radical individualism that overrides the claims of society itself. To the extent that feminism, like antislavery, has espoused those individualistic principles, it has condemned itself to the dead ends toward which individualism is now plunging.[23]

In contrast, the African-American women were publicly playful as well as nasty to each other, and about others, "because we love each other." Shermika told wonderful, vivid, outrageous tales, in part to "test" what the others would do, including, we believe, testing whether she was being classified as exotic, sexualized, or "other" as a specimen for the white women and the evening's analysis. Their school context made their bodies a matter of public talk. Exposed.

Shermika: I don't like my rear end. Guys are so ignorant. "Look at all that cake."

Pat: Maybe it's their problem.
Shermika: No, it *is* my problem. Because you see my butt before you see me.

Public talk could be aggression as well:
Damalleaux: I wouldn't talk to him [a stranger] and he got mad.
Shermika: I hate when they constantly talk to you and they get closer and closer.

The African-American women used and experienced conversation, public disagreements, pleasures, and verbal badgerings as ways to "try on" varied ways to be women.

During the second evening the four young women discovered and explored these differences through the metaphor of the "private" and "public" schools they attend.

Janet: I've got a question. At [your school, Shermika] are there kids who are like by themselves? Loners . . . who don't sit with anyone else, who nobody wants to sit with?
Shermika: Yeah but they can't because there's somebody always messin' with 'em, tryin' to get 'em to do something. So if they wanted to be by themselves they couldn't.
Janet: At our school it's so easy to get shut out when you're by yourself.
Sophie: You just kind of—disappear.
Janet: They don't say it [criticism or insult] in front of your face.
Sophie: You insult someone by not considering them . . . You don't consider their existence.
Shermika: Sometimes people need you to tell them how you feel.
Janet: For the most part when I'm mad at someone I don't say it to them.

Sophie: Only one on one. You don't say it to them in front of others unless you're joking. It's more private.

Shermika: But if you say it *to* the person, you avoid fights. If they hear you saying it behind they back, they wanna fight.

The four pursued this discovered difference between the "private" and the "public" school.

Shermika: Ain't nothin' private at my school. If someone got gonorrhea, everyone knows it.

Sophie: *Everything's* private at my school.

Janet: Cause nobody really cares about each other at our school.

Shermika: In our school, when I found out I had cancer, I heard about it on the loudspeaker. And everybody come and offer me help. When you're havin' problems in our school, people talk. That's why they're more mature at my school—excuse me. Say somebody poor, need name brand sneaks, they'll put they money together and give 'em some sneaks. And teachers do that too, if someone need food.

Sophie: We like to pretend that we're good to the neighborhood and socially conscious.

Over time, we came to see that "the facts" of these young women's lives were neither what we had invited them to reveal in our conversations, nor what they were giving us. Rather, we were gathering their interpretations of their lives, interpretations which were roaming within culture and class.

On Good and Bad Girls: Prospects for Feminism

"I consider myself a bad girl," Shermika explained, "but in a good sorta way."

Feminist scholars as distinct as Valerie Walkerdine, Carol Gilligan, and Nancy Lesko have written about polarizations of good girls and bad ones, that is, those who resist, submit, or split on the cultural script of femininity. Gilligan's recent essay, "Joining the Resistance," argues that at the outset of adolescence, young women experience a severing of insider from outsider knowledge, such that "insider knowledge may be washed away."[24] Gilligan and her colleagues have found that young women at early adolescence begin to submerge their interior knowledge, increasingly relying on "I don't know" to answer questions about self. They say "I don't know" at a rate amazingly greater the older they get—an average of twice at age seven, 21 times at age 12, 67 times at age 13. Gilligan and colleagues conclude, "If girls' knowledge of reality is politically dangerous, it is both psychologically and politically dangerous for girls not to know . . . or to render themselves innocent by disconnecting from their bodies, their representations of experience and desire."[25]

Nancy Lesko has written a compelling ethnography of gendered adolescents' lives inside a Catholic high school, where she unpacks a "curriculum of the body," mediated by class distinctions.[26] In this school, female delinquency was sexualized and "embodied." The genders segregated in high school by class, and created categories of behaviors to hang on to within these class groups. The rich and popular girls at her school paraded popular fashions, spoke in controlled voices, muted their opinions, and worked hard at "being nice." If they pushed the boundaries of wardrobe, it was always in the di-

rection of fashion, not "promiscuity." The "burnouts," in contrast, were young women who fashioned their behaviors through smoking and directness. They rejected compulsions toward being "nice" and excelled at being "blunt." Refusing to bifurcate their "personal" opinions and their public stances, they challenged docility and earned reputations as "loose" and "hard" (like Leslie Roman's working-class women who displayed physicality and sexual embodiment[27]). Social class, then, provided the contours within which a curriculum of the body had its meaning displayed, intensifying within gender oppositions, and undermining possibilities for female solidarity.

Departing somewhat from Gilligan and Lesko, Valerie Walkerdine sees adolescence for young women as a moment not to *bury* the questioning female "self," but a time in which young women must *negotiate* their multiple selves, through struggles of heterosexuality, and critiques of gender, race, and class arrangements. In an analysis of popular texts read by adolescent women, Walkerdine finds that, "heroines are never angry; most project anger onto others and suppress it in self, yielding the active production of passivity."[28] She asks readers to consider that "good girls are not always good, [but] when and how is their badness lived?" Interested in the splitting of goodness and badness we, like Walkerdine, asked these young women that question. When Shermika said, "I consider myself a bad girl, but in a good sorta way," she was positioning herself in our collectively made feminist context where *good girls* follow femininity rules, and *bad girls* don't. This good kind of bad girl plays by male rules of friendship, risk, danger, and initiative.

Within five minutes of our first meeting, the four girls discovered they all liked football, *playing* football, and they eagerly described the joys of running, catching the ball, tackling, and being tackled. Only Janet drew the line at being tackled, citing a "300-pound-boy" in her neighborhood. As an explanation for their preferred identities as "one of the guys," football exemplifies "masculine" values of gamesmanship. It is a game with rules and space for spontaneous physicality, with teamwork and individual aggression in rule-bound balance, and with maximum bodily access to others of both sexes, without fear about sexual reputation or reproductive consequences. When asked why they trust and like boys over girls, they cited boys' risk-taking making them more fun, their ability to "be more honest" and not backstab, "be more accepting." "You can tell when a guy's lyin'." "First of all they won't even notice what you're wearing and they won't bust on you." Shermika bragged that all of her boyfriends said they valued her most as a friend, not merely a girlfriend. The behavior, clothing, and values associated with such identification with boys and sports suggests both a flight from the "femininity" they collectively described as "wearing pink," "being prissy," "bein' Barbie," and "reinforcing guys all the time"—*and* an association of masculinity with fairness (vs. cattiness), honesty (vs. backstabbing), strength (vs. prissiness, a vulnerability whether feigned or real), initiative (vs. deference or reactionary comments), and integrity (vs. the self-doubt and conflicting loyalties dividing girls). The four girls' risk-taking behaviors—

driving fast, sneaking out at night—reinforced identities as "one of the guys." Such are the Bad Girls.

But being "one of the guys" makes for a contradictory position of self versus "other girls." Sophie mocked the femininity of good girls, at its worst when she said dismissively, "You should sit and wait in your little crystal palace" rather than "chase after guys." This constructed difference between self (the good kind of bad girl) and other girls (the bad kind of good girl) is an essential contradiction of identity that all four girls were struggling with. Valerie Hey, in her study of adolescent female friendships, calls this "deficit dumping": "all the 'bad' bits of femininity, social and sexual competitiveness, placed upon the 'other'," that is, other girls.[29] Sophie, like the girls in Hey's study, excepted her best friend along with herself from the generality of femininity: "It's different though with best friends. I mean like girls in general." Shermika likewise excepted Damalleaux when Michelle asked whether *no* other girls were to be trusted. "She a boy," Shermika countered, raising a puzzled laugh. But when Shermika's boyfriend likened her to a body builder when she was running track, she felt ashamed to "feel like a boy . . . like a muscle man."

Sophie confessed ruefully, "I'm certainly no bad girl," and Janet taunted her, "Sophie has a little halo." Certainly Sophie's good grades, good works, politeness, friendliness, and trustworthiness were acceptably "good" to both adults and peers, even if the popular crowd had not approved or welcomed her. "I don't want that image," Sophie told Janet about the halo. Goody-goodyism would be unacceptable to *all*

peers. Good-*girl*ism—Sophie's uncomfortable state—seems "good" for her conscience and adult approval, but "bad" for approval by the popular set, whose upper-class drink-and-drug-induced party flirtations and sexual liaisons Sophie disapproves of. The meaning of Sophie's good-girl image is, however, quite class-specific, as Mary Evans describes in her analysis of middle-class schooling:

> As far as possible a "good" girl did not have an appearance. What she had was a correct uniform, which gave the world the correct message about her, that is, that she was a well-behaved, sensible person who could be trusted not to wish to attract attention to herself by an unusual, let alone a fashionable, appearance.[30]

Signaling her acceptance of the career-class uniform, Sophie could not also signal her interest in boys. Indeed, she walked away from her body, except as an athletic court. "Other girls" dressed either "schleppy" (the androgynous or indifferent look) or "provocative." Sophie's neat, "sporty" look (tights and a lean body made her miniskirt look more athletic than hooker-inspired) seems designed to be comfortable and competent as one of the guys while ever so casually gesturing toward femininity (no dykey trousers). Her dress is designed to bridge the contradiction of middle-class education and femininity, as Evans describes it in her own schooling in the 1950s:

> To be a successful [prep] school girl involved, therefore, absorbing two specific (but conflicting) identities. First, that of the androgynous middle-class person who is academically successful in an academic world that is apparently gender blind. Second, that of the well-behaved middle-

class woman who knows how to defer to and respect the authority of men.[31]

Feminists have altered, over history, their terms of deference to men, their ability to name sexism and resist. But our four young women do not seem to have revised the categories of "gender" or "body" at all. What seems intact from the 1950s is their terms of respect for the authority of men as superior and normal forms of human beings. What seems distinct in the 1990s is that these young women think they have a right to be like young men too.

Damalleaux's example of her own goodgirlism shares some of Sophie's dilemma of being a good student at the expense of peer popularity. But Damalleaux resolved this tension differently, as Signithia Fordham would argue is likely to happen among academically talented low-income African-American students.[32]

Damalleaux: I used to be a straight-A girl and now I'm down to B's and C's. I used to be so good it's a shame . . .

Pat: What changed?

Damalleaux: I couldn't help it any more. When I got straight A's they'd call me a nerd and things. But I'd be happy because my mother would give me anything I want for it. Mom [would say to teasing brothers] "Leave my first girl alone!" [Then] I got around the wrong people, I don't study so much.

Pat: Is it uncool to be a girl and get good grades?

Damalleaux: Yes, it is. I'll do my work and they'll say "Smarty Pants! Smarty Pants!"

Janet gave an example of "acting stupid" with peers, which seemed to be her manner of flirtation. Sophie pointed out that Janet could afford to because everyone already knew she was smart. Sophie clearly felt more trapped by being a smart and a good girl.

Girls can be good, bad, or (best of all) they can be like boys. This version of individualized resistance, or feminism, reflects a retreat from the collective politics of gender, and from other women, and an advance into the embattled scene of gender politics— alone, and against boys, in order to become one of them.

The End of the Second Pizza

We heard these four women struggling between the discourses of feminism and adolescence. Perhaps struggling is even too strong a word. They hungered for a strong version of individualistic, "gender-free" adolescence and had rejected that which had been deemed traditionally feminine, aping instead that which had been deemed traditionally masculine. Delighted to swear, spit, tell off-color jokes, wear hats and trash other girls, they were critical of individual boys, nasty about most girls, rarely challenging of the sex/gender system, and were ecstatic, for the most part, to be engaged as friends and lovers with young men. But we also heard their feminism in their collective refusal to comply with male demands, their wish for women friends to trust, their expectations for equality and search for respect, their deep ambivalence about being "independent of a man" and yet in partnership with one, and their strong yearnings to read, write, and talk more about women's experiences among women. They appreciated our creation of a context in which this was possible. "The women of Michelle's place," Shermika called us at the end of one evening, prizing our collectivity by adapting the title of a black woman's novel.

Barbara Hudson describes part of the task of feminist work with girls as follows:

> The public terms of the discourse of femininity preclude the expression of deviant views of marriage, motherhood, and the public terms are the only ones to which girls have access. Part of the task of feminist work with girls is thus, I would suggest, giving girls terms in which to express their experiential knowledge, rather than having to fall back into the stereotyped expressions of normatively defined femininity in order to say anything at all about areas of life which vitally concern them.[33]

Through *critical and collaborative group interview* we evolved a form of conversation (what Hudson might call feminist work) with these four young women which allowed us to engage in what we might consider *collective consciousness work* as a form of feminist methodology. Our "talks" became an opportunity to "try on" ways of being women, struggling through power, gender, culture, and class.

With Donna Haraway's notion of "partial vision" firmly in mind,[34] we realized that in our talk, no one of us told the "whole truth." We all occluded the "truth" in cultured ways. The conversation was playful and filled with the mobile positionings of all of us women. While we each imported gender, race, class, culture, age, and bodies to our talk, we collectively created an ideological dressing room in which the six of us could undress a little, try things on, exchange, rehearse, trade, and critique. Among the six of us we were able to lift up what had become "personal stories," raise questions, try on other viewpoints, and re-see our stories as political narratives.

> As a critique of the excesses of individualism, feminism potentially contributes to a new conception of community—of the relation between the freedom of individuals and the needs of society. The realization of that potential lies not in the repudiation of difference but in a new understanding of its equitable social consequences.[35]

We could recount together how alone and frightened we have each felt as we have walked down city streets and are watched; how our skin tightens when we hear men comment aloud on our bodies; how we smart inside with pain when we learn that other women define themselves as "good women" by contrasting themselves with our feminist politics; how we make fetishes of those body parts that have betrayed us with their imperfection. Within the safety of warm listening and caring, yet critical talk, we attached each of these "secret" feelings to political spaces defined by culture, class, and gender contours of our daily lives. This method moved us, critically and collectively, from pain to passion to politics, prying open the ideologies of individualism, privacy, and loyalty which had sequestered our "personal stories."

After our second dinner, stuffed and giggly, tired but still wanting just one more round of conversation, we (Pat and Michelle) realized that the four young women were getting ready to drive away. Together and without us. Before, Pat had driven Shermika and Damalleaux to and from Michelle's home. But now

they were leaving us behind. Stunned, we looked at each other, feeling abandoned. We thought we were concerned about their safety. Four young women in a car could meet dangers just outside the borders of Michelle's block.

We turned to each other realizing that even our abandonment was metaphoric, and political. These four young women were weaving the next generation of feminist politics, which meant, in part, leaving us. We comforted ourselves by recognizing that our conversations had perhaps enabled this work. No doubt, individual interviews with each of the four would have produced an essay chronicling the damages of femininity: eating disorders, heterosexual traumas, perhaps some abuse or abortion stories—deeply individualized, depoliticized, and atomized tales of "things that have happened to me as an adolescent female." What happened among us instead was that a set of connections was forged between personal experiences and political structures, across cultures, classes, and politics, and within an invented space, cramped between the discourses of a rejected *femininity*, an individualized *adolescence* and a collective *feminism as resistance*.

> Resistance is that struggle we can most easily grasp. Even the most subjected person has moments of rage and resentments so intense that they respond, they act against. There is an inner uprising that leads to rebellion, however short-lived. It may be only momentary, but it takes place. That space within oneself where resistance is possible remains: it is different then to talk about becoming subjects. That process emerges as one comes to understand how

structures of domination work in one's own life, as one develops critical thinking and critical consciousness, as one invents new alternative habits of being and resists from that marginal space of difference inwardly defined.[36]

In our finest post-pizza moment, we (Pat and Michelle) realized that as these women drove off, they were inventing their own feminist legacy, filled with passions, questions, differences, and pains. We were delighted that we had helped to challenge four young women's versions of individualistic feminism, without solidarity, by doing the consciousness work of our generation. We taught, and relearned, feminism as a dialectical and historical discourse about experience and its interpretation, a collective reframing of private confessions. As we yelled, "Go straight home!" to their moving car, for a moment we felt as if the world was in very good hands.

Notes

1. Michael Payne, "Canon: The New Testament to Derrida," *College Literature* 18, no. 2 (1991): 18.
2. Barbara Hudson, "Femininity and Adolescence," in *Gender and Generation*, edited by Angela McRobbie and Mica Nava (London: Macmillan Publishers, 1984), p. 35.
3. Michelle Fine and Adrienne Asch, eds., *Women with Disabilities: Essays in Psychology, Culture, and Politics* (Philadelphia: Temple University Press, 1988); Gelya Frank, "On Embodiment: A Case Study of Congenital Limb Deficiency in American Culture," in *Women with Disabilities*, edited by Michelle Fine and Adrienne Asch, pp. 41-71; Kathryn Corbett, with Susan Klein and Jennifer L. Bregante, "The Role of Sexuality and Sex Equity in the Education of Disabled Women," *Peabody Journal of Education* 64, no. 4 (1987): 198-212.

4. Linda Brodkey and Michelle Fine, "Presence of Mind in the Absence of Body," *Journal of Education* 170, no. 3 (1988): 84-99.

5. Susie Orbach, *Hunger Strike: The Anorectic's Struggle as a Metaphor for Our Age* (New York: W. W. Norton, 1986).

6. Susan Bordo, "Reading the Slender Body," in *Body/Politics: Women and the Discourses of Science*, edited by Mary Jacobus, Evelyn Fox, and Sally Shuttleworth (New York: Routledge, 1990), pp. 31-53.

7. See Elijah Anderson, *Streetwise: Race, Class, and Change in an Urban Community* (Chicago: University of Chicago Press, 1990).

8. Elizabeth Spelman, *The Inessential Women* (Boston: Beacon Press, 1988), p. 13.

9. Michelle Fine, *Framing Dropouts: Notes on the Politics of an Urban High School* (Albany, NY: State University of New York Press, 1991); J. Halson, "Young Women, Sexual Harassment, and Heterosexuality: Violence, Power Relations, and Mixed Sex Schooling," in *Gender, Power, and Sexuality*, edited by Pamela Abbott and Claire Wallace (London: Macmillan Publishers, 1990).

10. Houston Baker, personal communication, 1989.

11. bell hooks, *Feminist Theory from Margin to Center* (Boston: South End Press, 1984); Paula Giddings, *When and Where I Enter: The Impact of Black Women on Race and Sex in America* (New York: Bantam, 1984).

12. And, although not at the table, it is still another thing to construct a sense of womanhood by and for women whose disabilities socially and sexually "neuter" them, propelling them out of any presumed relation with men, and depriving them of the many burdens of being female, including the privileges that come with those burdens, in experiences such as sexual harassment, motherhood, sexuality, having others rely on you, etc. Disabled women's identities are rarely positioned under, against, or with men's. As Kathryn Corbett, Adrienne Asch and Michelle Fine, Harilyn Rousso, and others have written (see Adrienne Asch and Michelle Fine, "Shared Dreams: A Left Perspective on Disability Rights and Reproductive Rights," in *Women with Disabilities: Essays in Psychology, Culture, and Politics*, edited by Michelle Fine and Adrienne Asch [Philadelphia: Temple University Press, 1988], pp. 297-305, it is no blessing for the culture to presume that because you are disabled, you are not female; not worth whistling at; not able to love an adult man or woman; not capable of raising a child; not beautiful enough to be employed in a public space.

13. bell hooks, *Yearning: Race, Gender, and Cultural Politics* (Boston: South End Press, 1990), p. 42.

14. Gloria Joseph and Jill Lewis, *Common Differences: Conflicts in Black and White Feminist Perspectives* (Boston: South End Press, 1981). p. 94.

15. Ibid., p. 79.

16. Rachel T. Hare-Mustin, "Sex, Lies, and Headaches: The Problem Is Power," in *Women and Power: Perspectives for Therapy*, edited by T. J. Goodrich (New York: Norton, 1991), p. 3.

17. Joseph and Lewis, *Common Differences*, p. 125.

18. Bordo, "Reading the Slender Body."

19. Celia Kitzinger, "'It's Not Fair on Girls': Young Women's Accounts of Unfairness in School" (Paper presented at the British Psychological Society Annual Conference, University of Leeds, April, 1988).

20. Liz Kelly, *Surviving Sexual Violence* (London: Basil Blackwell, 1988), p. 41.

21. Charles Vert Willie, *Black and White Families: A Study in Complementarity* (Bayside, NY: General Hall, 1985).

22. T. Robinson and J. Ward, "A Belief in Self Far Greater than Anyone's Disbelief," in *Women, Girls, and Psychotherapy*, edited by Carol Gilligan, A. Rogers, and D. Tolman (New York: Harrington Park Press, 1991), p. 9.

23. Elizabeth Fox-Genovese, *Feminism without Illusions* (Chapel Hill: University of North Carolina Press, 1991), pp. 240-241.

24. Carol Gilligan, "Joining the Resistance: Psychology, Politics, Girls, and Women" (Essay presented as the Tanner Lecture on Human Values at the University of Michigan, Ann Arbor, MI, March 1990).

25. Carol Gilligan, Janie Victoria Ward, and Jill McClean Taylor, *Mapping the Moral Domain* (Cambridge, MA: Harvard University Press, 1988), p. 33.

26. Nancy Lesko, "The Curriculum of the Body: Lessons from a Catholic High School," in *Becoming Feminine: The Politics of Popular Culture*, edited by Leslie G. Roman, Linda K. Christian-Smith, and Elizabeth Ellsworth (Philadelphia: Falmer Press, 1988), pp. 123-142.

27. Leslie G. Roman, "Intimacy, Labor, and Class: Ideologies of Feminine Sexuality in the Punk Slam Dance," in *Becoming Feminine: The Politics of Popular Culture*, edited by Leslie G. Roman, Linda K. Christian-Smith, and Elizabeth Ellsworth (Philadelphia: Falmer Press, 1988), pp. 143-184.

28. Valerie Walkerdine, "Some Day My Prince Will Come: Young Girls and the Preparation for Adolescent Sexuality," in *Gender and Generation*, edited by Angela McRobbie and Mica Nava (London: Macmillan Publishers, 1984), p. 182.

29. Valerie Hey, "'The Company She Keeps': The Social and Interpersonal Construction of Girls' Same Sex Friendships" (Doctoral thesis, University of Kent at Canterbury, England, 1987), p. 421.

30. Mary Evans, *A Good School: Life at a Girls' Grammar School in the 1950s* (London: Women's Press, 1991), pp. 30-31.

31. Ibid., p. 23.

32. Signithia Fordham, "Racelessness as a Factor in Black Students' School Success," *Harvard Educational Review* 58, no. 1 (1988): 54-84.

33. Hudson, "Femininity and Adolescence," p. 52.

34. Donna Haraway, *Primate Visions: Gender, Race, and Nature in the World of Modern Science* (New York: Routledge, 1989).

35. Fox-Genovese, *Feminism without Illusions*, p. 256.

36. hooks, *Yearning: Race, Gender, and Cultural Politics*, p. 15.

 Article Review Form at end of book.

Why do the women who claim to be feminists but, according to Faludi, really aren't, get so much media attention?

"I'm Not a Feminist But I Play One on TV"

Susan Faludi exposes the newest crop of media darlings.

Susan Faludi

Susan Faludi is the author of "Backlash: The Undeclared War Against American Women" (Crown). She is working on a book on masculinity.

According to the latest lifestyle headlines and talk-show sound bites, from *USA Today* to *Good Morning America,* we are witnessing the birth of a new wave of feminism. It's "like a second revolution in the women's movement," the Washington *Times* enthused, referring us to one of the nouveau revolution's adherents, who "compares her position with the 1970s feminists who burned their bras." The neo-rebel tells the *Times,* "I feel the same as I did when I was 19 years old during the women's liberation movement"; she confides she even had a 1970s-style "'click' moment" of feminist revelation.

The evidence for what the Washington *Times* calls "a nationwide trend"? New "feminist" organizations called the Women's Freedom Network, the Independent Women's Forum (IWF), and the Network for Empowering Women (or NEW, which, to hear its organizers tell it, will soon be displacing NOW). New inspirational "feminist" tracts like *Who Stole Feminism?* and *Feminism Without Illusions.* New "feminist" voices from a younger generation, like Katie Roiphe, author of *The Morning After: Sex, Fear, and Feminism,* and Rene Denfeld, author of *The New Victorians: A Young Woman's Challenge to the Old Feminist Order.* And members of a new "feminist" intelligentsia like philosophy professor Christina Hoff Sommers, hailed in the Boston *Globe*'s headlines as A REBEL IN THE SISTERHOOD who WANTS TO RESCUE FEMINISM FROM ITS "HIJACKERS."

That feminist leaders don't seem to be embracing these new reinforcements does give the trend's reporters pause—but only momentarily. Feminist standoffishness must just be jealousy—or, as the Chicago *Tribune* put it, "sibling rivalry."

But big-sister envy is not the problem here.

Perhaps the nature of the "click" experienced by the Washington *Times*'s "feminist" heroine should have been a clue: she says she sprang into action after she became outraged . . . by a feminist colleague's joke about Dan Quayle. Or perhaps the fact that the Washington *Times* was tickled pink over this new feminist birth in the first place should have been the tip-off; this conservative and Moonie-funded paper is not known for its enthusiasm over the women's movement. Cheap broadsides against Anita Hill are more in its line of work.

What is being celebrated is no natural birth of a movement—and the press that originated the celebration is no benign midwife. It would be more accurate to describe this drama as a media-assisted invasion of the body of the women's movement: the Invasion of the Feminist Snatchers, intent on repopulating the ranks with Pod Feminists. In this artificially engineered reproduction effort, the press has figured twice: the right-wing media have played the part of mad-scientist obstetrician-cum-spin doctor, bankrolling, publishing, and grooming their pod women for delivery to a wider world of media consumption. And the mainstream media have played the role of trend-hungry pack-journalism suckers; in their eagerness to jump on the latest bandwagon, they have gladly accepted the faux feminists' credentials without inspection.

If journalists were to investigate, they would find the "new" feminist movement to possess few adherents but much armament in the way of smoke and mirrors. The memberships of such groups as NEW are each in the low to mid three-digits, compared with NOW's 250,000. And they wouldn't find these women out on the hustings, in the streets, guarding a family planning clinic from antiabortionist attacks, or lending a hand at a battered women's shelter. Instead, if the media were to take a closer look, they would find a handful of "feminist" writers and public speakers who do no writing, speaking, organizing, or activism on behalf of women's equality at all. A review of their published writings unearths not one example of a profeminist article or book.

They define themselves as "dissenters" within the feminist ranks, but they never joined feminism in the first place; they have met each other mingling at conservative academic gatherings (like the "anti-P.C." National Association of Scholars) and conservative Washington networking circuits, not the feminist trenches of pro-choice demonstrations and clerical unionizing meetings. They define themselves as politically diverse, but the leadership of the Women's Freedom Network, the IWF, and NEW is overwhelmingly rightward leaning. And when one looks back at where these women were launched as writers, it is, over and over, conservative antifeminist journals like *National Review* and *Commentary,* or the, of late, feminist-bashing pages of *The New Republic.* They define themselves as representing "the average woman," but they are privileged women who rarely stray from their ivory-tower or inside-the-Beltway circles; they are in touch with "the average woman" only to the extent that such a phrase is a code word to signal that they themselves are white and middle- or upper-class. And their opposition to government assistance for women who need help with child care, education, basic shelter, and nutrition betrays a lack of concern, and a buried well of racially charged and class-biased ill will toward women who don't fit the narrow confines of their "average woman." They define themselves as feminists, but their dismissive-to-outright-hostile attitudes toward feminist issues—from sexual harassment to domestic violence to rape to pay equity to child care to welfare rights—locate them firmly on the antifeminist side of the ledger.

Yet their rallying cry—or more precisely, their resting cry, their call to disarm—appeals to some women for its comforting message of female victory and

From sexual harassment to eating disorders to rape to adolescent girls' low self-esteem—the pods say it's all hot air and hype.

success. Christina Hoff Sommers, author of *Who Stole Feminism?,* and her pod sisters—columnist Cathy Young; history professor and *Feminism Without Illusions* author Elizabeth Fox-Genovese; former *New Republic* writer Karen Lehrman; and writer Katie Roiphe, who, as a graduate student at Princeton, brought us *The Morning After,* to name the prime anointed media stars—maintain that sufficient progress has been made and that now should be a time of back-patting and "reconciliation" with men. Their conferences aren't planning sessions to advance women's rights; they are well-heeled business-card-swapping events where conservative luminaries speak from the podium about how feminism has gone too far—and how women should quit pressing for their rights and start defending men's. Women shouldn't try to spark social change; rather, as the Women's Freedom Network's mission statement asserts, "male and female roles should be allowed to evolve naturally"—that is, without a political shove in a feminist direction. Of course, as the most casual student of women's history could tell you, allowing gender roles to evolve "naturally," without the aid of political agitation, means allowing gender roles to evolve not at all.

Theirs is a beguiling line of argument because it is (a) positive, in a rah-rah "Year of the Woman" way, and (b) nonthreatening. NEW, et al., aren't encouraging women to pursue social change, and they certainly aren't asking men to change. It is no-risk feminism for a fearful age: just post your achievements, make nice with men, and call it a day. The Power of Positive Thinking will take care of the rest.

Ever since the media discovered feminism in the mid-nineteenth century, they have been more inclined to denounce it than study it. In the last round of feminism's revival, in the late sixties and early seventies, the "grand press blitz" lasted all of three months. By 1971, the press was calling the women's movement a "fad," a "bore," and "dead"—and taking a rather active role in hastening the movement's last rites. At *Newsday*, a male editor dispatched a writer on the story with the directive, "Get out there and find an authority who will say this is all a crock of shit."

In these times of sophisticated sophistry, the presentation of it's-a-crock-of-shit authorities has reached a high art of subtlety and obfuscation. One might say that the strategies used by 1980s political campaign handlers have now found reemployment in that long-running campaign—the one against feminism. Just as the Republicans hoped to hollow out the liberal Democratic message of compassion and human rights and replace it with Bush's "kinder, gentler" pod world, so do opponents of the women's movement seek to empty out the feminist message of sisterhood and women's rights and replace it with the pseudofeminists' co-opted language of "empowerment" and "reconciliation."

The podding-of-feminism phenomenon is most publicly demonstrated on the talk-show sets and lifestyle pages. In the past, when the media broached the topic of feminism, they often rigged the outcome by throwing their support to the antifeminist camp, but at least they clearly labeled the two sides. But over the past decade, the rigging has been obscured by a blurring of the lines.

First, around about the mid-eighties, the media began replacing the curmudgeonly feminist baiters like Norman Mailer and George Gilder (who actually seem rather endearing now, with their frank grumpings about independent women) with either a younger male model of the slickly earnest, collegiate variety—typically a Dinesh D'Souza-type editor of the *Dartmouth Review* or some other "anti-P.C." college paper kept afloat by right-wing foundation largesse—or with an older female model of the pursed-lipped Phyllis Schlafly variety, who claimed to be the real spokeswoman for the "average" middle-American female. By the late eighties, both of these representatives of the far right were displaced on our talk-show sets by the young college woman eager to say, "I'm not a feminist, but . . ."—as in "I'm not a feminist, but . . . I sure expect to get equal pay, equal opportunity, and reproductive rights." She seemed an ideal decrier of the women's movement because she had no political allegiances; she was just a neutral party, representing Every-woman—or rather, Every White Middle-Class College-Educated Woman. But having her eschew the women's rights struggle still wasn't as delicious as the ultimate in feminist denouncers: a woman who would actually call herself a feminist. Now, there would be a coup.

Come the nineties, a handful of women came forward to volunteer for such a part—and soon found themselves inundated with media casting calls. These women take the opposite tack of the young women who preceded them. Their slogan is "I am a feminist, but . . ."—as in "I am a feminist, but . . . I don't believe women face discrimination anymore; I don't see any reason for women to organize politically; I don't think the pay gap, sexual harassment, rape, domestic violence, or just about any other issue feminism has raised are real problems; I don't see why we even need to bother with gender analysis anymore; and, on the whole, I find feminists to be little more than victim-mongering conspiracy nuts." These are "feminists" who weigh in to the debate only to speak out against feminism's "excesses." None has yet to appear on a talk show to take any profeminist position—although they have devoted considerable energy to promoting their "pro-men" platform. NEW, for instance, holds that women's most "urgent" need now isn't economic or political progress but making amends with those poor feminist-bashed men. (It's even the slogan printed on NEW's business cards.) IWF is producing a video and a helpful media guide listing several hundred women who are ready and willing to hit the talk shows to dispute the "old" feminists. Their brand of feminism doesn't appear to run deeper than a surface gimmick to get airtime. Maybe their slogan should be "I'm not a feminist, but I play one on TV."

The precursor to the pods, the mother of all "I'm a feminist, but . . ." declaimers, is that made-for-TV antifeminist feminist Camille Paglia, whose latest "book," *Vamps and Tramps*, is an exhaustive, and exhausting, gaze into the mirror of her many media moments. She differs from the antifeminist feminists who came in her wake in that she is more of an attention-seeking generator of outrageous one-liners than a conservative in feminist costume. She dons

None has yet to appear on a talk show to take any profeminist position—yet they've devoted considerable energy to promoting their "pro-men" platform.

and discards so many masks—from drag-queen celebrator to bondage 'n' leather poster girl—that it's hard to say whether under her many veils a person with a coherent set of political beliefs really exists at all.

Paglia's tactic of labeling herself a "feminist, but . . ." has been followed, without the wit, by a small cast of media stars who emerged in the early nineties. Most prominent is Sommers, who says she's a feminist, but . . . has mass-marketed her belief that feminists should just shut up now because women have pretty much attained equal opportunity and anyone who claims otherwise is a liar and a whiner. Joining her in deputy status is Roiphe, who calls herself a feminist, but . . . has peddled the idea that acquaintance rape is really a minor problem that feminists have exaggerated all out of proportion. Then there's Cathy Young, who says she's a feminist, but . . . has convicted feminist leaders on the false charge of having crowned Lorena Bobbitt as Feminist of the Year. And there's Elizabeth Fox-Genovese, who says she is a feminist, but . . . was most eager last year to testify in court (and later, at greater length, in the conservative *National Review*) against women's admission to the Citadel, the state-supported all-male military academy in South

Carolina. There's Karen Lehrman, a journalist and author of a forthcoming book on what she calls "postideological feminism" (whuh?), who says she's a feminist, but . . . has tarred all of feminist scholarship with her sneering accounts of a few instances of excessive touchy-feeliness and self-involvement in the women's studies classroom.

The cherry-picking of "feminist excesses" is a favored strategy—and an effective one, because there *are* some feminists (particularly on campus, where many of the pod feminists reside) who say "all men" are creeps, or who jump down your throat for less than perfectly P.C. terminology, or who get mortally offended over minor slights, or who want to "share" tedious personal revelations in the classroom. Surely one can always find psychobabble and navel-gazing in an undergraduate population . . . or even in gatherings like, ahem, the pod feminists' "International Gender Reconciliation Conference" last September, which offered such sessions as "Looking at Yourself," "Women's Wounds," "Emotional Support," and even a "Healing Break." Every movement with a membership larger than ten will have such folks, but the women's movement has consistently been tarred in the press for the overzealous or dippy remarks of a very few. The media have exploited these "excesses," distorting them into an emblematic portrait of the movement. And so, when the pod feminists come along and decry such behavior, it rings true for many readers and

viewers who get their portrait of the women's movement from the media—and hence have come to believe that feminism is, in fact, overpopulated by shrieking ninnies.

If the pod feminists have adopted the strategy of cooptation pioneered by conservative advisers to George Bush, they also have echoed another behavioral pattern of recent vintage among right-wing pols: projection of their sins onto their opponents. Just as family-man-from-hell Newt Gingrich charged Democrats with home wrecking, just as illegal-immigrant-employing senatorial candidate Michael Huffington accused Democrats of illegal-alien coddling, so have the pseudofeminists laid at feminism's doorstep an indictment that could more properly be served on them. The main charges on their citation sheet: (1) feminists stifle the views of dissenting women; (2) feminists are paranoid whiners who like to imagine all women as helpless victims; (3) feminists spread falsehoods and myths about women's condition.

Take point one: feminists stifle diversity of thought. The "statement of principles" issued by the Women's Freedom Network asserts its intent to combat this number one crime: "We do not expect uniformity of opinion among women. Our commitment to genuine diversity is reflected in our advisory board, where libertarians, liberals, communitarians, and conservatives are all active participants." But the "diverse" leadership of the network, like that of its sister organizations such as NEW, is solidly conservative, typified by such luminaries as Jeane Kirkpatrick of the American

Enterprise Institute; Ricky Silberman, Equal Employment Opportunity Commission vice chairwoman under Bush and a vocal booster of Supreme Court Justice Clarence Thomas; and Mona Charen, feminist-bashing columnist. As one member of the IWF told the press, "This group represents an opportunity for folks who don't fall into a particular camp to get involved in an intellectual way in policy issues." But this member most definitely did fall into a camp: he was Tom Boyd, an assistant attorney general in the Reagan and Bush administrations. And IWF forums are notably feminist-free: they showcase such conservative litmus-test passers as Diane Ravitch, Bush's former undersecretary of education, and Mary Ellen Bork, antifeminist activist and wife of you-know-who. This spectrum of views on the subject of feminism is about as diverse as eighties Republicanism was a "big tent" (to quote the late Lee Atwater) for opinions on abortion. What Lehrman wants to label "postideological feminism" is just right-wing thought undercover. It's enough to make you yearn for the unvarnished anti-feminist tirades of Jerry Falwell—at least he was honest.

While the pods don't seem to tolerate much dissent in their own ranks, they still succeed in exploiting the claim that feminists stifle contrary views. There are indeed feminist activists who think only their opinions are the right ones and get hot under the collar when questioned. This phenomenon is typically portrayed in the media as the hip-booted feministo crushing her sisters under her iron-tipped heel. What this portrayal misses is that for every feminist trying to dictate policy in one direction, there's another challenging her. Heated exchanges, not censorship, characterize feminists' approaches to difficult subjects like pornography, surrogate motherhood, or RU 486. These differences of opinion—and the willingness to argue passionately over them—are precisely what strengthen the vitality of the women's movement, or any movement. But these points are quickly lost in the pods' endless loop of logic, which goes something like this: the antifeminist feminists say feminists stifle disagreement. A feminist disagrees with this statement. She must be trying to stifle dissent. And so on.

O.K., take point two: feminists are paranoid whiners who like to imagine women as helpless victims. The pseudofeminists maintain that feminist books like Naomi Wolf's *The Beauty Myth* and, well, my own *Backlash*, bellyache about a fantastical conspiracy plot hatched behind the scenes by mustache-twirling misogynists who have succeeded in brainwashing a mass female population. But both of these works took pains to spell out how this cultural counterreaction to feminism is "not a conspiracy." Moreover, the pseudofeminist critics missed a recurring theme, underscored rather obviously, I thought, in the conclusion of *Backlash*: women have resisted efforts to discourage them from pursuing their rights and independence; far from embracing victimhood, they have fought challenges to their freedoms tooth and nail. I would go one step far-ther here and argue that women's unladylike, un-victim-minded response to a backlash is, in fact, the enduring legacy of feminism. If feminism stands for anything, it is the belief that women can and must stand up and speak out. Feminism identifies victimization not so we can wallow in it, but so we can wallop it. Indeed, once feminist voices were able to force their way through the 1980s' right-wing wall of sound and make themselves heard in the bookstores, the cinema, and, most important, on live television (Anita Hill before the Senate Judiciary Committee), masses of women responded not with sniffling victim whimpers but with roaring outrage that found its outlet in historic-sized pro-choice rallies and historic gender gaps at the voting booths.

On the other hand, let us look at the pod feminists' own paranoia about—and now *this* is fantastical—the machinations of a "feminist-dominated" establishment. (Would it were true!) Christina Hoff Sommers writes that "clever and powerful feminists," backed by "well-funded, prestigious organizations as well as individuals," are pulling the wool over women's eyes and tricking them into believing that such a thing as the patriarchy still exists. She presents herself as a brave lone crusader (well, not that lone: she did receive the generous monetary backing of the well-endowed, right-wing Olin and Bradley foundations) going up against the reigning feminist matriarchy, venturing into, as she puts it histrionically, "the very dens of the lionesses." These lionesses, to hear Sommers tell it, have U.S. women under their intimidating thrall. To hear the pseudofeminists tell it, feminists

It's enough to make you yearn for the unvarnished antifeminist tirades of Jerry Falwell—at least he was honest.

are the ultimate string-pullers and women their victimized puppets: women are so defenselessly stupid, these writers suggest, that they'll swallow any mind-clouding swill that feminism dishes out. Women easily fall prey to feminists' trickery, and once under their spell, Sommers writes, women are "primed to be alarmed, angry, and resentful of men" and even "ready to fabricate atrocities." Now who's talking victimology?

The pod feminists themselves are not above whining, not to mention complaining to the press that they are victims—of that big, bad feminist establishment, of course. Roiphe has reportedly griped to journalists that she is the victim of feminist threats; she's even "heard," she reports with high melodrama, that "they" wish a rape on her. When you cross the feminist cabal, she whimpered to the Cleveland *Plain Dealer*, "all the guns are taken out."

This brings us to point three: feminists spread falsehoods and myths about women's condition. The pod feminists argue that the feminist "establishment" exaggerates women's inferior social and economic status to generate attention and support for its cause. From sexual harassment to eating disorders to rape to adolescent girls' low self-esteem—you name it, the pods say, it's all hot air and hype. Furthermore, they say that feminists manage to pass off this malarkey as truth because the feminist-blinded media just buy what the women's movement has to sell without examining it.

But if the media have failed to challenge anyone, it's pseudofeminists like Roiphe and Sommers, whose books are packed with misleading and false information. When this is pointed

out to the members of the media, they tend to show a remarkable lack of interest. I learned this for myself when, several months back, I made the mistake of agreeing to go on *Good Morning America* with Roiphe, in hopes I'd get the chance to explain how her book misrepresented rape statistics. But the moment I began to discuss the flaws in her statistical model, the host, Charlie Gibson, cut me off, saying he wanted "to nip in the bud" any tiresome foray into facts and figures. I had a similar encounter with a *Newsweek* researcher reporting a story about Roiphe's "findings": a few sentences into the interview, she ended it, explaining forthrightly that she needed to quote feminists who agreed with Roiphe. (So far, she noted, she only had one: Camille Paglia, who, in spite of her utter lack of knowledge on rape research, was the first person the *Newsweek* researcher called.)

Actually, there are many in the media who do agree. While the Roiphes and the Sommerses claim to be going against the cultural grain, they are really auditioning for the most commonly available, easiest parts to get in the pop culture drama: the roles of the good girls whose opinions are dutifully in line with prevailing prejudice. The problem is not their contrariness—feminism is lucky to be full of contention, and there are feminists I admire whose opinions differ vehemently from my own. The problem is reductionist, erroneous, easy opinions parading as serious and daring ideas. A case in point is Roiphe's claim that date rape is rare and that feminist rape researchers ex-

aggerate the numbers. That is, simply, wrong. Her book cites one so-called expert, who has never actually done any research on rape and is notably biased; he has a record of crusading against feminist legislation. Roiphe ignores a dozen studies, conducted by feminist and nonfeminist social scientists alike, that find that between one in four and one in 12 women will experience an attempted rape or a rape in the course of their lifetimes. But Roiphe never reviews the statistics on rape, never interviews any rape researchers, never talks to a single woman who has been raped. The only "evidence" she marshals to disprove the statistic that one in four college women experience a rape or an attempted rape is her astonishing remark that, as far as she knows, none of her college girlfriends has ever been raped. Yet, none of this low-rent logic seems to faze the media—and why should it? They, after all, haven't bothered to do any serious reporting on the prevalence of rape either.

Sommers, likewise, claims to be a debunker. But if you look closely at her sources, you find she is not doing original research; she is drawing her "facts" from the claims of the same antifeminist men who, a few years ago, would have been the ones sitting in her seat on the talk shows. She claims, for example, that the feminists are foisting upon the U.S. a massive $360 million bureaucracy that will place gender equity and sex harassment police in every high school and college. In fact, the program, the Gender Equity in Education Act, is slated to cost $5 million, features a

> They call themselves feminists, but their dismissive-to-outright-hostile attitudes locate them on the antifeminist side of the ledger.

bureaucracy of one, and has no provisions for such gender police. Where did she get this idea? Not from reading the legislation, but from reading an opinion column by a conservative male pundit.

For the sake of full disclosure, I should say that I'm one of the many feminists to land on the Sommers hit list, and so I have some experience with her technique, which amounts to a full-blown denunciation based on nitpicks. One of her most blazing broadsides against my book, in fact, involves a few words that appear in parentheses. But that seems to characterize the tactics of the antifeminist feminists, who are forever combing the footnotes of feminist works till they find a typo and declaring, "Aha! The whole thesis must be bunk!" The point isn't who's right and who's wrong in the error department. Surely all books have mistakes. The point is: Do the errors undermine the central thesis of the author? And are the media, in promoting the antifeminist feminists' gleeful announcements that they found another boo-boo in a feminist work, trading in real ideas—or simply playing a game of gotcha journalism?

In *The Grounding of Modern Feminism*, historian Nancy Cott recounts how a group of women writers got together and produced a journal that proclaimed, in words that echo the position of the Women's Freedom Network, "We're interested in people now— not in men and women." These writers wanted to drop gender analysis and make nice with men. They had a name for their new posture: "postfeminist." The year was 1919. As Cott observes about the career women of the post-

World War I era: "Professional women . . . might enthusiastically support equality of opportunity and yet frown on feminism. Among ambitious young careerists who intended to seize the main chance and relied on advancing by their individual talents, feminism was a 'term of opprobrium,' journalist Dorothy Dunbar Bromley found in 1927."

It's no less true today. The nineties-style post/pod feminists favor advances not for other women but for themselves. In making the argument that women have already achieved equality, Sommers draws most of her evidence from the upper-middle-class rungs of the socioeconomic ladder. "Women have made great advancements toward full equality in every professional field," she argues in her book, pointing to medicine, law, and business. Conveniently left out are all the unglamorous occupations where the vast majority of the rest of the female population works. Or maybe the omission is not so much convenient as it is the result of simple blindness. It is that inability to see and identify with other women, to take the empathetic and affiliative leap that leads to a sense of sisterhood, that is, above all, the reason why the "I am a feminist, but . . ." crew are not feminists at all. They frown on any feminist display of political passion or anger; they are cool mouthpieces, appropriate for the cool media to which they aspire. It is this lack of heat and passion, this lack of anger, that gives them away. As the heroine in *Invasion of the Body Snatchers* says of the clone-like pods supplanting the real town citizens: "There's no

emotion. The words are the same, but there's no feeling."

The pseudofeminists do see how feminism can help them. They see how they can use feminism—or, more often, cultural antagonism to feminism—to turn the media spotlight their way. It is telling that the Women's Freedom Network's "Statement of Principles" promises to pursue not social change for women but "speaker placement on television and radio talk shows." Sommers revealed more than she intended in this regard during an interview on *CNN Crossfire*. In a rare moment of media skepticism, cohost Michael Kinsley pressed her: "Aren't you a little bit alarmed by the new allies you've found in this argument? People like Pat Buchanan and magazines like the *National Review*. If it were up to them, what you call the good kind of feminism—equal-rights, equal-pay feminism—would never have happened at all. Doesn't that worry you, make you suspicious?" She responded by citing a "favorable" review of her book in *Newsweek*. When Kinsley arched a brow at this statement—the review was quite unfavorable—a rattled Sommers let slip, "Well, [the reviewer] called it the most talked-about book."

To be "the most talked about" is the ultimate goal of mass marketing, whether the product marketed is pantyhose or punditry. Soon after the emergence of the second wave of the women's movement in the early seventies, Madison Avenue sought to convince women that they could attain feminist objectives via the marketplace. They could achieve the right independent lifestyle and "have it all" if they bought the right products, drank the right diet drinks, smoked the right cigarettes. Feminism, reinterpreted by advertising's creative directors, was simply a form of narcissism that could be sated in the shopping mall and the mirrors of mass media. The pod feminists of the nineties, in a sense, embody that seventies consumerist reinterpretation of feminism. By posing for the TV cameras with their "postideological" message that women have "made it" and can relax, they have become the nineties real-life equivalents of the blissed-out fashion models adorn-ing the old Virginia Slims ads. They, too, gaze into the camera lens and congratulate themselves for having "Come a Long Way, Baby." This is Madison Avenue-hatched "feminist" celebrity come home to roost on the editorial pages: in place of rights, we'll give you a makeover and your moment in the klieg-light sun. But it is a promise that leads nowhere, as the pseudofeminists may discover when the ever-restless media move on in search of new spectacles.

Like the seedless pods of that B-grade horror film, the pod feminists are incapable of bring-ing new life to the women's movement. Theirs will always be a stillborn form of feminism, because it is an ideology that will not and does not want to generate political, social, or economic change. The pods do not look forward to creating a better future, only inward to the further adulation of self as this year's "most talked-about" model. No matter how many times they replicate themselves on the television screen, they will never produce a world that is wider or fairer for their sex.

 Article Review Form at end of book.

Along with women in general, what other groups have struggled for access to the power of naming, which is the power of the patriarchy?

Men's Power to Define and the Formation of Women's Consciousness

Gerda Lerner

In Volume One I described the creation of patriarchy, which took place prior to the formation of Western civilization. Patriarchal concepts are, therefore, built into all the mental constructs of that civilization in such a way as to remain largely invisible. Tracing the historical development by which patriarchy emerged as the dominant form of societal order, I have shown how it gradually institutionalized the rights of men to control and appropriate the sexual and reproductive services of women. Out of this form of dominance developed other forms of dominance, such as slavery. Once established as a functioning system of complex hierarchical relationships, patriarchy transformed sexual, social, economic relations and dominated all systems of ideas. In the course of the establishment of patriarchy and constantly reinforced as the result of it, the major idea systems which explain and order Western civilization incorporated a set of unstated assumptions about gender, which powerfully affected the development of history and of human thought.

I have shown how the metaphors of gender constructed the male as the norm and the female as deviant; the male as whole and powerful; the female as unfinished, physically mutilated and emotionally dependent. Briefly summarized the major assumptions about gender in patriarchal society are these:

Men and women are essentially different creatures, not only in their biological equipment, but in their needs, capacities and functions. Men and women also differ in the way they were created and in the social function assigned to them by God.

Men are "naturally" superior, stronger and more rational, therefore designed to be dominant. From this follows that men are political citizens and responsible for and representing the polity.

Women are "naturally" weaker, inferior in intellect and rational capacities, unstable emotionally and therefore incapable of political participation. They stand outside of the polity.

Men, by their rational minds, explain and order the world. Women by their nurturant function sustain daily life and the continuity of the species. While both functions are essential, that of men is superior to that of women. Another way of saying this is that men are engaged in "transcendent" activities, women—like lower-class people of both sexes—are engaged in "immanent" activities.

Men have an inherent right to control the sexuality and the reproductive functions of women, while women have no such right over men.

Men mediate between humans and God. Women reach God through the mediation of men.

These unproven, unprovable assumptions are not, of course, laws of either nature or society, although they have often been so regarded and have even been incorporated into human law. They are operative at different levels, in different forms and with different intensity during various periods of history. Changes in the way in which these patriarchal assumptions are acted upon describe in fact changes in the status and position of women in a given period in a given society. The development of concepts of gender should therefore be studied by any historian wishing to elicit information about women in any society.

In Volume One I concluded that women had a relationship to History and to historical process different from that of men. It is helpful to distinguish between history—events of the past—and recorded History—events of the past as interpreted by succeeding generations of historians. The latter is a cultural product, by which events of the past are selected, ordered and interpreted. It is in recorded history that women have been obliterated or marginalized. In this second volume, I attempt to define the nature of the difference between these two concepts more precisely and to show how the construction of recorded History has affected women.

The archaic states of the Ancient Near East which developed priesthood, kingship and militaristic elites did so in a context of developing male dominance over women and a structured system of slavery. It is not accidental that the time, leisure and education necessary for developing philosophy, religion and science was made available to an elite of priests, rulers and bureaucrats, whose domestic needs were met by the unpaid labor of women and slaves. In the second millennium B.C. this elite occasionally included female priestesses, queens and rulers, but by the time patriarchy was firmly established, approximately in the 6th century B.C., it was always male. (The appearance of an occasional queen to substitute for a missing male heir only confirms this rule.) In other words, it is patriarchal slave society which gives rise to the systems of ideas that explain and order the world for millennia thereafter. The twin mental constructs—the philosophical and the scientific systems of thought—explain and order the world in such a way as to confer and confirm power upon their adherents and deny power to those disputing them. Just as the distribution and allocation of resources give power to the rulers, so do the withholding of information and the denial of access to explanatory constructs give power to the system builders.

From the time of the establishment of patriarchy to the present, males of non-elite groups have struggled with increasing success for a share in this power of defining and naming. The history of the Western world can be viewed as the unfolding of that class-based struggle and the story of the process by which more and more non-elite males have gained access to economic and mental resources. But during this entire period, well into the middle of the 20th century, women have been excluded from all or part of that process and have been unable to gain access to it.

Not only have women been excluded through educational deprivation from the process of making mental constructs, it has also been the case that the mental constructs explaining the world have been androcentric, partial and distorted. Women have been defined out and marginalized in every philosophical system and have therefore had to struggle not only against exclusion but against a content which defines them as subhuman and deviant.[1] I argue that this dual deprivation has formed the female psyche over the centuries in such a way as to make women collude in creating and generationally recreating the system which oppressed them.

I have shown in Volume One how gender became the dominant metaphor by which Aristotle defended and justified the system of slavery. At the time of Aristotle's writing of *Politics* the question of the moral rightness of slavery was still problematical. It was certainly questionable in light of the very system of ethics and morals Aristotle was constructing. Why should one man rule over another? Why should one man be master and another be slave? Aristotle reasoned that some men are born to rule, others to be ruled. He illustrated this principle by drawing an analogy between soul and body—the soul is superior to the body and therefore must rule it. Similarly, rational mind is superior to passion and so must rule it. And "the male is by nature superior, and the female inferior; and the one rules and the other is ruled; this principle, of necessity extends to all mankind."[2] The analogy extends also to men's rule over animals.

And indeed the use made of slaves and of tame animals is equally not very different; for both with their bodies minister to the needs of life. . . . It is clear, then, that some men are by nature free, and others slaves, and that for these latter slavery is both expedient and right.[3]

The remarkable thing about this explanation is what is deemed in need of justification and what is assumed as a given. Aristotle admitted that there is some justification for a difference of opinion regarding the rightness of enslaving captive peoples in the event of an unjust war. But there is no difference of opinion regarding the inferiority of women. The subordination of women is assumed as a given, likened to a natural condition, and so the philosopher uses the marital relationship as an explanatory metaphor to justify slavery. By his efforts at justifying the moral rightness of slavery, Aristotle had indeed recognized the basic truth of the humanity of the slave. By denying and ignoring the need to explain the subordination of women, as well as by the kind of biological explanation Aristotle offered elsewhere, he had fixed women in a status of being less-than-human. The female is, in his words, "as it were, a mutilated male."[4]

More remarkable than Aristotle's misogynist construction is the fact that his assumptions remained virtually unchallenged and endlessly repeated for nearly two thousand years. They were reinforced by Old Testament restrictions on women and their exclusion from the covenant community, by the misogynist teachings of the Church fathers and by the continuing emphasis in the Christian era on charging Eve, and with her all women, with moral guilt for the Fall of humankind.

More than two thousand years after Aristotle, the founding fathers of the American republic debated their Constitution. Once again, a group of revolutionary leaders, defining themselves as republicans and devoted to the cre-

ation of a democratic polity, was faced with the contradiction of the existence of slavery in their republic. The issue of how to deal with slavery was hotly contested and highly controversial. It ended in a pragmatic compromise which perpetuated a major social problem in the new republic.

The Declaration of Independence which states, "We hold these truths to be self-evident that all men are created equal and are endowed by their Creator with certain unalienable Rights, that among these are Life, Liberty and the pursuit of Happiness," implied that by natural right all human beings were endowed with the same rights. How were such principles to be upheld in the face of the existence of slavery in the Southern states? The issue surfaced in the constitutional debates on laws regulating the slave trade, assigning responsibility for the return of fugitive slaves and apportioning voting rights. The last issue proved to be the most difficult, the Northern states holding that slaves should be counted as property and not counted at all in voting apportionment. The Southern states wanted slaves to be counted as though they were citizens, with their votes being wielded by the men who owned them. What was at issue, more than the abstract principle of how to regard the Negro, was the relative regional strength in Congress. Since the Southern population including slaves was more numerous than the population of the free states, this would have given the Southerners predominance in the House of Representatives. The irony in the debate was that the proslavery forces argued the humanity of the slaves, while antislavery forces argued for their status as property.

Definitions, in this case, were determined not by reason, logic or moral considerations, but by political/economic interest.

The compromise which was finally incorporated into the Constitution was couched in a language as devoid of concreteness and as abstract as possible. "Representatives and direct taxes" were to be apportioned by adding to the number of citizens in each of the states "including those bound to Service for a Term of Years, and excluding Indians not taxed, three fifths of all other Persons." In plain words, a slave was to be counted three-fifths of a man for purposes of voting apportionment. Implicit in both language and debate was the recognition that the Negro, although a chattel, was indeed human. The founders' uneasiness with the slavery issue was expressed in the outlawing of the external slave trade in 1808, which most men believed would doom slavery to wither of its own accord. It also found expression in the terms of the Northwest Ordinance of 1787, which explicitly stated that the territories then defined as the Northwest would remain free. This laid the basis for the constitutional argument of the antislavery campaigns of the antebellum period, that the power to keep slavery out of the territories lay with the Congress. Thus the Constitution in its unresolved contradiction over the slavery issue not only presaged the Civil War but set in motion the ideas and expectations that would fuel the struggle for the slaves' eventual emancipation and their admission to full citizenship.

It was different for women. There was no controversy or debate on the definition of a voter as a male. The American

Constitution embodied the patriarchal assumption, shared by the entire society, that women were not members of the polity. It was felt necessary by the founders to define the status of indentured servants, persons "bound to Service for a Term of Years," and of Indians in regard to voting rights, but there was no need felt even to mention, much less to explain or justify, that while women were to be counted among "the whole number of free persons" in each state for purposes of representation, they had no right to vote and to be elected to public office (U.S. Constitution, Article I, 3). The issue of the civil and political status of women never entered the debate, just as it had not entered the debate in Aristotle's philosophy.

Yet women in large numbers had been involved in political actions in the American Revolution and had begun to define themselves differently than had their mothers and grandmothers in regard to the polity. At the very least, they had found ways of exerting influence on political events by fund-raising, tea boycotts and actions against profiteering merchants. Loyalist women made political claims when they argued for their property rights independent of those of their husbands or when they protested against various wartime atrocities. Several influential female members of elite families privately raised the issue of women's rights as citizens. Petitioners of various kinds thrust it into the public debate. Unbidden and without a recognized public forum and emboldened by the revolutionary rhetoric and the language of democracy, women began to reinterpret their own status. As did slaves, women took the pre-

amble of the Declaration of Independence literally. But unlike slaves, they were not defined as being even problematic in the debate.[5]

The well-known exchange of private letters between John Adams and his wife Abigail sharply exemplifies the limits of consciousness on this issue. Here was a well-matched and loving couple, unusual in the wife's political interest and involvement, which would find active expression during her husband's later term as President when she handled some of his correspondence.[6] In 1776 Abigail Adams urged her husband in a letter to "remember the ladies" in his work on the legal code for the new republic, reminding him that wives needed protection against the "naturally tyrannical" tendencies of their husbands. Abigail's language was appropriate to women's subordinate status in marriage and society—she asked for men's chivalrous protection from the excesses of other men. John's reply was "As to your extraordinary code of laws, I cannot but laugh. . . ." He expressed astonishment that like children and disobedient servants, restless Indians and insolent Negroes "another tribe more numerous and powerful than all the rest [had] grown discontented." Chiding his wife for being "saucy," he trivialized her argument by claiming that men were, in practice "the subjects. We have only the name of masters."[7] A problem outside of definition and discourse could not be taken seriously. And yet, for an instant, John Adams allowed himself to think seriously on the subject—her code of laws, if enacted, would lead to social disorder: "Depend upon it, we know better than to repeal our Masculine systems."[8]

Here we see, in its extreme manifestation, the impact on History of men's power to define. Having established patriarchy as the foundation of the family and the state, it appeared immutable and became the very definition of social order. To challenge it was both ludicrous and profoundly threatening.

At the time Aristotle defined the rightness of slavery, the issue of the humanity of the slave was debatable but not yet political. By 1787 the founders of the new republic had to recognize the humanity of the slave and deal with its denial as a controversial political issue. The statement that the slave may be fully human yet for purposes of political power distribution (among the masters) may be counted as only three-fifths human and not at all as a citizen, was so profound a contradiction in a Christian nation founded on democratic principles that it made the end of slavery inevitable in less than a century. But for women nothing at all had changed in terms of the debate since the time of Aristotle. As far as the definition of humanity was concerned, they were still defined as incomplete and marginal, a sort of sub-species. As far as the polity was concerned, they were not even recognized sufficiently to be coddled with the sop of "virtual representation." The issue defined as a social problem can enter political debate and struggle. The issue defined out, remains silenced, outside the polity.

This ultimate consequence of men's power to define—the power to define what is a political issue and what is not—has had a profound effect on women's struggle for their own emancipation. Essentially, it has forced thinking women to waste much time and energy on defensive arguments; it has channeled their thinking into narrow fields; it has retarded their coming into consciousness as a collective entity and has literally aborted and distorted the intellectual talents of women for thousands of years.

In the literature dealing with the subject of women in history the emphasis has been on the various discriminations and disabilities under which women have lived. Structural, legal and economic inequalities between men and women have held the focus of attention, with educational deprivation seen mostly as yet another form of economic discrimination in that it restricted women's access to resources and self-support. I focus in this study on the educational disadvantaging of women as a major force in determining women's individual and collective consciousness and thus a major force in determining women's political behavior.

The systematic educational disadvantaging of women has affected women's self-perceptions, their ability to conceptualize their own situation and their ability to conceive of societal solutions to improve it. Not only has it affected women individually, but far more important, it has altered women's relationship to thought and to history. Women, for far longer than any other structured group in society, have lived in a condition of trained ignorance, alienated from their own collective experience through the denial of the existence of Women's History. Even more important, women have for millennia been forced to prove to themselves and to others their capacity for full humanity and their capacity for abstract thought. This has skewed the intellectual development of women as a group, since their major intellectual endeavor had to be to counteract the pervasive patriarchal assumptions of their inferiority and incompleteness as human beings. It is this basic fact about their condition which explains why women's major intellectual enterprise for more than a thousand years was to re-conceptualize religion in such a way as to allow for women's equal and central role in the Christian drama of the Fall and Redemption. Women's striving for emancipation was acted out in the arena of religion long before women could conceive of political solutions for their situation.

The next issue through which women's quest for equality found expression was the struggle for access to education. Here, again, women were forced for hundreds of years not only to argue for their right to equal education, but first to prove their capacity to be educated at all. This exhausted the energies of the most talented women and retarded their intellectual development. Further, up until the end of the 19th century in Europe and the United States, women in order to be educated had to forgo their sexual and reproductive lives, they had to choose between wifehood and motherhood on the one hand and education on the other. No group of men in history ever had to make such a choice or pay such a price for intellectual growth.

For many centuries the talents of women were directed not toward self-development but toward realizing themselves through the development of a man. Women, conditioned for millennia to accept the patriarchal definition of their role, have sexually and emotionally serviced men and nurtured them in a way that allowed men of talent a fuller development and a more intensive degree of specialization than women have ever had. The sexual division of labor which has allotted to women the major responsibility for domestic services and the nurturance of children has freed men from the cumbersome details of daily survival activities, while it disproportionately has burdened women with them. Women have had less spare time and above all less uninterrupted time in which to reflect, to think and to write. The psychological support from intimacy and love has been far more readily available to talented men than to talented women. Had there been a man behind each brilliant woman, there would have been women of achievement in history equal to the numbers of men of achievement.

On the other hand it can be argued that throughout the millennia of their subordination the kind of knowledge women acquired was more nearly correct and adequate than was the knowledge of men. It was knowledge not based on theoretical propositions and on works collected in books, but practical knowledge derived from essential social interaction with their families, their children, their neighbors. Such knowledge was its own reward in making women aware of their essential role in maintaining life, family and community. Like men of subordinate castes, classes and races, women have all along had thorough knowledge of how the world works and how people work within it and with each other. This is survival knowledge for the oppressed, who must maneuver in a world in which they are excluded from structured power and who must know how to manipulate those in power to gain maximum protection for themselves and their children. The conditions under which they lived forced women to develop interpersonal skills and sensitivities, as have other oppressed groups. Their skill and knowledge were not made available to society as a whole because of patriarchal hegemony and instead found expression in what we now call women's culture. I will show in this book how women transformed the concepts and assumptions of male thought and subtly subverted male thought so as to incorporate women's cultural knowledge and viewpoint. This tension between patriarchal hegemony and women's re-definition is a feature of historical process we have hitherto neglected to describe and observe.

Women have also been deprived of "cultural prodding," the essential dialogue and encounter with persons of equal education and standing. Shut out of institutions of higher learning for centuries and treated with condescension or derision, educated women have had to develop their own social networks in order for their thoughts, ideas and work to find audiences and resonance. And finally, the fact that women were denied knowledge of the existence of Women's History decisively and negatively affected their intellectual development as a group. Women who did not know that others like them had made intellectual contributions to knowledge and to creative thought were overwhelmed by the sense of their own inferiority or, conversely, the sense of the dangers of their daring to be different. Without knowledge of women's past, no group of women could test their own ideas against those of their equals, those who had come out of similar conditions and similar life situations. Every thinking woman had to argue with the "great man" in her head, instead of being strengthened and encouraged by her foremothers. For thinking women, the absence of Women's History was perhaps the most serious obstacle of all to their intellectual growth.

Notes

1. An excellent discussion of the philosophical inadequacies of the patriarchal system of ideas, which corroborates my thinking, can be found in Elizabeth Kamarck Minnich, *Transforming Knowledge* (Philadelphia: Temple University Press, 1990).
2. Aristotle, *Politica* (tr. Benjamin Jowett), in W.D. Ross (ed.), *The Works of Aristotle* (Oxford: Clarendon Press, 1921), I, 2, 1254b, 4–6, 12–16.
3. *Ibid.*, 1254b, 24–26; 1255a, 2–5.
4. J.A. Smith and W.D. Ross (tr.), *The Works of Aristotle* (Oxford: Clarendon Press, 1912), "De Generatione Animalium," II, 3, 729a, 26–31.
5. See Linda Kerber, *Women of the Republic: Intellect and Ideology in Revolutionary America* (Chapel Hill: University of North Carolina Press, 1980) and Mary Beth Norton, *Liberty's Daughters: The Revolutionary Experience of American Women, 1750–1800* (Boston: Little, Brown, 1980).
6. Kerber, *Women of the Republic*, p. 82.
7. L.H. Butterfield et al. (eds.), *The Book of Abigail and John: Selected Letters of the Adams Family, 1762–1784* (Cambridge: Harvard University Press, 1975). First quote, Abigail Adams to John Adams, Braintree, March 31, 1776, p. 121; second quote, John Adams to Abigail Adams, April 14, 1776, p. 123.
8. *Ibid.*

Article Review Form at end of Book

WiseGuide Wrap-Up

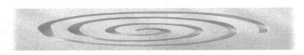

- The system of patriarchy benefits men by controlling and containing women.

- Feminist movements work for the equal rights of all women.

- Women who self-identify as feminists are not all the same but

are almost always characterized as bad girls, outside of the social order.

R.E.A.L. Sites

This list provides a print preview of typical **coursewise** R.E.A.L. sites. (There are over 100 such sites at the **courselinks**™ site.) The danger in printing URLs is that Web sites can change overnight. As we went to press, these sites were functional using the URLs provided. If you come across one that isn't, please let us know via email to: webmaster@coursewise.com. Use your Passport to access the most current list of R.E.A.L. sites at the **courselinks**™ site.

Site name: Library of Congress: Votes for Women: 1850–1920
URL: http://lcweb2.loc.gov/ammem/vfwhtml/vfwhome.html
Key topics: Feminism, History, Suffrage
Why is it R.E.A.L.? This site is one of the most comprehensive sites about women's history in the United States. The Library of Congress has digitized some of its large collection of primary documents.
Activity: Search the site by subject; then choose one subject that interests you. Read all of the historical documents in the area; then do a search from the home page for pictures that illustrate the main points you uncovered in your subject. Develop a simple web page using the historical documents and images that highlight those main points.

Site name: Women's Studies Resources
URL: http://www.inform.umd.edu/EdRes/Topic/WomensStudies
Key topics: Feminism, Education
Why is it R.E.A.L.? As a pioneering site in the field of instructional uses of the Internet, this database provides access to the most recent developments in the discipline of women's studies.
Activity: Read through the syllabi in the database; then evaluate each one for content, teaching strategies, and whether you think students will understand feminism after taking the course. Write your own syllabus for an Introduction to Women's Studies class, using ideas from the syllabi you find the most effective in your evaluations.

Site name: Guerrilla Girls
URL: http://voyagerco.com/gg/gg.html
Key topics: Patriarchy, Discrimination, Art
Why is it R.E.A.L.? The Guerrilla Girls combine theory and activism. Their web site contains a number of their posters designed to expose sexism in the art world.
Activity: Print out one or more of the Guerrilla Girls' posters, show the posters to a sample of students on your campus, and record their responses. Write a brief article for the campus newspaper, detailing your findings and making an argument about sexism and feminism on your campus.

Notes

Reading 9

1. Jeffreys, 1985, p. 47
2. Ibid, p. 32
3. Ibid, p. 97.
4. See for example Ferguson, 1984 and Sawicki, 1988.
5. Seidman, 1992, p. 187.
6. Davis, 1990, p. 35.
7. Steinem, 1978, p. 54.
8. Elshtain, 1988, p. 535.
9. Morgan, 1977, p. 181. Several critics have called this "femininism": "The femininist view of sex is . . . women have sex as an expression of intimacy, but orgasm is seen as a male goal"; Rubin, 1982, p. 215.
10. Interview with Ariane Amsberg, 1944, Amsterdam.
11. Barry, 1979, p. 270.
12. Ibid, p. 205.
13. Barry, 1995, plenary address at the Nordic Prostitution Conference, Helsinki, Finland, May, 1995. Emphasis mine. Barry opened her remarks with a strongly worded denunciation of conference organizers' decision to include a condom in conference packets: "The packet of material I received this morning [had] a condom in it which I assume is either part of the approach to normalization of prostitution or is it indeed a suggestion to those of us who have received it that we should be using it that way? I find this not at all cute or funny. I find it not at all educational or productive. I find it insulting."
14. For a conference report, see Kulp and Mudd, 1987, p. 6.
15. Kulp and Mudd, 1987, p. 6. Emphasis mine.
16. Ibid, p. 7. Emphasis mine.
17. Ibid. Emphasis mine.
18. Pateman, 1988, p. 208.
19. Fraser, 1993, pp. 174, 176.
20. MacKinnon, 1987, p. 149.
21. Ibid, p. 148.
22. Davis, 1990, p. 26.
23. Southern Women's Winters' Collective, 1987, p. 3.
24. Ibid.
25. Ibid, p. 4.
26. Ibid.
27. Dworkin, 1987, pp. 134–5. Emphasis mine.
28. Dworkin, 1979, p. 203.
29. MacKinnon, 1987, p. 59.
30. Barry, 1979, p. 218.
31. Barry, 1992.
32. Ibid.
33. MacKinnon notes that "Marxism teaches that exploitation and degradation somehow produce resistance and revolution. It's been hard to say why. What I've learned from women's experience with sexuality is that exploitation and degradation produce grateful complicity in exchange for survival," MacKinnon, 1987, p. 61.
34. Ibid, p. 148.
35. Seidman, 1992, pp. 187–8.
36. Ibid.
37. Wells, 1994, p. 132
38. Ibid.
39. Ibid, p. 58.
40. Other writers challenging so-called "victim feminism" include American feminists Katie Roiphe, 1993, and Naomi Wolf, 1993. In her version of "power femininism," Roiphe, for instance, scrutinizes rape and other crimes of male violence against women for evidence of women's own complicity. A similar strategy is at work in current attempts to redefine racism as a question of individual failure; see D'Souza, 1995.
41. hooks, 1994, p. 80.
42. Vance, 1984, p. 1.
43. Sheiner, 1994, p. 4. It is interesting to note that the author of the offending piece defends his work in a reply to Sheiner by arguing that she misinterpreted his intent: "I was trying to convey exactly the sense of revulsion at the use of Third World women [in sex tourism]. I agree completely with those who deplore it, and always have. The sexual image in this piece was intended to be grotesque."
44. Lilly, 1991, pp. 1–3.
45. Sawicki, 1988, p. 185.
46. Bhaba, 1987.
47. Califia, 1980, p. 27.
48. Marlatt, 1991, p. 260.
49. de Lauretis, 1984, p. 5.
50. Warland, 1991, p. 263.
51. Shange, 1994, p. 34.
52. Ibid, pp. 38–39.
53. Califia, 1980, p. 197
54. McClintock, 1993, p. 192.
55. Ibid, p. 113.
56. Connell, 1995.
57. Taussig, 1987, p. 16.
58. Kaplan, 1994, p. 22. Kaplan's suggestion that whores and dykes create sexual anxiety in men seemed to be confirmed at the 1995 U.N. Women's Conference in Beijing. The question of prostitutes' and lesbian rights proved to be among the most controversial considered at the conference. One government representative from Bangladesh insisted that an acknowledgment of lesbian rights would "open the floodgates for all kinds of behavior we can't accept. It is not innocent behavior." A delegate from Belize compared homosexuality to "prostitution and strip-tease dancing." See Burdman, 1995. p. 1.
59. Califia, 1988, p. 20.
60. Ibid, p. 22.
61. Duggan, et al., 1985, p. 145.
62. Levine, 1992, p. 47. Levine is coauthor with Robert Stoller of the book *Coming Attractions, The Making of an X-Rated Video*, 1993.
63. Interview with Carol Queen, 1992, San Francisco, CA.

Reading 19

1. Quoted in Catherine Gewertz, "Surrogate Mother Sues to Keep Couple's Child," *Los Angeles Times*, August 14, 1990. AI.
2. Ibid., A22.
3. Although Johnson may have been approached by various talk shows, in point of fact, she appeared only on *Donahue* in order to counter what she took to be widespread media misrepresentations of her claims. Although Johnson apparently received payment for her appearance—forty-six hundred dollars, or precisely the amount she required to repay Social Services— she testified that she knew nothing of this payment and did not personally receive it. Although this

seems, on the surface, to be somewhat far-fetched, it is entirely possible that any fee Johnson received for her appearance was negotiated by and channeled through her lawyers. Contrary to public perceptions, talk-show guests rarely receive compensation for their participation beyond airfare and hotel accommodations.

4. Catherine Gewertz, "Surrogate Mother in Custody Fight Accused of Welfare Fraud," *Los Angeles Times,* August 16, 1990, A10.

5. Wahneema Lubiano, "Black Ladies, Welfare Queens, and State Minstrels: Ideological War by Narrative Means," in *Race-ing Justice, En-gendering Power: Essays on Anita Hill, Clarence Thomas, and the Construction of Social Reality,* ed. Toni Morrison (New York: Pantheon, 1992), 338–39.

6. See Kobena Mercer, *Welcome to the Jungle: New Positions in Black Cultural Studies* (New York: Routledge, 1994), especially chap. 5.

7. Michael de Courcey Hinds, "Addiction to Crack Can Kill Parental Instinct," *New York Times,* March 17, 1990, A1.

8. On illegitimate birthrates, see Susan Faludi, *Backlash: The Undeclared War against American Women* (New York: Anchor, 1991), 34.

9. Lubiano, "Black Ladies," 331.

10. The significant passage of the act upon which Johnson's lawyers depended provides that the relationship "between a child and the natural mother may be established by proof of her having given birth to the child."

11. "In the committee's view, the genetic link between the commissioning parent(s) and the resulting infant, while important is less weighty than the link between the surrogate mother and fetus or infant that is created through gestation at birth. Thus, in the analysis and recommendations that follow, no distinction will be drawn between the usual pattern of surrogate parenting and surrogate gestational motherhood." "Ethical Issues in Surrogate Motherhood," trial exhibit, *Johnson v. Calvert,* Office of the Supreme Court, California (1990), 2.

12. Gina Kolata, "Menopause Is Found No Bar to Pregnancy," *New York Times,* October 25, 1990. A1.

13. "That the egg is not their own is a detail; what counts is that they are able to have a profound and transforming life experience, to bond prenatally with their baby, and reproduce the genes of their husband," Katha Pollitt, "When Is a Mother Not a Mother?" *The Nation,* December 31, 1990, 844.

14. Interview with prolife activist in Kristen Luker, *Abortion and the Politics of Motherhood* (Berkeley: University of California Press, 1984), 159–60.

15. Joseph C. Fletcher and Mark I. Evans, "Maternal Bonding in Early Fetal Ultrasound Examinations," *New England Journal of Medicine* 308 (1983): 392.

16. For a fuller discussion, see Rosalind Petchesky, "Fetal Images: The Power of Visual Culture in the Politics of Reproduction," in *Reproductive Technologies: Gender, Motherhood, and Medicine,* ed. Michelle Stanworth (Minneapolis: University of Minnesota Press, 1987), 59.

17. Carol Whitbeck, "Fetal Imaging and Fetal Monitoring: Finding the Ethical Issues," in *Embryos, Ethics, and Women's Rights,* ed. Elaine Hoffmann Baruch, Amadeo F. D'Adamo Jr., and Joni Seager (New York: Harrington Park, 1988), 56.

18. "Three natural parents is not in the best interest of the child. . . . I think it invites emotional and financial extortion situations." Trial transcript, *Johnson v. Calvert,* 1488.

19. Ibid., 1489–90.

20. Ibid., 1489.

21. Ibid., 1483–84.

22. Janet L. Dolgin, "Family Law and the Facts of Family," unpublished manuscript (1992), 34. A version of this paper was published as "Just a Gene: Judicial Assumptions about Parenthood," *UCLA Law Review* 40 (1993): 637–94.

23. Trial transcript, *Johnson v. Calvert,* 1490.

24. Ibid., 1487, 918–20.

25. "Who we are and what we are and identity problems particularly with young children and teenagers are extremely important. We know that there is a combination of genetic factors. We know more and more about traits now, how you walk, talk, and everything else, all sorts of things that develop out of your genes, how long you're going to live, all things being equal, when your immune system is going to break down, what diseases you may be susceptible to. They have upped the intelligence ratio to 70 percent now. Then there is environment. Over the years the experts flow back and forth between how much is genetics and how much environment after you're born. But, genetics and what happens to you after you're born are the primary factors, as I understand it, of who you are and what we become." (Ibid., 1486). Note that the terms in which Judge Parslow renders his story of human development fully eclipse gestation as a meaningful, relevant, or apparently even necessary interval.

26. Dr. Justin David Call, in ibid., 918.

27. Robert A. Jones, "Another Sorry Story for Solomon," *Los Angeles Times,* September 25, 1990.

28. Martin Kasindorf, "And Baby Makes Four," *Los Angeles Times Magazine,* January 20, 1991, 33, 11, 31.

29. Trial transcript, *Johnson v. Calvert,* 914–17, 1486.

30. Cited in Dolgin, "Just a Gene," 687.

31. Pollitt, "When Is a Mother Not a Mother?" 842.

32. Neil Gotanda, "A Critique of 'Our Constitution Is Color-Blind,' " *Stanford Law Review* 44, no. 1 (1991): 1–68.

33. Lubiano, "Black Ladies," 332.

34. On the condensed meanings of the category "welfare mother," see Patricia Hill Collins, *Black Feminist Thought: Knowledge, Consciousness and the Politics of Empowerment* (New York: Routledge, 1990), 67–90; Patricia J. Williams, *The Alchemy of Race and Rights* (Cambridge: Harvard University Press, 1991); Lubiano, "Black Ladies," 323–44.

35. Toni Morrison, *Playing in the Dark: Whiteness and the Literary Imagination* (Cambridge: Harvard University Press, 1993), 21.

36. Consider a story that was carried by the Associated Press and appeared in a small local newspaper under the headline "Mother Loses Third Son to Inner-City Violence" (*Santa Cruz Sentinel,* July 9, 1993). The story itself presents a curiously confused and inconsistent picture of a woman's failed effort to protect

her third and last child from the random street violence that claimed her first two sons. By her account, all of her sons did not deal drugs or carry guns and were the innocent victims of random shootings, but, according to this report, a preliminary police investigation, at least in the case of the youngest, suggested otherwise. Noting that the life expectancy of young black men is "down to less than 65 years, 10 years below the average for all Americans," the story then moves to the home of the dead son's grandmother, where relatives have gathered ostensibly to mourn. Notice, however, the way in which the scene of "mourning" is both staged and described:

Outside, barefoot kids eating grape popsicles inspected the score of quarter-size pockmarks pounded into steel security doors by the previous day's gunplay.

Inside, no tears were shed. Mrs. Davis' sisters watched "All my Children" and braided their daughters' hair. The grandmother, 62-year-old Clara Saunders, wandered around the apartment in slippers and railed about drug dealers. (A3)

37. George J. Annas, "Crazy Making: Embryos and Gestional Mothers," *Hastings Center Report* 21, no. 1 (1991): 37.
38. Jana Sawicki, *Disciplining Foucault: Feminism, Power, and the Body* (New York: Routledge, 1991), 88.

Index

References in bold are Readings authors.

E

Earnings, women's vs. men's, 4
Eating
    among adolescents, 164
    guilt over, 35
    restrictions on Bengali widows, 159-62
Eating disorders, 164, 168-69
Eco-feminism, 155
Economic growth, and women's education, 65-66, 69-70
Edathil, Jocelyn, 78
Education
    denial to women, 190
    effect on income and employment, 5
    effect on infant mortality, 65, 68
    gender equity in, 85
    of girls in Third World countries, 63-71
    about science, 83-84
    teacher sex biases in, 73, 74-75
Electronic Frontier Foundation, 21
Elementary school teachers, earnings of, 4
Elshtain, Jean Bethke, 48
Embryonic development, and hermaphroditism, 44
Emma, case history of hermaphroditism, 44-45
Enloe, Cynthia, 133
Entrepreneurs, 5
Environmental protection, as barrier to free trade, 150
Escort work, 10-17
Estrogen replacement therapy, 131
Ethnic Woman International, 156
Evans, Mark, 117-18
Eve Online, 155
Excerpt: Forever Barbie, 40

F

Factories, working conditions in, 133-38, 139-43
Faludi, Susan, 178
Families
    changes in, 86
    gay and lesbian, 88, 122
    "natural" form of, 121
    violence in, 97, 122, 170
Family values rhetoric, 87-88
Family Violence Prevention Fund, 122
Fat, social images of, 35-36
Fathers
    dominating, 89-94
    importance to families, 87-88
bf/Fausto-Sterling, Anne, 42
Femininity
    and adolescence, 163-76
    and disability, 177
    stereotypes of, 28
Feminism
    adolescents and, 163-76
    conservative infiltration of, 178-85
    development of, 157
    early opposition to, 184
    inconsistencies in, 7-9

Radical, 47, 48-51
    as resistance, 176
    Sex Radical, 47-48, 51-56, 96-97, 99-100
Feminist Majority Foundation, 122
Feminists
    becoming, 89-94
    phony, 178-85
    views of sexuality among, 47-56, 99-100
femxpri, 23-24
Fertility, effect of education on, 64, 65, 68-69, 70
Fetal alcohol syndrome, 108
Fetishes, sexual, 13-14, 100, 104
Fine, Michelle, 163
Fletcher, Joseph, 117-18
Folic acid, 129
Food
    guilt over, 35
    politics of, 144-51
Football, adolescent girls' liking for, 174
Foreign investment, and female literacy rates, 71
Fourth World Conference on Women, 152-54
Fox-Genovese, Elizabeth, 179, 181
Free trade, effect on Third World agriculture, 144-51
Freewoman magazine, 47
Fried, Susana, 152
Fritson, Naomi, 79-80
Full-time employment, percentage of women with, 4

G

Garment industry, overseas movement of jobs, 138
Gender, meaning of, 41
Gender and Sexuality, R.E.A.L. site, 60
Gender bias
    perceptions among teenagers, 73-80
    in schools, 73, 74-75
Gender differences
    in household chores, 74
    in patriarchy, 186-91
    perceptions among teenagers, 73-80
    persistence of, 81-82
Gender equity
    in Beijing declaration, 153
    in education, 85
    in medical research, 131
    in schools, 61
    in sports, 79-80
Gender Equity in Education, R.E.A.L. site, 85
Gender Equity in Education Act, 183-84
General Agreement on Tariffs and Trade (GATT), 138, 144-45
General office clerks, earnings of, 4
Genetics, and parental rights, 115-21
Genital Abnormalities, Hermaphroditism and Related Adrenal Diseases, 44
Geok-lin Lim, Shirley, 158
Gestational surrogacy, 115-21
Gilligan, Carol, 173

Gingrich, Newt, 181
Girls, education in Third World countries, 63-71
"The Goddess in Every Woman's Machine," 25
"Good girls," images of, 173-75
Gordon, Ronald R., 45
The Great Divide survey, 73-80
Gross national product (GNP), and female literacy rates, 71
Guerilla Girls, 192

H

Hadden, Kenneth, 63
Hare-Mustin, Rachel, 167
Health
    and dieting, 36
    effect of maternal education on, 65, 69
Health aides, earnings of, 4
Health studies, for women, 131-32
Heart disease, among women, 127-30
Hermaphrodites, 42-46
Hermaphroditus, 43
Heterosexuality, radical feminist views of, 49
Hill and King study, 67, 70-71
Hindu Widow Remarriage Act, 160
Historic Supreme Court Cases, R.E.A.L. site, 60
History, women's image in, 187, 190
Holloway, Denise, 77-78
Holloway, Sabrina, 77-78
Homosexuality
    and family values controversy, 88
    and hermaphroditism, 46
    See also Lesbianism
Homosysteine, 129
hooks, bell, 32, 52
Hormone replacement therapy, 131
Hudson, Barbara, 163, 175
Huffington, Michael, 181
Human rights, 154
Hunger, and free trade, 146-47
Hynde, Chrissie, 30-31
Hyperlink to Donna Haraway, 155

I

Identity, among adolescent girls, 165-68
Income, by sex and education level, 5
Independent Women's Forum, 178, 179, 180
Index of Net Social Progress, 66
India
    impact of GATT on, 145-46
    restrictions on widows, 159-62
    women in agriculture, 144-45
Indian Child Welfare Act, 107-8
Individualism, among adolescents, 167, 171-72
Indonesia, shoemakers' move to, 136
Infanticide, 158
Infant mortality, and maternal education, 68, 69, 70
Intellectual property rights, 148-50

Putting it in *Perspectives*
-Review Form-

Your name:_____   Date: _____

Reading title: _____

Summarize: Provide a one-sentence summary of this reading. _____
_____
_____
_____

Follow the Thinking: How does the author back the main premise of the reading? Are the facts/opinions appropriately supported by research or available data? Is the author's thinking logical?

_____
_____
_____
_____
_____

Develop a Context (answer one or both questions): How does this reading contrast or compliment your professor's lecture treatment of the subject matter? How does this reading compare to your textbook's coverage?

_____
_____
_____
_____
_____

Question Authority: Explain why you agree/disagree with the author's main premise.

_____
_____
_____
_____
_____
_____

COPY ME! Copy this form as needed. This form is also available at http://www.coursewise.com Click on: *Perspectives*.